# MODERNITY
# AT GUNPOINT

*ILLUMINATIONS: CULTURAL FORMATIONS OF THE AMERICAS SERIES*

John Beverley and Sara Castro-Klarén, Editors

# MODERNITY AT GUNPOINT

## FIREARMS, POLITICS, AND CULTURE IN MEXICO AND CENTRAL AMERICA

SOPHIE ESCH

UNIVERSITY OF PITTSBURGH PRESS

Published by the University of Pittsburgh Press, Pittsburgh, Pa., 15260
Copyright © 2018, University of Pittsburgh Press
Manufactured in the United States of America
Printed on acid-free paper
10 9 8 7 6 5 4 3 2 1

Cataloging-in-Publication data is available from the Library of Congress

ISBN 13: 978-0-8229-6538-1

Cover design by Melissa Dias-Mandoly

For Daniel

# CONTENTS

# *ACKNOWLEDGMENTS*

This book was initially conceived during a period of intense reading in New Orleans. While reading one revolutionary and postwar account after another, firearms and bullets kept on staring at me. And the imagery lingered. This ultimately led to the questions addressed in this book.

But that is just one way to tell the story of this book. The book might have also have been conceived years earlier, when I was sitting in my attic room in Berlin, listening with my dear friend Diana to the songs of the Sandinista Revolution, as we tried to decipher and transcribe the lyrics. Back then the Internet was not yet the place where one could turn for answers to all one's lyrics-related questions. Or the seeds of this book might have been planted during my time at the Lateinamerika-Institut of the Freie Universität Berlin: by my mentor, Marianne Braig, and her contagious fascination with the Partido Revolucionario Institucional (PRI), and her ability to teach how to tease out one's *Erkenntnisinteresse*, one's underlying epistemological interest; by Barbara Dröscher and her insightful teachings on Central American literature; and by Günther Maihold and his lectures on Latin American political thought and nonviolent state actors.

Or maybe this book was born many years ago when I visited the Museum of the Revolution in León, Nicaragua, which featured a few photocopies of photos, a painting of Sandino, and a Molotov cocktail. Or perhaps during the "Zapatour" through Morelos, organized by my dear friends Alejandra and Álvaro, or during a visit to Villa's hacienda in Chihuahua, again with Diana. Or while attending one of the meetings of La Otra Campaña with the *batucada*, the percussion group, watching the Zapatista *comandancia* plus armed guards arrive, as villagers and visitors alike rushed to try to catch a glimpse of El Sup.

The evolving thought process for this book encompassed multiple stories, events, and experiences, and most certainly this book would not have taken shape without the help of many minds.

At Tulane University, I am most grateful to Idelber Avelar, an enthusiastic mentor and a meticulous reader who always knew the right questions to ask and the right books to suggest. My thanks go to Yuri Herrera, Fernando Rivera Díaz, and Maureen Shea for reading my work and offering thoughts and encouragement. To have these four stellar academics read and comment on my work was a true privilege. Many thanks to them for their generosity of time and thought! For their help along the way, I also thank Laura Bass, Chris Dunn, Antonio Gómez, and Amy George-Hirons. I am forever indebted to Adam Demaray for his thorough reading of an earlier version of this manuscript and for our enlightening exchanges. Many thanks to *los detectives astutos*, Camilo Malagón, Catalina Rincón, Estefanía Flores, and Carlos Capellino, and all the smart and boisterous *compañerxs* who shared the good times and the bad times in beautiful New Orleans: Ana Villar, Caroline Good, Kate Richardson, Katharina Kniess, Luciana Monteiro, Brandon Bisbey, Giancarlo Stagnaro, Kurt Hofer, Katie Sawyer, and Nick McCulloch. Vital support for this project was received through the Monroe Fellowship, two Summer Merit Awards, and the vast resources of the Latin American Library at the university's Howard Tilton Library.

Also, thank you to New Orleans—I will forever miss your live oaks and magnolias. Gratitude is owed to other writing locations, too: Managua, Mexico City, Boston, Taos, Albuquerque, and Fort Collins.

At Colorado State University, a special thanks to Francisco Leal—a friend and one of the best intellectual interlocutors, mentors, and readers I could have hoped for. For their advice and their personal and intellectual support, I thank Mary Vogl, Silvia Soler Gallego, María del Mar López-Cabrales, Fernando Valerio-Holguín, Antonio Pedrós-Gascón, and Maite Correa. For their help and collegiality, I thank Jonathan Carlyon, Codi Delgadillo, Peter Erickson, Frédérique Grim, Carol Hughes, Brian Hull, Jourdan Jiruska, Rachel Kirby, Kaity Lewis, Andrea Purdy, Gretchen Suechting, and Esther Venable. The Department of Languages, Literatures, and Cultures offered financial support for image rights for the book. Special thanks to my writing group peeps: Alexus McLeod, Josh Sbicca, and Dustin Tucker for the stimulating exchanges and Susan Delong, Mackenzi Pergolotti, and Deanna Worley for being such an inspiring group. I thank Kristina Quwynn of CSU Writes for creating spaces for writing, and Jimena Sagás from Morgan Library for her help. The College of Liberal Arts supported this book through a Faculty Development Award as well as several Professional Development grants. My students at Colorado State University helped me think through many of the ideas presented in the book.

I am particularly indebted to the many colleagues at other universities who have inspired and helped this book with their comments, readings, and generous advice—in particular, Ileana Rodríguez, Ignacio Sánchez Prado, and Juan Pablo Dabove. Jorge Aguilar Mora read an earlier version of the introduction. Since my reading of the literature of the Mexican Revolution built on his, it was an honor to receive his scintillating comments. My most heartfelt gratitude goes to Alicia Miklos, with whom I have wandered this journey of academia together ever since we met in Nicaragua in 2012. Thank you for our trips, our talks, and for always being there when I needed a thorough read with a short turnaround (ahem, preferably tomorrow). I am grateful to Christian Kroll Bryce for his thorough and helpful comments on chapters 3 and 4. I thank him and fellow *centroamericanistas-mexicanistas* Nanci Buiza and Carolyn Fornoff for helping me think through the question of working on Mexico and Central America together.

I would like to express my gratitude to the many people who in conference settings or other contexts have offered comments and advice: Oswaldo Zavala, Magdalena Perkowska, Niamh Thornton, Rafael Acosta, Ana Patricia Rodríguez, Yansi Pérez, Isabel Díaz, Erin Gallo, Gaëlle Le Calvez, Carmen Díaz, Pedro Caro, Arturo Arias, Verónica Ríos Quesada, Leonel Delgado, George Yúdice, Debbie Rusch, William Clary, Andrew Ascherl, Alexandra Ortiz Wallner, Pablo Hernández Herández, Sebastian Pfotenhauer, Adriana Ortega, Everardo Pérez Manjarrez, Mary Addis, Nicole Caso, Miguel Cabañas, Santiago Vaquera-Vásquez, Leila Lehnen, Jeremy Lehnen, Zachary Brittsan, and the many others with whom I crossed paths over the years. I am very grateful to the anonymous readers of this manuscript. Their insightful comments were invaluable.

In Nicaragua my wholehearted gratitude belongs to Carlos Mejía Godoy, Luis Enrique Mejía Godoy, Sergio Ramírez, and former guerrilla commanders Dora María Tellez and Hugo Torres for sharing their memories with me. Many thanks also to the Instituto de Historia de Nicaragua y Centroamérica (IHNCA) and the Grupo de estudio sobre pensamiento latinoamericano for welcoming me with open arms in Nicaragua.

For his guidance and help in getting this book into shape, I thank my editor Josh Shanholtzer at the University of Pittsburgh Press. My gratitude also belongs to John Beverley and Sara Castro-Klarén for including this book in the Illuminations Series.

I want to express my thanks to the Fototeca of the Instituto Nacional de Antropología e Historia (INAH), the Museo Nacional de Arte (MUNAL), the Banco de México, *La Jornada*, and Magnum Photos for allowing me to reproduce several images in the book. For having granted me a permit to visit the Museo de Enervantes and to take pictures of the exhibit, I thank the Secretaría de la Defensa Nacional (SEDENA). I thank Luca Fiorentini for his help with the table in the introduction. I thank the *Revista de Estudios Hispánicos* for granting me permission to reprint parts of the article "In the Company of Animals: Otherness, Empathy, and Community in *De fronteras* by Claudia Hernández," previously published in volume 51, no. 3 (2017), in chapter 5 of this book. Some of the ideas presented in chapter 5 previously appeared in Spanish and under a Creative Commons license as "Rambo pinolero y Robocop guanaco: La novela del desmovilizado en la literatura centroamericana de posguerra," in the June 2016 issue of *AFEHC* (journal of the Asociación para el Fomento de los Estudios Históricos en Centroamérica). Also, chapter 6 includes parts of my article "In the Crossfire: Rascón Banda's *Contrabando* and the 'Narcoliterature' Debate in Mexico," which appeared in volume 41, no. 2 (2014) of *Latin American Perspectives*. It is reprinted here with permission of SAGE Publications.

A most heartfelt thank you is due to my parents, siblings, and friends in Germany for always supporting my path and maintaining conversations and closeness across the Atlantic.

There is one person I cannot thank enough: Daniel. He is the biggest fan of this research and by now knows many songs of the Mejía Godoys by heart. He has carried this work alongside me—through the Deep South, New England, and the Southwest—and throughout the process of writing and rewriting, he was a true partner, *compañero*, interlocutor, listener, *asesor*, translation consultant extraordinaire, proofreader, Linux technical support guy, travel companion, and so much more. *Por las horas compartidas*, for your generosity of heart, soul, and mind, *für deine Ruhe inmitten meines Sturms*, thank you, Daniel.

Finally, a thank you goes to *el gato*, Ernesto, my constant writing companion.

# MODERNITY
# AT GUNPOINT

## *INTRODUCTION*

# *FIREARMS AS SYMBOLS OF INSURGENCY AND MODERNITY*

Weapons come into focus as easily as they slip out of it. Weapons are often at the center of history, yet the stories we tell of war and revolution tend to focus on people, dates, and events—not objects. Many times, it is the weapons, especially firearms, that bring particular significance to images, songs, and novels of war, yet rarely do we discuss their symbolic meaning. What could we learn if we examined violent conflict through a cultural analysis of its objects? Firearms are widely available, controversial, and iconic tools of violence, and analyzing them means confronting violence in its most concrete but also most symbolic terms. Tools for killing, firearms are also crucial artifacts and tropes for understanding narratives of insurgency and modernity. By analyzing novels, songs, and photographs through the lens of the firearm, *Modernity at Gunpoint* provides new angles for understanding different armed conflicts and their cultural expressions in Mexico and Central America.

The first and second chapter of the book discuss the Mexican Revolution (1910–1940), both vilified and glorified. Since it involved large segments of armed peasants, elites and media outlets responded to the revolution with fear and contempt. Yet later on, as the elites converted it into a moderate project for a postrevolutionary mestizo state, the revolution was exalted as a source of national pride. The third and fourth chapter of the book discuss the Sandinista Revolution (1970s–1980s), often idealized as a utopian project, in which different strata converged to create a new society built on egalitarianism, religion, and arts. However, the project collapsed under its unacknowledged militarist authoritarianism and a US-financed counterrevolution. The fifth and sixth chapters of the book examine the diffuse current postwar and drug-related conflicts in Central America and Mexico. All of these conflicts have been fought and debated through the use of specific weapons.

### *On Firearms*

Human development and war technology are intrinsically linked. In *Speed and Politics,* Paul Virilio has argued that "history progresses at the speed of its weapons systems" (90). Progress, he writes, has been made possible largely due to advances in weapons technology, which have become increasingly fast and dynamic: from weapons of obstruction to weapons of destruction and communication (*Desert Screen* 6–7; *Speed and Politics* 62, 149). This describes the development from walls and forts to cannons, firearms, and satellites—and most recently to drones, a combined weapon of destruction and communication.

The firearm is a prime artifact of modernity.[1] Modernity understood in Weberian and Virilian terms is a process of rationalization in the context of the development of the nation-state and a market economy—oftentimes through the organization of war and concurrent technological innovation (Virilio *Speed and Politics*; Weber "Wissenschaft als Beruf"). Robert Kurz goes so far as to call the discovery of gunpowder in Europe in the fourteenth century the "big bang of modernity" and the firearm the "fundamental innovation of modernity." He argues that in Europe these inventions led to the development of an early military industry that resulted in an increased urbanization followed by the imperialist expansionism of Europe.[2] European colonialism lead to divergent experiences of modernity across the globe. In the Latin American context, in particular, modernity was mediated through the experience of the violence of colonialism and intrinsically tied to lettered culture as an influential practice of power (Mignolo; Quijano; Rama; Ramos).[3]

When addressing Europe's military evolution, it is quite common to overstate the importance of firearms in the early conquest of the American continent. In the narrative of the conquest, the firearm becomes the symbol of technological superiority, a simplistic and misleading way of explaining the defeat of the Aztec and Inca Empires. Most readers probably learned at some point that the Spaniards were able to conquer the American peoples and territories because they had firearms. Yet this myth of the conquest has been largely debunked (Restall 139–41). Other factors played a comparatively larger role, including germs and the inner conflicts between and within the different indigenous societies. Technology was a factor too, but not firearms. Steel weaponry and armor (against obsidian and bronze weaponry and light armor), crossbows, riding and shipping equipment, and the printing press were the key technologies, as explained by Restall (142–43) and Camilla Townsend (661, 677).

These factors gave the Spaniards a crucial advantage in the conquest; not their few, error-prone harquebuses, which according to Jared Diamond functioned poorly when wet, took a long time to reload, and probably required tripods to fire (76). Cannons played a role in the ambush Francisco Pizarro prepared for Inca ruler Atahualpa in 1532, but the defeat of the empire happened because of the Inca internal war, differences in war tactics and ethics, and the Spaniards' long, pointed steel weapons (77). This does not mean that the firearm was not crucial for *later* wars and conquests—in particular, in the nineteenth century, when rifles began to be more efficient and mass-produced. Rifles were key in the nineteenth-century imperialist-colonialist expansion of the United States. The 1873 Winchester rifle, for example, is mythicized from an Anglo perspective as "the gun that won the West." Yet in the conquest that took place three hundred years earlier, the firearm was not yet an important factor.

The ingrained myth of the importance of firearms for the Spanish conquest illustrates that the firearm's functional value is often superseded by its symbolic value. In societies shaped by war, a weapon is never just a tool to kill. A weapon, and the firearm in particular, wields enormous symbolic power. In further elaboration of Jean Baudrillard's object value-system, I distinguish between different values of an object: its functional value as a tool, its economic value as a commodity, its spectral value as an echo in the wounds it leaves behind, and its symbolic value as an artifact, trope, or prop. In *For a Critique of the Political Economy of the Sign,* Baudrillard discusses the different values of objects in the context of consumption. He distinguishes between the use, exchange, symbolic exchange, and sign value of objects. Following his logic, weapons can be a mere instrument to kill ("functional logic of use value"); a commodity ("economic logic of exchange value"); a symbol in an exchange where the other values of the object are of little importance, such as the rendering of arms ("symbolic exchange"); or a sign that is directed toward other subjects in order to differentiate oneself, such as the AK-47 as a status symbol ("sign value") (67). Baudrillard's conception of the sign value was an important step beyond the Marxist fixation on the use and exchange value of objects, but his main concerns were, as Tim Dant has highlighted, "function and ostentation" (508), which are not sufficient to grasp the full scope of an object's *symbolic* values.

Nor is the terminology of fetishism. Many readers may expect a book on weaponry to be in part about fetishism, since the association of firearms with gun lore and the phallus are so immediate. Fetishism is the attribution of power or value to an object, which seems to operate by itself isolated from its context. However, I purposely avoid this terminology and focus instead on the symbolic values of such objects. Fetishism originates from a colonial gaze, in which, as William Pietz has pointed out, it stood for the "pure condition of unenlightenment" (136). In later theoretical developments by Karl Marx and Sigmund Freud, "fetish" never completely loses the connotation of being a *mistaken* attribution to an object. Even more current anthropological takes on fetishism by Michael Taussig (xviii) and Matthew Carlin (508) are still very much focused on drawing a line between a supposed material or empirical essence of an object versus its cultural or decontextualized meaning. Although I am interested in the tension that arises between the functional and the symbolic values of the firearm, the potential falsity of a value attribution is not my concern.

Never merely tools to kill, what makes firearms such symbolically complex objects is precisely their functional value, creating an important interplay between function and symbolic meaning. The object's only function is to harm or kill, and as such firearms are tools for attack; they are also tools of deterrence, yet the deterrence comes from the fact that they are lethal tools, built with only one purpose in mind. Cars can kill, but this is not their main function; primarily they are tools of transportation, whereas firearms are tools of death and harm. This is where the spectral value of weaponry comes into play. Often, the weapon is no longer physically present, but it manifests itself in the physical and psychological trauma it leaves behind—an echo of its main function: harm. The firearm's functional value creates a particular tension and significance when it appears as a symbol. I distinguish between three symbolic dimensions of firearms: the object as artifact, trope, and prop. While all three refer to the symbolic level, they have a different relation to the principal function of the object (table I.1). With "artifact" I describe the sociocultural value of an object in relation to its function and to the subject using it. With "trope" I refer to the allegorical value of an object, a metaphorical, generally more abstract or broad meaning, that is still related to the object's function. With "prop" I refer to the performative value of an object, when the object is used for theatrical purposes—like a stage prop—and furthest removed from its original function.

The aforementioned harquebuses were the lethal yet fickle tools of the conquistadors as well as commodities produced and traded in Europe; as cultural artifacts, they were not overly important at the time, since for the Spaniards they were an unreliable piece of armament that provided a short-lived moment of surprise; as tropes, they are still used today to narrate the conquest as a story of technological superiority. I am unaware of concrete examples of firearms being used as props during the conquest, but one possible deployment would have been the simulation of firepower with dysfunctional cannons or harquebuses—that is, posing with firearms that have lost their lethal quality. As echoes, they appear in the collective memory of Amerindian defeat and loss—but in the nineteenth century, not in the sixteenth century.

To extrapolate these different values of firearms, I analyze a vast cultural corpus ranging from literature and music to visual culture.[4] This provides a

| The Values of an Object: The Firearm as Example | | |
|---|---|---|
| Functional Value<br><br>What is it used for? | Tool | Instrument to kill |
| Economic Value<br><br>How is it produced, obtained, and traded? | Commodity | Technological and coveted product to be produced and traded |
| Spectral Value<br><br>What does the object leave behind when it is no longer there? | Echo | The object is no longer present but it appears as an echo through what it left behind as a direct result of its functional value |

Symbolic Values—Dimensions: *What does it symbolize or stand for?*

Function ⟵⟶ Symbol

Artifact — Trope — Prop

| Sociocultural Value | Artifact | The object's sociocultural meaning in relation to its function and the subject that holds it, e.g. the firearm makes a person a combatant |
|---|---|---|
| Allegorical Value | Trope | The metaphorical meaning adjudicated to the object, further removed from its function and the individual subject, e.g. the rifle as liberation |
| Performative Value | Prop | The performative significance of the object, used like a stage prop, furthest removed from its lethal function, e.g. a dysfunctional rifle used for deterrence or decoration |

particular take on weaponry and on material culture in general, as something created and negotiated in text, sound, and image. I touch upon the object's physical materiality, but I am mainly concerned with its symbolic construction within cultural expressions. Songs, photos, and novels are prime vehicles for the communication and contemplation of violence, and the weapon acquires its sociocultural significance through them. But I also relate the symbolic meaning back to the object's functional-technical and economic aspects.

## Tools and Commodities: Death, Technology, and Trade

In the conflicts discussed throughout this book, several firearms stand out: for the Mexican Revolution, the US American Winchester Model 1894, called the *treinta-treinta* for its use of .30–30 cartridges, as well as German Mauser models and early machine guns; for the Sandinista Revolution, the FAL (Fusil Automatique Léger), a Belgian battle rifle; for the ensuing Contra War, Soviet

AK-pattern rifles; for the drug war, assault rifles such as AK-47s and AR-15s. The types of firearms reflect both the available technology and the means of production and trade at each time. Local firearms production in Latin America has been limited, but there have been some symbolically significant instances of the development of artisan weaponry. Most firearms in Latin America have been imported from countries with big military industries such as the United States, the former Soviet Union, and Western European countries. The rifles and cartridges used during the Mexican Revolution were the result of many nineteenth-century innovations in weapons technology that had made the old front-loaded muskets obsolete. These inventions included cartridges, which encased bullet, powder, and primer in a metal container instead of having to put them separately into the barrel; breech-loading rifles, in which the ammunition was inserted into the rear part rather than from the muzzle; as well as repeating rifles, which contained several rounds of ammunition (Bull 55, 217). Breech-loading, the *treinta-treinta* Winchester was a lever-action repeating rifle and the Mauser a bolt-action rifle. These innovations meant that the firearms used during the Mexican Revolution were more powerful and easier to handle. Mass production made them more accessible.

Following a long-standing pattern, the Mexican rebels acquired most of their firearms in US border towns.[5] The history of the US-Mexican borderlands is inseparable from that of arms trading. During the Mexican Revolution, US merchants readily provided firearms. Many hardware stores along the border became gun shops (Díaz 75). US companies targeted Mexicans in their ads: "Do you want a good rifle? Remember that an unarmed man is of no value. Write today. . . . It is our desire that each Mexican has a rifle" (quoted in Díaz 75). The arms trade was "funded by a booming export economy (guns for cattle, guns for oil)" (Lomnitz 383–84). In many ways, it determined the military power of the revolutionary factions. The Villistas in the Mexico's north went through great efforts to protect their railway lines to the border and thus secured their arms' supply for several years. In contrast, the Zapatistas in the central Mexico struggled to obtain weapons because they did not have such supply lines. The Orozquistas never managed to grow into a bigger movement because anti-US sentiments prevented them from trading (Aguilar Camín and Meyer 30). In response to the Orozco rebellion in 1912 and 1913, the US Congress prohibited arms exports to countries in the hemisphere with internal conflicts, but despite that, arms still passed the border (Díaz 74).

President Woodrow Wilson tried to influence the revolution by controlling weapon flows, at first during the summer of 1913 by giving only Huerta access to legal weapon imports (while other factions had to smuggle theirs). In early 1914, however, flows to all factions were opened. The US occupation of the port of Veracruz in part had to do with impeding the arrival of a German ship full of arms for Huerta (Katz, *Secret War* 167, 184–86, 196; Knight, *Mexican Revolution: Very Short Introduction* 52). In November 1914 the US forces abandoned Veracruz, leaving behind massive arms supplies. Some historians argue that this was to aide the Carrancistas (Joseph and Buchenau 73), whereas others say it was just "another episode in the long history of US forces mislaying military hardware" (Knight, *Mexican Revolution: Very Short Introduction* 64). Only when World War I increased the demand, did the arms trade in the United States become more difficult for Mexicans. Only the Carrancistas, one of the triumphant factions, were successful in running their own munitions factories (Katz, *Life and Times* 489).

Other important nineteenth-century innovations that played a role in the Mexican Revolution were smokeless powder, machine guns, and trains. Built under the Díaz regime to modernize Mexico, the railway system was appropriated by the rebel troops and used for the swift transportation of troops and weapons. This made the Mexican Revolution a modern violent experience in the Virilian sense, characterized by speed and war logistics. The "scale of the killings was unprecedented, and it reflected in a perverse fashion the depth of the Porfirian progress" (Lomnitz 383). With a death toll of more than one million people, the revolution presaged the two world wars to come: modern wars with swift massive troop movements and high casualties.

Whereas the Zapatistas were severely affected by their lack of trains and firearms, the Villistas "developed an awe-inspiring professional war machine" (Aguilar Camín and Meyer 43). Villa's massive army, the División del Norte, had at some point more than seventy thousand fighters, including a powerful cavalry. The Villista movement swiftly adopted many aspects of modern warfare, such as international trade, machine guns, trains, and strict military organization with ranks and pay grades (44). Yet they did not adapt quickly enough to the changes in combat tactics that followed the invention of smokeless powder; reducing visibility by means of trenches, ditches, and dust clouds became key (Aguilar Mora, *Una muerte sencilla* 62–63). General Álvaro Obregón had studied the Boer War and the beginning of World War I, and during the 1915 battles of the Bajío, he defeated Villa's powerful cavalry with trenches, barbed wire, and machine gun nests (62).

The Villistas tended to blame ammunition shortages for their loss, but their defeat had more to do with tactics as well as internal quarrels (Katz, *Life and Times* 492; Knight, *Mexican Revolution* 2:324–25). Villa's large, well-equipped, and reckless army had been successful against the federal and Huertista forces from 1910 to 1914, but its massive force was relatively powerless against this different style of warfare: "the élan vital of massed cavalry charges

. . . proved suicidal in the face of Obregón's well-organised, scientifically generalled army" (Knight, "Peasant" 46). Thousands died during the 1915 battles, and this bitter defeat of the División del Norte irrevocably changed the course of the revolution. Many fighters went home, and Villa turned to guerrilla warfare. In the end—after many more years of fighting—the more moderate elite forces, not the peasants and peons, won the war.

By offering these glimpses of the relation between war technology and the Mexican Revolution, I do not want to exaggerate the importance of weaponry over other political dimensions of the conflict, both internal and external. Realism in political science and international relations can be too simple, as it appears to reduce politics to counting weapons—that is, whoever has more weapons has more power. Yet, as DeLay puts its, the "arms trade emerges as a necessary, if insufficient, factor shaping first-order events in Mexican history. Again and again, the shifting architects of Mexico found their plans dependent upon, deformed, or demolished by arms flows from the U.S." (8). Weapons technology itself shaped the development of conflicts. Without explaining conflicts in their totality, highlighting these connections provides insights into how the weapon as tool and commodity affected the Mexican Revolution as well as conflicts that followed throughout the twentieth century.

Sixty years after the end of the main armed phase of the Mexican Revolution, the political and economic landscape of Latin America had changed considerably. The two world wars and the ensuing import substitution industrialization (ISI) policies had lessened Latin America's dependency, and Latin America was in the process of a rapid urbanization. What had not changed, however, was the profound inequality. At this junction, for progressive and poor segments of Latin American societies the Cuban Revolution and Marxism presented instances of intense hope that conditions could change, whereas conservative elements saw Leftist ideologies as an immense threat. This threw Latin America in the midst of the bipolar confrontation of the inaccurately called Cold War: in most world regions except Europe, the United States, and Australia, it was an intensely fought "hot" war—in desperate need of arms supplies.[6] Unlike the rebels of the Mexican Revolution, the guerrilla groups in Central and South America did not have direct access to the US market. Cuba became their main supply channel. After the Cuban Revolution had triumphed in 1959, Cuba, following an internationalist tradition, tried to export and aid guerrilla movements around the world, particularly in Latin America. Aid came in the form of training, advice, provision of a place to rest and plan on the island—and of course weapons. Usually those firearms were produced in Western Europe or in the Soviet Union and then channeled to Latin American guerrillas.

The Sandinistas, for example, smuggled weapons provided by Cuba into Nicaragua via Panama and Costa Rica (Castañeda 59). They also received generous gifts of arms from Venezuela and Panama, made deals with merchants from the Middle East, and got unexpected help from the *caudillos* of "peace-loving" Costa Rica, who in the 1970s dug up their hidden weapons arsenals for the Sandinistas, remembers Sergio Ramírez (*Adiós* 127–28, 249–50). When the Frente Sandinista de Liberación Nacional (FSLN) split in three different factions—Guerra Popular Prolongada, Tendencia Proletaria, and Tendencia Insurrecional—the pluralist Tendencia Insurrecional, or Tercerista, the one focused on creating broad alliances, was most successful in obtaining weaponry. It also acquired the most political power.

For the Sandinista guerrilla the most important rifle was the Belgian FAL, a powerful fully automatic battle rifle. The National Guard in general was better equipped than the FSLN, but the guerrilla force's acquisition of fully automatic weapons made them a serious opponent for the first time. Overall, however, the Sandinista guerrilla remained poorly armed in comparison to the military power of the Somoza regime, which did not hesitate to bomb entire cities and to use tanks and machine guns to attack Sandinista hideouts in urban spaces. The Sandinistas used any weapon they could get their hands on: AR-15s, M-1s, pistols. In 1978 a lack of firearms prompted people to take production into their own hands. In particular in Monimbó—an urban, indigenous neighborhood of Masaya famous for its artisan craftsmanship—people used their skills and the gunpowder from fireworks to make homemade bombs and resisted the National Guard with nets, masks, and marimbas. Celebrated by the Sandinistas as a heroic symbol of indigenous resistance in Nicaragua, the use of such weaponry shows the extreme precariousness of the fight.

Many people assume that the global weapon of insurgency, the AK-47, was also the most important firearm of the Sandinista guerrilla. Relatively simple in its technical aspects, it has become one of the most commercially successful weapons worldwide because it is easy to use and fares well under difficult environmental conditions. From the Kalashnikov of the Soviet Union, it became the rifle of liberation struggles in Africa, Asia, and Latin America, making it even onto the flag of independent Mozambique. However, the AK-47 only entered Nicaragua on a large scale in the 1980s, once the guerrilla force had become the regular army. The AK-47 was the weapon of the times of the Contra War. Financed by Nicaraguan elites and the United States, the Contra War erupted shortly after the Sandinistas took power and lasted through the 1980s. The US government under President Ronald Reagan was a powerful, ruthless enemy that did anything to provide the counterrevolutionaries with arms, as evidenced by the infamous 1985–86 Iran-Contra affair. During this episode, members of the Reagan administration illegally sold arms to embargoed Iran to continue financing the Contras, which had been prohibited by the US Congress. The Sandinistas, turned from an insurgent guerrilla into a revolutionary state party and military fighting counterrevolutionary insurgents, answered with an arms buildup.

In the meantime, conflicts in other Central American countries—in particular, El Salvador and Guatemala—intensified, as conservative authoritarian military regimes cracked down on guerrilla organizations and civilians. In the 1980s the Central American armed forces grew from forty-eight thousand to two hundred thousand members and US military aid to Central America's military governments grew exponentially (Pearce, "From Civil War" 594–95). The Salvadoran guerrillas started to receive arms from across the world, including Ethiopia and Vietnam, smuggled through Cuba and Nicaragua (Castañeda 98). The Western solidarity movements also chipped in. The radical left in West Germany, for example, started a fundraising campaign called Weapons for El Salvador and collected more than 3 million deutsche marks for the Salvadoran guerrillas. The Salvadoran guerrilla became one of the world's best equipped guerrilla movements. Whereas both Cuba and Nicaragua fought "relatively short, small-scale guerrilla wars, with less than a few thousand poorly armed combatants" (Castañeda 102), in El Salvador the war turned into a drawn-out conflict between two heavily armed armies. In Guatemala, where the guerrillas were never very strong in size and equipment, the Guatemalan military used the threat of the guerrillas to militarize the country and slaughter the civilian indigenous population, under the pretense that they were base communities for the guerrillas.

In all of Latin America, between 1959 and 1990, an estimated half a million people were killed "mainly by counterrevolutionary violence" (Beverley 58). In Central America alone, more than three hundred thousand people were killed and over two million displaced (Kurtenbach 95), of these over two hundred thousand in the Guatemalan genocide. With regard to the Sandinista Revolution, an estimated ten thousand to thirty-five thousand people died during the fighting in the 1970s and another ten thousand to forty-three thousand died during the Contra War in the 1980s (Lacina 405). In the early 1990s peace agreements were reached in Nicaragua, El Salvador, and Guatemala; disarmament and demobilization processes began thereafter. Tens of thousands of combatants from both sides were demobilized and thousands of weapons destroyed or sold. Yet the violence did not end. Central America still feels like a battlefield, only that now the lines have become blurrier. Throughout Central America, especially in El Salvador and Honduras, homicide rates are among the world's highest. Governments have responded with militarist tough-on-crime *mano dura* politics to the gang violence that emerged in the

FIGURE I.1. Diego Rivera, *Paisaje Zapatista El Guerrillero*. Banco de México Diego Rivera Frida Kahlo Museums Trust, México, D.F./Artists Rights Society (ARS), New York (reproduction rights); Museo Nacional de Arte (MUNAL) (provided high-quality image).

poor neighborhoods as a result of Latino gang members deported from the United States; however, the major drug-trafficking organizations have been allowed to operate in the region with impunity. The precariousness of many of the youth gangs has manifested in the return of artisan makeshift weapons: easily discarded cheap pistols made out of metal tubes and springs, called *armas hechizas* or *chimbas* (Godnick 8).

The leftover weapons from the wars in Central America have sometimes ended up in the Mexican drug war, a conflict that has been brewing since the 1970s but escalated in 2006 when President Felipe Calderón declared a war on drug trafficking. The main source for the weapons used in the drug war is the US retail market. According to a 2013 edition of *Small Arms Survey* ("Captured and Counted" 295), an estimated 68 percent of the firearms used by drug-trafficking organizations in Mexico come from the United States. Assault rifles such as the AK-47 and the AR-15 are the order of the day. The AK-47 is the most important weapon associated with Mexican narcos; many narcocorridos sing of the AK-47, affectionately calling it "goat's horn" due to the rounded shape of the magazine. Yet the firepower acquired officially by government forces far supersedes that of alleged criminal insurgents. Since 2007 Mexico has undergone a process of heavy militarization. Human rights violations and disappearance have increased exponentially. Many people have died in this conflict: an estimated 170,000 people dead and counting (*El País*). In both Mexico and Central America, military spending is on the rise. As the Cold War confrontations fade into memory, the region still operates under the sign of the rifle.

## Artifacts and Tropes: Citizenship, Militancy, and Modernity

The meaning of firearms as artifacts and tropes goes to the heart of my analysis. The firearm appears as an artifact of participation within state and modernity in texts about the Mexican Revolution, as an artifact of militancy and a trope of modernity in texts about the Nicaraguan Revolution, and as a confusing sign in the current drug war. These symbolic meanings relate to the question of the use of force in politics, the dangers of militarism and revolutionary justice, and the complex interactions between gender and weaponry.

### The Rifle as Artifact for Participation within State and Modernity

Diego Rivera captured the symbolic significance of weaponry in *Paisaje Zapatista El Guerrillero,* one of his earliest paintings of the Mexican Revolution (figure I.1). He painted it in 1915, after a momentous encounter with the young writer Martín Luis Guzmán. Rivera was at the time studying painting in Europe. Guzmán, recently exiled from Mexico, visited him at his studio in Paris and gave him a riveting firsthand account of the rebel campfires and the Villista and Zapatista occupation of Mexico City. Rivera would later judge the cubist painting to be his "most faithful expression of the Mexican mood" (cited in Ades 129). Except for the still volcanoes in the background, everything in this painting is in turmoil, floating in an upside-down world: the shadows in the painting are white, not black, and through the cubist technique of faceting, most objects appear in pieces. There are fragments of a colorful serape and a tall wide-brimmed hat. The Mexican peasant attire points to a rural context, but no person takes shape. Only two objects appear intact: a rifle in the center and an empty paper note seemingly nailed to the right corner of the canvas. Amid the upheaval, the rifle is the only thing that is distinguishable, the only object that stands out clearly. Meanwhile, the empty paper note—somewhat detached from the painting because of its trompe l'oeil three-dimensionality—is a reminder of the tasks ahead: to write the story of the revolution, to give it shape, to make sense of the turmoil. This story must necessarily start with the rifle.

The multiple uprisings and diverse events commonly referred to as the Mexican Revolution involved local and national elites, but it was also one of the most important peasant insurgencies in Latin America, encompassing indigenous and mestizo peons and small farmers in the south as well as cowboys, settlers, and rural workers in the north. This is what lurks behind the rifle: a new political entity. Through the rifle the peasant enters the political arena and national consciousness. The rifle at that moment stops being just a tool of violence or a commodity and becomes an artifact. It is the rifle as artefact that Rivera captures in his painting and that appears in so many other cultural expressions of the revolution. By joining *la bola*—the revolution's mobile collective of insurgents traversing the country—the combatants realized their self-worth and affirmed their presence. *La bola* gave them, as Aguilar Mora puts it, "the precious gift of finding their place; of finding that . . . with just a Winchester rifle as their sole property, their life was pertinent precisely because of the fact that they owned it" (*El silencio* 126).[7] Equipped with a rifle and draped in cartridge belts, these peasant insurgents manifested themselves within the nation and became visible as social and political subjects.

Gayatri Chakravorty Spivak has famously argued that subalterns cannot speak since they are not being heard, in the sense that subalterns rarely manage to imprint their subjectivity within history. But to some extent, they do speak when they carry a rifle—even more so when their images circulate widely, as was the case during the Mexican Revolution, the first modern mass-mediated revolution. In *Mexico's Once and Future Revolution,* Joseph and Buchenau caution against overstating the influence of the Mexican Revolution, arguing that in terms of impact it "pales by comparison to the Cuban Revolution" (9). Arguably, the Cuban Revolution had greater global repercussions, but the symbolic and hemispheric significance of Mexico's massive peasant insurgency should not be underestimated, especially because of its powerful iconography. Therefore, throughout this book the Mexican Revolution is the starting point for all inquiries into the meaning of firearms in the region. The rebels, especially the Villistas, had photographers, writers, and film crews at their disposal, enabling them to project to a broader audience. The rebels thus imprinted their peasant-popular political subjectivities into the collective imagination, and these images were taken up in songs, novels, paintings, and movies, traveling far and wide.

The rifle as artifact carried other important symbolic significance. It meant a visible participation within modernity. Generally dismissed as backward and stuck in tradition, peasants were handling rifles, mounting machine gins, riding trains, and having their picture taken. Thus they undeniably participated in modernity in all its swiftness and belligerence, as theorized by Virilio (*Speed and Politics* 62, 149). Appropriating modern technology, these peasants rose to resist an elite project of modernity and demand an alternative one built around social justice and identity politics.[8] Violence can also be seen as a "communicative exchange . . . in which destruction of property and the infliction of physical harm (sometimes unto death) is the essential mode of signification" (McDowell 19), and the firearm is a pivotal object in this exchange. Letting the arms speak in the form of an insurgency, a collective revolt against authority, is a form of negotiation, an act both vis-à-vis and within the state: part negotiation with the state apparatus, part participation within the state's formation.[9]

In cultural expressions from or about the Mexican Revolution, the firearm appears as such an ambiguous artifact of communication—from the corridos about the *treinta-treinta* to the novels of the revolution such as Mariano Azuela's *Los de abajo*, Nellie Campobello's *Cartucho*, Martín Luis Guzmán's *El águila y la serpiente*, and Rafael Muñoz's *Vamónos con Pancho Villa*. Often these depictions are not necessarily positive or affirmative. In fact, many novelists appear horrified by the unruly peasant armies, their frenzied violence and never-ending firing squads. Horacio Legrás, for example, has pertinently argued that most *novelas de la revolución* "express such dismay at the lack of moral or ideological convictions involved in the revolution that one is forced to wonder in what sense these are novels *of* the revolution" (*Literature and Subjection* 112–13, italics in the original). Subaltern studies generally advocates turning to court cases and other archives to surface subaltern thought and talk, yet we can also analyze fiction created by elites and read it against the grain to excavate the subaltern thought imprinted within it. Legrás as well as Juan Pablo Dabove in *Nightmares of the Lettered City* and Max Parra in *Writing Pancho Villa's Revolution* have offered such against-the-grain readings of novels of the Mexican Revolution. My book does so as well, but by focusing the reading on the main instrument of expression of the insurgents. In many of these texts, writers fixate on weaponry, trying to discover its deeper meaning. This representation has two sides: the political-performative reality of the peasant insurgent and his firearm manifest in the literary piece, and the mediation and interpretation by elite discourse.

As the meaning of the revolution reveals itself in the firearm or is sought in the firearm, we as readers can sense both the firearm's potent political-symbolic significance and the powerful form of myth-making in relation to the firearm. Weapons become a means to mediate the political, not in the sense of the often negatively connoted "party politics" within a representative democracy, but rather "the political" as the sphere of actions, attitudes, and processes that revolve around forms of social organization, generally in the form of a state, and around power. What is peculiar about the symbolic significance of weaponry in the cultural expressions of the Mexican Revolution is that firearms do not primarily appear as artifacts to take over the state apparatus but as artifacts to affirm one's presence vis-à-vis the state and society, to become and to be recognized as a social and political subject—a prosthesis for citizenship.

The use of force in the realm of politics is a topic hotly and long debated in philosophy and political science. There are those who see war as the natural order of things (Thomas Hobbes) and those who see war as the "continuation of politics with other means" (Carl von Clausewitz), or its inversion by Michel Foucault—namely, politics as "the continuation of war by other means," ("Society" 15) or politics as a field of friends and foe with the latent possibility of war (Carl Schmitt), so violence as inherent to politics. There are those who warn firmly against its use and perils, who warn not to confuse violence with power (Hannah Arendt), and those who theorized and embodied non-violence as a powerful tool (Mahatma Gandhi). Then there are those thinkers who to varying degrees defend revolutionary political violence as a means to bring about change—in particular, to end the harm inflicted by capitalism and colonialism (Karl Marx; Friedich Engels; Frantz Fanon). As Idelber Avelar illustrates in *The Letter of Violence,* the legitimation of the use of force in Marxist political thought is based on the axiom "that revolutionary violence brings with itself, by definition, the promise of an end to violence as such" (5). The idea that revolutionary violence is redeeming constitutes the "*ethical* basis for the vindication of violence" (5, italics in original). Yet from today's perspective, it is questionable whether revolutionary violence can "be neatly separated" from other types of violence (6). Also, spirals of violence after the triumph of an insurgent group and authoritarian tendencies of many left-wing revolutionary movements and regimes have cast doubt on this utopian disposition and possibility.

"Violence" is a slippery word as it encompasses many more aspects than direct or physical violence, which is physical harm against people and property. Johan Galtung coined the term "indirect violence" (83), violence that materializes in poverty, inequality, and dependency. Spivak described epistemic violence (76), which is exerted through language, knowledge systems, and their assertions and negations. Slavoj Žižek called the former "systemic violence" and the latter "'symbolic' violence" (1–2, 9). Revolutionary violence is often directed explicitly against direct—as well as indirect and epistemic— violence and can in turn exert its own direct, indirect, and epistemic violence. Throughout the book, my main focus is direct violence, although I keep these overlapping yet different types of violence within analytical view. I attempt to ground the discussion of political violence by focusing primarily on physical violence and one of its main tools and artifacts.

While this book does not propose a solution to the conundrum of the use of force in the political realm, it offers an exploration of the complex and contradictory nature of insurgent violence by pointing to its instrumental, economic, symbolic, and traumatic dimensions. For that purpose I analyze the firearm as the object through which these dimensions of direct insurgent violence are expressed and negotiated—within the particular discursive space opened up by cultural production. I turn to Walter Benjamin, who developed a complex take on violence in the political realm. He questioned the nexus between ends and means when it comes to the justification of violence. According to Benjamin, this nexus is the most common but flawed construction within natural and positive law. Written before his immersion within Marxist thought and under the impression of the writings by anarcho-sindicalist Georges Sorel, Benjamin's 1921 essay "Critique of Violence" offers a critical evaluation of violence in relation to the state, in particular to the law. Often misunderstood, partly because in German the word *Gewalt* simultaneously means force, violence, coercion, and power, the essay points to the violence underlying any conception of law. Benjamin distinguishes between three different types of violence/power/force: law-making (*rechtsetzend*), law-preserving (*rechtserhaltend*), and law-destroying (*rechtsvernichtend*). He criticizes law-making and law-preserving violence but exalts law-destroying violence because it destroys the violence of the law and does not intend (yet) to impose a new order, to become law-making violence. Whereas law-making violence is menacing, bloody, avenging (*sühnend*), and concerned with affirming its own power, law-destroying violence is striking (*schlagend*), sovereign (*waltend*), expiatory-absolving (*entsühnend*), and life-affirming (59–60, 64).

Law-destroying violence, also called divine violence by Benjamin, is a pure, cataclysmic violence that erases what was before. Divine violence is violence that just is. It is only means and does not need to express an end. In many ways the armed violence of *la bola* is an expression of this violence. It appears most clearly in Mariano Azuela's *Los de abajo*, the most canonical novel of the Mexican Revolution. In the book men take up arms and they continue to fight, all the while refusing to explain why. The peasant insurgents compare themselves to a stone that keeps on rolling (Azuela 207). Fighting and moving is paramount (209), and what comes after is of lesser importance. By pointing to the stone metaphor or to the law-destroying violence present in narratives of the Mexican Revolution, I by no means want to repeat the dismissive gesture of the fiction itself, where this representation served the purpose of highlighting the peasants' lack of political conviction or consciousness. There exists a generalized tendency in politics and historiography to depoliticize, minimize, or criminalize peasant insurgency. Ranajit Guha has argued most compellingly against this tendency, since it takes subjecthood away from the peasants in the very moment that they manifest themselves as subjects through insurgency (*Elementary Aspects* 3). Analyzing the case of peasant insurgency in colonial India, Guha pointed out that this "was a motivated and conscious undertaking on the part of rural masses" ("Prose of Counter-Insurgency" 46) and cautioned against narratives of spontaneity about peasant insurgencies where these appear as natural phenomena without direction; Guha cautioned that generally peasants had too much at stake to rise in an act of "absent-mindedness" (*Elementary Aspects* 9; "Prose of Counter-Insurgency" 45–46). For the Latin American context, Florencia Mallon has argued against the idea that peasants in the long nineteenth century (1820s–1930s) did not have a conception of the nation and argued for a historiography that "accounted for the active participation and intellectual creativity of subaltern classes in processes of nation-state formation" (3).

The metaphor of the stone appears to deny subjecthood to the peasant, and Azuela's oeuvre is full of these natural metaphors to describe the masses (Dabove, *Nightmares* 256). Yet, in a Deleuzian reading, Dabove has compellingly argued that the political dimension of the "nomadic politics" of *la bola* lies precisely in the rebels' refusal to explain the purpose of their insurrection (253–54). Dabove sees the political dimension of the insurgency in *Los de abajo* in the fact that the peasant insurgents "never appeal to 'Mexico' as the final cause of the war" (254), meaning that they operate outside of the conceptual confines of the nation-state. Yet if we add Benjamin to the mix, we see the state dimension of their acts, since the destructive dynamic of *la bola* makes away with one of the pillars of the state: the violence of law. Azuela wants to highlight the unjustified, directionless violence of these peasants, especially in the more negative second edition.[10] However, Benjamin helps us to see the acts of this small *bola* not as a lack of conviction or ideology but as a manifestation of divine violence—a violence that destroys the previous regime but that is nonviolent in its affirmation of life versus the blood violence of the law.

Benjamin's defense of insurgent violence, however, is not a defense of revolutionary terror. In fact, he explicitly criticizes executions as violent means of positing law ("Zur Kritik der Gewalt" 43). When revolutions start to judge and execute people for the purpose of establishing their own *Gewalt*, they cease to be an instrument of law-destroying violence and become an instrument of a new violent law-making and law-preserving force. This is crucial as we think through the issue of what has wrongfully been called "revolutionary justice," but which is rather utterly problematic revolutionary law making. The French Revolution's guillotine and the Mexican Revolution's endless firing squads stand as a reminder of the violence directed against supposed internal and external enemies. So do the Cuban Revolution's televised executions of former henchmen and the instances of guerrillas turning against their own, which are among the most chilling and disturbing moments of the Latin American left (Franco *Cruel Modernity* 120–51).

The Sandinistas wanted to escape this dangerous circle of revolutionary law-making violence. The expression by FSLN founder Tomás Borge that his "personal vengeance would be the right of his torturer's children to schools and flowers" sums up the FSLN position and myth on that subject: in this revolution, from a position of moral superiority, there would be no acts of vengeance or execution. While there were instances of executions in the aftermath of the war, the Nicaraguan Revolution was a revolution that in general "refused the temptation of the *paredón*" (Gould 13, italics in original).[11] Yet the Sandinista Revolution fell prey to another form of law-making violence: militarism. Benjamin specifically warned against militarism. Based on the definition by Martina Klein and Klaus Schubert (196), I understand militarism as the organization of the state and society according to military ideals and values, including bellicose categories of thought (the necessity of war, hierarchy, discipline, and obedience) and the glorification of military culture through marches and the display of uniforms and weaponry. Benjamin defined it more broadly as "the compulsory, universal use of violence as a means to the ends of the state" ("Critique of Violence" 241) and used it to establish the critical interrelation between violence and law.[12] Militarism uses violence to preserve and to make law and subordinates the citizen, in particular through conscription, under the law for a "legal end" ("*Rechtszweck*," "Zur Kritik der Gewalt" 40). Quite pointedly, forced conscription under the Sandinistas (the Servicio Militar Patriótico established in 1983 in the midst of the Contra War) is one of the main reasons that the Sandinistas lost popular support. This is the danger when the revolutionary violence starts to establish itself, when it becomes the new regime: it oozes its own law-making and law-preserving violence and thus becomes violent again, because it no longer suspends the violence of law-making. Militarism is an imminent internal danger of regimes that have come to power through armed conflict or that are, or feel they are, under attack by internal or external enemies.

Since Benjamin's text is not a theory of revolution but a *Kritik* (a critical evaluation of different forms of violence), and because he defends an undirected pure-means violence, Benjamin seemingly does not offer an answer to the possible organization of a postrevolutionary regime. There is, however, a hint of how he interprets the meaning of insurgent violence for the order that follows it in his criticism of representative democracy. Benjamin criticizes parliaments for offering a "woeful spectacle because they have not remained conscious of the revolutionary forces to which they owe their existence" ("Critique of Violence" 244).[13] It would be a mistake to simply see his frustration as an example of the German mistrust of democracy in the context of the Weimar Republic, as Avelar has pointed out (*Letter of Violence* 97). Rather, it is a call for more radical politics, for a legislature that makes laws according to the force/violence/power (*Gewalt*) of the people that created it. Benjamin's is a call for more daring, radical politics, "worthy of the violence" ("dieser Gewalt würdig") ("Zur Kritik der Gewalt" 46) that created the parliament in the first place. On the one hand, he wants to point out that it is a fallacy that parliaments are nonviolent means for making politics, since "positing law is positing power and as such an act of immediate manifestation of violence."[14] But on the other hand, there is a hope in the text, however vague, that parliaments use their power to develop a radical revolutionary political agenda. It is unclear how that would work, but if we go back to the only violence that Benjamin exalts (law-destroying violence), it would need to be leveling, absolving, life-affirming, and always destroying its own authority.

In the cultural production analyzed throughout *Modernity at Gunpoint*, the firearm is the symbol and a reminder of the need for such insurgent politics—meaning that the violent, radical, precarious gesture of armed insurgency appears as a call for a politics that levels. As such, the firearm appears as a prosthesis for citizenship, a means for people to affirm themselves as political and social subjects. That a firearm functions as a prothesis of citizenship is far from ideal—and through the notion of the firearm as echo, I discuss many of the harmful effects of this violent conception of politics. Yet it has to be seen within the postcolonial reality of countries built on feudal-capitalist and racial hierarchies. Within these structures the majority has always been excluded from positions of power within the state and market, and as such the firearm becomes a means to be seen or heard.[15]

## Rifles and Gender

This participation within state formation through firearms is also, unsurprisingly, deeply tied to questions of gender.[16] Often the people affirming themselves through firearms are men, and with the firearm they affirm themselves both as men and as citizens. That power, state formation, and citizenship are so often played out through men and arms has consequences. Within armed conflict an "extreme masculinity" can emerge (Franco, *Cruel Modernity*). Based on "an idealization of the dominating and ruthless male figure," this form of masculinity uses "massacres, rape, and desecration" for internal cohesion of groups of aggressors who are trained to become oblivious to acknowledging the body's vulnerability (*Cruel Modernity* 15). Rape of women and men, dead or alive, is used to denigrate the enemy and impose one's masculinity. In this context the rifle is not only an important artifact and trope of masculinity; it can also become a menacing repurposed tool and trope of sexual violence.

Extreme masculinity is not the only masculinity that emerges when it comes to armed conflict. In the cultural expressions studied here, two main types of masculinity are at play: the virile masculinity of the man of arms, both desired and feared; and the frail masculinity of the man of letters, fearful or effeminate, mocked but also affirmed. These are symptomatic of the gender and class dimensions at work when it comes to masculinity, weaponry, and politics in Mexican and Central American cultural production. The men of arms often come from a peasant or generally lower social background than the intellectuals, and the awareness of class and education distances them, frequently giving a patronizing tone to the intellectual's maneuvers. In many novels the intellectual appears as being drawn to the man of arms, his violence and virility, but also as trying to position himself outside of the violence, portraying himself as a pillar of reason amid frenzied action. The intellectual figure tends to flaunt his lack of dexterity with the gun, but he also needs the firearm or the man of arms to substantiate his revolutionary status and virility. It seems like the frail, seemingly nonviolent masculinity of the intellectual is often devalued. Yet the power-savvy rationality and linguistic capacity of this masculinity is also reaffirmed as the form that will prevail and shape the future of the nation: exalting the war masculinity but administering it from afar.

When it comes to women and war, things become even more complicated: often women are either absent from war narratives or the woman with the rifle is a highly ambiguous and controversial image. There is a deep interconnection between gender roles and war. Across cultures and history, war and gender have always mutually influenced each other (Goldstein 9–10). At the core of the correlation lies the pattern that in order to "help overcome soldiers' reluctance to fight, cultures develop gender roles that equate 'manhood' with toughness under fire" (9), whereas they keep "women away from killing roles" (127). The military relies on women but also needs to keep them away from "combat"—a term that "is usually conveniently vague in definition" (Enloe 13). By maintaining "combat" as a male domain, men can continue to "claim a uniqueness and superiority that will justify their dominant position in the social order" (15). Throughout history, however, women have changed and subverted gender roles in relation to war by participating in numerous ways and adopting combat roles (Cooke and Woollacott 323). By constantly redefining "combat" and the "front," the military has used the essential services supplied by women for a smooth functioning of the war machine but still managed to make women appear as "creatures marginal to the military's core identity" (Enloe 6).

There is an assumed gendered division of labor during war that equates the military sphere with public-masculine and the civilian sphere with domestic-feminine. Mary Louis Pratt has pointed out that within this common misconception the military sphere is the space where history is made by men-citizens who carry out productive (war) activities: they fight, they are soldiers. The civilian-domestic sphere is outside of history, constituted by women-noncitizens who carry out reproductive activities in the home: they wait, they are daughters, wives, girlfriends, sisters of soldiers ("Mi cigarro" 159). Yet while war narratives often operate with these dichotomies, the history of war tends to be more complicated than simple oppositions (Cooke 31).[17] There is an enormous dependency and permeability between the two spheres. During armed insurrection, spaces of participation can open up for women, but they are generally still determined by patriarchal structures of power, and there is an enormous economic and social pressure to remain in the civilian-domestic sphere. While the rifle in the hands of a woman intrigues societies and artists, it breaks gender roles so drastically that it seemingly always needs to be qualified, chastised, or restrained. The woman with the rifle threatens both the gender and the war system; thus, the weapon generally appears as an uncertain or transient artifact in the hand of a woman.

At the same time, the female element can be used to legitimize war, which was the case especially among the Sandinistas. One of the most iconic photographs of the Sandinista Revolution is that of a breastfeeding woman with a broad smile on her face and an AK-47 on her shoulder: "La miliciana de

Waswalito" taken in 1984 by Orlando Valenzuela.[18] This image has been used multiple times in political campaigns and murals and is still commonly sold as a postcard in Nicaragua. It is a powerful image because of the unselfconscious naturalness of the breastfeeding woman and because of the simultaneous presence of a baby and a rifle. Liberation and joy emanate from the photo.

The problem, however, was that even though the woman in arms was celebrated, her own liberation was not necessarily part of the Sandinistas' agenda. The photo has hence been criticized for "harnessing women for war without altering fundamental gender relations" (Goldstein 81) and for initiating the de facto return of women to the domestic sphere after the war (Enloe 166). The figure of the emancipated female combatant soon gave way to the conventional one of the mother producing warriors for the nation, as both Goldstein (81) and Sofia Montenegro have pointed out. The photo can be viewed in two ways. One possible reading shows that women can be both mothers and warriors, simultaneously carrying a baby and rifle, thus allowing for complex identities. In the other interpretation, the revolutionary gesture is celebrated, but the radicality of the armed woman is reined in by the presence of the baby and the rifle is a temporary accessory, a prop in a photo op.

Regardless, overall there is a strategic use of women in the Sandinista discourse. Through the presence of women, Sandinista songs, posters, and literary texts underscored that their violence was different from that of reactionary forces and right-wing dictatorships. It could not be the same if women were a part of the fighting. Ileana Rodríguez offers an extensive analysis of this in *Women, Guerrillas, and Love* and cautions that "the revolutionaries deluded themselves in believing that by proposing an 'alternative maleness,' one incorporating female traits such as *tendresse,* they would deliver the New Man" (33, italics in the original). In a way the focus on *tendresse* made the Sandinistas overlook their own authoritarianism and militarist machismo. The relationship between sandinismo and women (particularly feminist struggles) is an often disheartening tale (Kampwirth; Randall, *Sandino's Daughters Revisited;* Montenegro; Heumann; I. Rodríguez), but for many women the participation in the insurgency was nonetheless a pathway for personal liberation (Belli, *El país;* Randall, *Sandino's Daughters*). Despite the limitations and obstacles that women faced within the guerrilla organizations, it is certain that the Central American guerrillas saw a proportionally much higher number of women in combat and leadership roles than in previous insurgencies.

## The Rifle as Artifact of Militancy and Trope of Modernity

In the second half of the twentieth century, as guerrilla movements erupted across Latin America, there were more active fighting roles for women, but this was not the only change. While the peasantry was the main agent in the early twentieth-century insurgencies, in the guerrilla period it was the middle class—at times in broad alliances with peasants and elites—that took up arms. The Cuban Revolution (1956–59) and the Guevarian theory of the *foquismo* became the example to follow: a small group of insurgents fighting a guerrilla war in the mountains creates a focus that then supposedly triggers a general insurrection. The triumphant Cuban Revolution did not invent armed struggle, there was a long tradition across Latin America, but the Cuban regime "refined a tradition, and made it a policy of state and party" (Castañeda 69) and "affirmed armed struggle as the only way to bring about change" (Franco *Decline and Fall* 88).

Given that the Cuban Revolution became the example and supporter of many armed movements in the world, it is curious that the revolution's iconography rarely features weapons. Rather, the militarist and masculinist elements of the guerrillas in the Sierra Maestra are encapsulated in the men's beards, uniforms, and cigars—attributes with which Fidel Castro and Che Guevara rarely parted throughout their lives after the Sierra Maestra. Only a handful of photos exist that feature Guevara with a firearm. The rifle only becomes central after the triumph of the Cuban Revolution as the artifact that turns men and women into *guerrilleros* and *guerrilleras* and that bestows true militant status. Even though the FSLN eventually moved away from the Guevarian focus theory, the Sandinista militants aspired to be like El Che. The rifle as artifact became a prosthesis for militancy. It showed one's will to use violence but, more important, one's willingness to sacrifice, to take on the hardship and danger of guerrilla warfare, in the mountain or the city, and to live in the proximity of death. The rifle was a symbol—artifact, trope, prop—of one's conviction. Holding it therefore brought one closer to El Che, whose emaciated cadaver, whose sacrifice as Latin America's very own Messiah, was the example to follow.

Whereas the rebels of the Mexican Revolution spent little time justifying violence, the Central American guerrillas did. In the Sandinista discourse there were many very deliberate and careful attempts to justify the use of violence. In this context the rifle often got detached from its lethal function and instead became a trope of the new dawn. Although the Sandinista Revolution did not have a deep grounding in Marxist thought and the revolutionaries took a certain pride in not being theoretical nor dogmatic, they still operated under the Marxist notion of revolutionary violence as redeeming (Avelar, *Letter of Violence* 5). The promise of the Sandinista Revolution was an end of violence. Through armed struggle, Nicaraguan society would be cleansed of its long history of both indirect and direct violence. The revolution was also aimed at ending epistemic violence—that is, it was going to give agency and a voice to subaltern people so that the nation could come into its own.

In the Sandinista discourse the projection of a nonviolent future materializes in what I call an enchanted modernity. This concept, discussed in detail in chapter 4, appears vividly in the songs of Carlos and Luis Enrique Mejía Godoy, Nicaragua's most famous singer-songwriters. Contrary to Max Weber's well-known conceptualization of modernity as characterized byan increasing rationalization that leads to disenchantment ("Wissenschaft als Beruf"), in the Mejía Godoy brother's songs a vision appears in which armed struggle brings about a romantic, egalitarian, nonsecular, nonpositivist and hence enchanted society. This ideal is embodied and symbolized by the metaphor of a rifle that shoots auroras.

While the Sandinista Revolution differs in many aspects from the Mexican Revolution, it was also haunted by its powerful iconography. The Sandinista discourse similarly harbored the idea that the rifle as artifact could function as a prosthesis for citizenship. The song "Asalto al Palacio" from *Canto épico al FSLN* retells the events of the spectacular seizing of the Nicaraguan Congress in August 1978 by a Sandinista commando. A corrido composed and written by Carlos Mejía Godoy but sung by Mexican singer Amparo Ochoa, the song activates the memory of the Mexican Revolution. It celebrates the firearm as the object that gives people the power to exercise their political rights, to effectively become citizens: "when the furious rifle roared . . . for the first time, the citizenry was truly in session."[19] In the song, true citizenship starts with the roar of the rifle. The difference is that most Sandinista militants were not subaltern subjects trying to affirm their presence through the rifle. These were generally men and women already constituted as political subjects by their class or formation; however, the Somoza regime had made their citizenship and life—and those of others—precarious. Whereas the Mexican rebels rose to negotiate and participate within state formation, the Sandinistas rose with the explicit aim to take over the state apparatus. The rifle was an expression of militant citizenship, of insurgents who wanted take control of the state apparatus because it had lost legitimacy and represented an exclusive, repressive, and exploitative elite project.

### The Rifle as Blurry Sign: Neoliberalism and the Citizen as Violent Entrepreneur

In the context of today's drug war in Mexico and Central America, the connection between rifle and citizenship appears less evident. More than a hundred years after Rivera's 1915 painting, the rifle again is the only thing that stands out sharply, but what lurks behind it is far less clear. This is partly due to the conflict being current, since it tends to be easier to evaluate events in retrospect. But the blurriness also has to do with the conflict and the times themselves. The current drug war is alternately seen as a criminal insurgency, a civil war, or a conflict through which a state tries to control its market share via counterinsurgent techniques. Granted, the Mexican Revolution was also an all-out civil war, utterly confusing and with shifting alliances, different rural and local concerns, and state and nonstate forces overlapping and changing. Yet the issue with the current drug war is that no clear political identity seems to lurk behind the rifle but the narco—a nebulous shape of ruthless capitalist interests and desperate attempts of survival and consumption. However, this does not make the conflict any less political.

Including the narco complicates things because it seems to not quite fit. My main concern in this book is insurgency by violent nonstate actors, but sometimes these cannot be so easily distinguished from paramilitaries and state actors.[20] Battle lines are often blurry as insurgents take on state functions, counterinsurgents disguise or see themselves as insurgents, or a state creates supposed insurgents. In the current armed conflict, any ideological underpinning other than neoliberalism is hard to see, and the narcos are certainly not a leftist group trying to take over the state via armed struggle. But the lack of a clear political ideology does not make the thousands of civilians, paramilitaries, private security guards, and state forces who are currently under arms in the region any less real. This urges us to think about the narco phenomenon in relation to state formation, citizenship, and modernity.

Including the narco phenomenon helps us to see that these conflicts are not as separate as some would make them out to be. It helps to see continuities, similarities, and differences. There have been overlaps between insurgency, counterinsurgency, and the drug business. During the Cold War, for example, drugs were used to finance insurgent and counterinsurgent actions (Andreas 283; Valenzuela Arce 20). Once the Cold War was over, drugs replaced guerrillas on the US radar; drugs have been a welcome reason to stay involved in the region and have dominated relations and military aid since the 1990s (Andreas 285, 288). Meanwhile, the state apparatus in most Latin American countries has responded to drug-trafficking organizations in the same manner as it did to the guerrillas: counterinsurgency warfare, often euphemistically called low-intensity warfare. Dawn Paley has argued that a greater historical awareness, especially of the "US-backed counterinsurgency war in Central America," helps to elucidate the drug war in Mexico since the Central American wars are "part of the repressive memory that has been activated in order to carry out the ongoing 'war on drugs'" ("Repressive Memories" n.p.). Unsurprisingly, many former elite soldiers from Central America and Mexico now work for drug-trafficking organizations.

In the current conflict there appear to be very few insurgents; most of the men with guns appear to be state forces or paramilitaries, meaning that they are violent actors operating in relation to the state or taking on state functions. Thus the rifle as a prosthesis for a citizenship constructed within insurgency does not quite fit. But maybe the firearm in the narco context is precisely that appropriately nebulous artifact for intervening within a receding state in a neoliberal, postmodern context. The citizen has become an entrepreneur, and the narco is a good market-citizen in the sense that he uses all means—exercising violence and embodying other state functions—to make a profit. In this conflict the rifle is, above all, a blurry sign. As such, it appears as a tool of violence and an artifact of a neoliberal conception of citizenship and modernity but more often as a mere prop.

## Props: Theater and Truth

When a firearm is used for perfomative purposes, it becomes a prop; the firearm's symbolic significance is paramount and it is furthest removed from its lethal function. In photos of the Mexican Revolution, the firearm is both artifact and prop, when Zapata, Villa, and rank-and-file rebels pose with firearms and cartridge belts strapped across their chest. The use of the firearm as prop becomes even more evident in the hands of women, which in turn underscores yet again the ambiguity of the female combatant. There are photos from the Mexican Revolution of women "armed" and uniformed through *rebozos* crossed over the chest, emulating the men's cartridge belts. In her memories of the Sandinista Revolution, Gioconda Belli recalls that during the early days after the triumph, she and other Sandinista militants who had not actively fought in the guerrilla went through Somoza's arsenals to equip themselves with the all-essential rifle dangling from their shoulder. This use of the firearm as a revolutionary accessory makes it both artifact and prop, a sociopolitical and performative symbol of militancy (*El país* 329).

The use of firearms as props becomes most visible in the violent contexts that emerged after the end of the Cold War. One example are the *neozapatistas*. In the early 1990s, President Carlos Salinas de Gortari deepened the neoliberal restructuring of Mexico and all seemed quiet. The revolutionary fervor seemed a sentiment of the past. But in 1994 an indigenous group from Chiapas disguised with ski masks and armed with a few rifles erupted onto the world scene and declared war on the Mexican government. The Ejército Zapatista de Liberación Nacional (EZLN) laid down their arms but never surrendered them and turned into what Anne Huffschmid has called a "discourse guerrilla." They invoked Zapata and demanded that this time not the generic peasant but the indigenous subject be recognized as a citizen of the nation. The new Zapatista army was poorly armed and used the rifle more often as a prop than a tool; several members marched only with wooden rifles. By quickly ceasing fire but without rendering their arms, they garnered widespread global support. Yet it was the memory of the previous massive insurgencies that gave power to a group that defined itself as speaking through "the fire and the word" ("el fuego y la palabra"). This made their performative politics so forceful. The new Zapatista army used the ski mask as a sly reference to the bandit trope so often applied to armed peasant insurgents and as a conspicuous artifact to underscore the invisibilization of indigenous people within the Mexican nation-state. The insurgents used the real and wooden rifles as a reminder of the violent potential of the people and the need for more radical politics. The rifle as symbol, once converted into a prop in the form of a wooden rifle, became not obsolete but rather symbolically more powerful without obliterating the threat of insurgency.

But such a wooden prop is also a sign of the precariousness and lack of funds of the Zapatistas. The wooden rifle is as much a symbol of power as it is of powerlessness. It is the prop of defense of the losers of colonization and globalization. The wooden rifle also appears on La Bestia, the cargo trains used by Central American immigrants in desperate attempts to cross Mexico and migrate to the United States to escape violence and poverty. It is a dangerous trip, and the trains are repeatedly attacked by gangs and security forces. So the migrants use sticks as props for deterrence, as Oscar Martínez observed on his travel on La Bestia: "A Guatemalan indigenous man holds a stick, which he holds as if it were a rifle and aims at the darkness. The silhouette deceives" (72).[21]

These wooden "rifles" contrast sharply with another prop prevalent in current times: the lavishly decorated golden and silver assault rifles and pistols displayed in narcocultural expressions. Golden AK-47s appear on album covers of narcocorrido singers and on Instagram accounts of self-denominated narcos. Similarly, the Mexican government under Calderón spent much time and energy on elaborate displays of confiscated weapons obtained in government raids of houses of alleged narcos: always the most powerful sniper rifles up front, boxes full of ammunition, and soldiers holding up golden assault rifles and pistols for the press. The government used these weapons arrangements to showcase and exaggerate the firepower of narco organizations but also to underscore their cultural-moral threat, their exotic otherness and ostentatious indecency. In narcoculture—the cultural and material production around the real and imagined traits of the lifestyle of those involved in the illegal drug business—the not necessarily functional golden rifles are objects of a different performance than that of the government. The objective is to underscore virility and to display social mobility through an unapologetic consumerism. Different parties thus use the rifle as prop to stage different "truths" about the drug war, which makes it one of the most important but also most confusing signs of the war.

## Echoes: Trauma and Legacy of Insurgency

Firearms are not only present as tools, commodities, and symbols; they also manifest themselves when the object itself is no longer present. They acquire a spectral value in the wounds they leave behind. They leave a trace, an echo, in the body and the mind. In Nellie Campobello's *Cartucho*, for example, the echo of the firearm manifests itself in numerous ways; weaponry appears as the source of physical and psychological trauma. Campobello's book is full of the echoes of violence, full of corpses left behind by battles and executions, full of desecrated bodies, full of cruel and senseless violence, and full of women like Nellie's mother who is "tired of hearing the 30–30s" ("cansada de oir los 30–30") (84) and whose eyes have grown big and hard during the revolution pressed against "a rifle of her memory" ("un rifle de su recuerdo") (83). The cartridges and Winchester rifles leave an indelible echo in the text. Both Margo Glantz (47) and Jorge Ruffinelli ("Nellie Campobello" 64) have argued that bullets and rifles are the true protagonists of *Cartucho*. They can be sensed and heard within the rhythm, the sonority, and the constrained rapid fire lyricism of the narration. Thus Campobello re-creates the atmosphere of war and the penetration of senses and thoughts by weaponry.

Published during the Calles era (1928–1935), *Cartucho* was explicitly written against the then common vilification of Villa (Parra 51–52), and in defense of the insurgent gesture of so many rank-and-file rebels who took up arms to affirm their presence before state and society. But the book also shows the brutal and traumatizing reality of revolutionary war. The book "is a haunting and haunted text" (Linhard *Fearless* 175). An acute sense of trauma runs through the text, which speaks from the wound (178). *Cartucho*'s main narrator, a little girl, is haunted by the firearm as echo. For example, in the vignette "Desde una ventana" (Campobello 88), the girl appears fascinated with and haunted by a corpse that for days lies on the street in front of her window. When people take the corpse away, the girl hopes that they execute another one close to her window. Weimer sees this attitude as a normalization of violence (112), but I find that the narrator's apparent nonchalance is also a way of dissimulating her trauma and compassion. The girl's tone suggests that *el muerto* does not affect her, but she feels compelled to look at the corpse all the time, especially because he "seemed so afraid" ("parecía que tenía mucho miedo"). She cannot sleep thinking about the "doodle of his body" ("garabato de su cuerpo"), the echo of the armed violence, imprinted on her mind.

Along these lines, Martín Luis Guzmán's *El águila y la serpiente* dedicates a chapter to the wounds left behind by firearms. At the military hospital in Culiacán, Sinaloa, the novel's protagonist is shocked to see the manifold wounds inflicted by "the imagination of the bullets" ("imaginación de las balas") (144). So shocked is he that he intellectualizes the horrors by anthropomorphizing the bullets, complaining that not all dutifully fulfill their lethal duty. He had always believed that bullets would have "a certain sensitivity, a certain conscience" to follow their "exclusively deadly mission" ("de cierta sensibilidad, de cierta conciencia . . . su misión exclusivamente mortífera") (144). But now he finds that bullets are more imaginative, humorous, and playful, inflicting great pain, mutilating and leaving terrible and ridiculous wounds: a perforated abdomen, cerebral and spinal wounds, a missing eye, slicing the earlobe (145). The talk of the "good humor" ("buen humor") (147) of the bullets is contrasted with the scenes of agony that surround the protagonist in the hospital. Memoirs by Sandinista militants, too, are full of echoes of armed violence—in particular, the ghosts of the fallen. Sergio Ramírez recounts the anguish when he received yet another call about a slain militant and how he lived in constant company of death: "There was a smell of formaldehyde in the air" ("Había un olor a formol en el aire") (*Adiós* 46). The many deaths incurred in the guerrilla years led to a fervent death cult for the revolution's martyrs. When Salman Rushdie visited Nicaragua in 1986, he found the country "full of ghosts" (7).

Current postwar and war literature, less nostalgic and more disenchanted and angry than the Sandinista memoirs, are equally haunted by the echoes of war: the hurt bodies, the traumatized minds, and the demobilized combatants who, afloat after the peace agreements, are ever ready to return to their weapons. Militarism is the specter of these novels. In Horacio Castellanos Moya's *Insensatez,* fragments of terrible witness accounts and a paranoid yet justified fear of the Guatemalan militarist-racist police state haunt war victims and the protagonist. In Víctor Hugo Rascón Banda's *Contrabando,* about the Mexican drug war, an eerie Rulfian atmosphere reins where villagers tell stories of incursions by armed men as well as dead and disappeared relatives. The firearm as echo in these texts reveals armed insurrection as a precarious political gesture, desperate, overshadowed by the possibility of one's own death and that of others. This echo in these cultural expressions enables us to see a complex dynamic in which the firearm becomes a means for political or socioeconomic participation within unequal societies, which leaves behind wounds and voids: physical and psychological trauma and loss as well as political and social trauma due to a drastic militarization of society during conflict.

## Chapter Summaries

Chapter 1, "Carbines and Cartridge Belts: Affirming One's Presence," examines the prominence of rifles and cartridge belts in songs and Campobello's *Cartucho*. From the perspective of a little girl, *Cartucho* tells of the local and quotidian aspects of the Mexican Revolution in Chihuahua. The book presents the most complex depiction of revolutionary war, as it fully embraces the revolution's contradictory nature: brutal, precarious, dignified, and traumatic. The firearm appears as an artifact and echo of dignity and pain. *Cartucho* as well as several corridos tell a story of the Mexican Revolution, in which the masses primarily used firearms not to take power but to affirm their social and political presence. *Cartucho* illustrates the insurgent gesture of the many, often anonymous, rank-and-file rebels who died during the revolution, commemorating their precarious life and death. Drawing on ideas by Walter Benjamin, I show that Campobello represents the insurrection of the people of northern Mexico as constituting an imperative for more radical politics. There is an intent in Campobello's text to incorporate women in the same radical democratic state-building, but often the rifle has not the same meaning for women. For women the rifle tends to be not an artifact of empowerment but a trope for male violence. This representation has to do with historical realities as well as with Campobello's literary-political project. On the one hand, she celebrates and defends the revolutionary armed gesture of the brave men of the north, but, on the other hand, through the presence of women, she highlights nonviolent means for state-building: compassion and story-telling.

Chapter 2, "Pistols and Paredón: Violent Politics of Affect and Modernity," examines the relationship between war technology and modernity in Guzmán's *El águila y la serpiente*. The novel narrates the experiences of an intellectual who between 1913 and 1915 accompanies the rebels, first in the north and then in Mexico City. The novel's main focus, however, is Pancho Villa and his pistol. Again and again the narrator turns to the famously irascible and affectionate rebel leader. Villa's politics of violence and affect are both appalling and appealing to the intellectual. His pistols and firing squads implode the intellectual's primary ordering principle: the dichotomy between barbarism and civilization as the pillar of Latin American political thought. Instead, the novel leads the intellectual to the unfathomable realization that there is a deep interconnectedness between modernity and violence. The intellectual experiences the Mexican Revolution as a modern event of speed (through trains, telegraphs, photographs, and moving images), which all point to a modern rural political subjectivity that the intellectual cannot quite grasp.

Chapter 3, "Riddled by Bullets: Weaponry, Militancy, and People in Arms as Desire and Enigma," discusses the importance of weaponry in autobiographical texts of Sandinista militants. In such books as *La montaña es algo más que una inmensa estepa verde* by Omar Cabezas, *Adiós muchachos* by Sergio Ramírez, and *El país bajo mi piel* by Gioconda Belli, the firearm is the artifact that makes a person a *guerrillero* vanguard. The bourgeois protagonists of the texts have to create their militant identity in relation to the firearm, even though not all had active combat roles. The chapter traces the disintegration of the Sandinista trope of the "people in arms," when peasants took up arms against the revolution during the Contra War.

Chapter 4, "Songs of Guerrilla Warfare and Enchantment: Popularizing and Legitimizing Armed Struggle," analyzes the one medium that was specifically aimed at reaching "the people"—the music of Carlos Mejía Godoy and Luis Enrique Mejía Godoy. Widely popular but understudied, their music was a central medium for the communication of the ideals and the self-conception of the Sandinista insurgents. In particular, the albums *Guitarra armada* and *Amando en tiempos de guerra,* launched during the intensification of the fighting in 1979, popularized and legitimized armed struggle by teaching listeners how to use firearms such as the FAL (the Fusil Automatique Léger) and, more significantly, by sanctifying, zoomorphizing, gendering, and sexualizing armed struggle. The firearm is intrinsically linked with the Sandinista vision for an enchanted modernity. Analyzing their 1981 post-triumph cantata-suite *Canto épico al FSLN,* I highlight the intersection of utopian, Catholic, romantic, and militaristic discourses in this vision for a future society, which like a phoenix was to emerge from the ashes of violence. This vision of modernity materializes in pastoral images: biblical rivers of milk and honey; fallen guerrillas turned into birds and trees; and an aurora-shooting carbine.

Chapter 5, "Hidden Arsenals: Demobilized Combatants and the Postwar State of Mind," examines the significance of weapon arsenals in contemporary Central American postwar fiction. Hidden caches and depots with grenades, assault rifles, and rocket launchers appear as tropes and echoes of the unresolved legacy of war and the pressing postwar violence. They belong to demobilized combatants from both the right and the left. So prominent is the figure of the ex-combatant in this literature that I have identified an emerging subgenre that I call the demobilized combatant novel. Former fighters roam Central America equipped with a heavy arsenal in such novels as Horacio Castellanos Moya's *El arma en el hombre* and Franz Galich's *Managua, salsa city* and *Y te diré quién eres.* While these novels about vi-

olence workers offer an astute critique of the devastating and violent effects of neoliberal modernity, because of their uncritical adoption of an action movie aesthetic, they fail to develop a more critical engagement with
the legacy of militarism. I contrast these texts with Claudia Hernández's
short stories from *De fronteras,* which lay bare the emotional and societal
trauma of war precisely by not featuring violent showdowns or high-tech
firearms.

The flashy aesthetics and flamboyant uses of weaponry are the focus of
chapter 6, "Golden AK-47s and Weapon Displays: The Props of the Drug
War." The chapter examines literary texts, songs, and visual materials about
the Mexican drug war to highlight the different meanings of firearms in this
conflict. The firearm often becomes a nebulous artifact, identifying people
as participants in the conflict but not their affiliation. In Víctor Hugo Rascón Banda's novel *Contrabando,* armed men repeatedly attack settlements
in the Chihuahua mountains, but it is unclear whether they are narcos or
state forces or both. Weapons are used for performative purposes within
official government discourses and within narcoculture. In this theater of
war weapons become props to create dangerous, exotic criminals, to present
the government as a pillar of righteousness amid moral decay, or to display
manly prowess and unapologetic consumerism in the context of a violent
life.

### Looking at and through the Barrel of a Gun

My cultural analysis of weaponry provides new perspectives on violence, material culture, and state-building. I trace how firearms are used to narrate and
negotiate insurgent and counterinsurgent violence. Many scholars have studied representations of armed conflicts in Latin American texts and songs, yet
they have devoted little attention to the tools of violence such as firearms.
Curiously, two important studies of the objects of modernity in Mexico forgo
firearms, focusing instead on seemingly more innocuous or less politically
charged objects. The recent *Technology and the Search for Progress in Modern Mexico* by Edward Beatty focuses on technologies of industrialization in
nineteenth-century Mexico: the sewing machine, the glass bottle–blowing industry, and the cyanide processes for gold and silver refining. Rubén Gallo's
*Mexican Modernity,* a seminal study on objects of modernity, focuses on the
Vanguardist fascination with cameras, typewriters, radio, cement, and sta-
diums—after the armed phase of the Mexican Revolution. This is a curious
omission because for Mexican avant-garde artists, the firearm was an important point of reference. Campobello not only wrote a book titled after the rev-

olution's cartridges, and which featured bandoliers on the cover, but she also put on a massive ballet with more than a thousand dancers called *30–30,* after the revolution's Winchester rifles. Famous Italian-American photographer Tina Modotti during her time in postrevolutionary Mexico took still life pictures with cartridge belts. There is also the oft-overlooked radical art movement ¡30–30!—recently analyzed by Tatiana Flores in *Mexico's Revolutionary Avant-Gardes.*

*Modernity at Gunpoint* puts the firearm—the object that most clearly encapsulates the violence inherent in projects of modernity—in the center of analysis. It starts right between Beatty's and Gallo's books, when the rifle changed the face of Mexico. Next I analyze the object's role in the region's other cataclysmic conflicts. I build on the exceptional work done by scholars of literature, culture, history of the Mexican Revolution (Aguilar Camín and Meyer; Aguilar Mora *Una muerte, El silencio;* Arce; Dabove *Nightmares;* Gollnick; Knight "Peasant"; Legrás *Literature and Subjection;* Linhard; Lomnitz; Noble; Parra; Pratt; Ruffinelli). For the Sandinista Revolution, I build on several important studies (Chávez; Franco *The Decline and Fall;* Henighan; I. Rodríguez; Saldaña Portillo) and scholarship by Leonel Delgado and T. M. Scruggs. With regard to Central American postwar literature I draw on William Castro, Beatriz Cortez, Misha Kokotovic, Catalina Rincón Chavarro, and many others. Finally, for narcoculture and narconarratives, the scholarship of Luis Astorga, Shaylih Muehlmann, Juan Carlos Ramírez-Pimienta, Omar Rincón, and Oswaldo Zavala has been indispensable.

Violence in Latin America has been and continues to be a topic of widespread public, political, and academic concern. In the midst of an abundance of academic studies on violence in Latin America, often with a high level of abstraction, critical voices have called for "more grounded" studies on such topics as cruelty and weaponry (Pratt "Violence and Language"). While several outstanding and chilling books have done so by analyzing torture, such as Franco's *Cruel Modernity* and Elaine Scarry's *The Body in Pain,* mine is the first book specifically devoted to the cultural meaning of firearms in the Latin American context.

Writing *Modernity at Gunpoint* has brought me to places where few scholars in the humanities have ventured, and lesser so female ones. The research brought me, among other places, to a shooting range in New Hampshire as well as to a tucked-away section of the library, dark stacks with no trace of human traffic: classification U, about military science. The editors of *A Cultural History of Firearms in the Age of Empire,* a study of the cultural symbolism of weaponry in the context of Anglo-American expansionism, say that they put their book together to take "firearms from the clutches of encyclopediasts and technical enthusiasts" and to study them beyond their technicalities and as artifacts central to "class, gender and ethnic identities in both the metropolis and the colonies" (Jones, Macola, and Welch 1). Similarly, my book works to bring the critical study of weaponry into the realm of the humanities. It provides a different angle by thinking about weapons and gun culture in relation to cultural production and in relation to political and criminal violence in Latin America. The aim is to establish a dialogue with scholars in the humanities and social sciences and show how cultural production shapes the sociocultural significance of objects. Many historians of the Mexican Revolution happily cite novels as part of their sources or to illustrate points. In much historical scholarship one notoriously finds a reference to the most famous chapter of Guzman's *El águila y la serpiente,* "The Fiesta of Bullets" (Joseph and Buchenau 2, 55; Knight *Mexican Revolution: Very Short Introduction* 1, 54) analyzed in detail in chapter 2 of this book. Historians use Guzman's novel as a striking or problematic metaphor to describe the revolution but do not engage with the literary construction of this most controversial chapter. Yet we have to analyze cultural texts as products in their own right, as distinct discourses, pivotal to myth-making and state-building.

Text, music, and visual culture constitute different means to aid, condemn, understand, or represent armed conflict, and they touch the audience on different aesthetic, affective, and sensory levels. Weapons acquire meaning through cultural expressions and, in turn, give meaning to them. Several photographs of revolutions have become iconic, first and foremost, because of the presence of weaponry; and throughout songs resound the roars and bursts of the rifle. Then there is the firearm to which novelists return again and again as the object harboring a deeper meaning about insurgency. All these cultural expressions make the firearm such a polemic and formative object.

## *Looking at Mexico and Central America Together*

*Modernty at Gunpoint* shows that the firearm has shaped sociopolitical developments and literary traditions of Central America and Mexico in the twentieth and twenty-first century. This book thus brings together two neighboring regions that are rarely studied together: Mexico and Central America. A look at the shared and divided history, politics, and literature of Mexico and Central America illustrates the profound cultural-political impact of national revolutions within the region as well as the interconnectedness of these conflicts. It highlights similarities and discontinuities in armed negotiations of politics and modernity and offers a better understanding of their rich literary traditions, as they relate to insurgency and beyond.

## History and Politics: Differences and Connections

When looking at Mexico and the seven Central American countries together, one faces blurry demarcations.[22] Mexico, Guatemala, Belize, Honduras, El Salvador, Nicaragua, Costa Rica, and Panama are ethnically and linguistically diverse countries that share history, culture, and politics. However, nationalist attitudes as well as the sheer geographical, demographic, and economic size of Mexico in contrast to the Central American countries have impeded attempts to compare them or to think about them together. Often these countries are viewed as completely separate entities, with Mexico occupying the position of the powerful empire in the north and the Central American countries that of the poor, troubled, small countries to the south. Mexican political and academic life tends to be fixated on national history, combined with an often imperial attitude toward the isthmus. In Central America, Mexico is admired but also eyed with suspicion given its regional power. At the same time, discussions about the lack of Central American regional integration and unity or each country's national history, tend to be more important than Mexico. For both Mexico and Central America, ultimately the difficult relationship with the big imperial power further north—the United States—tends to be more decisive for their outlook on foreign and internal affairs than the relationship between Mexico and Central America.

Both regions have been impacted by their proximity to the United States. Since the nineteenth century, they have suffered US military, political, and economic interventions. The resulting deeply ingrained anti-imperialism notwithstanding, Mexico and several Central American countries have seen substantial flows of immigrants to the United States and rely heavily on their remittances. Yet the topic of migration often divides rather than unifies the regions. Mexico has acted as the extended arm of the United States, charged with impeding Central American immigrants who traverse the Mexican territory from making it to the US-Mexico border. In the United States, Central American immigrants often become invisible because they are mistaken for Mexican Americans or nullified by Latino discourses (Arias *Taking Their Word* 186–87).

Internally, Mexico and the Central American countries are organized around powerful discourses of *mestizaje,* often designed to negate the indigenous and Black elements in nations ruled by white and mestizo elites. Furthermore, both Mexico and the Central American countries were repeatedly unsettled by divergent projects of development and social justice: liberalism versus conservatism, or export-oriented elitist regimes versus protectionist-nationalist, egalitarian projects. As such, Mexico and Central America share a history of armed conflict and insurgency. The Mexican Revolution served as an inspiration for Central American movements and the postrevolutionary regime as a place of rest and material support. The postrevolutionary regime in Mexico, even though often repressive toward its interior, became a safe haven for political exiles from Central America. One of them was Nicaraguan guerrilla leader Augusto C. Sandino, who during his fight against US marines (1927–33) went into exile in Mexico in 1929. Yet because he was there during the Maximato—a time of consolidation of a more moderate revolutionary project—Sandino failed to secure real support from the Mexican government.

In the 1980s the Sandinistas encountered a more favorable Mexican government. The memoirs of Sergio Ramírez contain various episodes that recall the generous help from the Mexican government. In July 1979, Mexican president José López Portillo sent the government airplane Quetzalcoatl II to fly the provisional Nicaraguan government from San José to Managua (Ramírez, *Adiós* 266). In the 1980s the representative of the Mexican Partido Revolucionario Institucional (PRI) in Managua would always encourage them to ask for more supplies: oil, construction material, helicopters, medicines, and teaching materials: "That's very little, add more. Don't be shy" ("Es muy poco, agréguenles sin pena") (74). In 1982, when López Portillo himself visited Nicaragua with his cabinet, one of his ministers asked what treatment Nicaragua should receive. López Portillo responded: "That of a state of Mexico" ("El de un estado de México"). This affirmation did not offend anyone, Ramírez writes; "rather it flattered us" ("más bien nos halagaba") (74). It is a telling tale that illustrates the complex mix of dependence and solidarity between two (post)revolutionary governments unequal in size and power.

Mexico was an important point of reference during the Central American wars. Guerrilla fighters from El Salvador, Guatemala, and Nicaragua fled to Mexico and regrouped there, under the watchful eye of the Mexican state.[23] The Lacandon jungle on the Mexican side was a point of entry for guerrilla excursions into Guatemala as well as a refuge for civilians from Guatemala. Later in the 1980s, through the Contadora group, the Mexican government acted as an important mediator in the Central American conflict. The support was not limited only to the level of government. Many Mexicans were inspired by this new revolution in the region and came to Nicaragua to help with the war effort or the coffee harvest. Just as the Mexican revolution had inspired Central American leftists, now the Nicaraguan revolution inspired Mexicans and other internationalists. Managua became an artistic and intellectual hub similar to Mexico City, albeit on a smaller scale. The Nicaraguan Revolution, often seen as the last Third World revolution and the last modern revolution, had an enormous appeal across the world and sparked solidarity movements worldwide (Delgado, "Memorias apocalípticas" 108; Henighan 508).[24] This appeal was owed in part to the strong presence of poets and priests, and it marked a clear contrast to the Cuban Revolution: "Nicaragua brought together, as Cuba did not, the poetics of the avant-garde with the vanguardism of the revolution and the messianism of liberation theology" (Franco, *Decline and Fall* 111–12).

In the meantime, and in the same Chiapanecan jungle to which the Guatemalan refugees fled, the Zapatista Army of National Liberation (the EZLN) carefully studied the shortcomings and successes of the Sandinista Revolution. The Zapatista concept of "mandar obedeciendo," leading while obeying the will of others (Subcomandante Marcos), can be seen as an attempt to curb the authoritarianism and militarism that plagued the Sandinistas. Following the example of the Sandinistas, the Zapatistas knew that a strong global solidarity was key for the guerrillas' success. They called for "intergalactic" meetings in Chiapas, and people from across the world answered the call. Thus it was in Mexico in 1994, after the end of the Cold War and the supposed end of the grand ideological narratives, that the armed subaltern rose again, informed by the Central American experience.

Now, in the new millennium, as Mexico finds itself in the worst armed conflict since the Mexican Revolution—the drug war—the collective memory of counterinsurgency in Central America might hold the key to better understand the conflict. After all, arms flows and the flow of violence workers in the region are connected. Former elite soldiers from Central America and Mexico—from the Guatemalan Kaibiles and the Mexican GAFES (Grupo Aeromóvil de Fuerzas Especiales)—have joined the drug business in such groups as Los Zetas (Paley, *Drug War Capitalism* 175). The former soldiers employ counterinsurgent techniques learned and refined during the guerrilla period.

Thinking about these seemingly disparate regions yields new perspectives and unexpected discoveries. The South-South comparison destabilizes the often monolithic notions of nation-states and challenges the often limited view of national history. When one looks from the center, one tends to only see the capital or the national territory. But when one observes from the margins, one can see complex interactions and unequal relationships within the South: the wall between Guatemala and Mexico, for example, or the poor treatment of the many Nicaraguan immigrants in Costa Rica. Also, one can see what happens beneath the level of government. Nongovernmental solidarity becomes visible: revolutionary-internationalist solidarity or the solidarity of the poor, as epitomized by Las Patronas, poor women in Mexico who help the Central American immigrants on passing cargo trains by throwing food and water to them. Exploring from the margins and through connections complicates national and imperial storytelling, and so does writing and reading from the real and imagined margins occupied by Mexican and Central American literatures.

## Grappling with Insurgency and the Lettered City

The lettered city plays out differently in Central America and Mexico. The term "lettered city" refers to the combination of institutional, discursive, and individual practices in Latin America, which since the Spanish colonization have cemented a power structure around and through the written word (Rama; Dabove "Ciudad letrada" 56). In Mexico for a long time the lettered city corresponded to the colonial and modern power and splendor of Mexico City—challenged over the past two decades through the emergence of a prolific literature in the north. From the times of the viceroyalty to today, Mexico has boasted a vast array of literary productions, which circulated widely in the Spanish-speaking world. In Central America the lettered city generally saw itself in a more precarious role. The image propagated by Nicaraguan Vanguardia poet José Coronel Urtecho of his "library in the jungle"—filled with North American classics—is emblematic of this notion (Coronel Urtecho; Delgado, "La biblioteca" 35). The lettered city was seen as a small, erudite, cosmopolitan fortress.

A sense of marginality tends to dominate discourses on Central American literature, since the region suffers a double marginalization within the global North-South divide and Latin America itself (Arias, *Taking Their Word* xii). Literary production from the isthmus often seems to become invisible next to the economic and social capital of Mexican and South American letters, their big transnational publishing houses, and their famous boom authors. Yet I find this view too limited. Central American literature is the foundational literature of Spanish-American modernism; it brought about the second Latin American Nobel Prize winner of literature; it was at the center of the debates on *testimonio;* and the poetry and narrative that emerged in relation to the conflicts in Nicaragua, El Salvador, and Guatemala was widely read. Nowadays, Central American literature is at the center of a renaissance of Maya literature and it boasts a prolific postwar literature, often published by such big publishing houses as Tusquets and Alfaguara. This necessarily incomplete list of some of the most prominent literary milestones and contributions shows that these successes are not an exception to a rule but a sign of the consistent and innovative literary production by Central American writers. Given the difficult economic and political conditions for the production and distribution of literature from Central America, the richness and vastness of this cultural production is nothing but astounding.

Mexican literature has for a long time enjoyed considerable state support and a high level of institutionalization (Sánchez Prado, Nogar, and Ruisánchez Serra 11).[25] In Central America, state support of the arts has generally been scarce—with some exceptions, like the Sandinista regime, but which was severely affected by economic scarcity. Despite these differences in terms of literary institutions, there are many connections between the two literary traditions. Mexican literature has for decades benefited from the presence of Central American writers in Mexico. Mexico City was a hub for Central American intellectuals. There in exile or to study, they made essential contributions to intellectual life in the Mexican capital.[26] Central American literature has also benefited from the Mexican infrastructure, in particular through book fairs which provided space and financial support.[27] Meanwhile, in Central America the yearly meetings titled Centroamérica cuenta and organized under the auspices of the novelist Sergio Ramírez have provided an important space for better recognition and exchange among Central American writers; several Mexican writers are always in attendance, too (Centroamérica cuenta).[28]

Central American and Mexican literature share certain thematic and aesthetic concerns. For one, writers often have felt torn between a desire for universalism and cosmopolitanism and for nationalist or politically committed literature. Rubén Darío's swans and princesses and his anti-imperialist poetry in *Prosas profanas* and *Cantos de vida y esperanza* visualize the two sides of the spectrum. Moments of insurgency were always key moments for literature, since the revolution unsettled the nation-state, catapulted the countries onto the world stage, and created a need for the narration and interpretation of these events for a national and international audience. This also meant a possibility for the writer to position or create himself or herself in this context. This built a complex relational quadrangle of writer-state-people-violence in modern Mexican and Central American literature. Both literary traditions have key narrative moments that have to do with this relationship between the writer, popular sovereignty, state logic, and violence. Just as Mexico and Central America share a history of insurgency, they also share a literary history of grappling with the figure of the insurgent.

The Mexican Revolution constituted one of the most powerful hemispheric memories of peasant insurgency, and it haunted the guerrilla movements and their readings during the Cold War period. Yolanda Colom from the Guatemalan guerrillas recounts that in the mountains they read books from the Mexican Revolution: Guzmán's *El águila y la serpiente,* John Reed's *Insurgent Mexico,* and several novels from B. Traven's revolutionary mahogany cycle (228–29). The Central American guerrilla movements yearned for the cultural and political legitimacy of the figure of the peasant-in-arms, even though their actual relationship with the peasantry was often fraught with distrust. They encountered in the literature of the Mexican Revolution this desired political subjectivity—mediated through a literary form that had revolutionized Latin American literature.[29]

In Central American literature, however, it was ultimately not through the *novela de la revolución* as such but through poetry, testimonial literature, and later memoirs that writers and militants took on the role of narrating and interpreting the Central American insurgent gesture. In Central American literature, the aim hereby was always to bridge elite and subaltern forms of literary expression (Arias *Taking Their Word* xiv).

Music constituted another point of connection between Mexico and Central America, and between lettered and folk-popular spheres. Sandino's army fought against US marines in Nicaragua singing "La Adelita" in the mountains of Segovia. Mexican rancheras were immensely popular in Nicaragua and later the Mejia Godoy brothers made other musical connections through *mazurcas, romances,* and corridos.[30] Lyric-centered genres like the corrido and *nueva canción* constituted effective, affective, and lyrical means of communication and representation of insurgency in a largely illiterate context.

Many noteworthy instances invite us to think about connections and comparisons between Mexican and Central American literature and music in this book and beyond.[31] Even though I highlight connections, I discuss each literature and each insurgency in separate chapters in order to explore them in their specificity. This book thus offers not a straightforward comparative analysis but rather a complementary look on Mexican and Central American literature as an invitation to think about two neighboring regions and literatures together to see connections, influences, entanglements, or overlaps. It is an invitation to read from the margins and centers occupied by these literatures.

Despite the homogenization processes brought on by big publishing houses, contemporary Mexican literature, due to the vastness of production and presses and decentralization processes, is characterized by an "unprecedented diversification and proliferation" (Sánchez Prado, "Mexican Literature" 375). The situation is not unlike similar processes taking place in contemporary Central American literature, where some authors routinely publish with Alfaguara and Tusquets, whereas others publish with small publishers in El Salvador and Guatemala. Furthermore, the Central American literary output of the past two decades has been characterized by a forceful and plentiful return of experimental fiction (Ortiz Wallner).

This rich history and prolific diversity warrants further study, yet both literatures are to varying degrees still marginal within the English-speaking academia. Mexican literature, while read and studied in Mexico and Latin America, in English-speaking academia was "for many years eclipsed by Chicano studies or by the dominant interest in the Southern Cone" (Sánchez Prado, Nogar, and Ruisánchez Serra 1). Only in the past decade or two has it "grown and evolved considerably" (1), while also pushing beyond the previous fixation on questions of *mexicanidad* (3). Central American literature, however, is still often seen as peripheral in US academia (Arias, *Taking Their Word* 186). This marginalization is a problem given the immense cultural production of both Mexico and Central America and the entangled relationship between these countries and the United States. The Anglo-American, Mexican American, and Central American student body at US institutions deserves to be introduced to this rich literary tradition and to know more about the often painfully shared history of the United States, Mexico, and Central America.[32]

There are signs of improvement, though, in particular because students and faculty have fought and worked for greater visibility.[33] The spaces for academic reflection on either Mexican or Central American literature are growing.[34] Now it is time to bring the two together. I hope *Modernity at Gunpoint* is one of many more studies that explore a transnational, complementary, or comparative angle, to help us better understand Mexico and Central America, their stories, and imaginations—in their disparity and their connectivity. Much remains to be done.

FIGURE 1.1. Emiliano Zapata in his headquarters in Cuernavaca, 1911. Secretaría de Cultura, INAH, México.

*CHAPTER 1*

# CARBINES AND CARTRIDGE BELTS

## AFFIRMING ONE'S PRESENCE

There is no image of the Mexican Revolution more iconic than that of the revolutionary with at least two cartridge belts crossed over his chest and a rifle in his hand. The famous portrait of Emiliano Zapata (figure 1.1) is just one of many individual and group photographs of insurgents with their weapons. Bandolier and rifle encapsulate the fundamental raison d'être and meaning of the Mexican Revolution. For decades, peasants had been marginalized within Mexico's feudal-capitalist system and repressed by authoritarian elites. But with rifles in their hands, they could no longer be ignored. Through the firearm, these men became visible within the political arena. By massively taking up arms, they affirmed their presence before the state and society. Zapata's portrait shows a strong sense of self. In its aristocratic posture, aided by the sable and the tricolor sash, it bears a resemblance to the portraits of Louis XIV. Only that in this case it is the peasant leader who declares: "I too am the state."[1]

The bandolier and rifle are key to the image and to this message. Firearms were at the center of the revolutionary experience and figure prominently in images, songs, and novels. For the creators of these cultural expressions, firearms become key artifacts and tropes through which to capture and ponder the meaning of the revolution. Read in this way, songs and novels tell a tale of peasants and other subalterns who take up arms not to take over the state apparatus but to affirm their presence as political subjects. This is particularly the case in Nellie Campobello's *Cartucho: Relatos de la lucha en el norte de México.*[2] Narrated from the point of view of a young girl named Nellie, the book describes the lived experience of revolutionary war within the beleaguered town of Parral, Chihuahua: minor battles, firing squads, and the actions of women, men, and children. Cartridges and rifles are woven throughout the text: metallic, loud, intriguing, penetrating. It is a text that smells of gun powder.[3]

*Cartucho* not only situates the reader in the immediacy of armed insurgency but also offers its most complex political depiction: insurgency as a dignified, precarious, brutal, and traumatizing political gesture. Taking up arms appears as a call for more egalitarian and inclusive politics. This chapter explores two main aspects of that book: first, the functional, symbolic, and spectral role of weapons as tools, artifacts, and echoes in the push for recognition by the male insurgents; second, the ambiguity of rifles in relation to women. In *Cartucho,* for women the rifle is not an artifact to affirm their political and social presence but rather a trope of male violence. This has to do with historical realities and with Campobello's literary-political project. She celebrates and defends the revolutionary armed gesture but, through the presence of women, she also highlights the trauma of war and offers other nonviolent means to affirm one's presence and participate in revolutionary state-building. Those means are compassion and storytelling.

## The Power of la bola

The Mexican Revolution constituted a complex historical phenomenon characterized by "kaleidoscopic variations" (Knight, *Mexican Revolution* 2). The conflict lasted for decades and was marked by shifting alliances and projects, some national and some local in scope. To date, the revolution figures as the most violent period in the history of Mexico as a nation-state. The war decimated the country's population, with an estimated 1.4 million war-related deaths (McCaa 396). Almost all key revolutionary figures were assassinated: Francisco Madero in 1913, Emiliano Zapata in 1919, Venustiano Carranza in 1920, Francisco Villa in 1923, Álvaro Obregón in 1928. The main armed phase (1910–20) was characterized by massive violence and battles, carried out primarily by rural groups. During the second phase (1915–40) the revolutionary project was consolidated by the elites (Katz, "Violence" 45–56).

The initial insurrection was directed not merely against the reelection of Porfirio Díaz, who had ruled Mexico for over thirty years, but also against his technocratic, authoritarian, and criollo-elite version of modernity. Díaz had modernized Mexico with an iron fist. His regime disenfranchised peasants, workers, and miners. Furthermore, he angered those parts of the oligarchy since some were excluded from the circles of power. These very different strata of society temporarily joined forces to overthrow the by-then eighty-year-old Díaz. Yet the elites did not expect that what was meant to be a swift coup d'état turned into a massive peasant insurgency. When Madero, a member of the disgruntled elites, called for an insurrection, he envisioned only a "nineteenth-century political rebellion" and not, as happened, a "twentieth-century social revolution" (Aguilar Camín and Meyer 22). The insurgent peasants wanted profound political *and* social changes—a different project of modernity. The following declaration attributed to Zapata highlights the contrast between the liberal rhetoric that prevailed throughout the nineteenth century in Latin America and the social reality of the country: "freedom of the press for those who can't read, free elections for those who don't know the candidates, fair legal procedures for those who have never had anything to do with an attorney" (quoted in Katz, *Secret War* 260). Social reforms were necessary in order to create a citizenry capable of enjoying its liberal rights. Neither positivist authoritarianism nor idealist liberalism constituted an acceptable political project for the insurgent masses. Instead, they demanded social justice and more inclusive national identity politics.

The peasant segments did not win the war, but echoes of these demands can be found in the consolidation of the revolutionary process by the elites. The progressive Constitution of 1917 legally protected community lands (*ejidos*), and the presidency of Lázaro Cardenas (1934–40) implemented far-reaching land and labor reforms and nationalized petroleum. The postrevolutionary art and public education system celebrated a Mexico of heroic mixed-race peasants. The sole exaltation of the mestizo is, of course, problematic as it tends to celebrate the indigenous past but not the indigenous present. It, nevertheless, constitutes a profound change from the criollo fixation on Europe and whiteness. After the massive peasant uprising, the face of Mexico could no longer be the same.

These accomplishments notwithstanding, a great ambivalence characterizes most evaluations of the Mexican Revolution. Historians disagree on whether peasants or elites were the true agents and beneficiaries of the revolutionary process. Some say it was a revolution controlled by regional and national elites, while others stress the profoundly popular and peasant character of the revolution.[4] Overall the perception in Mexico is that the institutionalization of the revolution through the party that eventually adopted the name Partido Revolucionario Institucional (PRI) cemented a new power structure benefiting mainly a set of former and freshly minted elites. Constructed around authoritarianism and corporatism, the postrevolutionary regime co-opted revolutionary symbols, social agents, intellectuals, and artists. One of the ironies of the (post)revolutionary process is that while many insurgents rose in defiance of the increasing concentration and expansion of power in a the centralist Porfirian state apparatus, the revolution ended up creating "a powerful state" (Knight, "Peasant" 19).

The elites' appropriation and recent dismantling of the revolutionary legacy under President Enrique Peña Nieto (2012–2018) obscure the decidedly peasant and popular-subaltern dimension of the original uprisings.[5] Yet rural groups bore the "burden of the revolution—the long campaigns, the guerrilla wars, the pitched battles which toppled first Díaz, then Huerta" (Knight,

"Peasant" 21). Their revolution from below, in the form of the "radical and eternal novelty of *la bola*" ("la radical y perenne novedad de la Bola") (Aguilar Mora, *El silencio* 141) traversed the country and demolished the old regime. Even though all men of legal age nominally had voting rights since the 1857 liberal constitution, many of these men had been *ninguneados* (ignored and denied recognition). Through *la bola* and their rifles, however, they affirmed themselves as social and political subjects before themselves, before others, and before the state apparatus.

Many of the insurgents were not necessarily aiming to take power. Rather, they wanted to establish their presence before the state and within modernity. Just as Villa and Zapata entered the capital, took a picture on the presidential seat, and shortly thereafter left again, many revolutionaries were not seeking to take over the state apparatus.[6] This does not mean that those insurgents did not have a conception of the state or nation, as has been argued by Aguilar Camín and Meyer (56). Rather, the insurgents either displayed a libertarian preference for self-government, or they wanted a more just society and a state that would guarantee liberal and social rights. There were two main popular movements. The first group roughly corresponded to the "peripheral peasant-ry" (Knight, "Peasant" 27), who were generally landless peasants organized around Villismo in the north and who wanted fewer taxes and less govern-mental control. The second group consisted of members of the "middle peas-antry," who (had) owned land but had been dispossessed or were under threat of dispossession. This group, mainly located in central and southern Mexico, aimed at restitution and redistribution of lands and was organized within the Zapatista and other *agrarista* movements (Knight, "Peasant" 22f, 27). For these men, the *patria chica* (their regional community) and personal bonds were central categories. Yet that does not mean that they had no conception of the state. Rifle in hand, these insurgents actively participated in the contin-uous process of state formation and exhibited a clear sense of self. Through the massive uprising, they manifested themselves as vocal constituents of the Mexican nation-state. The firearm became the prosthesis for citizenship, not de jure but de facto. Now, for the first time, these men had to be recognized and taken into account.

## Corridos and Carbines

This sense of identity had an important vehicle: music. The corrido is *the* mu-sical style associated with the Mexican Revolution. Constituting a vague and heterogeneous genre, these folk ballads became particularly popular during the war.[7] Many sang of the heroic deeds of the insurgents, whereas other famous corridos of the armed phase, such as "La Adelita" and "La Valentina," are songs of courtship in times of war.[8] These corridos came to express the moment of revolutionary upheaval. Their catchy tunes heralded a sense of change in the air. These were the songs of a young generation that was rebelling against Porfirio Díaz's gerontocracy (Aguilar Camín and Meyer 13). As the insurgents traveled across the country within the unruly troop collective of *la bola,* these songs accompanied them, sung by the insurgents and played at dances. The *corridos de la Revolución* constitute a complex cultural form: an expression of the turbulent times and a product for mass consumption; a means for the rebels to express political ideas but also a space of projection of political ideas onto the insurgents.

Corridos are often perceived as an authentic expression of "the people," a pure genre that becomes corrupted by professionalization and the market (V. Mendoza 111; Simonett, "Transnational Dimension" 223); but in truth the "corrido developed out of complex interactions among publishers, performers, and market demand" (Frazer 135). Many of the corridos' anonymous, amateur composers wrote them in part to earn a few *centavos,* while others performed at country fairs or were directly employed by revolutionary leaders, such as Marciano Silva, who produced corridos *por encargo* for Zapata (V. Mendoza 111; Héau 108, 111). Corridos were anchored within oral culture but also tied to lettered culture. Two major printers in the capital—Antonio Vanegas Arroyo and Eduardo Guerrero—were involved in producing corridos with their own crew of corrido writers for their broad sheet production, which were sold as illustrated loose-leafs and handbills at markets and events (Frazer 133–35). While corridos can constitute an important rural and mestizo perspective from below (Giménez and Héau 364; Simonett, "Transnational Dimension" 223), one should not "simply assume their authenticity as a complete and unequivocal vox populi" (Frazer 133). Composed and written by mostly anonymous artists across several decades, corridos developed both organically and commercially from the campfires as well as from Mexico City's printing houses.

The corridos of the revolution contemplated violence by singing of battles, executions, and weapons; they glorified and vilified rebels. Corridos about armed men had existed before. Américo Paredes's famous study of the legendary border figure Gregorio Cortez is famously called *With His Pistol in His Hand,* and horse and pistol are common motifs of nineteenth-century bandit corridos (A. González "El caballo y la pistola"97). But in the corridos of the Mexican Revolution, the formulaic expression of "with my rifle/pistol in my hand" or, better yet, "with my bandolier and my rifle" acquired a new dimension. It no longer referred to the lone bandit fighting an injustice. In revolutionary corridos the individual was an insurgent within a collective; he had *la bola* behind him or was about to join *la bola*. Through the armed collective, the insurgents manifested their *political* subjectivity. The weapon facilitated the process of becoming a political subject.

In a Zapatista corrido by Marciano Silva the chorus states that the rebel figure singing the song is a Zapatista from Morelos proclaiming the Plan of Ayala and of San Luis. Also, it says that if those in charge do not keep their promises to the people "with arms we will make them keep them" ("sobre las armas los hemos de hacer cumplir"). The insurgent presents himself with a particular identity defined by several coordinates of belonging: home state, political agenda, and armed collective. In this song the political subjectification of the peasant rebels vis-à-vis the state does not manifest itself in a demand for power but rather for accountability. The state is now accountable to *them*.

The importance of the rifle as an artifact of political subjectivity appears in one of the corridos dedicated to the revolution's most widely used rifle: the Winchester Model 1894, called the *treinta-treinta* for its use of .30–30 cartridges. The revolutionary song "Carabina .30–30" establishes a keen awareness of history and collectivity in relation to the carbine, as the singer sings about marching with his .30–30 to swell the ranks of the rebellion and to make a sacrifice for the nation. Sung in a pleading yet determined tone, the prevailing notion is not so much to take power or to overthrow the state but to join *la bola,* to be part of the insurgent movement. Just as the periodization of this song is uncertain, there is disagreement with regard to the meaning of a line in the song that states the Maderistas said that they did not kill anyone with these .30–30 carbines.[9] Some say that the line has to do with the Winchester rifle's many technical defects (Kohl 68). Others suggest that the song conveys a more radical anarchist Orozquista/Magonista perspective, and that it is thus a critique of the Maderistas not being radical enough (Guerrero Aguilar). I see it as indicating that the functional value of the Carabina .30–30, a tool for killing, was not as relevant as its sociocultural value as the artifact of a collective armed uprising. The song expresses a longing to follow suit, to join *la bola*. In that quest it does not matter if one might kill or die because the most important act has already been carried out: to join *la bola* and to affirm one's presence within state and modernity through the carbine.

### *Cartridges and Cadavers*

The aesthetics of corridos, carbines, and cartridges run through Nellie Campobello's *Cartucho*. Written by a dancer and collector of folk music, the text has a particular rhythm and sonority; throughout it resounds the revolution's "song of bullets" ("canto de balas") (142). Rifles and bullets are omnipresent as toys, shiny objects, intimate things, instruments of oppression and liberation, without being detached from their functional logic. They are artifacts, tropes, and props but also tools and echoes. The book's visual language contains many images of death featuring ammunition: bodies riddled with bullets or burned by them, bullets squeezed by flesh, men forever put to sleep by bullets. In the form of a nonchronological collage of over fifty vignettes, the text observes the comings and goings of the revolution in the northern mining town Hidalgo de Parral mostly during the revolution's particularly violent period in Chihuahua from 1916 to 1920. The book's three parts center around weaponry: "Men of the North," "Shot by Firing Squad," and "In the Line of Fire" ("Hombres del norte," "Fusilados," "En el fuego").

The text is about the dignity of all the nameless insurgents, the nobodies, who, with their bandoliers strapped to their chests, constituted *la bola,* and whose stories did not happen on the main stage of history. It is about the rank-and-file rebels who *appear* to have become cannon fodder: empty vessels, disposable bodies, spent cartridges, *cartuchos.* Although Campobello plays with the notion of cannon fodder, the author does not want the nameless revolutionaries to have been only carnage. Instead, she highlights and recuperates the dignity and humanity of all the anonymous—generally male—combatants who took up arms to affirm their presence. Firearms and cartridges make these nobodies visible; their insurgent act dignifies them. Through firearms, they affirm their presence, but at the same time the firearms threaten their very existence: many insurgents in the text die in front of a firing squad. The text retains the actions of insurgents both behind and in front of the rifle to capture the precarious and violent political gesture of this peasant insurgency.

*Cartucho* presents firearms as simultaneously empowering and traumatizing artifacts. By focusing on the political subjects and on the cadavers produced by bullets and rifles, the text offers a particular approach to the complex politics of *la bola*. It is the revolutionary novel that is "most challenging to bourgeois concepts of violence" (Gollnick 26), since it does not condemn violence but sees violent acts as exemplary moments (27). I argue that *Cartucho* dares to fully embrace the complex and contradictory nature of revolutionary war as a simultaneously brutal, dignifying, and traumatic experience. Rifles and cartridges are the artifacts through which these ideas are expressed.

In his well-known essay "Critique of Violence," Walter Benjamin criticizes parliaments for not having "remained conscious of the revolutionary forces to which they owe their existence" (244).[10] Rather than simple antiparliamentarism, it is a call for more radical politics, for a legislature

that makes laws according to the *Gewalt* of the people that created it—
*Gewalt* simultaneously meaning "force," "violence," and "power" in German.[11] *Cartucho,* which appeared a decade after Benjamin's essay, can be
seen as a literary-political attempt to remind the postrevolutionary Mexican state of the revolutionary *Gewalt* to which it owes its existence. Published during the Calles era, *Cartucho* opposes the common vilification
of Villa but also the nascent incorporation of his figure into a docile state
narrative of the revolution (Legrás, *Literature and Subjection* 146; Parra
51–52).

Campobello once declared that she wrote *Cartucho* to "avenge slander"
("vengar una injuria") (cited in Aguilar Mora, *El silencio* 101). This avenging voice sometimes manifests itself explicitly in the text. In these moments
the narrator leaves the carefully constructed child's perspective, and an
adult voice comes to the fore. Campobello was writing against the contempt
for Villa but also against the omission of the original and originating violence within the hegemonic discourses about the revolution, against "the
attitude of the few that tried to split the triumphs of the majority among
them" ("la actitud de los pocos que pretendieron repartirse los triunfos de
la mayoría" (*Cartucho* 66). By spotlighting and remembering the revolution
of the common man, their individual and collective armed act, Campobello ultimately frames this peasant insurgency and its law-destroying violence
as a quest for democratic politics built around social justice and identity
politics.

In this interpretation of the Mexican Revolution, the insurgent gesture is
not only a call for liberty and equity but also of difference, since *Cartucho*
specifically defends northern culture. Regional autonomy within the nation-state, singularity within the collective, a leader as one among equals as
well as the reminder of the dignity and death of all the nobodies who affirmed
themselves through insurgency, are key elements in the radical literary-
political project of state-building that Campobello proposes with *Cartucho.*
In this rewriting, in a first instance, *Cartucho* challenges the criminalization
of revolutionary figures from northern Mexico. The text points to the political
act of affirming one's individual but also regional presence through taking up
arms. The narrator recounts that the Carrancistas called the Villistas bandits,
but that the people in Parral knew that they were "men of the North" ("hombres del Norte") (119). The insurrection in the north signified an affirmation
of regional presence and autonomy against a centralist state. The fact that the
narrator always gives local details about the revolutionaries such as their village, their relatives, their peers "conjures up the image of a *patria chica,* or
regional homeland" (Parra 58).

*Cartucho* thus reflects the autonomous and militarist frontier history of the north, which was impacted and shaped through numerous armed conflicts between indigenous tribes and nonindigenous peasant settler-fighters. Sanctioned by the Mexican state, these "peasant warriors" came to violently occupy the land of indigenous peoples (Alonso 7). Ana María Alonso points out, that the centralist Mexican state and society at first viewed these settlers as "agents of civilization" against the indigenous "savages," but when they started to resist the capitalist and centralist processes of state formation in the late nineteenth century, they became the "barbarians" who needed to be civilized (7). The "violent tradition of frontier culture was fully reactivated during the revolutionary war, and Villismo was to be the insurgent movement that best embodied the bellicose and territorial mentality of the military colonists" (Parra 59–60). *Cartucho* is written from this strong sense of northern settler identity, which is pitted against a foreign, centralist state symbolized by the Carrancistas, which were perceived as no more than "an occupying army" (Parra 60). In *Cartucho* the Villistas are the embodiment of an exemplary northern heroism and masculinity: possessing a cheeky, daredevil attitude, and a particular calmness with which to express "their truths" ("sus verdades") (Campobello 159). By contrasting the narratives from the north and the center, Campobello insists on truth and knowledge as defined by position. As such, *Cartucho* stands not only as a challenge to the criminalization of northern rebels by the center but also as a demand for space for other positions and cultures within the nation-state.

Consequently, the book does not end with Villa's death in 1923, but rather in 1917 with one of the few big battles that were still won by Villista forces in the late 1910s: the Battle of Rosario in March 1917, during which over two thousand Carrancistas died (León Diez n.p.). The people in Parral are celebrating the defeat of the Carrancistas and a collective longing for northern culture and autonomy concludes the narration: "The horse hooves would resound again. Our street would liven up again" ("Volverían a oírse las pezuñas de los caballos. Se alegraría otra vez nuestra calle") (Campobello, *Cartucho* 161). This conforms with Alonso's anthropological findings, which show that the "discourses of resistance were informed by a frontier ideology of honor and a utopian memory of the past" (11).

Yet while *Cartucho* shows with regard to *el Norte* a "nostalgic desire for epic greatness and regional autonomy" (Parra 61), it also expresses a distrust of the epic and the heroic. The resolute intensity of this narration about war and death is often attenuated by a notion of play and playfulness that runs through the entire text: the revolution oftentimes appears as a game of *traviesos,* of cheeky men, as Kristine Vanden Berghe has indicated ("Alegría" 157–

58). The playful irreverence of these nobodies delights the narrator. Although the book is written in defense of Villa and stresses the closeness of the girl's family to the revolutionary leader (Campobello, *Cartucho* 71, 83, 119, 123), the girl's true sympathy lies with the *cartuchos,* who, like her, are outside of history (Pratt, "Mi cigarro" 158). Several critics have argued that *Cartucho* democratizes war by focusing on the rank and file (Pratt, "Mi cigarro" 165; Ruffinelli, "Nellie" 65). This is further enhanced by another democratizing feature of the book: iconoclastic attitudes toward Villa, who is presented as one among equals. Death hereby serves as a democratizing reminder of the ephemeral nature of rule.

There are two vignettes that deal with the mortality and death of Pancho Villa. In the vignette "El coronel Bustillos" the Colonel says that he does not like that they eulogize Villa, since he is just like everybody else. Bustillos names one of Nellie's mother's doves Pancho Villa, the one that "beat everyone, [which] was so fierce that all the others had grown terrified of it" ("que aporreaba a todos, [que] era tan bravo que se había hecho el terror de los demás") (51). This characterization of the terrifying Villa-dove is a mocking gesture, caught between awe and irreverence. Nellie's mother, who becomes cross if anybody dares to disparage Villa, does not say a word about this naming but starts to give the fierce Villa-dove special treatment. The girl recounts that one day the Villa-dove is shot dead: "with a bullet, they blew off his head. Mamá got very angry; we roasted him in the yard" ("le volaron la cabeza de un balazo. Mamá se puso muy enojada; nosotros lo asamamos en el corral") (51). The demystification is presented in a laconic staccato. Villa has become a little bird, hardly enough to fill their empty stomachs during the economy of scarcity of war. This displays an iconoclastic attitude toward the rebel leader, which once more underscores the democratic intent of the book. Campobello wrote *Cartucho* explicitly in defense of Villa, but she also insists on stressing his ordinariness. Villa is as singular but also as "shootable" and as mortal as everyone else.

This democratizing attitude is also present when it comes to narrating Villa's death in 1923. His death is almost hidden in a vignette called "El cigarro de Samuel" in the third part of the book about "Men of the North." Instead of focusing on Villa, the narrator talks about the death of the timid Samuel Tamayo, who was sitting in the same car as Villa when the assassins came. The narrator does not tell us about Pancho but instead tells us about Samuel. With empathy, the narrator talks about Samuel's particular character and captures his last gesture at the moment of death. This can be seen as a way of evading the pain of narrating Villa's death, but I read it as an attempt to show that Samuel's life and death were no less significant than those of Villa. *Cartucho* repeatedly stresses the collective over the leader. Yet the collective is not an indiscernible, diffuse multitude but a group made up of singular individuals with their own stories and personality traits. The firearm is an artifact to affirm this singularity within the collective, just as it serves as the reminder of the precariousness of the body. In an empathetic tone, the narrator stresses Samuel's particular character and highlights how even this timid man affirmed his social presence by taking up arms. Stressing the singular and collective dignity of the *alzados* and *fusilados* is key in reminding the state of the violent foundational act of the revolutionaries. The first vignette, "Él," about the revolutionary named Cartridge, announces and encompasses the idea of affirming one's social presence through weapons by exploring and establishing the different meanings of "cartridge." It thus serves as an introduction and guide for the stories of the homonymous book—named for this anonymous insurgent and the nineteenth-century innovation in weapon technology.

Cartridges are central to the imagery of the Mexican Revolution. Men and women draped in one, two, or more cartridge belts became the iconic image of the revolution. The "surplus of cartridges" ("lujo de cartuchos") (Quevedo y Zubieta 47) had practical and political reasons. Clip-fed firearms (those with magazines holding multiple rounds of ammunition) were still less common and the cartridges were still relatively big, so the heavy cartridges had to be carried somehow. The belts also identified one as a fighter in lieu of proper uniforms.[12] Yet the bandoliers also became artifacts of a political statement, expressing defiance and one's will to affirm one's political and social presence. In the vignette "Él," *cartucho* means many things, both literal and figurative: a nickname, ammunition, an unimportant container, cannon fodder, a flicker, a blast. The man named Cartridge is just one of the many individuals making up *la bola*, one of the many cartridges in the revolutionary enterprise, one tiny element loaded into the revolutionary rifle. Yet he was also an individual, not just part of an indistinguishable mass. The opening sentence, "Cartridge didn't say his name" ("Cartucho no dijo su nombre") (*Cartucho* 47) reveals the narrative project of the book: naming the anonymous (Ruffinelli, "Nellie" 65). Even though he only appears under his nickname, through this story the insurgent named Cartridge enters the history of the revolution and ceases to be unknown. Through the child narrator the reader learns that Cartridge was carefree, playful, and always had a song on his lips.

That war and its objects imprinted themselves on Cartridge in the form of a nickname highlights once more the importance of weaponry in this political act. He "finds himself" through weaponry and through the collective of insurgents (Aguilar Mora, *El silencio* 100–101). After a battle between Villistas and Carrancistas ensues in the streets of Parral, the insurgent Cartridge is last seen shooting his rifle in a street corner, but then he disappears. A man called José ponders the fate of Cartridge, who is probably dead. However, José is not too worried because, as he declares, "Cartridge already found what he wanted" ("Cartucho ya encontró lo que quería") (*Cartucho* 47). Cartridge, keenly aware of the historical moment and the value of his life, already succeeded in establishing his social presence through the rifle and through participating in the collective uprising (Aguilar Mora, *El silencio* 89, 97, 100). The vignette ends with José philosophizing that all insurgents are, in fact, "cartridges" while he resolutely tightens a cartridge belt (*Cartucho* 48). José's act of buckling up is an expression of awareness of the destiny that awaits the rebels. The insurgents are all cartridges, probably destined for death, but they affirm their existence through this collective act, consciously assuming their loss of life as a possibility. The act of buckling up is also an act of memory, of symbolically carrying his fellow-cartridges with him, of carrying on in memory of those cartridges already spent. The notion of risking or giving one's life in order to affirm it seems contradictory, but it points to the dignity and the precariousness at the core of the act of taking up arms. Born out of precariousness, insurgency is a desperate and extreme political gesture framed by death—of others and of oneself.

This notion of precariousness manifests itself in the narrator's many musings about the beauty of corpses and firing squads. Earlier readers condemned the book as inhumane (M. P. González *Trayectoria* 289), while later critics have argued to the contrary. I, in agreement with the latter, see the portrayals of the dead as explicitly dignifying and humanizing gestures (Pratt, "Mi cigarro" 166; Aguilar Mora, *El silencio* 96). The narrator describes these "cartridges," their personalities, their last actions before death, and their poses as cadavers in order to preserve their memory and the dignity of their political act. By telling us their names and anecdotes about their lives, the text reenacts their affirmation of presence through the firearm. Aguilar Mora argues that the ritualistic actions of the *fusilados* in *Cartucho* affirm their human dignity as disenfranchised people in front of an oppressive state and a disdainful society. The life of the *fusilados* is taken away violently, but as Aguilar Mora points out, they keep a level of control over it by deciding *in which way* they will face the firing squad. Their life might be the only thing they own, but they attempt to determine it to the very end (*El silencio* 96). They try to finish a novel, look up into the sky while others express their infinite anger or clasp their shirt when they give their life away (Campobello, *Cartucho* 65, 69–70, 90, 100). Or there is the story of Perfecto Olivas, who is not given last words nor time to finish his cigar, but who still tries to die with a dignified gesture. He extends his serape and leaves his forehead uncovered, looking at the firing squad, "as if he were to have a picture taken" (como si se fuera a sacar un retrato") (109). Although, as the text says, "the cameras of the rifles" ("las cámaras de los rifles") destroyed his pose (109), by recounting his actions, the narrator recuperates his intentions and his dignity.

The theatrical gestures of the *fusilados* notwithstanding, their deaths are not always a heroically defiant act of affirmation. Sometimes they merely reflect the cruel, baffling nature of war and its perpetrators. The narrator, for example, recalls the *fusilamiento* of Rodolfo Fierro's chauffeur in "The Sorrows of *El Peet*." The nameless chauffeur accepts the rules of the game: "It's okay, I'm going to die, this is *la bola*" ("Está bueno, voy a morir, andamos en la bola") (Campobello, *Cartucho* 93). But the fact that he apparently dies for the trivial reason that his boss bumped his head causes grief and shame among the revolutionaries (94). Campobello stresses the dignity of the act of taking up arms, but she also stresses the nonsensical workings of revolutionary war. Gollnick compares the book's gore and graphic content to a "literary snuff film" (27), but I see the curious and morbid gaze as one that is ultimately touched and empathetic. The vignettes of all the *fusilados* are written against the war machine, *la bola,* that was so quick to execute: "That was a mess; they went in and out, they yelled, went around, argued, and always the same: 'execute them, execute them'" ("Aquello era un reborujo; entraban y salían, gritaban, hacían, discutían y siempre lo mismo: 'fusílenlos, fusílenlos'") (*Cartucho* 123). Against the agitated state (the *reborujo*) of the revolutionary war, the child narrator records the names of the revolutionaries, be they Villistas, Urbinistas, or Carrancistas. She holds on to their image, even to their dead bodies. The descriptions of the beauty of corpses creates a contrast with their brazen treatment and desecration, as, for example, in the vignette about the guts of General Sobarzo (*Cartucho* 85). The author does not shrink away from the abject; she confronts the reader with the precariousness of the human body (Cázares 91; Vanden Berghe *Homo ludens* 54).

The vignette "Desde una ventana" (*Cartucho* 88) is emblematic for the text's tendency to simultaneously work toward an affirmation of human dignity in revolutionary war and toward an expression of the enormous physical and psychological trauma it produces. The vignette deals with the girl's fascination with a corpse that for days lies on the street in front of her window: "I felt that dead one was mine. . . .He was my obsession during the nights, I liked to look at him because it seemed to me that he was very afraid" ("Me parecía mío aquel muerto. . . Era mi obsesión en las noches, me gustaba verlo porque me parecía que tenía mucho miedo" (88). She feels compelled to look at him and cannot sleep, thinking about the odd shape of his body and his scared appearance. The infantile, curious gaze is mixed with a maternal one that seeks to comfort the dead body and to return dignity to him.

There is a strong determination to highlight the humanity of the dead bodies and to treat them with respect and compassion. This becomes especially clear in the girl narrator's reaction to the execution of her friends, "Zafiro y Zequiel." The two insurgents Zafiro and Zequiel come from the Mayo/Yoreme people, a northern indigenous nation who, like the Yaquis and the Apaches, were under siege by settlers throughout colonial times and the nineteenth century. Zafiro and Zequiel appeared in Parral and Nellie used to play with them, squirting water at them from her window. This was their only way of interacting since they did not speak one another's languages, Spanish and Mayo. When the little girl hears that the two have been executed (no reason is given for why or by whom), she expresses profound sorrow and trauma by portraying her efforts to maintain composure in the face of extreme violence. Nellie pretends not be affected: "My heart didn't jump, nor did I get scared, nor did I become curious; that's why I ran" ("No me saltó el corazón, ni me asusté, ni me dio curiosidad; por eso corrí"). She finds them next to each other: "They had their eyes open, very blue, dull, it looked as if they had been crying. I could not ask them anything" ("Tenían los ojos abiertos, muy azules, empañados, parecía como si hubieran llorado. No les pude preguntar nada"). She counts their gunshot wounds, turns Zequiel's head, and cleans the dirt of his face: "I was a little bit moved and told myself within my heart three and many times: 'poor, poor boys'" ("me conmoví un poquito y me dije dentro de mi corazón tres y muchas veces: 'Pobrecitos, pobrecitos'") (*Cartucho* 64). She notices that the blood has frozen, so she gathers it and puts it in the pocket of Zequiel's blue linen jacket. The act of gathering Zequiel's blood and putting it into his pocket reveals a sense of wanting to make them whole again, returning life to them, holding on to their life.

This vignette alludes to the partially racial roots of the conflict, not only in southern Mexico but also in the north. The presence of these young men is a reminder of the violent pacification of the Mayo/Yoreme and Yaqui/Yoeme communities under the Porfiriato. The state *campañas* against these people constituted "a bloody war that disrupted the organizational forms of both tribes, rejected their ancient rights, and transferred their lands [among the most fertile in the desert] to white domination" (Aguilar Camín and Meyer 5). Hence these two indigenous men had also joined *la bola* to affirm their presence. They were treated with little respect in both life and death, but this little girl, in grieving for them and holding on to their image, gives them the dignified treatment that they deserve as human beings. Through her caring gestures, she repeats the gestures of other women in in the book who take in the dead bodies that are left exposed (*Cartucho* 73, 104). Treating them with respect and grieving for them makes them not be simple cannon fodder. They are not corpses; they are Zafiro and Zequiel—two individuals, two humans who died in the revolution. They were *ninguneados* by the Mexican nation-state, but by taking up arms they affirmed themselves, and they confronted a capitalist state that mistreated them due to their race and class. A little girl, another nobody, testifies to the value of their lives and their existence by remembering them.

At the core of this representation lies a necessity to recognize the human in the other, both in war and in politics. Weapons in hand, poor peasants and indigenous peoples—often branded as "savages" or "outlaws"—manifested themselves as political subjects. *Cartucho* reminds the reader of each insurgent's singularity. Written during a time when postrevolutionary elites were interpreting and writing the story of the Mexican Revolution at their will, *Cartucho* aims to rescue the radical traits of the revolution. Weapons in *Cartucho* appear as empowering and dignifying but also traumatizing. The firearms leave behind an echo: traumatized and hurt bodies and minds, bodies full of bullets, corpses in odd shapes. This is the violence that the Mexican postrevolutionary needs to be reminded of; it needs to hear the echoes to make politics worthy of this violence and pain. Through their violent acts and suffering, these people helped create the new state, and thus politics must be made according to their insurgent potential and humanity. The state's law-making power has to be employed in accordance with the people's law-destroying power. *Cartucho* advocates that it is not simply a matter of symbolically incorporating these people in the state's cultural politics. Rather, it is a call for more radical politics in accordance with the dignity and trauma of the insurgent gesture: embracing difference, dissent, and the other.

Weaponry was key for establishing this individual and collective sense of political self. Analyzing literary and political texts of the Mexican Revolution, Joshua Lund and Alejandro Sánchez Lopera criticize "the delusions of Revolution that equate social justice with the legitimate force of men with guns" (n.p.); instead, they highlight later postrevolutionary texts that try to envision nonviolent politics of social justice. While I share their valid concern about the fomentation of militarist forms of political action, in this case it obscures the symbolic meaning of the firearms of the Mexican Revolution. Whether we agree or not, firearms were the artifacts through which peasants and subalterns became visible as political subjects. Through firearm the insurgents expressed a demand for recognition and for social justice, but not necessarily for power as defined by the gun. The firearm as artifact is a symbol of the violent potential of the people and thus a reminder to make politics according to their complex and multivocal bidding: not a quest for authoritarian politics in the name of social justice but for socially radical and democratic politics.

FIGURE 1.2. Revolutionaries and *soldaderas*, portrait. Secretaría de Cultura, INAH, México.

## Rifles and Rebozos: *Female Agency and War*

While it was possible for a man—be he poor, indigenous, *norteño*—to affirm his presence through the rifle, this did not necessarily apply to women during the Mexican Revolution. In early twentieth-century Mexico, women were not recognized as political subjects, and the revolution did not change that fundamental fact. Admittedly, women in Mexico acquired the right to divorce in 1914 and more equality before the law through changes in the civil code throughout the 1920s. Yet in its formulation and definition of citizens as *mexicanos,* the constitution of 1917 implicitly denied women the right to vote (Olcott 19), thus excluding women "from full citizenship" (36). Carlos Monsiváis even goes so far as to say that the constitution declared women "to be social and political 'minors'" ("When Gender" 10). The governors of San Luis Potosí and Chiapas conceded to women the right to vote in 1923 and 1924, yet a similar federal initiative by Cárdenas in 1937 did not pass the Chamber of Deputies. Although in 1946 women obtained the right to vote and hold office at the municipal level, it was not until 1953, thirty-three years after the end of the armed phase—that Mexican women obtained the right to vote in federal elections (Macías 145; Monsiváis, "When Gender" 15, 17).[13]

There are many reasons for this belated granting of full political rights to women. Among them were deeply ingrained patriarchal prejudices and a widespread concern about the perceived conservatism of many women, who opposed the anticlericalism of the 1920s and 1930s governments and thus presented a threat to the revolutionary modernizing plans. It also had to do with the complex agenda of Mexican feminist movements, in which suffrage was only one of many concerns (Macías 25, 104–21, 137–46)—just as political demands were only a part of the many social demands of the revolution's insurgents. Ultimately, the female presence in *la bola* did not translate into women being recognized as political subjects. For many men the Mexican Revolution meant to turn a de jure citizenship into a de facto citizenship; for women the revolution did not even result in de jure political rights. This does not mean that they did not also affirm their social presence during the revolution; however, these affirmations tend to be complex and heterogeneous. Women played an important role in the revolutionary process, both as supporters and opponents of the revolution and its political aftermath. The images and stories of women in the revolutionary process tend to be diffuse and their achievement of political agency dubious. Particularly when it comes to women and weaponry, and to women in combat roles, what predominates is great ambiguity.

This chapter opened with the hypermasculine portrait of Zapata: rifle, bandolier, and sable operating as key artifacts for Zapata's phallic affirmation of political presence. I would like to juxtapose this with another photo. In this photo from 1915 from the Casasola Archive, two men and two women face the camera with equally stern looks and polished clothes as Zapata (figure 1.2). The men flaunt the typical cartridge belts and rifles of the revolution, whereas the women emulate the cartridge belts by crossing a traditional shawl, a *rebozo*, over their chest. This photo probably most adequately encapsulates the complexity of female participation and agency during the Mexican Revolution. Although they were present, uncertainty shadows over the question of the use of force. Many societies construct gender roles through keeping women away from active combat, meaning lethal, roles (Goldstein 127). In this image both masculinity and femininity are at play—ultimately reinforced through the gendered division of labor. Yet by emulating the cartridge belts, by uniforming themselves through the *rebozos*, by using weaponry as a prop, the women signal their participation. It shows that the advent of the revolution meant a push for women into the public sphere; the upheaval not only mobilized men but also women.

The use of the cartridge belts as props makes for complex identity politics. There existed during and after the revolution a particular type of photo, in which middle- and upper-class women from rancher families "pose in soldadera attire, with rifles in one hand and cartridge belts crossing the bosom of their immaculate dresses" (Legrás, "Seeing" Women" 10). The photo described above might be one of them since all four wear spotless clothes and the portrait is thoughtfully arranged with a careful use of props: firearms, *rebozos,* and hats. It certainly differs from other famous photos of generally poor *soldaderas* riding or sitting in a chaotic disarray on trains. Yet contrary to the unclear class dimension of this particular portrait of the two women and the two men, the use of the bandolier-rebozo could also be seen as a reference to indigeneity. Christine Arce argues that in this photograph the *rebozo*, often used to carry foods and babies, signals indigeneity and points to the importance of women for the food logistics of the war and the sustenance of life (75–76).

Whatever the historical truth behind this particular photo, it points to the heterogeneous and often contradictory nature of female participation and affirmation during the revolution. We are left to speculate about the class of the two women as well as their relationship with the men standing next to them; we also do not know the circumstances and purpose of this posed photo. As Andrea Noble has pointed out, "illuminating and accounting for female agency in the revolution remains a methodologically challenging task" (101).[14] She warns against using photos of women in the revolution just for the sole purpose of offering proof that women were present, since "seeing women in the photographic record of the revolution is far from straight-forward" (102). Such an approach, which is merely focused on presence or participation, does not see the "conflicts and tensions that relate to issues of sexual difference" (103). The ambiguity of this photo reflects that. Posing with the *rebozos* points to sexual difference. Furthermore, it also reveals Zapata's and Villa's photos as performances, in which the firearm is just as much a lethal, political artifact as well as a theatrical prop. The *rebozo* as stand-in for weaponry hints at the fact that, despite her later mythification, the woman with the rifle was actually rare.

Today, when people think about women and the Mexican Revolution, original photographs of stern, rifle-toting women or later sexualized images come to mind, such as María Félix as the erotic warrior woman in the movie *Cucaracha* or comics of a lascivious Adelita. These are the predominant associations of the word *soldadera* nowadays: heroic, armed women, often objectified.[15] But *soldadera* means, first and foremost, "camp follower." It comes from a long tradition in Mexico of women and children accompanying the troops throughout the nineteenth century (Reséndez Fuentes 530). Women received part of men's pay—the *soldada*—in exchange for domestic services, therefore they were called *soldaderas*. The main role of the women was foraging and preparing food. Other functions included sexual and nursing services. Sometimes this was paid labor; in other instances this was unpaid, domestic work performed by wives or daughters, or forced labor of abducted women (Salas 36, 39, 43, 120).

The *soldadera*, the female camp follower, thus should be distinguished from the female combatant. *Soldaderas* at times would carry rifles, bring ammunition to the battle field, or smuggle firearms (Reséndez Fuentes 546). But their main task, and central for the war effort, was in food logistics. They represented "a domestic sphere at the edge of the military sphere" (Pratt, "Mi cigarro" 158). During the revolution, female combatants existed, some rising to captains and colonels. These few female combatants, sometimes cross-dressing, tended to garner a lot of attention by the media and thus made their way into popular imaginaries (Reséndez Fuentes 524, 545f; Salas 48). They were then often called *coronelas* and not *soldaderas*. The *coronelas*, however, were the exception rather than the rule. The image of the fierce, female combatant of the Mexican Revolution was popularized mainly through later postrevolutionary representations, in movies for example, but more often than not this image reflects later emancipatory processes instead of the realities of the armed phase. These later representations used the symbolic power of the rifle and the revolution to *retroactively* affirm women's presence within the postrevolutionary nation.

We have to be careful with these distinctions though, because, as Cynthia Enloe has pointed out, the military depends on women yet needs to define them as camp followers and constantly redefines combat in order to maintain "the front" a male-only domain (1–17). Distinguishing between camp followers and combatants might run the risk of repeating a patriarchal-militarist logic that wanted to confine a historical phenomenon that challenged so many confines and institutions.[16] However, because of the postrevolutionary prominence of the idea of the heroic warrior woman in media and memory, it is hard to decipher the legacy and meaning of the many different types, circumstances, and motivations of *soldaderas*. As Monsiváis aptly puts it, *soldaderas* "were the force that the makers of History ignore in order to avoid complications" ("When Gender" 9). Monsiváis warns not to overly romanticize or idealize *soldaderas*. Poor and without rights, women were treated poorly within the troop, where they "suffered rape, rejection, and victimization" ("When Gender" 8).

Despite the importance of women for war logistics, many revolutionary leaders were scornful of the camp followers that slowed down their army. Villa despised the female presence in his troops; he wanted a male-only army. There are anecdotes of Villa threatening and killing *soldaderas* who attempted to participate in battle, and of Obregón using women and children as human shields (Salas 47). By 1915, as Villa resorted to guerrilla tactics and Obregón tried to shrink and professionalize his troops, the number of women among the troops was declining rapidly (Reséndez Fuentes 548f). In 1925 the postrevolutionary government banished women from the troops and barracks (Salas 47, 49). The difference between *soldaderas* and female combatants and the lack of female autonomy are reflected in several corridos. The most famous songs associated with *soldaderas*, "La Adelita," was about a woman *accompanying* men: there to be courted, enhance their companions' masculinity, and mourn the brave dead men. The corridos about Adelita—"crazy in love with the sergeant" ("locamente enamorada del sargento")—and Valentina—"a passion dominates me" ("una pasión me domina")—can be seen as attempts by a patriarchal society to come to terms with the female presence in *la bola* by objectifying women and placing them within a romance narrative (Herrera-Sobek 104). These songs also celebrated the subtle sexual liberation taking place and furthered homosocial bonding through the collective devotion to these idealized female figures—similar to later uses of pinups.

Next to Adelita, the sweetheart of the troops, whose name became synonymous with the *soldadera,* exist a few corridos about female combatants with firearms. However, this image—present in such songs as "Juana Gallo" and "La Chamuscada"—seems to be a later development (Herrera-Sobek 110). The production or release dates of these two songs are unknown, but since both songs have a more complex dramatic and melodic composition than the more monotonous corridos of the armed phase, I assume they are songs from after 1920, maybe even produced in relation to two films of the same name: *Juana Gallo* (1961) and *La chamuscada* (1971). These later images of female combatants correspond more to a mythical archetype of the warrior woman than to the historical figure of the *soldadera,* the camp follower (Herrera-Sobek 110; Monsiváis, "When Gender" 19). The character of Juana Gallo takes on a masculine perfomativity. She is always at the front of the troops fighting "like any Juan" ("como cualquier Juan"). One can see this as a gender-bending transgression, but I see it as an affirmation of the revolution's masculinist framework of bravado and honor. Named "cock" ("gallo"), a key symbol of masculinity in Mexico, and killing mercilessly "with her enormous pistol" ("con su enorme pistolón"), Juana's phallic masculine figure does not question the underlying gender norms; rather, it exalts prevalent ideas about masculinity. Moreover, her bravery is circumscribed within a romance story: she only fights to avenge her dead loved one.

Only "La Chamuscada" (literally "The Burned One" by the gunpowder) tells the story of a profound female emancipation: a woman follows her father into *la bola* but in the end she becomes a general. Emblematically, it is only after her father's death that she is freed from the patriarchal grip. She ceases to be a *soldadera,* a camp follower, and thereafter becomes a combat fighter: "since that day she was a *soldadera* no longer" ("desde aquel día jamás fue soldadera"). With her full bandolier and her rifle, she fights always at the front line, laughing at the bullets. She does not have or want a lover; she does as she pleases. She is sentimental and brave and rises to the highest ranks, becoming a general, as a result of her bravery. Covered in gun powder, and thus apparently unconcerned with appealing to imposed norms of female beauty, she is free. While this song can be understood as a feminist narrative of emancipation, it can also be read as yet another example of a woman with a rifle always being an objectionable figure within patriarchy. Herrera-Sobek argues that through her nickname "The Burned One," "this Woman Warrior is given from the inception of the song a tinge of the supernatural by association with the devil" (114). There is always an ambivalence and uncertainty when it comes to women and the rifle. Romanticized, masculinized, mythologized, yet ultimately nebulous.

The ambiguity of the armed woman is also manifest in literature. In the novels of the Mexican Revolution, women are either absent (Guzmán's *El águila y la serpiente*), killed to free men to go to war (Muñoz's *Vámonos con Pancho Villa*), or present but problematic when they bear arms (Azuela's *Los de abajo*).[17] *Cartucho* probably offers one of the most complex depictions of women (and children) during the Mexican Revolution.

The child perspective is key for the literary and political project of the text; it is not an autobiographical choice but a literary one. Even though Campobello wanted the text to be read autobiographically—suggesting that the homonymous author-narrator experienced the narrated events as a child—it is more likely that Campobello experienced the armed phase of the revolution as a teenager. This is part of several performative acts that the dancer Nellie Campobello staged during her lifetime. She was born in 1900 (documents say) or 1909 (she says) under the name María Francisca Moya Luna. She later adopted the last name Campbell from her stepfather and then hispanicized the name. She spent her youth in Chihuahua but, after her mother's death, she and her sister were moved to Mexico City, where they started successful dance careers (Aguilar Mora, *El silencio* 94; 114–19). Around the same time that she published *Cartucho*, her mass ballet *.30-30* premiered, employing one thousand dancers (Matthews, *La centaura* 73). Generally she is seen as the primary female—albeit marginalized—voice of the Mexican Revolution (Aguilar Mora, *El silencio* 137; Cázares 17), but in recent years has become one of the most canonized.[18]

In *Cartucho,* Campobello uses the child discourse strategically to erase any notion of intellectual or lettered discourse, which in her view suppresses the revolution from below (Peña Iguarán, "Auto-representación" 112). The text itself works outside of the categories of the lettered city, told from a village in the north and by a narrator who because of her age does not meet lettered criteria. The narrative perspective also gives the author a lot of freedom to speak from the amoral or innocent frankness of a child (Ruffinelli, "Nellie" 67). It makes for a peculiar limited point of narration and scope of action: the house, the window, the street, behind her mother's skirt. *Cartucho* tells the story of the revolution from a domestic view, or rather from the constant overlapping of the military-public and the civilian-domestic sphere. As such, it presents women as important contributors in the revolutionary process yet maintains an ambivalence and uncertainty regarding the woman and the rifle. Rarely is the rifle an artifact for empowerment for women; instead, it is often a trope for the domestic and sexual violence suffered at the hands of the insurgents.

Several vignettes talk about rebels trying to abduct women (*Cartucho* 54–55, 71; 120). In one of the most intense and cryptic vignettes, the rifle functions as a metonymy for the rape of Nellie's mother. In "El general Rueda," a Carrancista general storms the house with ten men in search of weapons because they know that Nellie's mother supports the Villistas. They search the house with bayonets, shove the children around, and threaten to burn the house down. The narrator recounts that her mother did not cry, pleading with them not to touch the children, saying that they could do what they wanted. "Not even with a machine gun could she have fought them off," says the narrator, adding "Mama's eyes, grown large with the revolution, did not cry, they had become hardened, pressed against the barrel of a rifle of her memory" (83).[19] The narrator tells us that she could never forget the image of her mother "stuck to the wall made into a painting" ("pegada en la pared hecha un cuadro") (83). Here the trauma is expressed through poetically vague language, and the rifle is a metaphor both for the woman's impotence in the face of ten intruders ("not even with a machine gun could she have fought them off") and for the sexual violence suffered at their hands. The rape is not explicit, and several critics do not mention the possibility of such a reading (Faverón-Patriau 63; Matthews, "Daughtering" 166; Parra 66), but Tabea Alexa Linhard has convincingly shown that the scene can certainly be read in this way and that these visual descriptions point "to a desolating numbness, often associated with the trauma of rape" (Linhard, "Perpetual Trace" 35). The rhythmic sentence about her mother becoming a still life—pressed motionless against the wall, with eyes wide open, the gaze hardened against the rifle—is a picture of rape. Here the firearm is a trope of an aggressive, phallocentric masculinity, and a metonymic placeholder for the unspeakable.

In the same vignette the rifle becomes the daughter's imagined artifact of revenge but continues to be a tool of men only. When Nellie sees the general two years later in Chihuahua, she wants to shoot him but her gender impedes her. She wishes she could "be a man, have my pistol and shoot him a hundred times" ("ser hombre, tener mi pistola y pegarle cien tiros") (*Cartucho* 84). Nellie's wish for retribution is only fulfilled when she reads in a newspaper years later that the general has been executed. She sees it as a form of restitution: "They killed him because he abused Mamá, because he was bad to her" ("Lo mataron porque ultrajó a Mamá, porque fue malo con ella") (84). Yet she can only imagine realizing revenge through a man and his firearm. The female narrator visualizes her imaginary pistol transformed into the soldier's rifles carrying out the order: "they had in their hands my pistol of a hundred shots, made carbine on their shoulders" ("tuvieron en sus manos mi pistola de cien tiros, hecha carabina sobre sus hombros") (84).

Throughout *Cartucho*, the firearm is an ambivalent object in the hands of a woman. The girls get bullets as presents (49) and are eager to see combat up-close (76), but they never transgress into a combat role. Another woman, Carolina, has a rifle that she uses to shoot into the air during the Mexican

Day of Independence, but she does not use it herself during the insurrection. Instead, she runs out of her house to give the rifle to Villa (120). Also, in the only vignette dealing with a female combatant, the one about *coronela* Nacha Ceniceros, the woman does not use her rifle in combat. Nacha shoots the man she loves, possibly by accident or out of jealousy, while he is talking to another woman in a different tent (66), and she is then put before the *paredón* on Villa's order. She receives the deadly charge crying and burying her face in her hands. In the second part of the vignette, this ending is recanted.[20] The narrator declares that everything she just narrated is not true; Nacha did not die. Disillusioned with the revolution, she simply left the army and went home. She returned to the domestic sphere and to reconstructive activities: "she started rebuilding the walls and covering the blast holes through which thousands of bullets had flown against the murderous Carrancistas" ("se puso a rehacer los muros y tapar las claraboyas de donde habían salido miles de balas contra los carrancistas asesinos") (67). The vignette explains that Nacha, because of her capabilities, "could have been one of the most famous women of the revolution" ("pudo haber sido de las mujeres más famosas de la revolución") (67), but instead she went home. The text ends with an again ambiguous "viva" for Nacha, *coronela* of the revolution.

Horacio Legrás sees the entire vignette as an example of Campobello "relinquishing of narrative authority" (*Literature and Subjection* 145), yet another sign of her "active resignation from the field of literary production" (142). While certainly Campobello's distrust of lettered principles comes to the surface here, I agree with Linhard that this scene is, first and foremost, about the difficult space occupied by women in war history (*Fearless Women* 164, 171). Nacha's whereabouts are uncertain. Her actions within the military sphere are decidedly nonheroic—although they could have possibly been heroic because, as the vignette explains, Nacha was an exceptional rider and had technical skill. Yet her most noteworthy act is to conform to conventional gender roles: to go home and mend the holes the men produced with their rifles. Legrás makes another valid point about this vignette: that it can be read as revolutionary death—before the firing squad—being a privilege reserved for men ("Seeing Women" 20n20).

One could criticize a book like *Cartucho* for not being more revolutionary with regard to its gender framework. It is, after all, revolutionary and radical in its style and content, the first work about the Mexican Revolution authored by a woman and narrated by a female voice—a voice that is often transgressive, cloaked in the supposed innocence of a child. However, such a critique would not correspond to the historical realities of the time nor to the literary intentions of the author. Few women participated actively in combat. *Cartucho* was written, in part, to defend northern settler culture, a particularly masculinist and bellicose society. As Ana María Alonso wrote, "The colonial and Mexican states actively fostered a military investment of male bodies on the Chihuahuan frontier. [They] deployed a discourse that privileged masculine virility, valor, and fighting skills and constructed warfare in terms of the idiom of honor" (92). These sensibilities run through the text largely unquestioned. In general, Campobello's opus only voices a very subtle critique of patriarchal structures (Estrada 38–40). Most important, however, the text's ambivalence toward women with rifles reflects an attempt to present a nonviolent means of sociopolitical intervention. Through the actions of women, Campobello represents ways of affirming one's presence in war other than through the rifle.

This happens through constructive, humane gestures toward others. Nellie's mother in particular is a pillar of empathetic reason, defending and saving the lives of men, women, and children. After the battle of Torreón, Parral is full of injured Villistas, and the Carrancistas are on their way to finish them off. Nellie's mother arranges to move the injured to the hospitals of the nuns so they will not be killed. The mayor of Parral scolds her for helping to save "bandits" ("unos bandidos"), but she defends her actions by countering: "In this moment they are not even men" ("En este momento no son ni hombres") (118). Despite the fact that the men are eventually killed, hers is the word that brings a humanitarian reason to the often senseless experience of war. At this moment Nellie's mother affirms her social and political presence as woman. She speaks up and not even the Carrancistas dare to reproach her (119). She thus intervenes politically in the public space by showing compassion and by pointing to the dignity and humanity of these men and by embodying a revolutionary-political regime that embraces difference and dissent.[21]

In *Cartucho*, women participate by becoming the storytellers of the revolution. All the northern women are the "witnesses of the tragedies" ("testigos de las tragedias") (157). Nellie's mother continues to tell the stories of the revolution, even though she is tired of the sound of the Winchester rifles (84). The author Nellie Campobello repeats these gestures through writing *Cartucho*. Speaking up, telling the story, retaining the image becomes a different foundational act than that of the rifle. In a compelling reading of Campobello's other text, *Las manos de mamá*, Mary Louis Pratt contrasts the mother's Singer sewing machine—another mass-produced piece of suddenly widely available nineteenth-century technology—with that of the rifle: one used for creation, the other for destruction ("Mi cigarro" 170). In *Cartucho,* however, the symbol of sewing is less prevalent; here the constructive act has to do with storytelling. Pratt argues that, through being witnesses of history, women and children in *Cartucho* become "co-producers of History" with "a space of citizenship" opening up for them ("co-productoras de la Historia" . . . "un espacio de ciudadanía") (165).

I see the women in *Cartucho* as constituting an alternative form of archive. Roberto González Echevarría has argued that Latin American novels have the tendency to deny that they are novels and to pretend to be something else, mirroring legal, scientific, or anthropological texts. Novels thus take on the form of an archive and constitute authoritative, foundational acts within "the discourse of the modern state" (30).[22] Campobello's text is similar to the texts that González Echevarría analyzes in the sense that her work also denies being a literary text. It is not a novel, she claims: just *relatos,* memories. But her text differs fundamentally from the canonical texts González Echevarría examines. In *Cartucho* the archive being imitated is oral rather than written, constituted not through the authority of the written word of the lettered city but through the more collective and less authoritative oral tradition. Collective storytelling is presented as a nonviolent, democratic possibility for the foundation of state and society. It has the potential to affirm the social and political presence of not only men but rather all of humanity within state and society. It is a foundational act but, because of the collective and oral character of storytelling, it does not operate with the same epistemic violence that writing history generally implies.

*Cartucho* shows that the rifle is not the only means for political participation in the context of inequality. The role of women reflects this different, nonviolent means of inclusive, egalitarian state-building: not through the rifle but through compassion and storytelling. It is ultimately only through the presence of women, as contributors to and storytellers of the Mexican Revolution, that the most important insight of this peasant insurgency comes to light: revolutionary war as a political act that is simultaneously brutal, dignified, precarious, and traumatic. *Cartucho* introduces to the political and literary field a vision in which dissent and acceptance of difference become the pillars of the society to be constructed. This is the political legacy of the precarious politics of *la bola,* if told both through the rifle and the *rebozo.*

*CHAPTER 2*

# PISTOLS AND PAREDÓN

## VIOLENT POLITICS OF AFFECT AND MODERNITY

*La bola* that figures so prominently in Mariano Azuela's *Los de abajo,* Nellie Campobello's *Cartucho,* John Reed's *Insurgent Mexico,* or Rafael Muñoz's
*Vamónos con Pancho Villa* makes only rare appearances in Martín Luis Guzmán's novel *El águila y la serpiente* (originally published 1928). In the novel
the armed masses are always an indistinguishable mass, not really intelligible
to the intellectual protagonist. He narrates his two direct encounters, one with
drunken troops in Culiacán and one inside a messy train, with disgust and
bewilderment (113, 155). Because of these scenes, the novel has been criticized
for its disparaging view of the populace (Parra 88, 138; Shaw 3, 15) and viewed
as a narration by and about "los de arriba," in contrast to Azuela's *Los de abajo*
(Uribe Echevarría 39).[1] Yet this critique fails to see the novel's intricate pattern
of ambiguity, ambivalence, and uncertainty. The novel is an inquisitive and
often confused search into the meaning of the armed insurrection (Legrás,
*Literature and Subjection* 125).

The narrator reacts not only with disgust but also with a sense of awe at the
sight of the armed rebels—at least when he sees them from a distance. Seeing
the revolutionary campfires in the north, he senses a mystery and a deeper
meaning: "of some kind of essence of Mexico in the hustle of men who moved
around in the shadows, sure of their march, indifferent to their destiny and
with the rifle on the shoulder or the hip clad with the weight of the revolver.
An air of mystery, men of character and mysterious souls" (87–88).[2] Similar
to Campobello's *Cartucho,* but from a more aloof position, Guzmán's novel
presents the idea that weapons produce social and political presence. As Max
Parra puts it: "Guzmán evokes with a routine scene a simple but transcenden-
tal reality: that of the ragged, dark-skinned, anonymous masses up in arms,
dignified by the fleeting sight of their weapons" (83). Without the weapon, the
masses are tumultuous, incomprehensible hordes, but the weapon lets them
enter the political somewhat comprehensible sphere. Yet the armed populace,
while fascinating to the intellectual, continues to be an enigma. The novel depicts a *letrado* struggling to make sense of the armed insurrection—just as the
author himself had an ambiguous relationship with the revolution and the re-

gime that followed it.[3] His books are inquisitive searches into the meaning of the revolution that reveal him to be both enticed and appalled by the relation between violence, militarism, power, and politics. Intrigued and dismayed by the revolution and Villa, *El águila y la serpiente* constitutes Guzmán's first attempt to render them in literary form.

Similar to *Cartucho*, Guzmán's *El águila y la serpiente* works with the tension that arises from the possibility of an autobiographical reading and the illusion of veracity. Yet, just like Campobello's literary rendering, nothing in the 450 pages of *El águila y la serpiente* is happenstance or accidental. It is a carefully constructed episodic novel in which colors, sensations, and notions of light and shadow play an important role (Leal 72–74; Parra 81).[4] The recurrent plays of light and darkness in the novel are also present in its discourse itself, which has led some readers to read the novel in a Manichean manner. Yet the shadow plays are an expression of the ambivalences and doubts that run through the narration, characterized by "a dialectic process of illumination and ignorance" ("un proceso dialéctico de iluminación e ignorancia") (Aguilar Mora, *El silencio* 56). With *El águila y la serpiente,* Guzmán accepts the challenge that the massive armed insurrection represented to intellectual self-perception and goes on a "tentative and half-blind search for a new hermeneutics" (Legrás, *Literature and Subjection* 125).

The many people, events, and trips in the episodic novel create a sensation of being swept away by a mind-boggling process. The text begins after the assassination of President Madero by Victoriano Huerta in February 1913, which prompts the protagonist-narrator to flee to the United States and join Venustiano Carranza and Pancho Villa in their fight against Huerta. The first part takes place mostly in the US-Mexico border region and northern Mexico. It draws portraits of commanding revolutionaries and describes various facets of the movement of large armies: celebrations, conversations, executions, journeys, and care for the wounded. The second part deals with politics after Huerta's defeat in 1914; it portrays the Aguascalientes Convention, during which the different revolutionary factions tried to agree on a future leader and course for Mexico as well as the violent political life in Mexico City during its occupation by Convencionista troops.

The narrator wants to uncover the meaning of the armed populace, but he can never really distinguish nor understand them as a mass. So he singles out the most famous man of arms, Pancho Villa, to understand these new revolutionary politics and these new political subjectivities. The northern rebel leader, next to the protagonist itself, is the anchor point of the novel and the narrator returns again and again to him and his main instrument: the pistol.[5] Villa makes himself known through the pistol. Villa's firearm stands for violent, affective politics, which both fascinate and frighten the intellectual. The text is full of distancing and subalternizing gestures of the *letrado* toward the *armado,* but Villa's affection toward the intellectual inverts their roles and draws the intellectual closer to the violence. The novel grapples with the irruption of these new political, markedly rural, subjectivities. Witty, defiant, modern, traditional, and violent, the Villista and Zapatista troops bring through their rifles an intense affect to the political arena and also a keen eye for the performative aspects of rule. Firearms are thus key to reading Guzmán's novel as well as the Mexican Revolution itself.

By extension, one of the most iconic and brutal institutions of the revolution featuring firearms becomes another element for grasping the meaning of the revolution: the firing squad. Several firing squads figure prominently in the text, and together with the sensation of speed that permeates the text, reveal that the Mexican Revolution was not only a violent struggle for interpretative power over modernity but also an utterly modern experience in itself. Just as the technologically advanced gruesomeness of World War I ruptured the faith in the narrative of progress, the revolution's modern warfare reveals an unthinkable interconnectedness of violence and modernity, collapsing one of the most important ordering principles of Latin American intellectual thought: the dichotomy between barbarism and civilization.

## Villa's Pistols and Embraces

Guzmán's representation of Villa in the novel is shaped by two opposing movements. The first movement depicts Villa as an uneducated, unpredictable brute and the intellectual as superior, the voice of reason, who needs to civilize and domesticate the subaltern wielding the firearm. Contrarily, the second movement depicts Villa as an affectionate, savvy friend, knowledgeable in the current violent politics and the intellectual as the ignorant disciple who needs to be educated in the art of war and the use of the firearm. As such, the man of letters becomes the uneasy apprentice of the man of arms. Instead of difference and distance, encounter and intimacy characterize this second dynamic. A homosocial bond between the two is formed, primarily through Villa's physical and emotional signs of affection toward the intellectual.

The first dimension appears most clearly during their first encounter, as described in the chapter "Primer vislumbre de Pancho Villa." The protagonist visits Villa together with another *letrado,* Alfredo Pani, in Ciudad Juárez. They are greeted by defiant Villista troops laden with cartridge belts and cartridges (*El águila y la serpiente* 46). To the dismay of the intellectuals and the amusement of the reader, in this humorous scene the armed guards care very little about the ranks and titles of the *letrados*. Overall, this first encounter with the Villistas and Villa is characterized by distance and disdain. An enormous abyss separates them, this meeting putting "into contact two mental orders foreign to each other" ("en contacto dos órdenes mentales ajenas entre sí" (49–50). Villa appears as the animalized other, the uncontrollable savage; the narrator calls him a "beast in his lair" and a "jaguar" ("fiera en su cubil" "jaguar") (49–50).[6] For now, Villa is "domesticated" ("domesticado") (50) within revolutionary alliances, but it is uncertain that it will remain this way. Villa's bestiality has to be tamed and dominated by the civilizing powers of the intellectual. In many ways Pancho Villa was an epitome of popular anger (Gollnick 24–26). Yet the only reason that this popular anger had to be taken seriously is because of Villa's firepower, his and that of his men. During this first encounter the intellectual does not see Villa's firearm because Villa is lying back in his bed, but he senses it. Some of Villa's movements give away the presence of a firearm, he says (*El águila y la serpiente* 49). Throughout the book the negotiation of the meaning of Villa happens in relation to the firearm—and less so in relation to his imputed animality. More than a jaguar, or a centaur, he appears in the novel as a cyborg, as somebody who has become one with his firearm and, as such, can only be understood through the firearm.

At first, the intellectual is afraid of Villa's violence and his main instrument of politics, shrinking away from it: "The contact with the pistol burned me" ("el contacto de la pistola me quemaba") (255). But he nonetheless embarks on the endeavor of "taming" this violence. The *letrado* represents himself as stepping up to the task, using his power, the power of the word, to face the man of violence and arms. In the chapter "La pistola de Pancho Villa," the Guzmán character convinces Villa to present a possible ally, revolutionary leader Lucio Blanco, with his pistol as a token of his trust and alliance. Villa, persuaded by the *letrado*, hands the protagonist the pistol so he can give it to Blanco. Yet when Villa suddenly realizes that the unthinkable has happened— that he is unarmed—he becomes agitated and demands to be handed a pistol right away (255). He then holds the pistol to the intellectual's head because he holds him responsible for putting him into this vulnerable position. But the man of letters remains cool and manages to calm Villa with a joke. In the end the intellectual manages to disarm Villa, both literally and figuratively, because he manages to pacify the "brute" with words and reason (Parra 93). This violence-controlling, "disarming" function of the intellectual resurfaces several times throughout the novel (*El águila y la serpiente* 50, 255, 322). During all these episodes the intellectual remains superior and aloof.

This is not the only way the intellectual subject position is affirmed in the text. The novel vindicates the role of the *letrado* through the narration itself—

that is to say, through the extratextual figure of the author (Legrás, *Literature and Subjection* 125–26; Parra 97; Peña Iguarán, "Próspero" 95, 105). *El águila y la serpiente* is characterized by a heavy expressionist symbolism, and the eloquent use of language is a constant reaffirmation of the intellectual subject position. As Jorge Aguilar Mora has written, Guzmán's style "is an unequivocal and decided manifestation of the desire that he not be confused with the rabble, nor with the illiterate caudillos, nor the corrupt leaders of the Revolution" (*El silencio* 134).[7] It is the *letrado* Guzmán who is searching for the right language, the right genre, and embarking on the difficult task of deciphering the meaning of this new, political appearance. Given these affirmations of the figure and persona of the intellectual, the novel's representation of Villa has generally been read as an example of the controlling function of literature as a way to domesticate and delegitimize the popular violence Villa represents (Legrás, "Martín Luis Guzmán" 429, 452; Parra 93, 97). Parra has pointed out that the "systematic references to [Villa's] violent personal impulses are not innocently neutral, but integral to Guzman's ideological agenda," since it gives him "moral authority" over the man of arms (93). Parra argues that the novel's main objective is "to praise and bond with the spirit of the popular Other while politically delegitimizing it" (97). Legrás provides a similar argument while stressing Guzmán's difference from other nineteenth-century writers who just wanted to eliminate the barbarian element: "The violence and the barbarie itself, the animality with which Pancho Villa is represented, are not just rejected but rather reinscribed and reinterpreted through a discourse which at once incorporates and domesticates them" ("Martín Luis Guzmán" 452).[8]

Although these are compelling readings, more emphasis needs to be placed on the affective dimension of the relationship between Villa and the intellectual. This second dimension of their relationship undermines the intellectual's aloof position and puts him closer to the violence he has set out to control. The intellectual's immersion and growing comprehension of the social and political presence of the insurgent and his violent politics of affect leads to a dislocation of the intellectual and his civilizing project. The *letrado* becomes "civilized," educated, and transformed by the firearm, and the two men's roles become somewhat inverted. The intellectual becomes the friend and apprentice of the insurgent and at times even ends up acting like a bandit and "uncivilized" man, especially toward the end of novel. Where the first dimension of their relationship is characterized by disdain and distance, the second dimension is characterized by encounter, closeness, and affection. Parra acknowledges this dimension but sees it merely as an expression of "the fascination the sedentary intellectual often feels for the man of action, a sort of contemporary dependence and subliminal desire for the vitality of the 'low-Other'" (94). I side more with Legrás's reading that within this description lies an acknowledgment of this new political subjectivity.

The second dimension of their relationship showcases subaltern political knowledge, and the intellectual is drawn to the new Villista politics of the firearm. For example, during the aforementioned first encounter between Alfredo Pani and Martín Luis Guzmán with Villa, the latter requires an explanation of his two *letrado* visitors about their lack of action against Huerta, who has just assassinated President Madero and usurped the presidency: why did they not just shoot him (49)? The two intellectuals initially want to burst into laughter when hearing Villa's seemingly guileless question, but at that moment they realize that it is not such a naïve question after all. They comprehend that killing Huerta would have been a possible political solution, realizing, as Legrás puts it, that "Villa's innocence is only comparable to their own" ("Martín Luis Guzmán" 436). Hesitantly, the *letrados* agree with the logic of the insurgent peasant leader. This is a moment when not only the political presence of the man of arms is recognized, but so too is his political reasoning: "Guzmán sees beyond his own prejudice, and what he discovers in the figure of Villa is the rising of a new form of sovereignty whose exact formula [the text] strives to decipher" (Legrás, *Literature and Subjection* 130).

The Mexican Revolution took *letrados* by surprise. Under the assumption that the educated city dwellers were the ones in charge of steering the nation's fortune, the lettered elite was astonished when through the revolution, new primarily rural political subjectivities emerged on the national stage. Recognizing the political presence and reasoning of the man of arms from the lower classes represented an immense challenge to the Mexican intelligentsia, not least because many forms of armed collective action had been routinely criminalized as banditry throughout the entire nineteenth century. Widespread banditry represented a major interior and exterior political concern.[9] The elites never conceived of banditry as having a political dimension on behalf of the perpetrators. Rather, they used the trope of the bandit to envision a powerful state, a "civilized" nation, and above all themselves in opposition to an undesired, atavistic, innately criminal other (Dabove, *Nightmares* 3–7, 29; Frazer 9, 12, 21). Thus it was practically incomprehensible for the elites when one of these bandits rose to the national stage and became a key power broker. This tendency still held true after the armed phase: "In postrevolutionary Mexico, particularly among the upper and middle classes . . . , politics was still perceived to be a matter for 'civilized' men. And Villa, a semi-literate, rough man from the countryside, did not belong in that category" (Parra 20).

Since it was such a common trope to criminalize organized, collective armed action as banditry, revolutionaries such as Madero and Zapata were at some point labeled bandits (Frazer 188, 190). But Villa had indeed been a bandit, making a living by stealing cattle. Suddenly, political activity in the 1910s was deeply impacted by the actions of this former bandit, who at some point during the revolution commanded more than seventy thousand fighters (Frazer 195). Friedrich Katz's extensive opus on Pancho Villa and Paco Ignacio Taibo II's long biography are signs that this figure continues to be an enigma even today. This is partly due to Villa's charisma and his unpredictable—both irascible and kind—character. But it is also a result of what Villa stands for: the rise of the disenfranchised rural armed man to the national political arena. Through Villa, the uneducated cowboy from the north, the "barbarian" marches into the lettered, "civilized" city, with little care for its rules and concerns. In Guzmán's novel this inconceivable political subjectivity of the armed rural man from the north expresses itself through the firearm: "This man wouldn't exist if it weren't for the pistol. . . . The pistol is not only his tool for action: it is his fundamental instrument, the center of his work and his game, the constant expression of his intimate personality, his soul materialized" (*El águila y la serpiente* 253).[10]

The pistol is also an expression of affect, understood here as an emotional and relational charge full of bodily and affectionate intensity.[11] Villa's pistol appears as an affective extension of Villa's being, and a tool and artifact of his violent, affective politics: "When shooting, it won't be the pistol firing, but he himself: the bullet must come from his own guts when it leaves the sinister barrel. He and his pistol are one and the same. His pistol has borne and will bear his friends and his enemies" (253).[12] Concerned but intrigued by this fusion of man, machine, and affect, the man of letters is also drawn to these politics and their virility, which manifests itself in detailed, eroticized descriptions of Villa with his pistol and cartridges, "big, reminiscent of torpedoes" ("grandes hasta recordar los torpedos"): "nothing stood out more in his entire figure than the enormous pistol which hung from his hips deep into a very ample holster" ("nada resaltó tanto en toda su figura como el enorme pistolón que le bajaba desde la cadera hasta lo hondo de una funda holgadísima"). The narrator notes that the handle plate appeared shiny because of frequent use and that it did not have "the effeminate shimmer of what exists only to show off" ("el resplandor afeminado de lo que sólo es para lucir") (252). This erotic gaze that focuses on Villa's phallic, virile masculinity—"enormous," "deep," "torpedoes"—stands in contrast to the aforementioned first dimension in which the man of letters works hard to keep a distance. Here, the gaze is full of admiration, aesthetic appreciation, and desire. As Héctor Domínguez-Ruvalcaba puts it, "Villa's body is placed in the liminality between eroticism and politics that defines desire in the novel" (59).

Villa's violence and virility draw the intellectual closer, but it is ultimately the affection that Villa displays toward him that completely "disarms" the intellectual. In the chapter "El arte de la pistola," Villa entertains himself with shooting games and is surprised when he hears that the protagonist is indeed a very poor shot. Incredulous at the intellectual's lack of dexterity with the gun, Villa becomes very concerned about his "amiguito" (*El águila y la serpiente* 344). It is the intellectual who apparently needs to be educated about politics. How can he be in a revolution without knowing how to use a gun? In a tender, paternal manner, Villa tells him: "one of these days they will kill you" ("uno de estos días me lo matan") (344). The affection is contained in the pronoun *me*. The presence of the indirect object pronoun in this construction expresses care, connection, a relationship. Villa does not say "they will kill you"; he says "they will kill you and take you from me." Worried, Villa becomes the intellectual's teacher (345). This is a symbolically significant inversion of roles. The *arielista* Guzmán, whose deep admiration for the figure of the teacher repeatedly resurfaces in the novel (*El águila y la serpiente* 404–406, 433; Peña Iguarán, "Próspero" 97), is taught and civilized in this new order of politics and modernity by the "barbarian" Villa, who turns out to be a very good teacher. He lets the intellectual in on his secret for a better shooting technique—use the ring not the index finger on the trigger—and encourages him to keep trying. This yields immediate results; the man of letters has better aim and he beams with pride (*El águila y la serpiente* 346). It is the rural man who teaches the man of letters, the urban man, how to properly use this artifact of modernity.

Alan Knight argues that intellectuals "saw in Villa an instrument to be used: the alliance was a calculating move, rather than a warm embrace; and towards Villa himself their feelings were often mingled fear and contempt" (*Mexican Revolution* vol. 2, 291). Yet what shines through in this passage is not disdain but sympathy and appreciation. Villa's affect changes the aloof position of the intellectual: a homosocial bond is formed, of which the *letrado* is obviously fond (*El águila y la serpiente* 257; 344–46). With a sense of wonder and pride, he narrates the physical affection Villa demonstrates toward him. He narrates how Villa put an arm around his shoulder, pulling him toward him and thus took him for a walk (344–45); and at another point he recalls: "I felt myself in his arms, lifted in suspense two quarters above the ground; put in an atmosphere where his breath and mine mixed" ("me sentí en sus brazos, levantado en vilo a dos cuartas del suelo, metido en una atmósfera donde su aliento y el mío se mezclaban") (462). Adela Pineda Franco argues that throughout the novel the protagonist tries to protect himself and his good judgment from the "unwholesome passions of those below" ("pasiones malsanas de 'los de abajo'") ("Afecto" 250), but their affect—their hugs, their breath, their warmth, their impulses, their expressions of affection—impedes his distancing acts. It is rather, as Legrás argues, that the affect destroys the distance and that Guzmán's discourse ends up being "permeated by the Villista indistinction between affect and violence" ("permeada por la indistinción villista entre afecto y violencia) ("Martín Luis Guzmán" 451).

There is a desire to be accepted by the man of arms. Since the Mexican Revolution, the masculinity of the *capitalinos* had been under attack. In 1914, Álvaro Obregón, among others, said that they were "sissies" wanting to sit out the revolution (Lear 185). In addition, in 1925 a debate raged in the feuilletons about the "effeminate" character of recent Mexican literature, singling out Azuela's *Los de abajo* as an example of truly "virile literature" (McKee Irwin 116–31). One of the main conflicts of *Los de abajo,* especially the second extended version, is the relationship between men of arms and men of letters. Several *curros* (city slickers) accompany the band of peasants under Demetrio Macías and their relationship is fraught with misunderstanding and distrust but there is also fascination for the capabilities of the others. The men of letters want to be accepted by the men of arms, but they flee from the violence those men represent; at the same time, the peasants admire, as Ángel Rama has pointed out, the intellectuals' linguistic power, "their almost magic power to practice writing and through it compose the justifying ideological discourse ('how well the city slicker speaks')" ("su poder casi mágico para ejercer la escritura y mediante ella componer el discurso ideológico justificativo ['¡qué bien habla el curro!']) (124).

Overall, through the *curro* characters the novel displays an ambivalent relationship with the revolution, its violence and its perpetrators: the at first intrigued and then disillusioned Alberto Solís, the opportunistic Luis Cervantes, who ends up making money in the United States, and the sensitive dreamy poet Valderrama, *el loco,* who sings of the revolution but, like the others, maintains a calculated distance from battles and firing squads. These figures are contrasted with the boisterous peasant rebels and their rifles. There is a wish to bring these different masculinities together, but generally class differences lead to a profound *desencuentro.* Even though the image of the *letrado* drawn is ambivalent, in the end the novel paves the way so that the men of letters can take over, precisely by giving the justifying discourse for the revolution; as such, they will interpret and manage the insurgent event for the postrevolutionary regime.

Guzmán's *El águila y la serpiente* also interprets the Mexican Revolution according to the relationship between *armado* and *letrado.* While it affirms the position of the *letrado,* it also shows, similar to *Los de abajo,* the intellectual's longing to be accepted by the man of arms. There is a desire in the novel to have one's masculinity affirmed through the other's approval. Villa's signs of affection toward the protagonist are combined with constant appraisals of his virility. For example, Villa calls the protagonist a civilian who is braver than a military man (257). The invitation to Villa's inner circle is an affirmation of the protagonist's virility: "only the men get in here" ("aquí no entran más que los hombres"; 463). It is accompanied with an admonition to adhere to a masculinist code of honor: "Talk to me like a man" ("Hábleme como los hombres"; 465). So while the *letrado* has interpretative power over Villa when he animalizes him and inferiorizes him, the *letrado* also depends on Villa, who has power over him because it is Villa who has the ability to confer onto the *letrado* the virile masculinity the intellectual so strongly desires. The intellectual becomes a *hombre,* a man, only through Villa. As most novels of the revolution equated Mexican national identity with virility (McKee Irwin 185), underscoring one's virility becomes a crucial element for the intellectual to maintain himself within the national project. The intellectual needs the armed man to teach him his virile violent ways.

All this brings Guzmán's man of letters far closer to revolutionary violence than he would like to admit. In the process of being taught by the armed man, the *letrado* himself ends up becoming a man of violence, a "bandit" even. When in the end the protagonist has to flee Mexico City, he impulsively stops a car in the middle of the street and confiscates it, citing necessities of war. He contritely concurs with the vehicle owner's accusations that his defense of the action displays the reasoning of "highwaymen" ("salteadores de camino"; 442). Although the intellectual ultimately returns the car to the owner, as he hastily clarifies (451), he is now operating within Villa's logic of affect and violence.

Yet ultimately the intellectual betrays the man of arms. When the protagonist flees the capital traveling toward Villa in Aguascalientes in a risky gamble to save himself, Villa welcomes the *letrado* as one of his own and affectionately embraces him. He declares that he knew that Guzmán would not abandon him (462). In a paternalistic show of affection, Villa declares that the intellectual will stay with him from now on: "I don't want you to be around those sons-of-bitches anymore" ("Ya no quiero que ande con jijos de la rejija"; 462). Guzmán asks Villa to be allowed to go in search of his family who had left the capital on a different train. Villa grants Guzmán permission while begging him not to abandon him. Villa gives him another hug and reaffirms their homosocial bond by warning the train driver to take great care of Guzmán because "he is one of my men" ("es de los míos"; 466). The *letrado* boards the train and slyly abandons his friend, sighing at the 1,400 kilometers that he still has to ride until getting to exile.[13]

Thus a tragic "image of desertion" ("imagen de deserción,") (Pineda Franco, "Entre el exilio" 40) closes the novel *El águila y la serpiente*. While the intellectual appears affected by the armed man on an individual and social level, Guzmán is ultimately unwilling to commit to him on the political and national level. It can be argued, as Domínguez-Ruvalcaba does, that this is due to the suppression of homoerotic desire. He argues that, unlike the heterosexual national romance novels of Doris Sommer's famous *Foundational Fictions*, in the novels of the Mexican Revolution the nation is founded on homosociality in which homoerotic desire cannot be explicitly expressed or consummated (Domínguez-Ruvalcaba 55, 59, 65). The national project is thus built upon "a homophilia continuously restrained by homophobia" (65). I believe that another fear weighs heavier than homophobia. The man of letters leaves Villa and his pistol because he is afraid of what his absolute immersion into the politics of affect and violence would ultimately entail: the definite collapse of the paradigm of civilization versus barbarism.

## The Tremendous Reality of Firing Squads

Several critics have argued Guzmán's *El águila y la serpiente* operates within and reiterates the Latin American ordering principle of civilization versus barbarism (Shaw 3; Espinosa 98: Parra 93). I, on the contrary, argue that the novel is not a vindication of this dichotomy but rather a testimony of its implosion. While certainly influenced by patterns of thoughts from Sarmiento's *Facundo* and Rodó's *Ariel*, Guzmán's novel actually shows how the powerful, rigid episteme starts to crumble under the impression of the "creative and destructive confusion of the Mexican Revolution" ("confusión creadora y destructiva de la Revolución Mexicana") (Domínguez Michael 210).[14] Just as he tries to uncover the mystery the men of arms represent, Guzmán also tries to understand the revolution through its most emblematic institution: the firing squad. During numerous wars in the nineteenth century, Mexico had already seen most forms of political violence that were employed during the revolution; firing squads were no novelty, and only political assassinations were new (Lomnitz 585).[15] In particular the 1867 execution of Emperor Maximilian had created a potent visual blueprint of the firing squad, which generally featured "the victim, the wall, the firing squad and onlookers" (Noble 91). Yet the sheer number of executions far superseded occurrences in previous conflicts and, as such, must have produced a strong impact. Throughout *El águila y la serpiente* different firing squads occurr: mass executions of prisoners of war as well as summary executions of common criminals or of individuals who offended the revolutionary troops in power. A master narrator, Guzmán paints an ambiguous picture of the institution of the firing squad and offers different aesthetic and moral-political takes.

There are those firing squads that happen during the Conventionalist oc-cupation of Mexico City, during which the rebels take over state functions, arbitrarily judging and executing. Álvaro Obregón's martial law orders are that anyone disturbing the public order shall be executed (*El águila y la ser-piente* 239). When two men are caught in the act of stealing and five men are caught for counterfeiting, they are "sentenced" without a trial. Everyone in-volved knows that what they are doing is wrong, and the doomed men plead not to kill them for a relatively minor offense, but those are Obregón's orders. The representation of this execution is not only a direct criticism of Obregón's institution of martial law during the occuption of the capital,[16] but it is also a more abstract reflection on the injustice of martial law and military men, since they are bound by duty and obedience to go against their inner convic-tions of right and wrong (242).

These episodes reveal two problems of so-called revolutionary justice: the use of capital punishment and militarism. Benjamin has pointed out that the use of the death penalty for property crimes only serves the purpose of posit-ing a new order and establishing power ("Zur Kritik" 43) and that militarism, in particular policing, leads to a suspension of the necessary distinction be-tween law-making and law-preserving violence ("Zur Kritik" 43–44). So here the insurgents are suddenly far away from their revolutionary law-de-stroying force and instead have become a highly problematic violent state force, one that simultaneously preserves and makes law. A common theme in these descriptions is the arbitrariness of these convictions. The *letrado* criti-cizes that those sentenced to death are behaving like the troops, taking what they want, and making their own money for personal gain (*El águila y la ser-piente* 249; 388). He highlights that at the moment of revolutionary upheaval, the lines between insurgency and delinquency are fluid. So who is supposed to make and impose law?

Yet the intellectual absolves himself from any responsibility. He places himself outside of the violence, more a philosophical observer than an actor, left to wonder not only about the irregularity of the events but also the "the monstrous irregularity" ("la irregularidad monstruosa"; 243) of the execution by firing squad itself, of having men shoot another man with his back against the wall and his hands tied. However, these episodes happen when he has been declared an interim police inspector partly in charge of reorganizing the met-ropolitan police amid the revolutionary upheaval. The *letrado* finds the execu-tion "abominable and perverse" ("abominable y perverso"; 249), yet he refuses to take on any personal responsibility or intervene since he is not a military man. He takes himself out of the equation because he is a civilian and this "is not a time for studied people" ("no es momento de licenciados"; 245). In both executions the Guzmán character does not intervene, or says he is unable to do so (390–91). In the end lie dead the cadavers of the two thieves—one still with an expression of pleading, the other resigned (249). In the other episode the *letrado* is left to look upon the sad caravan taking the five counterfeiters to the cemetery, their faces lost and acutely aware (392). Culpable of this monstrosity: men of arms.

Although these summary executions in the urban space are generally condemned, the firing squads after battles are far more ambiguous in their representation—in particular, as they relate to a realization of how violence relates to modernity. The Mexican Revolution was a modern experience, characterized by speed—in the form of swift transport of troops, information, images, and the "deployment of efficient mechanized killing" (Lomnitz 383). In *El águila y la serpiente,* characterized by a whirlwind of encounters and multiple journeys, speed becomes a principal sensation of the revolution: "Why were we going so absurdly fast?" ("¿Por qué íbamos tan absurdamente aprisa?"; 365). Modernity thus reveals itself as a combination of speed and violence.

One execution is not an actual execution but rather the spontaneous *fusilamiento* of a moving image of Venustiano Carranza during the Convention of Aguascalientes, which was called to decide the future course of the revolution but in which the most important leaders—Villa, Carranza, Zapata—were absent. A film is shown of the troops' entry into Mexico, and somebody from the audience shoots the image of disliked Carranza riding his horse, almost killing Guzmán and his friends, who were viewing the movie from behind the curtain. Pineda Franco argues that this affective gut reaction disturbs the intellectual, not only because of their near death but because mass media, the film, makes it possible that the revolutionaries react without the mediation of the intellectual ("Afecto" 249). Again, this execution reveals the violence of the Mexican Revolution as a modern experience, mediated through the swift immediacy of images and the firearm.

In another story, the chapter titled "Pancho Villa en la cruz," a telegraph is at the center of the tale. In this suspense story about a *fusilamiento,* Villa orders by telegram the execution of 170 prisoners of war. Making him more irascible but also increasing the moral dilemma is that these men once fought under him but once their leader, Maclovio Herrera, turned against Villa, the men became enemies. Guzmán and a fellow intellectual manage to convince Villa that it is wrong to execute men once they have surrendered, arguing that those who surrender save the lives of others by ceasing to fight and thus in turn should also be spared (361). Villa changes his mind and orders the suspension of the execution; contrary to other affirmations in the novel, this shows that one can reason with Villa. But it is unclear whether the order will reach the other side on time, since everything is mediated through the simultaneous swiftness and slowness of the telegram: "Tic-tic, tiqui . . . Villa did not take his eyes off of the movement that was transmitting his orders two hundred leagues to the north, and neither did we" (359).[17]

The tale suggests that Villa needs the intellectual to guide him because his original reaction was impulsive and violent: "But what else should one do than execute them? ("¡Pues ¿qué ha de hacer sino fusilarlos?!" 358). Yet the anecdote becomes "an exemplary tale of moral redemption" (Parra 92)—moral redemption of Villa but also of the protagonist himself whose inaction in Mexico City has not redeemed him nor absolved him of complicity. Yet it is also a story about the modernity of the revolution and how violence and modernity constantly overlap. The Guzmán character points to this by recalling that he "tried to guess the precise moment when the vibrations of the fingers spelled the words 'Execute immediately'" (359).[18] The experience of the Mexican Revolution as narrated in the novel exemplifies the intimate relationship between modernity, velocity, and military armament Paul Virilio has theorized. It is a "logistical" conception of modernity—one built around the process of preparing and organizing war (Bratton in Virilio, *Speed and Politics* 7).

Trains were one of the crucial components of the Mexican Revolution that made it a modern experience of logistics and velocity. The railroad system constructed under the Porfirian regime had been an important symbol of its "civilizing mission" (Matthews, *The Civilizing Machine* 11). It was also the regime's instrument of repression, since the trains were used to quickly send in federal troops to crush any flicker of discontent (Gilly 44). Now they were reappropriated by the same peasants the regime had sought to suppress.[19] During the revolution great numbers of troops were transported by rail and thus encountered a previously unknown country, learning, as Héctor Aguilar Camín and Lorenzo Meyer put it, "that they can travel throughout the country and make it their own" (51).

Many corridos also refer to trains, such as "Siete leguas," "La rielera," and "Máquina 501" ("The Railroad Worker" and "Machine 501"). The song "Aquí viene el tren" ("Here Comes the Train") from *Cantares de la revolución* by Dueto Rubén y Nelly shows how the train became an important means of war. The singer threatens the *pelones* (the federal army who had shaved heads) by announcing the arrival of the train, full of troops. The song expresses a thrill of speed and power, as it announces the arrival of the train at full speed: "The driver has started to pull the brakes, the rifles are already firing, the grapeshot is starting" ("El maquinista ya empezó a meter los frenos, ya los fusiles se disparan, ha empezado la metralla"). Thus modernity became a lived experience, in the form of war and speed.

In *El águila y la serpiente*, which notably starts and ends with journeys by train, significant negotiations of the meaning of the revolution happen aboard trains or in cars, with obstacles ahead or tumultuous situations inside the vehicles functioning as allegories for the mind-boggling revolutionary process (154–55, 171). Dazed by the revolution, dazed by the speed, for Guzmán the trains are not symbols of emancipation but of the upside-down world the revolution represents: people sit, lie, and eat everywhere; he is unable to distinguish between persons and objects; any "civilized" notion of decorum has disappeared due to the plebeian-revolutionary "de-civilizing wave" ("ola descivilizadora"; 156). On the train there is no longer any space for reason and arguing, only violence could have contained the chaos, he says (155–56)—a moment where we again see his permeation by the violent logic of the revolution. In these passages one can certainly see Guzmán's adherence to the civilizing paradigm in the narration and the narrator's classism (Parra 93; Ruffinelli, "Trenes revolucionarios" 289), but ultimately I read this episode as a testimony to the implosion of the old order, swept away by the modernity of the revolution.

Modernity often has a positive connotation. It is seen as a progressive process of increasing civilization, one that runs opposed to barbarism or violence. On the brink of World War II, Norbert Elias still published *Über den Prozeß der Zivilisation* (1939), which conceives modernity as a civilizing process in which the interlacing of personal and societal structural changes such as the increasing control of sexual, violent, and digestive activities are at the core of the increasingly less violent Western European modernity. But quite contrary to this powerful belief in the "civilizing," nonviolent tendency or effect of modernity, numerous thinkers have highlighted that modernity and violence are not opposed phenomena but that rather they are intrinsically linked. Decolonial thinkers such as Aníbal Quijano and Walter Mignolo have highlighted the intimate relation between modernity and the violence of colonialism. Zygmunt Bauman has demonstrated that the Holocaust was a product of modernity and not a barbarian slippage in the West's supposedly straight path to "civilization." Jean Franco has recently argued that the state-sanctioned atrocities committed in Latin America throughout the twentieth century are a regional expression of a general global tendency in which "the acceptance and justification of cruelty and the rationale for cruel acts . . . have become a feature of modernity" (*Cruel Modernity* 2). While Franco's analysis is compelling, it nonetheless leaves us with the question, When was modernity, built on the violence of colonialism, ever not cruel?

These studies show that modernity is not necessarily as civilized and non-violent as imagined. This realization jolts the "morally elevating story of humanity emerging from pre-social barbarity," which is the "etiological myth deeply entrenched in the self-consciousness of our Western society" (Bauman 12). For this reason, acknowledging the interconnectedness of modernity and violence continues to be a difficult task. Guzmán's *El águila y la serpiente* operates heavily within the dichotomy of civilization and barbarism, but both Villa with his pistol as well as the modern killings of the revolution collapse this dichotomy. While there are numerous descriptions of firing squads in the novel, the chapter titled "La fiesta de las balas" is the most significant because of its epistemic, ethical, and aesthetic dimensions. It is also the novel's most famous, most anthologized, and most controversial chapter. Here, Rodolfo Fierro kills hundreds of prisoners of war (Orozquistas) on Villa's orders. It is one of the few episodes in the book where Guzmán does not claim the status of an eyewitness. He explicitly says that what he is about to narrate is rather legendary and not necessarily historically sound. He adds, however, that he finds the legendary episodes, those with "the touch of poetic exaltation" ("el toque de la exaltación poética") more revealing, "more worthy to make History" ("más dignas de hacer Historia") (199). Let's remember that he is in search of the mystery and truth that these armed men represent, and this tale of a mythical mass execution is an important piece in this puzzle that the armed peasant insurgency presents to the intellectual.

The chapter does not depict a classical firing squad in the sense of a group shooting a man before a wall, *el paredón,* but rather a dynamic, cruelly designed mass execution lasting for several hours. Fierro tells the prisoners that they have a chance to escape if they manage to climb the wall and that he will be the only one shooting. But this is a deception, as others help to enclose the prisoners-turned-cattle with their weapons. Tricked by the false promise of a possible escape from death, the doomed men are hushed through several corrals and slaughtered by Fierro and a few men. Fierro, with the help of his assistant—who is in charge of reloading Fierro's weapons—shoots almost all prisoners, with two exceptions: one man manages to climb over the wall, only to be shot by another Villista, reasoning that the small moving point in the distance "looks bad" ("Se ve mal"; 209); another man survives under the dead bodies and, when he cries for water during the night, Fierro has his assistant kill him. After the massacre Fierro sleeps peacefully in the "crib" under the stars ("pesebre"; 211).

The entire episode is set up to hint at a deeper meaning or revelation: "it was like feeling within the soul the brush of a tremendous reality" ("era como sentir en el alma el roce de una tremenda realidad"; 199). Guzmán uses the ambiguous adjective "tremendous" to frame this tale, whose meaning ranges from "mighty" to "terrible" in Spanish, something worthy to be feared, respected, or revered (see Real Academia de la Lengua Española). The "tremenda realidad" that appears in his carefully constructed tale, strategically positioned at the end of the novel's first part "Revolutionary Hopes" ("Esperanzas revolucionarias"), is that modernity can be violent and cruel, that one can be civilized and barbarous at the same time. The scene displays behavior that is as cruel as it is "barbarous." The setup of the execution is a malicious endeavor bound to instill panic. On one side of the fence men are trying to flee the bullets, screaming and inevitably dying and on the other side men are pushing back against the riders rounding them up and forcing them toward the gate (208). The execution is carried out with absolute disregard for human dignity: the prisoners are dehumanized, converted into livestock ("rebaño de reses" 201; "como cabras" 206). The absolute lack of compassion and inhibition on behalf of the Villistas creates a situation in which the reader hopes for a redeeming moment. However, the story negates any redemption or catharsis. Fierro sleeps apparently guilt-free. His assistant does show some remorse as he crosses himself before going to sleep, but when during the night a lone survivor asks for human compassion and begs for water, the assistant follows Fierro's order and shoots the man.

This cruel mass execution is a modern killing, methodological and rational ("civilized"). It is not a furious killing by the "mob" but rather an organized, modern mass murder executed through the use of firearms—not a slaughter with the machete, a "premodern" killing tool. It might seem cynical to stress the type of weapon used, but many peasant and indigenous movements such as the Zapatistas, Sandino's peasant army in Nicaragua, or the doomed peasant insurgents of La Matanza in El Salvador were marked as barbarous and "premodern" in Latin America precisely because of the use of the machete and the disfiguration of bodies that such a weapon produces. Yet the modernity of this mass execution is not only related to the firearms. Overall, it displays key elements of a modern society, as defined by Max Weber (*Wirtschaft und Gesellschaft*): it is calculated, rationalized, organized, bureaucratized, and disciplined. The killers display methodological behavior as well as diligence and obedience. Fierro fulfills Villa's orders with "efficient diligence" ("eficaz diligencia"; 200); he is disciplined and duteous in following his superior's orders, and he is quite bureaucratic when inspecting the different corrals and setting up a meticulous, organized killing machine. This attitude is similar to the "honor of the civil servant," a Weberian notion that Bauman uses to describe how this sense of bureaucratic honor outweighs personal inhibitions toward violence in the context of a chain of command (22).

Although Fierro's assistant does not seem to enjoy Fierro's cruel fantasy, he still obeys. He devotes himself to the mechanics of putting bullets in Fierro's three pistols and avoiding seeing beyond his immediate task. He does not lift his eyes to see those falling and just focuses on the pistols he needs to refill (*El águila y la serpiente* 207). This relation between modern technology and death appears several times throughout the novel, reflecting the link between the immensity of the armed conflict and the previous modernization of the country. The actions of the assistant show that the technology permitted distancing oneself from the killing. The assistant's participation makes the mass execution an industrialized killing. Alberto Blasi has called this scene an "assembly line," a Fordist production of death (36). The alienation of the violence worker from the end product—the dead body—is thus a modern experience.

The cruel setup and execution alone could be seen as a conventional critique of revolutionary cruelty in which the barbarian element is stressed, thereby vindicating the need to civilize/control these elements. However, the reading of this chapter is complicated even more by its explicit aesthetization of the gruesome episode (Peña Iguarán, "Próspero" 99–100). Making use of different cinematic techniques, the narrator creates a spectacular scene of a mass execution in a corral at sunset (Duffrey 47–48). Like a canvas, tone and colors are arranged in harmony, including plays of color at the sunset and ending under an idyllic night sky and moonlight. Creating a sense of theatricality through a mix of long shots and close-ups, the narration describes a desolate yet awe-inspiring scene on the northern plain. The description of Fierro points toward the appearance of the sublime: "His grand and beautiful figure gave off a strange aura, something superior, something prestigious" ("Su figura grande y hermosa, irradiaba un aura extraña, algo superior, algo prestigioso"; 202). The plays of light and color add drama to the scene in which the weapon is transformed, irradiating and reflecting the light—light often symbolizing some superior truth in the novel: "The barrel of the weapon, long and polished, became a pink finger in the light of the sunset" ("El cañón del arma, largo y pulido, se transformó en dedo de rosa a la luz poniente del sol"; 203). As Luis Leal puts it: "And even the pistol, destructive weapon, is seen like an object of art" ("Y hasta la pistola, arma destructora, es vista como objeto de arte"; 75). It is beautiful, awe-inspiring, and epic, which draws the reader closer, making it hard to maintain a moralizing distance from the narrated events. Just as Villa's violence and affect draw the intellectual closer, here the author draws the reader closer into the violence.[20]

It is only through the "poetic exaltation" ("exaltación poética"), which is placed as a reading key at the beginning of the chapter, that Guzmán can express the "tremendous reality" ("tremenda realidad") of the firing squad and the revolution, a reality that cannot be captured by the dichotomy of civilization and barbarism. This frightening and confusing realization can only be expressed in the ambiguity of the novelistic form. The modernity and beauty of these actions topple the dichotomy. Suddenly, civilization and barbarity and, in this sense, modernity and violence, are not mutually exclusive anymore. The intellectual can insinuate but not explicitly formulate such a monstrosity. While it is certainly true that the novel searches for a new hermeneutic framework, as Legrás argues, Guzmán's most staggering discovery is ultimately too much for the intellectual. He is intrigued by the mystery of the masses in arms and gets dislocated by the affective relationship he develops with the individual man of arms. Accepting that modernity is violent, however, is too tremendous a reality, so in the end he flees the scene.

## The Dance of the Rifle: The Irruption of the Zapatismo

The Villismo represented a rural and regional identity heavily marked by the processes in northern Mexico, not unlike the development of the western United States: a bellicose settler mentality, individualism, cattle farming and mining, which made for many highly mobile, landless, or land-poor rural laborers. While the majority of *El águila y la serpiente* is dedicated to the Villista forces, a different political rural subjectivity appears a few times: the Zapatista rebel from Morelos, a more classical peasant than the Villista rebel, generally seen as more indigenous, more traditional and closer to the land, and more marked by the feudal relations of the Morelos sugar plantations but also by the encroaching capitalist land speculation. Representative of some of the most radical traits of the Mexican Revolution, which featured communitarian and anarchist elements, Zapata continues to be a folk hero but less of an official state hero. Whereas Villa's remains were eventually transported to the Monument of the Revolution to lie there in unity with his archenemies, and his spectacular hacienda museum is managed by the Mexican military, Zapata's remains continue to be in Cuautla and the museums dedicated to him in Morelos display an obvious lack of state funding.

The Zapatismo is repressed not only in national politics but also in literature. Most novels of the revolution are about the Villistas and not the Zapatistas. Guzmán in *El águila y la serpiente* only dedicates a few pages to the Zapatistas, and utter puzzlement characterizes their depiction: from the unnerving sound of the Zapatistas' *huaraches* in the National Palace to their insubordinate behavior during his time in the Ministry of War. Yet these short scenes are masterfully written and characterized by a similar dynamic as the depictions of Villa: a subalternizing gaze that nonetheless recognizes this new emergent subjectivity and the unclear position of the intellectual relative to this subjectivity. "Los zapatistas en Palacio" is probably the novel's second most anthologized and analyzed chapter after "La fiesta de las balas." Taking place during the Convencionista occupation of Mexico City, the chapter tells of the Zapatista occupation of this most important symbol of power: the National Palace. Eufemio Zapata, Emiliano's brother, greets the delegation to which Guzmán belongs and leads them through the palace.

Guzmán, being the narrator he is, fixates on senses, sounds, and dissonances to describe the political shock of seeing the building occupied by Zapatista forces, describing the contrast, the sheer "incompatibility" ("incompatibilidad," 395) between the refined colonial architecture and the coarse peasant clothes and hands of Eufemio. Guzmán describes two Zapatista rank-and-file wandering through the palace in silence and reverie, their presence "representing a truth" ("representaba allí una verdad," 396) and the troops getting drunk in the lower chambers. Christopher Domínguez Michael has rightly pointed out that this particular "chapter has been judged as the proof of Guzmán's 'petit-bourgeois' fury, his incomprehension in the face of the popular forces, when actually it is a formidable call of attention about the irruption of the others in the life of Mexico" (203–4).[21] In recent years, however, several scholars have offered subalternist readings (Legrás, *Literature and Subjection*, "Martín Luis Guzmán;" Moreiras; Williams, *Mexican Exception*). Gareth Williams sees the Zapatista insurgents in the palace as representing "the immanent egalitarianism of violent revolution and lawlessness" (50) and the interventions by Eufemio Zapata as affirming himself as a speaking subject (52).

There is another scene in the novel, rarely commented upon, in which the Zapatistas appear and affirm themselves a speaking subjects and as people wholly aware of power relations and the performativity of lettered political power in Mexico. In this scene military equipment is key. The *letrado* protagonist, from police inspector has now moved on to working in the Ministry of War and he has one job: to keep the Zapatista demands for trains and firearms at bay. If we recall his disarming function the *letrado* describes in relation to Villa, here it appears again, and it is literal: keep weapons away from the peasants. The Zapatista delegation comes to the Ministry of War to demand weapons, which they are expecting since the Aguascalientes Convention led to an albeit fragile alliance between Villista, Zapatista, and other more moderate forces. But instead of giving them weapons, the Guzmán character is in charge of avoiding just that. He entangles them "in the most intricate of discussions regarding the modern art of battling with cartridges and without cartridges, with rifles and without rifles, with trains and without trains" ("en intrincadísimas disquisiciones sobre el arte moderno de batallar con cartuchos y sin cartuchos, con fusiles y sin fusiles, con trenes y sin trenes") (*El águila y la serpiente* 409). In fact, the moderate forces to which Guzmán belongs are using the Carrancistas (their enemies) to fight against their allies Zapata and Villa in order to lessen their military power and thus strengthen the political power of the moderate group around President Eulalio Gutiérrez (408). The peasant insurgents see through these performances. Angry because they did not obtain the desired equipment, one group takes revenge by putting on an equally performative act. In front of the fifty people in the waiting room, they start to dance "something that could be called the 'dance of the rifle and the pistol'" ("algo que podría llamarse la 'danza del rifle y la pistola'" (409). Guzmán retells it with irony, but he unintentionally registers a political intervention. A *Bauernschläue* (peasant wit and shrewdness) shines through here, showcasing once more subaltern political knowledge.

In the first chapter in this book, on *Cartucho,* I mentioned the corrido "Soy zapatista del estado de Morelos" as a sign that now the peasants will hold the state accountable to them. This new confidence also appears in this episode. Another Zapatista general insists that he get a locomotive to help the village of Amozoc, under attack by Carrancistas. The *letrado* lies to him, saying that they do not have any, but the general enumerates all the locomotives and where he has seen them; so in the end the intellectual cedes him an old one, still running on wood. The Zapatista assents but not without a threat: "Okay, master: I take that one. But, son of a guava if they defeat me! . . . Because then I will come and smudge you" ("Bueno, patrón: me llevo ésa [locomotora]. Pero, !ay jijo de la guayaba si me redotan! . . . Porque entonces vengo y lo tizno"; 410). Hearing the insult, the protagonist challenges him with a paperweight: "Son of a what?" ("¿Hijo de qué?"). The Zapatista takes back the insult, apologizing to the "dear master" ("patroncito") but still threatens to come back and kill him if he is defeated because of the lack of good equipment (410). The use of *patrón* in this exchange is peculiar: the feudal term points to a conscience of the unequal power relations between them, and while the Zapatista general is behaving according to the linguistic formalism and deference, this does not mean that he will respect the physical integrity of the *letrado.* This new popular subjectivity, born out of armed insurgency, is no longer afraid, only angry at the deceit.

The novel is full of disdain about "the Zapata riffraff" ("las chusmas de Zapata"; 431), and even in a poetic description of their presence, the narrator cannot help but point out that they smell bad: "the *huaraches* made a soft sound; in marched, like big wheels over an invisible rail, the enormous wide hats, which produced when they moved a breeze of stuffy, impure air" ("hacían rumor suave los huaraches; desfilaban, como grandes ruedas sobre carril invisible, los enormes sombreros anchos, que producían al moverse brisa de aire confinado, impuro"; 409). Yet there is an acknowledgment of their presence, their cleverness. There they are. Less dangerous than Villa because of their lack of firepower but nonetheless an apparition. It is as if the *curro* sees them for the very first time, when they irrupt in his urban modern spaces. The scenes of the Zapatistas in the National Palace and in the Ministry of War described in the novel are comparable to the famous photo of the Zapatistas in the Sanborns: an irruption and revelation.

Guzmán, with his acute awareness for symbols, senses, truths, and virtues, wavers at their sight. Disgusted, afraid, but also fascinated. Their dance of the rifle and the pistol is a conscious irruption highlighting power relations and the performative character of politics. He searches and searches for a truth in this armed insurgency and makes distressing and surprising findings. He condemns the militarism and arbitrariness of revolutionary state-making, but he is, nonetheless, taken by the presence of the men of arms. Acutely aware of the continuous betrayal by the elites, his betrayal of his friend Villa, his mandated betrayal of the Zapatista generals and ranks, it is the irruption of the Zapatistas that mark a vision of truth. Poorly armed, there they are with their *huaraches,* their muslin, and their smell of rural poverty. Looking, speaking, and dancing.

## CHAPTER 3

# RIDDLED BY BULLETS

## WEAPONRY, MILITANCY, AND THE PEOPLE IN ARMS
## AS DESIRE AND ENIGMA

Rifles occupy a central position in the revolutionary and postrevolutionary Sandinista discourse. They appear throughout songs, photos, posters, poems, *testimonios*, novels, and memoirs. They are key artifacts, tropes, and props in the Sandinista political and cultural universe: from the early 1970s, when they appeared as killing tools mainly in the hands of the Somoza regime, which used heavy firepower against a then small Frente Sandinista de Liberación Nacional (FSLN), to the years of rural and urban guerrilla warfare, when they functioned as artifacts and props of virile militancy. Weaponry was central to one of the Sandinista main desires and enigmas: the people in arms. The aspiration was that "the people"—that inherently vague political category—would rise up in arms, which would fulfill the necessary shift from a Guevarian-focus guerrilla to a general insurrection.

When the Sandinistas triumphed over the Somoza regime in July 1979, they had reached power with the promise and hope that Nicaragua could be cleansed from its long history of direct, indirect, and epistemic violence. This would be achieved through a nationalist-progressive project deeply grounded in cultural institutions and aimed at far-reaching agrarian and social reforms. Many conceived of the Sandinista Revolution as a utopian political project in the sense that the revolutionaries wanted to create an ideal state and societal order.[1] The symbol of the new revolutionary times, which supposedly would bring an end to violence was, paradoxically so, the firearm. Until 1986 the logotype of each anniversary of the revolution featured stylized images of firearms or machetes (for the logotypes, see Bujard and Wirper 8).

In the 1980s the revolution's utopian aspirations were undone by the United States–backed Contra war, multiple errors in the political and economic administration, and an encroaching militarism. The militarization that started in the guerrilla years increased and became all-encompassing during the years following the triumph. With the placement of former *guerrilleros* in government positions came the army green fatigues and the obligatory rifle on the shoulder of the freshly minted bureaucrat as well as the de facto government of the nine former guerrilla commanders, the Dirección Nacional. With the Contra War came the arms buildup, which ultimately devoured most of the state's resources (Kruijt 124) as well as the creation of a mandatory military service for men in 1983, an unpopular political action with long-lasting effects. The Contra War also meant that peasants had taken up arms *against* the revolution. The revolutionary trope of the "people in arms" crumbled. As Nicaraguans grew tired of the war, the firearm started to become less prominent in the official discourse. In the late 1980s the logotype of the revolutionary anniversary no longer featured weaponry, with the exception of an adumbrated firearm in 1988—the year the peace negotiations began.

In 1990 the FSLN lost the election and ceded power. This was followed by reconciliatory politics and years of neoliberal, conservative policy-making dedicated to erasing the revolutionary experience from national memory. In 2006, Daniel Ortega and the FSLN returned to power with politics that, despite referencing the revolutionary symbols, are more concerned with retaining power for the Ortega-Murillo family than with far-reaching social changes. The red and black of the Sandinistas has been partly replaced by pink and yellow, and rifles have all but disappeared from the visual discourse, which still features Augusto C. Sandino and the FSLN founder, Carlos Fonseca. The rifle has been replaced symbolically by Tree of Life statues that First Lady Rosario Murillo had placed throughout Managua.

This chapter traces the distinctive, changing, and often contradictory symbolic significance of weaponry during and after the Sandinista Revolution by analyzing literary texts and photographs. I discuss the symbolic meaning of firearms in relation to different social actors in three separate sections: *guerrilleros* and weaponry; peasants, "the people," and weaponry; and militant intellectuals and weaponry. The starting point is Omar Cabezas's *La montaña es algo más que una inmensa estepa verde* (1982), Nicaragua's most famous *testimonio*, which relates the experience of becoming a *guerrillero*.

Whereas Cabezas's memoir appeared in the early 1980s, when the Sandinistas were still in power, about twenty years later—and ten years after the Sandinistas lost the election in 1990—there appeared several memoirs by leading Nicaraguan intellectuals constituting a postrevolutionary canon in which the memory of the revolution is "elaborated by the political and literary elite" ("elaborada por la elite política y literaria") (Delgado, "Memorias apocalípticas"; 109). Together with Ernesto Cardenal's autobiography, the memoirs by the country's most prominent novelists, Gioconda Belli and Sergio Ramírez, have had the biggest impact. Belli's autobiography *El país bajo mi piel: Memorias de amor y guerra* (2001) talks about the author's participation in the Sandinista Revolution, her writing, her relationships with different men, pregnancies, child rearing, and her current life split between Nicaragua and the United States. Ramírez's *Adiós muchachos: Una memoria de la revolución sandinista* (1999), a political memoir disguised as *crónica*, talks about the author's participation in the Sandinista Revolution, both in the 1970s and as vice president of Nicaragua in the 1980s. The book offers a reflection on the achievements and shortcomings of the Sandinista Revolution. Both works, published by big publishing houses such as Random House and Alfaguara, were quickly translated into English and German. They communicate with an audience both at home and abroad—in particular, with the solidarity movements in Europe and the United States. Written as a defense of the revolutionary project in the face of revolutionary simulacrum of a strengthened Orteguista Sandinism, these books have been criticized for their rather uncritical, nostalgic, and self-preserving gestures (Arias, *Taking Their Word* 21; Browitt; Mackenbach, "Mentiras"; Polit; Urbina). I am interested in the discursive role firearms play in these texts. Even though both authors did not engage in combat, firearms are an important element in their constructions of self.

## Muchachos *against Tanks and Men of Steel in the Mountains*

Central to the early Sandinista discourse is the representation of the firearm as a lethal tool in the hands of the Somoza regime. The weaponry of Somoza's National Guard appears as an echo in the riddled bodies of slain FSLN members: generally young men, *muchachos,* who died in unequal fights with the regime's tanks and airplanes. These bodies underscore the excessive use of force by the Somoza regime, which in return justifies the use of force by the Frente. Their ill-equipped but spirited and altruistic resistance contrasts with the dictatorship' plump use of force. Defiant, precarious, and full of bravado, these Sandinista militants sacrifice themselves for the nation. From these precarious beginnings emerges a heroic masculinity that is both fragile and strong—steeled through armed struggle and created in relation to the firearm.

When it comes to the men of arms in the Sandinista Revolution, *muchachos* is the key word that encases the discursively hegemonic masculinity of the revolution. It is no coincidence that Ramírez's postrevolutionary account is entitled *Adiós muchachos.* Referencing Carlos Gardel's tango "Adiós muchachos," the book announces Ramírez's retreat from political life. It is a farewell to former political comrade-in-arms, a farewell to youth and revolution. In the text he sighs at the fact that after the end of Sandinista rule and political-cultural restructuring of Nicaragua in 1990s, "the terms *muchachos,* and *com-*

*pañeros, compa, compita*, were lost" ("Los términos *muchachos*, y *compañeros, compa, compita*, se perdieron"; 56). The mourning for the revolution is encapsulated in the loss of these words. Whereas Ramírez focuses on the general use of the terms to express militancy and collectivity, I focus on one particular image: that of the *muchacho* facing off against the heavy firepower of the Somoza regime.

## Riddled Bodies and Defiance

These images and narratives generally concentrate on two young men who resisted the National Guard against great odds and at a moment when the FSLN was still a small organization: Julio Buitrago, killed in July 1969 at age twenty-five, and Leonel Rugama, killed in January 1970 at age twenty. In the case of Buitrago, hundreds of soldiers attacked a safe house of the Frente in Managua and, after two female militants managed to escape, he defended the house by himself for hours against tanks and heavy fire. The fight was mass-mediated too, as Cabezas narrates in his *testimonio*. The TV coverage did not have sound, but people could see "how the automatic weapons threw out the shells with great velocity, . . . how the pieces of concrete, cement, wood, glasses, paint, jumped when hundred thousands of bullet impacts hit the house" (34).[2] People also saw how, again and again, Buitrago appeared in a different window returning fire with his M-3 submachine gun. Cabezas recalls that then a small tank moved in and started firing and that Buitrago continued to return fire. Then a plane appeared and "all the guards, the tank insistently started to shoot against the house, and the plane, which almost touched the house, fired, and then we saw how they were reducing the house to rubble within seconds" (35).[3] Then Julio came out, still firing, until he was gunned down—in front of everyone's eyes: "We see Julio coming out of the house's main door, running, shooting in bursts against the Guard and seconds later, how Julio starts to bend, and shoots and bends some more and shoots and bends some more, until he falls to the ground" (35).[4]

The fragile body of the boy is shattered and brought down by the heavy armory, but he refuses to desist, his body still standing, his voice still shouting, his weapon still shooting. This was not just a war story; it was mass-mediated through photos and moving images. Maybe inexplicably from today's perspective, Somoza had the footage put on heavy rotation for days so that even people who did not own a TV were able to see it over time. It appears that he thought it was a potent show of force. Yet this backfired since to most people, Buitrago was the hero in this standoff. Cabezas narrates that he and other Sandinista sympathizers wanted to cry, but that that seeing Buitrago's death gave them a sense of "an indestructible strength" ("una fuerza inde-structible"; 35).

A couple of days later, and half a year before dying a similar death, Leo-nel Rugama went to the wrecked house where Buitrago died and to anoth-er safe house where several militants died and wrote the poem "Las casas quedaron llenas de humo." Among the images his poem describes are the holes produced by the Sherman tank, the Garand, the machine guns, "or by who-knows-what" ("o quién sabe de qué"; 69)—all the powerful weap-onry used against a few *muchachos*. The poem expresses admiration that they all died without saying a word (70). Yet Rugama himself became fa-mous for his last words before his death. In a safe house in Managua un-der heavy assault by the National Guard, Rugama, together with two other young men, resisted the attack. When asked to surrender, he yelled in de-fiant banter: "Let your mother surrender" ("Que se rinda tu madre"). After the fight ended, neighbors could not believe that the National Guard car-ried only three limp, light bundles out of the hollowed-out house (Ramírez, *Adiós* 40).

These representations endow the weapon with a highly significant and gen-dered value. The frail, thin, bullet-riddled cadavers highlight the dispropor-tionality of Somoza's reaction. His show of force becomes a sign of weakness exposing his fear of these *boys*. The deaths ridiculed the militarily superior National Guard and presented the Sandinistas as a youthful and out-gunned David against a heavily armed Goliath. Rugama's defiant response was an emasculation. It is David against Goliath, and Goliath had no balls. Rugama's skinny, intellectual, nonmasculine appearance works as a counternarrative to the masculinity of the bloodthirsty National Guard and the violent, deca-dent, and plump Somoza men. Ramírez narrates that Rugama "did not have the vignette of the heroic guerrilla of the trading cards" ("no tenía la estampa del guerrillero heróico de los cromos") (*Adiós* 39). He was a "poor seminary student" ("seminarista pobretón"), had big glasses, was always carrying books around. Rugama's youth and fragility as well as his nerdiness, religiousness, and poverty lessened his own use of force and heightened the violence of the regime.

These deaths exalted the masculinity of the Sandinista rebels. From this fragile masculinity, riddled with bullets and steeled through armed strug-gle, emerged the "New Man." This fragile albeit fearless masculinity, full of youthful recklessness and willing sacrifice, is espoused as the example to follow. It conforms to national ideals of masculinity. The dominant con-ception of masculinity in Nicaragua equates masculinity with a willingness to take "risks, to take chances, with all the bravado, flair, and even flamboyance that one can muster," as Roger Lancaster explains in his anthropological study *Life Is Hard* (196). Rugama's death expresses this desired masculinity—full of flamboyant bravado and defiant humor. His actions in the face of fire also fulfill the patriarchal notions that war brings out true men.

These ideas also appear in the song "No se me raje mi compa" from 1974 by Carlos Mejía Godoy, analyzed in greater detail in chapter 4. The song is in part about Rugama. It talks about him as the *muchacho* who sold tortillas and left the seminary to join the guerrilla, who "died like a man" ("Murió como todo un hombre"). The song is an exhortation of the determined serenity and vulnerability of the *muchachos* as well as of a desired masculinity that comes to full force in war. Through armed struggle, the boy becomes a man. The song reminds the listeners not to be "chusmón" (mediocre), a word that phonetically sounds like "cochón." *Cochón* is generally used for describing homosexuals that take a passive role in a homosexual intercourse; more important, *cochón* is "stigmatized for being less than a man" (Lancaster 274). So the song admonishes men not to be less of a man but manly just like the *muchachos*.

This desired war masculinity, fragile yet steeled and strong, also appears in two hypermasculine iconic photos of the Sandinista Revolution that became a symbol of the Frente. One is the famous photo of Edén Pastora after the successful attack on the National Congress in 1978, when a Sandinista commando took the congressmen hostage and had their demands fulfilled: ransom, liberation of prisoners, dissemination of their message, and free passage to Cuba. It was a risky and audacious act similar to that carried out by a small commando led by a Comandante Cero (Edén Pastora). They all wore masks, but Pastora could not resist the temptation to take his off before boarding the plane to Cuba. Arms stretched, rifle in one hand, beret, and two grenades on his shoulder, he became one of the most visible faces of the revolution. Pastora, who most wanted to be like El Che—later on he even left a farewell letter to Tomás Borge, similar to the one El Che wrote to Fidel—crafted a similar image. Yet he violated the Sandinista honor code of putting the collective before the individual; his grasp for fame and glory went against the ideals of asceticism: "His photograph traveled around the world, but his indiscretion was never forgiven" ("Su foto le dio vuelta al mundo, pero aquel desliz jamás le fué perdonado" (Ramírez *Adiós* 65). Another dimension conveyed by this photograph is that the Frente has graduated from *muchacho* to *hombre*, that it had become a powerful, armed organization capable of possibly overthrowing the Somoza regime.

FIGURE 3.1. *Sandinistas at the walls of the Esteli National Guard.* Photograph by Susan Meiselas. Susan Meiselas/Magnum Photos, 1979.

The second image is again that of a *muchacho*, fragile because of his skinniness, precarious and powerful at the same time because of his two weapons: a Molotov cocktail and a Fusil Automatique Léger (FAL). By famous war photographer Susan Meiselas from the urban battlefields of Estelí in 1979, the *muchacho* in the photo is Pablo de Jesús Arauz Mairena ("Bareta"), although few people know his name (Aragón Rodríguez); he is generally seen as an anonymous hero of the revolution, often only referred to as "hombre molotov." Wearing the obligatory Guevarian beret, the *muchacho* is throwing a Molotov cocktail, a FAL in the other hand, while a tank looms threateningly behind him: "He is a true *muchacho* and not a soldier, as demonstrated both by his youth and by his sorry excuse for a uniform" ("Es un muchacho de verdad, y no un soldado, como lo prueban tanto su juventud como su remedo de uniforme"), posits Alma Guillermoprieto. The photo suggests an enormous threat by the tank, but it had already been immobilized and rendered useless at the moment the photo was taken. The *muchacho*'s face seems contorted from the exertion of the fighting but also gives him an appearance of anger and determination. Although the Molotov cocktail shows precariousness, the rifle, as Guillermoprieto analyzes, is the "heart of the photograph: because although a *muchacho* with a Molotov cocktail would usually be doomed to failure, this one will succeed, because he has . . . a FAL" ("corazón de la foto:

pues aunque un muchacho con una molotov normalmente estaría condenado al fracaso, éste va a triunfar, porque . . . tiene un fal"). Without it, he would be a martyr, but with it, Guillermoprieto says, he becomes a hero.

It is significant that it is a FAL that appears in the photo; this was the rifle that turned the Frente and its *muchachos* into a force to be reckoned with. The FAL was one of the most symbolically significant rifles of the Sandinista Revolution. In a conversation with a former Sandinista guerrilla commander, the person explained that the Belgian FAL became a symbol of insurrection against the symbol of terror that was the National Guard's Garand. Although the loud roar of the semiautomatic Garand had always provoked great fear, when in the 1970s the Frente faced the National Guard with FALs, for the first time it was the Guard who retreated when it heard the sound of the fully automatic rifle. In general, the National Guard was better equipped than the FSLN, but the guerrilla force's acquisition of fully automatic weapons made them a serious opponent for the first time.

These two photographs are characterized by an imitation of Che Guevara, an aspiration to be like him. However, very few photographs exist of Che Guevara with a firearm. The iconic photographs of Che Guevara have more to do with his hair, his beard, his beret, his cigar, his smile, or, upon his death, his bare, emaciated chest. Sure enough, both photos of the Sandinista fighters feature the obligatory beret, yet it is the firearm that features here as the ultimate symbol of their conviction. It is the artifact of true militancy. Anyone can don a beret, but the willingness to fight and to sacrifice oneself is expressed in the rifle. The artifact demonstrates that they mean the Sandinista oath of wanting to die like El Che. Because as much as these images and narratives are about heroic behavior in a combat situation, they are more about sacrifice. These two photographs show the Frente as a serious force in the late 1970s, yet behind them lurk the images from the early 1970s, those of the riddled bodies. In terms of their political significance—for the conception of the FSLN, of a revolutionary masculinity and of armed struggle—these early images and narratives were the most formative and long-lasting.

These riddled bodies present a justification for the use of force and are also the beginning of a profound death cult among the Sandinistas. From this moment on, the image of the Frente was one of self-sacrifice. In Ramírez's post-revolutionary account *Adiós muchachos*, one of the key chapters, "Vivir como los santos," titled after another Rugama poem, centers on the deaths of these *muchachos* and the sacrifice that going underground represented. Going into the *clandestinidad* of urban guerrilla warfare meant to live in the proximity of death and was thus a sign of the ultimate sacrifice and renunciation: "Death never stopped being the path to absolute purification, the expiation of all sin, above all because it represented a deliberate sacrifice, wanted, sought, scapegoat and sacrificial lamb" ("Nunca dejaba la muerte de ser el camino de la purificación absoluta, la expiación de toda mancha, sobre todo porque representaba el sacrificio deliberado, querido, buscado, chivo expiatorio y cordero degollado") (Ramírez, *Adiós* 46). In a convergence of Catholic and Marxist thought, sacrifice and death were seen as an ethical choice that purified society from the vices of a flawed consumerist modernity (Franco, *Decline and Fall* 87).

This notion reminds of René Girard's work in which he concludes that ritual sacrifice has the purpose of channeling the communitarian violence onto a surrogate victim, which permits that the community "be reborn in a new or renewed cultural order" (255). In the foundational myth of the Sandinista Revolution, the *muchachos* offered themselves up as scapegoats. Sacrifice was one's offering for a better world. The chosen death, the willing sacrifice, was part of the guerrilla mystique that also allowed the FSLN to represent itself never as a perpetrator of violence but as its victim. If one is the sacrificed lamb, one is not the wolf. Armed struggle appeared not as an act of aggression but of sacrifice. Going underground, becoming the New Men through guerrilla warfare, be it in the city or the countryside, meant an enormous sacrifice: facing deprivations and living in close proximity to death. This sacrifice is also exemplified in *muchachos'* skinniness: the thin, dead bodies of Buitrago and Rugama and the gauntness of the guerrilla commanders, when they come out of the mountains, that surprises Régis Debray (Ramírez, *Adiós* 61).

### Forged by the Mountain

Most of the iconic images and narratives of the fragile, riddled bodies stem from the urban guerrilla warfare, yet the ultimate test and proof of masculinity happened in the mythical mountain space, from which men returned both emaciated and steeled. Cabezas's *testimonio* first tells of his urban heroes—Buitrago and Rugama—but then turns to his own steeling process in the mountains. *La montaña es algo más que una inmensa estepa verde* is about the self-construction of the man of arms. However, it hardly relates any direct battle situation of the protagonist. Instead, it is more about the "violent" and "traumatic" process of becoming a guerrillero (261), which is a necessary process to purify oneself from the vices of urban middle-class life, a leitmotif in the text (90, 95, 120, 159, 260–65). This is thus not a *testimonio* by a subaltern subject but a decidedly literary intervention by a militant.

Delgado points out that, in contrast to other views of the *testimonio* as expressing subaltern voices, *testimonios* in Nicaragua tend to be by the middle class, like this one by Cabezas (*Márgenes* 109). Instead of being a text that supposedly goes against the institution of Literature, as John Beverley has argued ("Margin at the Center" 37), it is a text that wants to be literary, that tries to position itself in front of the old lettered elites, still seeking their approval (Delgado *Márgenes* 109, 111, 113). The style is oral, conversational, buoyant, lyrical. The lyricism shines especially through in scenes of "virile sensibility" (Rodríguez, *Women* 47). According to Cabezas, the process of becoming the New Man requires "a mix of tenderness and violence" ("una mezcla de ternura y de violencia"; 122) as personified by René Tejada alias Tello, a *guerrillero* who subjects them to a hard military training but who also talks tenderly about the New Man to convince them that it is a necessary sacrifice. This scene with Tello is probably the most analyzed of the text. It constitutes a founding narrative of the nation organized around male homosocial bonds. It shows a dangerous tendency where the lines between love, tenderness, violence, and discipline become blurry (Rodríguez, *Women* 46).

The firearm is key for becoming the New Man. In Cabezas's enumeration of the countless sufferings in the mountains, the firearm appears as a key tool, artifact, and trope. In the *testimonio*, weapons are a means of getting closer to the Che Guevarian ideal of the New Man—"one has to be like El Che" ("Hay que ser como el Che"; 22) is the mantra of the text, passed on by Rugama. The process of becoming the New Man, of embracing this new politico-military subjectivity, means becoming one with nature, becoming one with technology, and becoming one with the people. While some rather uncritically read Cabezas's *testimonio* as a convincing Bildungsroman where *machista* tendencies are eliminated in the process of becoming the New Man (Orr), Rodríguez shows how the revolutionaries rely on traditional patriarchal images and conceptions (*Women* 31). George Yúdice has argued that Cabezas's *testimonio* "repeats patriarchal privilege in the guise of a Sandinista uniform" (44). As such, it might not come as a surprise that the rifle has quite a phallic conception in the *testimonio*.[5] It is the essential artifact and prop of the New Man in progress, both a prosthesis and a burden: "The rifle is part of you in the mountain, you sleep with your weapon, you walk with her, you wash yourself with her on the side, you do exercise with her, frozen weapon, oily weapon, weapon on the shoulder, weapon in the hand, weapon with dirt, support weapon, clean weapon, wet weapon. . . . In the mountain the weapon becomes a part of you, like another limb, and it is one of the most important members of your body" (Cabezas 197–98).[6] Key here is the conception of becoming one with the weapon. Daniel Chávez has analyzed how an important trope of the *testimonio* is communing with nature, becoming nature, becoming animal (184). Yet just as important is the communion with technology, becoming one with the firearm, knowing how to disarm it and load it in your sleep. To become a weapon. As mentioned, hardly any battle appears in these pages; true to Guevarian *foquismo*, the *guerrilleros* are more intent on avoiding the army than engaging in battle. As such, becoming one with the weapon happens through military training, but it is also expressed through iron and steel metaphors. The men are described as "a mettle of iron, of steel, a contingent of men with an unyielding strength between them" ("un temple de hierro, de acero, un contingente de hombres con una solidez gránica entre ellos"; 117) and "people with enough steel to maintain and develop this guerrilla" ("gente con suficiente acero para mantener y desarrollar esta guerrilla"; 130).

Cabezas also describes how the Sandinistas covered walls in the city with the acronym PLOMO (Patria Libre O Morir), meaning "lead" and "Free Fatherland or Die," and how these letters give him hope when his girlfriend leaves him (169). Alexandra Ortiz Wallner and Werner Mackenbach see in PLOMO "a metaphor, maybe unconscious but accurate, which describes the closed, militarist and patriarchal conception of the 'new' nation and the 'new' man" ("una metáfora, a lo mejor inconsciente pero certera, que describe la concepción cerrada, militarista y patriarcal de la 'nueva' nación y del hombre 'nuevo'") (84). This also shows the permeation of life by weaponry and a militarist logic and aesthetic. This political identity is not affirmed through weaponry; it is in fact constructed through it. This marks a clear difference to the symbolic meaning of weaponry in the Mexican Revolution. Where rifles and cartridge belts were an artifact for the peasant rebels to affirm their presence (as discussed in chapter 1), in the Sandinista Revolution political subjectivity is constructed through and in relation to the firearm.

## Peasant Arsenals: The People in Arms as Desire and Enigma

Despite its differences from the Mexican Revolution, the legacy of armed peasant insurgencies weighs heavy on the Sandinista Revolution. The firearm acquired another important symbolic meaning in relation to the other desired agents of the revolution: the peasantry, and more broadly "the people." The idea of "the people in arms" was one of the biggest desires of the Sandinista Revolution—both for its own legitimacy and because of its ideology of liberation—and one of the biggest frustrations, when an abyss opened up between Frente and the peasantry. The desire for the people in arms starts to unravel once peasants take up arms against the revolution in the Contra War of the 1980s.

### Sandinista Arsenals

The members of the Frente Sandinista de Liberación Nacional presented themselves as a direct continuation of Augusto C. Sandino's peasant insurgency against the marines in the 1930s—a construct developed by Sandinista leader Carlos Fonseca to give national legitimacy to the guerrilla and reflected in the name of the Frente (Villena Fiengo 20). In Cabezas's *La montaña es algo más que una inmensa estepa verde*, the firearm establishes the Sandinista lineage. It is a symbol for armed struggle as a national tradition, exemplified by the peasant combatants the *guerrilleros* encounter in the mountains. The peasants see the current Sandinistas as a continuation of Sandino's fight against the marines in the 1930s and willingly offer leftover weapons and other support. These peasant arsenals give legitimacy to the Sandinista fight. Even though most of the Frente's cadres stem from urban contexts, this support frames the Sandinista struggle as a continuation of earlier peasant insurgencies.

Cabezas narrates that most peasants fear the *guerrilleros* when they encounter them, knowing that the counterinsurgent repression will fall on them. Yet some "recognize" these new armed men as heirs of Sandino's Ejército Defensor de la Soberanía Nacional de Nicaragua (EDSN) and confuse them with Sandino's army. For example, there is Don Bacho, an old peasant, who on his first encounter with the *guerrilleros* exclaims that he knew that they would be back and that he has something for them, digging up an old bag full of bullets for the Lee-Enfield rifle used during the 1930s occupation by the marines. For decades he had been taking them out to dry "because he knew that one day the Sandinistas would come by again" ("porque él sabía que algún día iban a pasar de nuevo los sandinistas"; 224). The book ends with an encounter with another peasant: Don Leandro, who helped Sandino's army during those days. When he sees Cabezas's pistol, the old man asks him about all the long arms. He wants to know what happened to the Enfield, Mauser, and the *treinta-treinta* Winchester (283). Although Cabezas first thinks that the peasant is associating them with other FSLN combatants who passed through, he realizes that Don Leandro thinks that they are fighters of Sandino's army. Don Leandro says he can no longer fight, but he offers his sons to go with them (289). This encounter deeply moves Cabezas and, while he aspires to be like El Che, the true legitimacy lies here: in the peasant arsenals and the idea of a continuation of Sandino's anti-imperialist, anti-elitist peasant insurgency.

Analyzing writings by Che Guevara and Central American guerrilla narratives, among them Cabezas's *testimonio*, Ileana Rodríguez finds that in these "the struggle to come to terms with the concept of popular subjectivities is central" (*Women* 65). Although this is the subject that is supposed to be "liberated" by the guerrilla warfare, "the *campesinado* [appears] distant, detached, estranged from the guerrillas" (58). In Cabezas's *testimonio* there is also a distance between the peasants and the lower-middle-class white student from the city. The protagonist feels the distance and marks the distance, for example, when he tells of the peasant woman, Martha, a collaborator of the guerrilla, who thinks he is pulling her leg when he tells her that the earth is round. Here, Cabezas describes himself in a colonialist manner as "a super master man, far more educated than her" ("un hombre super máster, super más culto que ella"; 136). He does not know how to explain physics to her. There is only distance here between the guerillero and the peasantry. The distance "makes impossible the convergence of that masculine I-guerrilla and that collective subject-Masses/peasants, in whose name the revolutionary processes of agrarian societies speak" (Rodríguez, *Women* 60). The rifle, however, seems to connect the two worlds: the rural and the urban, the peasant and the middle class—or at least the male parts of this equation. It is a point of encounter and mutual recognition, and moreover, it gives the young man, so insecure about his standing in the mountain, confidence that he is on the right track, that the Frente is on the right track. The *testimonio*, published in 1981, tries to extend this popular-peasant legitimacy at a point when the cracks in these political constructions are already starting to show. The testimony brushes over these fissures and ends on an optimistic note. Rifle in hand and supported by peasant arsenals, they will finish Sandino's fight.

### The People in Arms I: Monimbó

The Sandinista discourse understood itself as a revolution of "the people in arms." The Tercerista faction of the FSLN successfully abandoned the Guevarian *foquismo* and advocated for broad alliances and a general insurrection. Although the Sandinistas never lost the notion of the vanguard necessary to lead the masses, the idea of "the people in arms" who acquire historical agency through revolution was a key trope of their discourse. The embodiment and realization of that myth was the popular uprising of Monimbó, an urban, indigenous neighborhood of Masaya. Using their artisan knowledge and gunpowder from fireworks, in February 1978 the people of Monimbó resisted the National Guard with homemade bombs (*bombas de contacto*) and spun nets over the streets to impede the entrance of tanks. To disguise themselves, they used indigenous masks. This was a precarious and heroic fight—immortalized through a renowned picture by Susan Meiselas of masked combatants with contact bombs in their hands.[7]

The indigenous element was key. Carlos Mejía Godoy in the song "Vivirás Monimbó" draws a lineage from the indigenous resistance against the *conquistadors* in this region to the indigenous resistance against Somoza. The song uses and celebrates the *atabales* (drums) and the marimba that were used during the fighting and celebrates it as a decolonizing fight, highlighting Monimbó's "obsidian heart" and "millenary presence" ("corazón de obsidiana," "milenaria presencia"). While there is in the song an *indigenista* tendency of celebrating the glorious indigeneous cultures of the past, the fight of Monimbó was very much about indigeneous cultures in the present. The urban-artisan resistance of the inhabitants of Moninmbó showed the indigenous population as part of the armed negotiation over the right project of modernity for the country. It was similar to cases of indigenous resistance such as Rigoberta Menchú in Guatemala and later the EZLN in Mexico, cases that "challenge a model of revolutionary subjectivity and a theory of agency not from a position of indigenous purity but from an indigenous and peasant subject position simultaneously produced by modernity and in reaction to its developmentalism" (Saldaña Portillo 12).

Monimbó was of great political importance for the Frente because it was one of the first popular uprisings—at which the organization was aiming— and it showed that "the people" were resisting Somoza by any means available. The Sandinista Revolution yearned to see the people in arms and Monimbó fulfilled this desire. Monimbó was a sign that the people were with the Frente and the indigenous element provided additional legitimacy.[8] In Monimbó it was no longer just the *muchachos* fighting against tanks but "the people." In the Sandinista rhetoric the "cult of the image of the people . . . acquired mythical proportions" (Chávez 214). One of the issues at hand, however, was the fuzzy figure of "the people" ("el pueblo"), "that elusive entity" (Franco, *Decline and Fall* 66). "The people" can refer to a "collective social actor" (Judson 212), "the common populace, or the popular/subaltern sectors of society" (Williams, *Other Side* 4), or a country's entire population.

These divergent notions stem from different European conceptions: the Enlightenment idea of the people as agents of political processes, the Romantic one of the people as agents of culture, and the introduction of a class dimension in Marxist and Anarchist thought (Martín Barbero, *Communication* 6, 13, 17). This medley of dimensions makes the concept of "the people" an utterly vague but politically powerful category. Williams sees it "as a potentially hegemonic formation designed to suture the totality of the nation's demographic and cultural differences to the formation and expansion of the nation-state" (*Other Side* 5). For the Latin American context, Franco points out that "the 'people,' [is] a term that in Cold War politics replaces 'the proletariat' so that it includes peasants in alliance with professionals and the intelligentsia" (*Decline and Fall* 70). Yet it is always a malleable construction thought from above and always changing according to the political necessity. "The people" is a construction that allows one to speak for a whole. In the Nicaraguan revolutionary context, the term *pueblo* has several different meanings depending on the context and the need. The term refers to the lower classes or subalterns (enabled through the revolutionary process), or it refers to the whole of the nation in the sense of *Volk: el pueblo nicaragüense.*

Jesús Martín Barbero points out how the Enlightenment thinkers saw a new legitimacy for power in the will of the people, but they also viewed the populace as a threat of disorder and irrationality (*Communication* 6). This ambiguity also shines through in the Sandinista discourse, even though it exalted "the people." In Ramírez's memoir there is a revealing scene when he talks about the other *pueblo*, the one not on the side of the Sandinistas. It tells the story of when he arrives with the Grupo de los Doce, a coalition for a transitional government, in Managua in 1978 and they are first greeted by Frentes Populares Somocistas. The description of this *pueblo* is one of scum: "horde of butchers drawn from the markets and comarcas" ("horda de matarifes sacados de los mercados y de las comarcas" (*Adiós* 173). Ramírez describes the leader of these popular Somocista goons, La Nicolesa Sevilla, as tacky and with animal attributes: "the Nicolesa, on her arm an enormous patent leather bag, seized us up, smiling and challenging, with her little mouse eyes" ("la Nicolesa, al brazo una enorme cartera de charol, nos escrutaba, risueña y desafiante, con sus ojitos de ratón"; 174). Tellingly so, she does not carry a firearm, but only an oversized handbag. This animalized, criminalized, gaudy, right-wing *pueblo* is contrasted with "el otro pueblo" that clamors outside and welcomes the arrival of the Grupo de los Doce. This shows that *pueblo* can mean an exclusive revolutionary construct: a part of the nation constituted by the lower classes and led by progressive-revolutionary Sandinista elites or vanguards.

### The People in Arms II: Contra War

These contradictions became apparent in the 1980s, as thousands of disgruntled peasants and indigenous and creole peoples from the north and the Caribbean started to take up arms for the counterrevolution. The Contra War was financed by the United States but drew many of its fighters from non-Pacific areas, whom the Sandinistas had tried to reach with their revolutionary project without respecting them as political subjects with specific concerns and cultural backgrounds. Sergio Ramírez eloquently reflected on this in an interview I conducted with him in 2012: "From the political discourse of the revolution, the poor people, the artisan people, peasants, marginalized people, is the *pueblo* that the revolution will redeem. The discourse of the revolution at the same time assumes that this *pueblo*, because the revolution will redeem them, this *pueblo* is on the side of the revolution, which is an a priori assumption that there is a symbiosis *pueblo*-revolution where they respond to each other, but this ends up being a fallacy, right? Because a part of that *pueblo* turns against the revolution in arms; the poor peasants take up arms against the revolution."[9]

Both the *testimonios* of Contra fighters in Alejandro Bendaña's *Tragedia cam-pesina* as well as the case study of Lynn Horton's *Peasants in Arms* show that the reasons why peasants took up arms against the revolution were numerous and heterogeneous (Horton 10–17, 173–92). The peasants who took up arms in the Contra War often saw the time before the Sandinistas as their own peaceful utopia, where they might not have had much but freedom to do as they chose with their land, produce and sell without the "damn cooperatives" ("menta-das cooperativas") (Bendaña 87) and other planned economy models. Also, the peasants often saw themselves fighting against the militarization brought to their lives by the Sandinistas (Horton 97, 205). Furthermore questions of kinship as well as being wedged between two fronts often gave the peasants no other alternative than to flee or to take up arms for one side or the other. This complex bundle of grievances led to "one of the largest armed mobilizations of peasants in contemporary Latin American history" (Horton xii). And with it, peasants effectively became architects of national history, as the Sandinistas had hoped, only their plans ran contrary to those of the Sandinistas. As María Josefina Saldaña Portillo points out, through taking up arms in the Contra War, peasants ultimately decided the political outcome of the revolution (112).

In her autobiography *El país bajo mi piel*, Gioconda Belli avoids this part of history almost completely. Her narrative in various moments reveals the dis-tance between her status and that of other women, but there is no critical re-flection about the Contra War, just the puzzlement that "people" turned their arms against the revolution and voted the Sandinistas out of office. In keeping with a generalized tendency in postrevolutionary autobiographies, the autobi-ography avoids any "profound political conflictivity" ("conflictividad política profunda") (Delgado, "Desplazamientos" 53). Belli hardly speaks about the Contra War; rather, in the so characteristic "will to elude the defeat" in Latin American literature (Avelar, *Untimely* 21), when she talks about the 1980s, she retreats into the problem of having a relationship with a US American in times of the Contra War.

Sergio Ramírez in his memoir talks more about the 1980s and the Contra War specifically, and there is a sincerity in his search for answers—centered around the ever so symbolic rifle. The public rendering of arms of reactionary peasants became a common ritual during the years of the Contra War. In two of his autobiographical books, *Confesión de amor* and *Adiós muchachos*, Ramírez recalls the same episode twice: that of a counterrevolutionary peasant handing him—the vice president—his FAL in a public act in the village San Carlos.[10] The rendering of arms reveals an abyss between the subaltern and the *letrado* and shows that there is no organic symbiosis between "the people" and the revolution. There is only the "intellectual puzzlement of a thinker trying to discern the subaltern" (Rodríguez, *Women* 63). In Ramírez's description the FAL, once the symbol of glorious insurrection of the Sandinistas, has lost all its virile glory. Ramírez describes the peasant as a "little, worn-out man, poorly dressed" ("hombrecito desmedrado, pobremente vestido") and his FAL as "old and rusted" ("viejo y herrumbrado") (*Confesión* 118–19). The rifle is no longer a sign of revolutionary belonging but one of poverty, distance, and mutual incomprehension between the Sandinista intellectual and "the people": "I saw him get up on the platform . . . dressed in rags and barefoot, the old rifle hanging from a cord not a strap. This is when I realized that between us there was an immense abyss difficult to overcome" (Ramírez, *Adiós* 230).[11]

The weapon is no longer a symbol of the new dawn, of modernity. It does not shoot auroras into the firmament, as envisioned in Carlos Mejía Godoy's songs (discussed in chapter 4). It has been demodernized through the peasant's *mecate* (the Nahuatl word for "cord"). The weapon has become a symbol of peasant stubbornness, frustrating the intellectual because the peasant does not understand that the revolution proposes to "save" him with modernity: "We proposed him the incomprehensible journey from the primitive to the modern, but he refused and had taken a weapon in opposition" ("Le proponíamos el viaje incomprensible de lo primitivo a lo moderno, pero él se negaba y había tomado un arma para oponerse") (Ramírez, *Adiós* 230). As Saldaña Portillo points out: "While the peasantry is not racialized as indigenous within Nicaragua, the Sandinistas nevertheless viewed peasant consciousness as a 'premodern' ethnos, as an obstacle to . . . development" (10). While there certainly is an "earnestness" in Ramírez's "bewilderment," as Ileana Rodríguez indicates (*Women* 62–63), this description nonetheless reveals a vision from the paternalistic, lettered center that looks at the peasantry as backward (Browitt). Here, the Sandinista discourse of the "people in arms"—which advocated armed popular insurrection and the agency of the subaltern—unravels because it only allows for political agency and behavior as defined by the revolution.

It also reveals, as Saldaña Portillo has shown, that even though the Sandinistas and other revolutionary movements in the Americas were against colonial power relations, they "shared a theory of human perfectibility" in which one had to transcend premodern ways and become universal by "leaving behind . . . one's own particularity" (7). This lack of recognition or embrace of difference denied the peasants political participation but enacted "paternalistic and coercive policies in agriculture," not unlike "liberal development schemes" (10). The Contra War produced a crack in the revolutionary ideologies, since, as Delgado points out, "the peasant army of the 'contra' would represent one of the most evident contradictions between revolutionary state reason and subaltern representation (or lack thereof)" ("Desplazamientos" 38).[12] Ultimately, the rendering of arms that happens throughout the 1980s and culminates in official peace negotiations in 1988 unintentionally produced a recognition of this failure.

The negotiations with the Contra in Sapoá in 1988 changed the political landscape of Nicaragua. Divisions blurred and the *"guerrillero* became a suited politician, and his new garb came to reinforce the image of the fading agendas of the revolutionary state" (Rodríguez, *Women* 4, italics in original). To lay down the firearm became the starting point for a transition to formal democracy. An important postwar discursive formation was the strengthening of Western political concepts. The idea of modernization through armed struggle was defeated and thus other approaches took over, generally "in ways that accord with the neoliberal paradigm of the post–Cold War world and the revitalized faith in Western concepts of liberalism and democracy" (Pearce, "From Civil War" 600). This also appears in Belli and Ramírez's texts, which circle around firearms and power, yet ultimately end up defending the revolution by stating that they brought democracy to Nicaragua—referring to the formal transition to democracy in 1990 when the Frente lost the election. Yet what they do not contemplate is whether they actually see "the people" or peasantry as citizens in their own right, forgetting that a true democracy is not based on formal elections but a firm concept of citizenship and participation. Delgado points out that Ramírez says the biggest achievement of the revolution was instituting in Nicaraguan politics a "sensibility for the poor" ("sensibilidad por los pobres"; *Adiós* 225) ("Desplazamientos" 40–41).

Yet this is again a malleable, vague category.[13] Delgado points out that thus "the marginalized/peasants formed, rather than a citizen presence in the modern sense, a kind of motivating sensibility" ("los marginales/campesinos conformaron, más que una presencia ciudadana, en sentido moderno, una especie de sensibilidad motivadora"; 49). Even though peasants took up arms for and against the revolution, the political and intellectual elites still struggle to see them as citizens, as political subjects of their own right. It appears that in the Sandinista Revolution and its aftermath, the political subjectivity of the peasant continues to be as blurry as ever, if not even blurrier. To the intellectual, it is the eternal enigma.

## Militant Memoirs: Rifles and Constructions of Self

From the focus on the collective during revolutionary times, in postrevolutionary texts such as Belli's *El país bajo mi piel* and Ramírez's *Adiós muchachos* returns with full force the individual I. And said individual has to negotiate his or her identity in relation to the most important symbol of revolutionary consciousness and belonging: the firearm. In both texts weapons are featured on the cover page and appear from the first pages on. The rifle is a crucial artifact and prop to showcase one's conviction, but it is also important to maintain a distance from it in order to successfully construct a *letrado* identity in postrevolutionary times. Both Belli and Ramírez reiterate the political necessity of armed struggle while stressing their personal dislike of and lack of dexterity with guns—a discursive device to position oneself away from the violence and closer to the new hegemonic discourse of liberal democracy.

Belli's *El país bajo mi piel*, in the Spanish and English versions by Random House, pictures a woman with high heels and an AK-47 on the front cover.[14] It is not a photo of Gioconda Belli herself—meaning that probably no such photo of her exists since several other photos of her are included in the book—but one of a Sandinista woman named Marta Lorena on guard duty, taken in 1984 by Jenny Matthews in Managua, Nicaragua (Field). Yet on the cover, Marta Lorena's head is not visible, probably because the publishers wanted to keep intact the illusion for the reader that this could be Gioconda Belli. The clipping turns this photo into a generic photo aimed to sell the book around several exoticizing attributes: a T-shirt featuring a tropical scene with palm trees, Catholicism encased in a chain with a little cross, high heels as attributes of femininity, and the Kalashnikov as symbol of Third World revolutions. What makes the paratext disturbing is that the woman appears headless, reduced to her body and accessories.

Belli herself never took up arms in combat, but she nonetheless arranges her life story around the firearm. The text starts with the smell and sound of guns, with her carrying an AK-47 and Fidel Castro looming in the background. The first chapter is titled "Here, with the smell of gun powder, begin these recollections" ("Donde dan inicio, con olor a pólvora, estas rememoraciones," all caps in the original). The first line reads: "With each shot my body disintegrated" ("Con cada disparo el cuerpo se me descosía"; 17). It tells the story of Belli together with other Sandinista militants receiving military training from the Cuban Armed Forces under the auspices of Castro. It is January 1979, a few months before the triumph of the revolution in July of the same year. Up until this moment Belli had only practiced with pistols, but now she wants to try out a rifle. Cuba is the playground that offers this possibility: "we all seemed like children in a toy store, touching and examining the automatic, semiautomatic rifles, the submachine guns and the pistols put at our disposal" (18). Describing the lure of firearms, Belli immediately adds how much she detested shooting and begrudgingly describes the unsettling effect shooting has on her body: "The bang shook all my articulations and

left an unbearable, sharp, disturbing ringing in my head" (17).[15] In this simultaneously mythical (Fidel, Cuba, AK-47) and demystifying ("I hate this")
tale a very complicated negotiation of subject positions starts, pivoted around
the rifle. One dilemma is that of the intellectual and the upper-class member
needing "to purge themselves of the original sin of being middle-class intellectuals" (Franco, *Decline and Fall* 88)—or upper class in the case of Belli—by
joining armed struggle. The rifle is the symbol of this conviction and so she
is ashamed and angry at herself when she is overwhelmed by the physical and
emotional sensations that shooting produces in her (*El país* 17, 115). While
one can see a demythifying dimension in these representations (Mantero),
the iconoclastic move against the rifle only happens in the postrevolutionary
account, over two decades later. Only then does she admit her dislike of the
prime artifact of the revolution, but while in Cuba that is impossible: "I would
have been ashamed" ("Vergüenza me habría dado") (*El país* 17). Instead, she
pushes through and continues to shoot, eyes closed.

This has to do with another dilemma—namely, how to transform her "intellectual conviction that the fight was necessary into the decision of making
use of force" ("convicción intelectual de que la lucha era necesaria, en decisión
de hacer uso de la fuerza"; 115). The shooting lessons—the first one, with a
pistol, she receives in August 1974 on a Pacific beach in Nicaragua, and the
one with assault rifles she receives in January 1979 in Cuba—are what turns
the theoretical into the practical, and it is disturbing: "the jolts of the deto-
nation destabilized not only the body but also the spirit" ("las sacudidas de
las detonaciones me desestabilizaban no sólo el cuerpo sino el espíritu"; 115).
But it is not only the physical dimension of shooting itself but also its lethal
significance that affects her: "I understood the dark power of life and death
which one feels when pulling the trigger" ("comprendí el oscuro poder de
vida o muerte que se siente al apretar el gatillo"; 115). This enters in conflict
with her other identity as a *letrada*—in particular, the sensibilities of a poet. A
safeguard from the violence is needed, so similarly to the Guzmán character
during the Mexican Revolution, she stresses her dislike of weapons: "Far from
feeling any pleasure, I experienced in an unequivocal manner the profound
repudiation which firearms created in me" ("Lejos de sentir ningún placer,
experimenté de manera inequívoca del profundo rechazo que me inspiraban
las armas de fuego"; 18). In another instance: "How could anyone in their right
mind actually enjoy this sensation?" ("¿Cómo podía alguien en su sano juicio
disfrutar realmente esa sensación?"; 115).

It also clashes with Belli's identity as a woman. Throughout her opus she
displays a strong cultural feminism—a feminism that harbors an essentialist
idea of femininity and believes in an inherent difference between men and

women. This is why she sees her dislike of firearms as a result of being a woman: "What a weird fascination men felt for arms, I thought" ("Rara fascinación la que sentían los hombres por las armas, pensé"; 114). While the men seem fascinated with firearms, during her different shooting lessons in Nicaragua and Cuba, she instinctively rejects them, as if they were a dangerous animal, "a tiger, a snake" ("un tigre, una serpiente"; 114). She wants to get rid of the rifle, as if it were something unnatural in the hand of a woman; she has a "desire to throw away the arm as if it burned, as if my body would be able to recuperate its integrity only if it could get rid of this lethal member" ("el deseo de tirar el arma como si quemara, como si mi cuerpo fuera a recuperar su integridad sólo cuando se despojara de ese miembro mortal"; 17). Here we see the complexity of the subject position and negotiation: Belli knows that as an attractive upper-class woman and poet, all eyes are on her, especially during training in Cuba. She has to prove herself within the collective, so she pushes through and starts to shoot with a Caliber .50 machine gun, the most powerful weapon available. She likes it because "the sound was dry and did not expand within me" ("el sonido era seco y no se expandía dentro de mí"; 18). Belli's phallic appropriation is noticed by Fidel, who tells her with sly innuendo that he heard she liked the heavy machine gun (18).

Belli's first novel of the revolution, *La mujer habitada,* published eleven years before her autobiography, tells the story of the conversion of a female upper-class protagonist into an urban guerrilla commando member, aided by the emboldening spirit of an indigenous warrior woman—a fictionalized account of the successful 1974 attack on the house of Somocista Chema Castillo. Vinodh Venkatesh has argued that in this novel the female protagonist appropriates a violent revolutionary masculinity that comes with "a renewed affinity for all things violent and combative" ("Mirrors" 501)—in particular, an appreciation of "the aesthetic beauty of the pistol" (502). An appropriation of that violent masculinity is also what Belli appears to be doing while in Cuba—"manning" and mastering a heavy machine gun—but the postrevolutionary account reveals more complexity and more fissures and cracks in that construction. In her autobiography Belli constructs herself as woman above any other subject position.[16] This reflects once more the dilemma and ambiguity of the woman with the rifle. The photo of Marta Lorena on the cover of *El país bajo mi piel* can also be seen as an implicit reference to the famous photo of the militia woman from Waswalito, mentioned in this book's introduction. Both photos point to the question of balancing and negotiating womanhood, femininity, war, violence, and revolution. The dilemma of balancing motherhood, militancy, and war is an important topic of Belli's memoir, which reflects on her pregnancies and difficulties as a mother of four children.

Delgado has criticized Belli's autobiography for "domesticating" and "privatizing" the history of the revolution ("Desplazamientos" 41, 53n47). This critique, however, dismisses the important political intervention of *El país bajo mi piel*—namely that, true to the important feminist motto that the private is political, it reviews recent Nicaraguan politics both from the domestic and the public spheres. The autobiography revisits the history of the revolution from a subject perspective often ignored in the hegemonic narratives of the revolution, which tend to "be formulated in a masculine I, aiming at narrating a collective subject that does not include women" (Rodríguez, *Women* xvii). Belli's autobiography is, of course, not that of a subaltern subject but one of a woman already constructed and perceived as subject and citizen through her race and class; nonetheless, the narrative offers a different epic than that of the mountain or the urban underground. It aims to tell the story of the revolution from a female perspective. She talks about her job, her work for the Frente, going through two marriages, several relationships with high-ranking guerrilla commanders, several pregnancies, as well as sexual advances by Latin American political leaders. Precisely by interweaving her personal history of liberation, Belli offers an account of the revolution focused on egalitarianism or lack thereof in all spheres of life. More often than not, she is an object of men's desire—until she finds a relationship that offers more equality, just like the revolution that was supposed to bring more equality. In the end she finds the desired egalitarian ideal only within the confines of an intimate relationship and not in the confines of a nation.

Belli formulates her political critiques of the revolution from that subject position of woman and lover. Fiercely critical of Daniel and Humberto Ortega and their ruthless clasp for power, she is also critical of the men with whom she has intimate relationships: Eduardo Contreras, alias Marcos, key thinker of the Tercerista faction; and Henry Ruiz, alias Modesto, crucial guerrilla commander of the Guerra Popular Prolongada (GPP) faction. Both men are supposed to be epitomes of the ascetic, utopian Guevarian New Man, but in the private sphere Belli reveals their many personal flaws and *machista* traits, undermining the egalitarian aspirations of the revolution.[17]

Belli critically reflects on what it means to take over power. The Sandinistas assumed that, after Somoza was ousted, the power would somehow be shared; but the hasty flight of Somoza and the National Guard left a power vacuum. Encountering a deserted state structure in Managua means that—despite the fact that they arrived at this point through alliances—the Sandinistas can take over: "taking power in such an absolute manner as we had done was nothing but mind-boggling" ("tomar el poder de forma tan absoluta como lo habíamos hecho, no dejaba de ser alucinante"; 330). Belli compares the sensation to a painting from her childhood with a girl on the grass looking at the landscape with the caption: "The world was mine and it all belonged to me." She continues: "In that same moment, I understood, physically, what it meant to 'take power.' I was overrun by an inexpressible feeling that was, at the same time, dazzle, pride, and humble gratitude for live to have granted me that day in my history. When one dreams with things like changing the world, there is no more splendid power than feeling that it is possible to do so" (328).[18] This (state) power has an allure, and Belli falls for it. She concedes that she stayed in an unhealthy relationship with Henry Ruíz because he was one of the nine commanders: it was the power that attracted her (344).

The Sandinista Revolution was a statist revolution, concerned with taking over the state. As such, Sandinista memoirs are, as Delgado has observed, often characterized by "a mourning for the administrative" ("el duelo por lo administrativo") ("Memorias apocalípticas" 119). This also applies to Belli's autobiography, in which the Sandinista Revolution appears—and is mourned—as one of an armed and uniformed citizenry but also of an armed and uniformed administration. The way the Frente took power was through the rifle. Instead of abandoning the rifle right away in order not to establish another authoritarian regime like the one they just defeated, the rifle, paradoxically so, thus became the symbol of the new times. This remains unquestioned in Belli's memoir and is powerfully reflected in the narrative, which starts with the smell of gunpowder. She acknowledges her intellectual and feminine dislike of firearms but still points out that later she became a good shooter, making second place in a shooting competition.[19]

Most of Belli's activities during the 1970s—using her upper-class upbringing and appearance, her whiteness—were in intelligence gathering and smuggling money and weaponry. She never engaged in combat, she never had to kill somebody directly. But the firearm is the artifact and prop of the time, of the ultimate commitment, of militancy, armed struggle, and solidarity with the poor. Therefore, she needs to get hold of one. When Belli enters Managua in July 1979, one day after the triumph because she was doing support work in Costa Rica, everyone calls her "Comandante Belli." She wants a rifle. Arriving at Somoza's bunker, a threatening symbol of his militarist power, she finds it full of gregarious militants kissing, hugging, destroying. Everyone wants to get a piece of his arsenal. Seemingly unaware of the irony and the militarist tradition that is continued here, they equip themselves with the weapons of the dictatorship.

Belli is happy with her loot: she gets a few uniforms, a submachine gun, and a box of ammunition (*El país* 329). The rifle is the prop of militancy. In a way the rifle is an accessory, part of the fashion of the new times, *militantisme oblige*: army fatigues and a firearm dangling over the shoulder. Yet guerrilla commander Bayardo Arce mocks her for wearing it in that manner: "Dressed in olive green with my submachine gun around the shoulder—Bayardo said that I wore it as if it were a handbag" (344). Despite the rifle, Belli cannot fully erase the stigma of being a woman and a member of the upper class.

The rifle and the uniform is the obligatory fashion for militants and freshly minted government officials. Belli likes the Sandinista female policewomen dressed in olive garb (one of the few spaces that opened up for women, since shortly after the triumph they were banned from most military positions): "I liked to watch the girls wearing olive green uniforms and impeccably polished military boots. Many of them wore lipstick and even red nail polish. They were the symbol of a new time for women in my country" (342).[20] Even though she is not in the police or the military, Belli, like other Sandinista officers, works in her administrative government role in military uniform.

Belli narrates that on 1979 New Year's Eve, people in Managua, dressed in uniform and black and red bandanas, fired machine guns, tracer ammunitions, and rockets into the air: "In the city everyone was armed to the teeth, and there was no weapon that was not fired" ("En la ciudad todos estábamos armados hasta los dientes y no hubo arma que no se disparara"; 373). The tools of death became symbols of joy: "The rattle of the automatic firearms resounded during at least fifteen minutes, deafening the city in a collective madness that was unforgettable, happy, and that was never repeated" ("El tableteo de las armas automáticas sonó durante al menos quince minutos atronado la ciudad en una locura colectiva que fue inolvidable, feliz y que nunca más volvió a repetirse"; 373). This embrace of weaponry and of military culture was different from the one promoted by the Somoza regime. Somoza relied on a paid troop and gala uniforms for building a brutal and repressive state with control from above. The Sandinista militarism relied, in the early years, on volunteers and militants. It was popular, colorful, and rebellious in spirit, but it was militarism nonetheless.

Jorge Castañeda has argued that to most observers the militarization of the Sandinista Revolution came as no surprise. Castañeda attributes the arms buildup of the 1980s to the substantial influence of Cuban militarism and the valid fear of a US invasion (110-11). He ascribes the Sandinista's militaristic logic to the region's *caudillista* legacy of politics through arms: "from time immemorial, the only source of power in Central American politics was the sword and gun" (109). The absolutism of Castañeda's statement is certainly questionable, but the importance of armed political intervention on the isthmus is indisputable. The Nicaraguan Revolution did have traits of *caudillismo*, but the underlying justification of violence was far more elaborate and the project in its national and collective scope was more far-reaching than most *caudillista* political interventions, which tend to arise from a mixture of localism and individual charisma.

The topic of militarism and *caudillismo* is a central topic of Ramírez's *Adiós muchachos*. He describes the Dirección Nacional as "a caudillo with nine heads instead of one" ("un caudillo con nueve cabezas en lugar de una"; 66). Composed of nine former guerrilla commanders, three of each Sandinista faction, all dressed in olive garb made in Cuba (288), became the de facto political-military centerpiece of a nation. Ramírez criticizes the militarism embodied by the Dirección Nacional, which cemented an authoritarian exercise of power in which military power equaled political power (106). He instead reasserts the civilian constellations that were meant to take over power, such as the Grupo de los Doce and the Junta de Gobierno. In this context Ramírez constructs himself as civilian and intellectual: not as vice president of a militarist revolutionary regime that fought a counterinsurgent war throughout its existence in the 1980s, but as *cronista* of the revolution. Similarly to Guzmán and Belli, Ramírez constructs a subject position by circling around the question of arms versus letters. He is not writing a memoir but a *crónica*, he says, comparing himself to the figure of Bernal Díaz de Castillo, chronist and simple soldier of the conquest of the Aztec empire.[21] In contrast to Díaz de Castillo, Ramírez presents himself as removed from the military sphere: "I did not take up arms in the revolution, I never donned a military uniform" ("No empuñé armas en la revolución, no llevé nunca uniforme militar"; 14). This affirmation is central to the text (Urbina)—as are firearms.

Ramírez's book also features rifles on its front cover: a famous picture by Pedro Valtierra from July 20, 1979, in which combatants on a tank in front of the Palacio Nacional in Managua raise rifles, fists, and flags into the air. In the text itself, however, Ramírez displays an aloof relationship with firearms, and throughout he flaunts his uselessness with arms. Nevertheless, he is adamant about the power and historical significance that the armed revolution implied: "Nobody would have taken up a rifle to do a revolution halfway . . . You also don't triumph with arms to take over power short term, when it is about doing away with history" (*Adiós* 226f).[22] Thus the weapon is always present as artifact and trope—part of the discourse, part of the politics—but Ramírez maintains a distance from it as tool.

Part of the importance of firearms in the narrative of a noncombatant has to do with the political rewriting that takes place in the book. Castañeda has noted that in the dominant Sandinista discourse, in textbooks but also in anecdotes, there existed "a clear tendency toward a systematic overvaluation of the military, epic, heroic facets of their victory, and a corresponding sublimination of political and international factors" (109). In many ways Ramírez's text is a political (not military) *crónica* of the victory. It does not narrate the battles but the meetings and scheming taking place at different moments; he rewrites Sandinista tradition by focusing not on the military aspects of the Tercerista faction (embodied by Daniel and Humberto Ortega) but on the political aspects. He dedicates an entire chapter to Eduardo Contreras, Comandante 0 of the important 1974 hostage commando, the Tercerista mastermind who advocated for making broad alliances but who died in 1976. In another chapter he writes of Pedro Joaquín Chamorro, the bourgeois opponent of the Somoza regime, whose murder in 1978 led to an uprising across Nicaragua.

Ramírez indicates that his lack of military accolades weakened him politically. Although he does become vice president, Daniel Ortega is opposed to him forming part of the Dirección Nacional. Substituting for his lack of combat experience, Ramírez strategically inserts memories of his son fighting in the Contra War at the beginning of the text. He thus shows that he did not use his power to save his son from the front and in a way offers his son's heroism and muscular masculinity as a surrogate for his own (Henighan 510). He tells his son's stories from the front, his experience of death of comrades, but he also highlights the strangeness of reading his impersonal, logistical letters from the front and of encountering his son on furlough in the bedroom, bare-chested with backpack and rifle next to him (Ramírez, *Adiós* 28, 30). As Stephen Henighan has pointed out: "*Adios muchachos* illustrates Ramírez's attempt to negotiate the gender contours of a longed-for yet unsettling identity as 'just a writer'" (511).

The text displays a mix of alienation, perplexity, and fascination when it comes to men of arms. Even Edén Pastora, longtime persona non grata among Sandinistas, appears in the text in a relatively positive light. Ramírez seems fascinated by Pastora's adventurous, virile manner: "he was born for boldness" ("había nacido para la temeridad") (*Adiós* 93). Yet, generally, Ramírez constructs himself as a *letrado* in distance to the firearm, the questionable power, whereas his power, the silent, lettered background appears as innocuous. The *letrado* Ramírez refuses the pistols and women the Panamanian general Omar Torrijos offers him in Panama (*Adiós* 131)—here it is telling to compare his experience to that of a woman, Gioconda Belli, who had to fend off Torrijos's advances (*El país* 275). Ramírez receives a private shooting lesson by Manuel Pinheiro, head of the Cuban intelligence agency DGI (Dirección General de Inteligencia) and a key figure for Latin American guerrilla movements. Ramírez comments on this shooting lesson with Pinheiro with self-deprecating, dismissive humor, saying that it did not yield "any results other than the bruise from the blow of the rifle's butt to the shoulder" ("sin más resultado que la magulladura del golpe de la culata en el hombro") (*Adiós* 171).

Jean Franco has written that during the Cold War period in Latin America "[p]ersonal experience of the armed struggle was the motor of transformation that created the new man" and that "militancy became the true test of the authentic intellectual" (*Decline and Fall* 88). Since Ramírez did not hold a weapon, he vindicates himself through other means, as father of a son who did fight in the Contra War and above all as *letrado* to whom violence and by extension political power are unnatural, a burden, something that can ultimately be shrugged away. The book, however, shows that it is not easy to let go of power after all. Ramírez's *Adiós* is yet another example of the mourning of administrative and political power common in Sandinista memoirs (Delgado, "Memorias apocalípticas" 119). Even though Ramírez depicts himself as a bystander in the text and as outside of the realm of politics, throughout the book he shows himself in the company of powerful men such as Pinheiro, Castro, and Torrijos, which leaves no other conclusion than that Ramírez himself was a powerful man (Polit 229; 231). And he was. For a decade Ramírez was a key member of the government of a country that played an important role on the world scene in the 1980s.

In the end, *Adiós muchachos* turns out to be less a mea culpa for the shortcomings of the revolution but rather a mournful apology for Ramírez's withdrawal from the political field in the mid-1990s. He therefore seeks the authorization of the men of arms to withdraw from active politics. The last chapter ends with an outlook of his return to literature. A portrait of Sandino points in the right direction, since in it the famous man of arms, who also wrote, is featured with the tools of writing: a pencil and a fountain pen. As Henighan puts it: "The message could not be clearer: Sandino is dispatching Ramírez back into private life to perform his revolutionary duty through his writing" (512). This seems to resolve Ramírez's dilemma—shared by many Latin American writers, often public intellectuals who at some point also held government positions—of having to navigate or choose between the literary and the political field. However, the image shows more than just Ramírez's revolutionary guilt and his absolution by Sandino. Ramírez is also aware of the power that lies in his withdrawal from politics. He ends up with one of the most important and theorized forms of powers of Latin America: the power of the written word. As Gabriela Polit has argued: "His words become, in effect, the memory with which Nicaraguans will surely remember the revolution and will recognize themselves as a nation" (228–29).[23] He never bids farewell to power itself. After insurgency, what survives is not the rifle but the pen. Literature is what remains, power is what remains, whereas violence vanishes.

## *Days of the Rifle*

Nowadays in Nicaragua it is common to hear comments arguing that those who "did not hold a weapon" should not give their opinion about the revolution and the war. It might be just a figure of speech favoring the firsthand witness or simply a synecdoche in which the firearm stands for militancy or participation. In theory this silences large parts of present-day Nicaraguan society. Ironically, many of the most important voices of the revolution—whose memoirs have been read by the largest audiences at home and abroad due to their literary talent and prominence—are Sandinista militants who did not take up arms in combat such as Ramírez and Belli. The firearm is nonetheless a complex and ambiguous artifact in the construction of self in their postrevolutionary accounts. And these accounts are often steeped in nostalgia. Belli, for example, remembers wistfully those "days when I transported weapons, those days when I had a rifle on my shoulder" ("días en que transportaba armas, los días en que anduve con una metralleta al hombro") (*El país* 407).

Meanwhile those who did not actively participate in the war—because they were too young, they were abroad, or they tried to remain uninvolved— are told not to opine about the revolution and the war. In Nicaragua it is difficult for younger generations to question the recent history and create their own narrative and position. There is the so-called lost generation ("generación perdida"), those born around 1979 or shortly thereafter, who have some faint childhood memories of the 1980s war but were too young to be part of the political struggle. One researcher from this generation, Juan Pablo Gómez, criticized the postrevolutionary storytelling in a 2012 editorial saying that it showed there was no will to critically review the past and to question "how deep the war has permeated as a means for political struggle and culture" in Nicaragua ("lo hondo que ha calado la guerra como forma de lucha y cultura política"). The Sandinista Revolution had an enormous impact, and before the younger generations lies the enormous task to make sense of it now, to analyze it on their terms. They are faced with the glory and nostalgia of the past leftist generation, the fervent anti-Sandinista discourses from conservative segments, the relative lack of peasant memories about these two insurgencies, as well as the revolutionary simulacrum of the Orteguismo. Even though rifles have all but disappeared from Sandinismo under Ortega, facing the almost oppressive ubiquity of rifles in the discourses of memory is key.

*CHAPTER 4*

# SONGS OF GUERRILLA WARFARE AND ENCHANTMENT

## POPULARIZING AND LEGITIMIZING ARMED STRUGGLE

Many revolutions have a song. The French Revolution has "La Marseillaise," a call to arms composed in the aftermath of the revolution, when France was battling other European powers. The Mexican Revolution has "La Adelita," not a war march but a love song that captured the spirit of the revolutionary masses traversing the country as *la bola*. The Nicaraguan Revolution did not have a song. Thanks to two highly prolific singer-songwriters, it had an entire soundtrack. Between them, Carlos and Luis Enrique Mejía Godoy composed so many songs that it seems as if there were a song for every moment of the revolutionary process: songs about Sandino; the 1972 earthquake; liberation theology; repression under Somoza; the indigenous uprising in Monimbó; songs about particular firearms and homemade bombs on the album *Guitarra Armada* (1979), made before the insurrection; songs about love, gender, and war in *Amando en tiempos de guerra* (1979), commemorations of battles and fallen guerrilla fighters; anthems for Nicaragua, the guerrilla organization Frente Sandinista de Liberación Nacional (FSLN), and the literacy campaign; and the cantata-suite *Canto épico al FSLN* (1981). Produced for the second anniversary of the revolution, *Canto épico* narrates the entire history of the Sandinista struggle in song format. Overall, the brothers' opus constitutes one of the most extensive musical sagas of armed struggle.

In this chapter, I argue that the music fulfilled the revolution's utopian aspirations in that it legitimized and popularized armed struggle through numerous stylistic devices involving weaponry. In their compositions the brothers legitimized armed struggle by sanctifying and gendering it, and by anthropomorphizing and zoomorphizing beings and objects involved in the struggle. The songs drew weapons closer through national(ist) and folk-popular tropes. They framed revolutionary violence as different from other forms of direct violence, a violence that would lead to an end of violence. This idea manifested itself most vividly in the metaphor of the rifle that shoots not bullets but auroras, the firearm as harbinger of the new dawn. The brothers' songs projected a future in which the contradictions of using violence to achieve an end of violence would be resolved. Rather than leading to disenchantment (to which modernity inevitably leads, according to Max Weber ("Wissenschaft" 510), this new order devised by the songs was a project of what I call an "enchanted modernity." It was utopia achieved at gunpoint. Though it emerged from violence, the promise was that in the end it would evanesce the violence, turning bloodshed into beauty, peace, serenity, enchantment. In the songs, fallen guerrilla fighters became birds and trees, nature and inorganic matter joined the fight, and even the firearms shot auroras. Notwithstanding these lyrical projections of an enchanted modernity, however, the songs perpetuated a militaristic logic that created a tension in the projection of a peaceful tomorrow.

## Music as a Popular Vehicle and as a Utopian Space of Revolution

The New Song movement was a vital vehicle for social and political commentary throughout Latin America during the Cold War. Nueva Canción, associated mainly with South America, especially Chile and Argentina, provided protest music with catchy tunes that drew on local folk-popular traditions.[1] Nueva Trova, associated primarily with Cuba, provided lyric-focused songs with a more experimental poetic and musical style. Generalizing, one could say that Carlos Mejía Godoy's music was closer to the South American folkloric roots of New Song, creating folk music with social content, accessible melodies, and witty lyrics. Meanwhile, Luis Enrique Mejía Godoy's music was closer to the more intellectualized style of Cuban Trova. The songs of the brothers moved from social commentary to overtly militant content as the fight against Somoza intensified and as their originally loose connection with the FSLN tightened.

South American and Cuban influences notwithstanding, the brothers' music formed a particularly Nicaraguan or Central American New Song movement that emerged parallel to the guerrilla movements on the isthmus—in particular, the Sandinista revolution. In Nicaragua of the 1970s and 1980s, several musical groups sprouted up: the Mejía Godoy brothers, the Dúo Guardabarranco, the Grupo Mancotal, and the Grupo Pancasán. This very own current of Nicaraguan New Song and Trova was sometimes referred to with the rather artificial term *Volcanto,* for the music coming out of the small country so marked by its volcanoes. The term never stuck, however. What stuck was the music. Next to Caribbean rhythms and Mexican *rancheras* popular across Nicaragua, the music of the two Mejía Godoy brothers was resounding everywhere, creating national and international affective spaces of identification. However, most scholars—with few exceptions such as the works by ethnomusicologist T. M. Scruggs—focused on the literature of the revolution, not the music.[2]

This is a curious oversight. Given its oral immediacy in a largely illiterate context and its widespread popularity in the 1970s and the first half of the 1980s, the music played an important role in the dissemination of the idea of armed struggle. In fact, it is probably one of the most beloved, utopian, and unchallenged spaces of the revolution. To this day, the brothers play weekly concerts. Even though their musical repertoire goes beyond the revolutionary songs, they still play many of those songs from the 1970s and early 1980s. They constitute an important space of revolutionary memory and nostalgia. Intellectuals and politicians in Nicaragua will, without any hesitation, affirm that especially Carlos Mejía Godoy's music was crucial for the revolution. In the early 1980s, Sergio Ramírez declared: "I don't know how much the revolution owes to the songs of Carlos Mejía Godoy, which managed to organize a collective sentiment of the people, extracting their themes and chords from deep down in our roots and preparing this sentiment for the struggle" (*El alba* 270).[3] In a 2012 interview, Ramírez reaffirmed that idea, saying that the revolution cannot be explained without Carlos Mejía Godoy's music.

The music is the essence of what the Sandinista Revolution wanted to be, the space where the revolution reached its own imagined utopian constitution—as illustrated in this episode from Ramírez's *Adiós muchachos*: "Today for many people, in- and outside of Nicaragua, the revolution remains in the nostalgias of the past and in long-gone memories, and is recalled like lost loves; but it has ceased to be a reason to live. Sometimes, at friends' houses abroad they play—like an homage they pay me and they pay themselves—the music of those times, the revolutionary songs of Carlos Mejía Godoy to which I listen with an oppressive sadness, with a feeling of something I sought and never managed to find" (17).[4] This frames the music as an emotionally charged space of collective belonging as well as nostalgia. The wistful lingering and longing for "something I sought and never managed to find" shows that music is intimately linked to affective and utopian notions of revolution. Within the music, utopia was attainable. The songs channeled the shared and lived experiences of a historical time period, similarly to Raymond Williams's concept of "structures of feeling." As Ron Eyerman and Andrew Jamison put it: "Music in a sense *is* a structure of feeling. It creates mood . . . and this way can communicate a feeling of common purpose, even amongst actors who have no previous historical connections with one another" (162).

Song in the context of the Nicaraguan Revolution was a highly effective and flexible medium that allowed an emotionally charged fusion of different societal spheres and actors: lettered, folk-popular, revolutionary, national, urban, and rural. It was a bridge that allowed the seemingly distant folk-popular and lettered spheres and circles to permeate each other. Carlos Mejía Godoy put poems by Rubén Darío, Pablo Antonio Cuadra, and Ernesto Cardenal to music. He offered a humorous yet critical reinterpretation of the lettered city in the song of "Terencio Acahualinca" from *Cantos a flor de pueblo*. In this song a squatter mocks the government employees conducting a census, asking him about his profession by showcasing his ability with the spoken word— through many puns—and contrasting the importance of *letrado* titles with his destitute situation. The squatter says that through his life he has earned "a bachelor's in poverty" and "a master's in malnutrition" ("soy licenciado en pobreza / master en desnutrición"). Critics laud Carlos Mejía Godoy's ability to fuse the lettered and the folk-popular sphere, writing that "his double artistic side—the learned and the popular—fuse in a single song" ("su doble vertiente artística—la culta y la popular—se funden en un solo canto") (Matus Lazo). In his songs he combines "a highbrow and often poetic language with a spontaneous and never forced use of the Nicaraguan speech" ("un lenguaje culto y con frecuencia poético con un espontáneo y nunca rebuscado uso del habla nicaragüense") (Mántica). Carlos Mejía Godoy managed to showcase the folk-popular sphere both in his lyrics and his melodies. Through multiple trips throughout the country, with the Brigada de Salvación del Canto Nicaragüense, created in 1973, and the Taller de Sonido Popular, created in 1975, Carlos Mejía Godoy started to collect rhythms, melodies, and genres such as *son nica* and *mazurka* from all over the country.[5] His great linguistic and musical capacity to incorporate the colloquial and the vernacular into his songs is part of his musical legend (Scruggs, "Socially Conscious" 42). Often he was seen as a vehicle for the voice of the people: "Carlos Mejía Godoy does not sing for the people. The people sing in him and for him and with him. The popular voice. Voice and song of the people" (as written by Julio Valle Castillo in the liner notes of the album *Monimbó*).[6]

Carlos Mejía Godoy, born to a family of musicians in 1943 in the northern village of Somoto, started to become successful through the radio, where he combined political cabaret with humorous songs with some social content, first in the 1960s with his radio personality "Corporito" and then in the early 1970s with the program "El son nuestro de cada día." The latter was a popular show and even the guerrillas in the mountains tuned in to hear the songs. Omar Cabezas, in his *testimonio La montaña es algo más que una inmensa estepa verde,* recounts how the guerrilla ritually gathered at 6:00 to listen to the radio program, which kept up their morale (143). These radio programs and Carlos Mejía Godoy's first album, *Cantos a flor de pueblo* (1973), are the foundation of his popularity, grounded in his ability to capture and reinterpret folk-popular culture. His album *El son nuestro de cada día* (1977), which celebrated both the linguistic and musical vernacular of Nicaragua, increased his popularity.[7]

The dictatorship did not quite know how to handle the dissident space that was opened up by the music (Scruggs, "Socially Conscious" 47–48). On the one hand, the radio station was fined several times for Carlos Mejía Godoy's mocking performances; on the other hand, members of the National Guard became fans of some songs because of the at times misleading double entendres and the picaresque style of the songs, which appealed to a sense of *nicaraguanidad* (Scruggs, "Socially Conscious" 49, 58; Landau 183). The rebellious content of his songs was packaged in a form that had enormous mass appeal, not only linguistically but also musically. Carlos Mejía Godoy, also a notable composer of radio jingles, presented the revolutionary ideas within very catchy melodies. Salman Rushdie in *The Jaguar Smile* points out that Carlos Mejía Godoy's "gift for the hummable tune might be envied by Paul McCartney" (60). Likewise, the journalist Edwin Sánchez has characterized him as "[t]he man who got the whole world to 'hum' the revolution" ("El hombre que logró que todo el mundo 'tarareara' la revolución") ("'F' de fuerza").

The combination of these factors explains why Carlos Mejía Godoy continued to be immensely popular, even after he turned to more overtly political content once he joined the FSLN ranks around 1975 (Landau 155; Scruggs, "Socially Conscious" 49, 52; Sturman 256). He started to give logistic support and play solidarity concerts abroad. Many of the later albums were recorded outside of Nicaragua—in Costa Rica, Mexico, and Spain. From Costa Rican territory they were transmitted via the underground Radio Sandino or smuggled into Nicaragua and secretly sung at mass (Luis Enrique Mejía Godoy, *Relincho* 300; Scruggs "Las misas"). His music became an increasingly important space of identification for the international solidarity movements, both in Latin America and Europe.[8]

His brother, Luis Enrique Mejía Godoy, born in 1945, had a different trajectory. Similar to his older brother Carlos Mejía Godoy, Luis Enrique launched his first album in the early 1970s: *Hilachas de sol* (1972). Yet Luis was lesser known before the triumph of the revolution, partly because since 1974 he had been living in exile in Costa Rica, where he had been a militant of the communist Partido Vanguardia Popular and had participated with his music in many union and protest events (L. E. Mejía Godoy, *Relincho* 297, 354). He did not come back to Nicaragua and join the FSLN ranks until 1979, after the triumph of the revolution, but together with his brother he participated in many crucial revolutionary compositions. Far more than his brother, Luis Enrique Mejía Godoy looked for inspiration elsewhere than in the folkloric traditions of the Pacific and of northern Nicaragua. He experimented with *trova*, rock, and Caribbean dance music. Scruggs argues that it is because of his playful, vital, folkloric style that Carlos was more successful in Nicaragua than Luis

Enrique and his more experimental style ("Socially Conscious" 55). Neverthe-less, Luis Enrique had several very renowned revolutionary song, too. Besides, both brothers are often confused, and the audience frequently does not know which song was written by whom (L. E. Mejía Godoy, *Relincho* 335), making it impossible to separate the two. Also, Luis Enrique Mejía Godoy should not be confused with Luis Enrique Mejía Lopez, a *salsa romántica* singer and nephew of the brothers.

The music of the Mejía Godoy brothers has a complex history within Nic-aragua as its context changed drastically over the years. From popular and traditional music, to subversive, at times clandestine means of protest and mobilization during the insurrection, it became the state-sponsored, insti-tutionalized music of the revolutionary state. Luis Enrique even became the director of the new revolutionary state music label ENIGRAC. The brothers say that they hardly ever wrote songs *por encargo,* on specific orders of the Frente. Only the "Himno de la Unidad sandinista" by Carlos was ever signed over to the FSLN. Yet it is safe to assume that the music was not composed in absolute independence because songs were often made with the help of com-rades to verify technical or historical detail (Landau 261). This was a delib-erate decision on behalf of the artists, but the music certainly corresponded to political needs of the moment.[9] Their music thus had a different path than the Cuban Trova, which was first viewed with suspicion by the revolutionary state and then appropriated (Moore 18–20, 22), but it also held a difficult posi-tion because of its proximity to power. As far as I know, neither the musicians nor the general public ever questioned this position during the revolutionary period.

It only became a sensitive issue after the FSLN had returned to power in 2006. In June 2008, Carlos and Luis Enrique Mejía Godoy, who had been ac-tive in the dissident party Movimiento Renovador Sandinista (MRS) in which many artists and intellectuals took refuge from the new Danielista politics, forbade the FSLN from using their songs in official party functions—except the aforementioned Sandinista anthem.[10] The FSLN then threatened to "con-fiscate" the songs, arguing that they "belonged to the people" (Rico). There was a flurry of media responses, and the brothers were applauded and criticized for their decision. In the end the FSLN recognized their authorship (C. Mejía Godoy "Interview"), but the matter was never fully resolved. By 2012, when I conducted my interviews, both musicians had retired from active politics. They were still giving their weekly concerts in their own venue in Managua, and the FSLN continued to use their songs.

The full extent of the conflict can only be understood if one takes the emotional value of these songs into consideration. Although the debate was framed in legal and economic terms, it was actually a moral one (L. E. Mejía Godoy, "Respuesta"). To many people, this music is of such integrity that they believe that the current FSLN does not have the moral right to use this symbol, while the Frente thinks of itself as a historical continuity of the revolution and therefore in its full right to use them.

The music of the Mejía Godoys had played a key role in the mobilizing efforts of the FSLN in the 1970s. Even though its importance waned in the mid-1980s, the music continued to be an important space of identification because like no other medium did it capture and express the utopian aspirations of the Sandinista Revolution. The convergence of lettered, folk-popular, rural, urban, Christian, national, and revolutionary spheres within the Mejía Godoys' music made the utopian ideal more tangible.[11] In *Women, Guerrillas, and Love,* Ileana Rodríguez analyzes writings by Che Guevara and Central American guerrilla narratives and states that in these "the struggle to come to terms with the concept of popular subjectivities is central" (65). Moreover, she perceives that despite the revolutionaries' desire to "be with the people," there is "a distress" when the revolutionaries talk about the popular subjectivities and themselves (75); their narratives display a "linguistic distancing" (43) from the popular masses; there is an "uneasiness" (47). This distance and distress is far less pronounced in the music of the Mejía Godoys since it features a lighthearted blending of different societal spheres. The popular-subaltern is neither suspect nor uncomfortably unknown as in Che's writings; rather, it seems to unfold in a colorful celebration of spoken language, humor, and melody. In their songs there is no distress. This is what Sergio Ramírez refers to when he talks about hearing something in the music, *something* he sought: the dream of utopia, a joyful march toward the promised land, a joining of forces to build a new revolutionary society. Within this affective projection of utopia the music popularizes and legitimizes the idea of armed struggle.

## Spreading the Revolutionary Word: Rifles, Women, Jesus, and the Nation

The Sandinista discourse was a predominantly utopian discourse in the sense that it centered around creating an ideal societal order. The promise of the revolution was that in Nicaragua's very own utopia, society would be cleansed of its long history of violence, both indirect and direct as well as epistemic violence. This utopian society was to be achieved through armed struggle. The use of force was seen as justified because it would bring about a nonviolent future. The Sandinista discourse thus operated with the common Marxist axiom of revolutionary violence always being a "redeeming violence" (Avelar, *Letter of*

*Violence* 5). But because not everyone would so easily subscribe to such an axi-om, the music became an important medium to spread the revolutionary word.

Within its own utopian constitution the music takes on the difficult task of spreading the revolutionary word and legitimizing it. In particular, the songs depict revolutionary violence as fundamentally different from other types of direct violence. For said purpose, the singers employ different tropes aimed at transforming armed struggle and firearms themselves. These range from sanctifying and gendering armed struggle to naturalizing it, presenting it as something organic to the Nicaraguan nation and nature.

"Cristo ya nació en Palacagüina" is an example of how the music legit-imized armed struggle by fusing Christian and revolutionary spheres. Lib-eration theology and the Christian base communities were central for the broad acceptance of armed struggle as proposed by the Sandinistas, and this song is "emblematic of the key role music played in the convergence of reli-gious-based morality with a mobilizing ideology for social change" (Scruggs, "Socially Conscious" 62).[12] It is an early revolutionary song from 1973, so firearms only make a tacit appearance. The carol tells the story of Christ be-ing born to the son of a washerwoman and a day laborer in the Nicaraguan village Palacagüina and ends with Jesus dreaming of becoming a guerrilla fighter. The song thus embeds the idea of armed struggle within Christian thought.

The song stresses liberation theology's preferential option for the poor by making the Bible relevant for the poor, relating it to their life experiences, interpreting it within their local context, and focusing on their empower-ment and liberation. It nationalizes and naturalizes the story of Jesus's birth by transporting it to Nicaragua, making it local. The song itself, whose cho-ral and harplike sounds of the guitar or *charango* chords make it suitable for mass, plays on the *son nica* genre (Scruggs, "Socially Conscious" 60–61). And the Nicaraguan-born Jesus, son of "some guy called Joseph" and "some wom-an named Maria" ("Chepe Pavón y una tal María"), receives humble local gifts such as string cheese, caramel candies, and pastries instead of gold, incense, and myrrh. Conforming with liberation theology's revolutionary gospel, the song emphasizes his parents' poverty and exploitation. Maria is a poor wash-erwoman working for the wife of the big landowner, and Joseph is sick from his job as a carpenter. The problem of inequality and landownership is stressed throughout the refrain, which repeatedly talks about the exquisite clothes of the landowner's wife that Maria washes.

As a result of witnessing these injustices, the young Jesus wants to become a guerrilla fighter. Connecting the idea of taking up arms with the figure of Jesus softens the implication of guerrilla warfare and sanctifies armed struggle as the only ethical response to injustice. Jesus's wish—"tomorrow I want to be a guerrilla fighter" ("mañana quiero ser guerrillero")—only appears once in the song but, in contrast to the melodic, tranquil voice and minor tonality in the rest of the song, this part is accentuated through a change in tonality to major and some hard strikes on the guitar (Scruggs, "Socially Conscious" 62). A pressed, guttural phonation expresses fierce determination. While the song comes to an end in a crescendo repeating the words "del terrateniente," the idea of wanting to become a guerrilla fighter continues to resonate in the listener's head long after the song is over. The idea of armed struggle is thus presented as the only logical consequence under the prevailing circumstances.[13]

Another important element in legitimizing armed struggle is through the presence of women. Often armed struggle becomes gendered or sexualized, and firearms figure both as artifacts of oppression and liberation. The military repression by the Somoza regime, especially of women in the countryside, is the topic of "Venancia," a song from 1975 that exists in different versions by Luis Enrique Mejía Godoy. Telling the story of "Venancia," the song is one of Luis Enrique's most dramatic. He composed it in response to the rape of the peasant activists María Castil and Amanda Pineda de Arauz by the National Guard (L. E. Mejía Godoy, *Relincho* 298). The peasant woman Venancia works as a messenger for the guerrilla, whose unionized brother was killed and whose mother was raped by the major. The song starts off with a dramatic rock-like riff, the rhythm of the song moves between fast and slow parts interrupted by individual drums that evoke bursts of shots being fired. The singer's voice alternates between lament, distress, and urgency. These elements make the song very theatrical and create a scenario of menace, tension, and woe, which seems as breathless as Venancia herself who hastily runs through the mountains to deliver the message to the guerrilla. The singing voice pleads her to be careful, because "They have a rifle" ("Ellos tienen un fusil"), while she has a dead brother because he was unionized and a mother whose clothes smell of those of the commander. The firearm stands for the threat posed by the army, a phallic threat extended by the rifle, made explicit through the mention of the rape of Venancia's mother. The continuous repetition of the line "They have a rifle" stresses the double danger for women, terrorized by both sexual and armed violence.

Although the woman seems victimized by firearm and phallus, Venancia also symbolizes resistance to this threat—through supporting armed struggle, not with a rifle but through her work as a messenger. Her figure is a prime example of the base communities necessary for the development of the *foquismo* model of a guerrilla. She is a daughter of the mountain and, as such, of the guerrilla. Venancia forms part of the mythical mountain space where, according to the Guevarian-Sandinista mystique, the guerrilla fighters were shaped. She also has the support of nature; the hill cheers her on and tells her that she is gutsy.

Sometimes the rifle and the woman also become a point of desire. "Muchacha del Frente Sandinista" is a bolero-style love song for the Sandinista militant, composed by Carlos in the late 1960s. Dedicated to Doris Tijerino, a militant tortured in Somoza's prisons, the song celebrates the figure of the female guerrilla (C. Mejía Godoy, "El verbo"). The Sandinista girl becomes the romantic symbol of military discipline and revolutionary freedom: boots and drill pants, rifle in hand, and long flowing hair. Here, the firearm is not threatening anymore but has become the symbol of liberation and desire. Despite Carlos's crooning—"Allow me to entangle in your carbine my love verses" ("Permite que en tu carabina enrede mis versos de amor")—the boyfriend of the *muchacha sandinista* will have to wait, says the song, because her real boyfriend are the Nicaraguan people who need to be liberated. In this instance, armed struggle is discursively softened through the female element. In most cultures war was generally considered a male-only affair (Braudy 21–22), so in these songs feminization is used to mark a difference with other forms of militarist violence. That is, it cannot be the same militarism as the dreaded right-wing dictatorships if women are a part of the fighting.

To present armed struggle as an act of love is a common element in Sandinista discourse. The idea of romance and love-making also appears in later post-triumph songs, when it is important to construct a national project out of the saga of armed struggle. In the songs "El Castillo de la Concepción," "Octubre," and "Estelí" from the album *Canto épico al FSLN,* guerrilla fighters are described as "lovers of the homeland" ("los enamorados de la patria") and as "armed to the teeth with tenderness" ("armados de ternura hasta los dientes") or as the "relentless guerrilla fighter, untameable, sweet, and fierce fighter of love" ("implacable guerrillero, indomable, dulce y fiero combatiente de amor"). Ileana Rodríguez has rightly pointed out that the idea of tenderness and love as the guiding principle of the Sandinista Revolution constitutes a fallacy in the construction of the New Man. (33). A lot of times love functions as "an exercise of power, authority, violence" (46). Yet it is certainly a useful metaphor when it comes to legitimizing armed struggle because it transforms the rifle from an artifact of violence into one of love.

In the Sandinista songs the act of love—armed struggle—becomes the means to refound the nation, similar to the "foundational fictions" Doris Sommer identified in nineteenth-century Latin American literature. The twentieth-century guerrilla movements see the earlier independence movements as incomplete and thus in their own names often feature the idea of "national liberation," a desire to free the nation from the colonial legacy. The song "Nicaragua, Nicaragüita" by Carlos Mejía Godoy, Nicaragua's unofficial national anthem, which also appears on *Canto épico,* mentions moments of indigenous resistance such as the Chorotega leader Diriangüén, who fought against the Spaniards in 1520s. The Sandinista Revolution is seen as fulfilling his legacy. Liberation becomes the constituting moment of the nation: "now that you're free, Nicaragüita, I love you even more" ("ahora que ya sos libre, Nicaragüita, yo te quiero mucho más"). With a slow rhythm the vocals changing between a sole tender whisper and multiple strong choral voices, the lyrics using the diminutives and the *voseo,* the *imagined community* "Nicaragua" becomes less abstract and more palpable, as if the revolution allows to establish a more direct and intimate relationship with the country and its people.[14] In the song "Yo soy de un pueblo sencillo," Luis Enrique Mejía Godoy draws a similar image of the Nicaraguan people coming into their own through the revolution when he sings that the Nicaraguan people are "born in between rifle and singing" ("nacido entre fusil y cantar"). Rifle and songs, armed struggle and affect, create a new nation.

The other figure of resistance used to legitimize armed struggle is, of course, Augusto C. Sandino, guerrilla general who fought against the US Marines in the 1920s and whose name the Frente Sandinista de Liberación Nacional took on. Through his figure, armed struggle is presented as something that lies within Nicaragua. This maneuver is very common in Sandinista political discourse, ever since the Sandinista leader Carlos Fonseca rediscovered and resignified Sandino's struggle for the FSLN. It is not only about following the Guevarian ideal of the New Man but also about following the example within the nation. "Eran 30 con él," from the album *Amando en tiempos de guerra* by Luis Enrique, sings about the small army of Sandino, which consisted of men, women, and children. It puts special emphasis on Sandino's peasant shrewdness; he learned from the mountain, the animal kingdom that the snake/politician needs to be slain. The song points out that although Sandino had been vilified as a bandit in the national discourse under Somoza, him taking up arms was the honorable thing to do—as opposed to being a politician, a treacherous, dangerous animal. In the song, taking up arms becomes the true, pure politics against the abomination of those in power. The song also refers to the Mexican Revolution, one of Sandino's role models, and incorporates parts of the famous *corrido* "La Adelita." This puts the Sandinista struggle in the continent's tradition of peasant insurgency, the tradition of politics from below. Armed struggle appears as righteous politics, both a continental and national legacy.

A musical reference to the Mexican Revolution also appears in "Asalto al Palacio," the only corrido from *Canto épico* (discussed in the book's introduction). The aim to evoke the Mexican Revolution shows the desire to legitimize the Sandinista Revolution as yet another revolution from below. Armed struggle is again seen as a democratizing act. The roar of the rifle erupts in the democratic farce of the National Congress and now, for the first time, the citizens are truly "in session," in power. But whereas in the Mexican Revolution peasants affirmed themselves as political subjects before the state, here this is taken a step further, since it is no longer about affirming oneself but about taking over the state. Again the firearm appears as a prosthesis for citizenship, imbued with a sense of righteousness. Not only does the rifle enable citizens; making people citizens for the first time, it appears as *the* artifact for true and righteous politics.

The Mejía Godoy brothers legitimized armed struggle by fusing it with national and Christian elements, highlighting repression under the Somoza regime, and associating armed struggle with women and love-making, presenting it as lying within the nation, as something organic. In the hands of the *guerrilleros* and *guerrilleras* the firearm transforms from the dirty tool of state oppression and rape to a symbol of change, resistance, love-making, and true and righteous politics. Legitimizing armed struggle thus meant the continuous detachment of the firearm from its functional logic. But in an attempt to popularize armed struggle, these songs of guerrilla warfare also had to focus on the lethal aspects of weapons.

## A Lullaby for a Rifle: Drawing Weapons Closer

As the fighting intensified, so did the music. Moving toward the general insurrection of 1979, the songs by the Mejía Godoy brothers no longer worked only toward a legitimization of armed struggle but also toward its concrete implementation. The need and aim was to draw firearms closer, to make them intimate tools and artifacts—in figurative and concrete terms. Luis Enrique Mejía Godoy even wrote a lullaby for a rifle ("Canción para un fusil") on the album *Amando en tiempos de guerra*. Accompanied by soft guitar chords, the singer caresses the rifle and tells the rifle to sleep now since the battle against the dictatorship is approaching and once in battle, he will not allow the rifle to rest. In the song the rifle has become an intimate artifact of the life of the militant: "Brother, comrade, friend, let me caress your so hard skin" ("Hermano, compañero, amigo, déjame acariciar tu piel tan dura").

Songs did not stop at metaphoric endeavors of drawing weapons closer. Carlos and Luis Enrique Mejía Godoy produced several songs that taught how to disarm, upkeep, and use specific firearms. Composed right before the general insurrection in 1979, the album *Guitarra Armada* aimed to popularize and implement armed insurrection by familiarizing people with firearms. The album features songs about the FAL, the Garand, the carbine M-1, the .22-caliber pistol, and different bullets as well as instructions on the preparation of homemade explosives, military discipline, and battle tactics; it closes with songs about martyrs and the Sandinista anthem. The songs were widely distributed through the clandestine Radio Sandino during the final insurrection, and some say that for many fighters it was the only military instruction they received (Dore 417; Landau 218). The brothers, however, deny the latter; they say that the purpose of these songs was complementary: to capture the spirit of the moment and to show people that they could resist Somoza's professional army with homemade weapons and that it was not so difficult to handle firearms (C. Mejía Goody, "Interview"; L. E. Mejía Godoy, "Interview").

In these songs the necessity for armed struggle is already assumed as a given; they are less about justifying armed struggle and more about implementing it. Still, the songs present complex expressions and negotiations of revolutionary violence. For one, they experiment with an array of strategies to use song to teach the handling of firearms: folksy and poetic tropes, mnemonic devices such as sing-along songs as well as vernacular, colloquial, conversational, or exhortatory forms of speech. In particular, the songs draw firearms closer by relating them to folkloric traditions and by animating them through zoomorphism and anthropomorphism. This is partly a didactic device—using metaphoric visual language—but it is also a continuation of the political discourse that revolutionary armed violence of the Sandinistas is a different type of violence. From this arises a certain tension. The songs are aimed at explaining the functional logic of the firearm, but simultaneously they have to constantly transform it into an artifact of righteous, legitimate violence, and the songs do so through lyrical metaphors. The firearm, here both tool and artifact, thus appears at the heart of revolutionary rhetoric, at the center of complex negotiations when it comes to actually popularizing armed struggle.

One element of the didactic poetics of implementing armed struggle is the incorporation of folk-popular tradition. In the song "Los explosivos," Carlos uses the folkloric tradition of *la gigantona* to explain how to build homemade bombs. The tradition of *la gigantona* dates back to colonial times: an enormous female puppet (*la gigantona*) representing Spanish colonial power dances through the streets accompanied by a drum player (*el tamborilero*), a person shouting popular verses (*el coplero*), and a small big-headed puppet (*el enano cabezón*), often thought to represent indigenous or mestizo culture. In this song, reenacting a call-and-response style within a circle of children, the *coplero* shouts different homemade recipes for bombs (the right proportion of aluminum, sawdust, ammonium nitrate, etc.), while explaining that the people have to prepare for the final offensive, contribute to the fight. The declamation of recipes is interrupted by dances of the *gigantona* to a rhythmic refrain of "coplas libertarias"—verses that call the people to arms.

Another common trope is to give weaponry a different meaning through feminization. The song "Las municiones" employs violin chords, shouts, and a refrain sung by male voices. Yet each single stanza is sung by a different female voice, representing different types of ammunition. Each bullet—the ordinary bullet, the perforating incendiary, the tracer ammunition, the blank propellant cartridge for the launching of grenades—presents herself in first person. The word "bullet" (*la bala*) is feminine in Spanish, so the use of female voices to represent them is a logical step, but the feminization goes beyond purely grammatical reasons. The Mejía Godoys often use feminization to transform the weapon. At the beginning of "Las municiones," a female voice explains that several cases of bullets were obtained in the fall of Matagalpa, but that now that the Sandinistas have them, they are not the same anymore because now they are used to fight for freedom. Here lies the eternal tension of armed, revolutionary struggle: the idea that weapons are different in the "right" hands. In terms of their functional logic, they are not different. Bullets are still objects that are inserted into a firearm to harm other individuals. They are tools of harm, yet from a political perspective they are artifacts of liberation. To make that semantic shift and to highlight them as artifacts of a revolution's "redeeming violence" (Avelar, *Letter of Violence* 5), the bullets have to be metaphorically transformed. Since the feminine is assumed distant from the logic of war, the feminization of bullets helps to transform the bullet from lethal object into a political artifact of a different kind of violence, a righteous violence.[15]

Zoomorphism is another trope used to draw weapons closer. In the songs the bullets describe themselves in a figurative, poetic language animating weaponry through the attribution of animal features. The ordinary bullet, for example, presents herself a "furious steed" ("corcel de furia") that will rush to kill the oppressor. The lethal qualities of the tracer ammunition are framed in equally lyrical terms. The ammunition explains that she does not have expansive qualities, but that she is armor-piercing and has a bright glow. Particularly useful at night, she describes herself as: "Happy firefly of the guerrilla, the compass of the sturdy projectile" ("Luciérnaga feliz de la guerrilla, soy brújula del recio proyectil").

The didactic lyricism also appears in the stanza about the grenade-launching blank cartridge, which appears as empowered by martyrdom. Its empty interior is filled with "the soul of the brother who has fallen," which will help to launch a fragmentation grenade" ("el alma del hermano que cayó"). This transforms the cartridge but also the death of the comrade; the act of mourning is mixed with a sense of resilience. Through this rhetoric device, Carlos is able to explain the technical aspect—the emptiness but effectiveness of this blank cartridge—and fill it with political meaning. These metaphorical animations draw the weapon closer. One could, of course, call this fetishism because of the attempt to animate things, but the critique of fetishism in my opinion adds very little to our understanding of the symbolic meaning of weaponry. Here the enchantment through women, animals, and souls is a literary device used for pedagogic and political purposes. Zoomorphism and anthropomorphism help explain technological aspects, but simultaneously draw away from the object's functional logic—its lethal purpose—as is the case with the tracer ammunition being represented as a "happy firefly." Also, animalization makes the ammunition less of a sterile cold, modern piece of technology and draws it more into the rural and natural sphere.

Zoomorphism is used to describe the FAL, the Sandinista guerrilla's preferred weapon. In the song "Qué es el FAL," animalization is used to explain technical aspects but also to present it as an invigorating, virile automatic weapon: "this animal fires everything" ("este animal tira todo"). Referring to the firepower and velocity of an automatic weapon, its sound is described as barks and its demeanor in combat as "trembling with emotion" ("charchalear"). This animal has to be tamed and controlled by strong men. As one can see, feminization is not always used; here a masculine aesthetic predominates. In a colloquial tone, sung only by male voices and interrupted by dialogues, the song explains in detail how to disarm the rifle, how to adjust the gas system, and how to switch from automatic into grenade-launching mode. The song praises the aesthetics, technicality, and vigor of the FAL—calling it a beauty and a modern powerful rifle for real men.[16] According to Landau, this song made the FAL a coveted status symbol in Nicaragua (250).

The main focus of the songs about rifles—the FAL, the Garand, the carbine M-1—is the proper disarming of rifles and doing things with care. For that purpose a vernacular style is used. Carlos Mejía Godoy himself called it *chapiollo* style, a Nicaraguan Spanish word that refers to something being local, vernacular, often used pejoratively but here meant as something that will appeal to "the people."[17] The song "Carabina M-1" by Luis Enrique starts with a burst of the carbine shots and then breaks into a mazurka rhythm accompanied by joyous shouts. Explaining how to use and clean the weapon, Luis imitates an off-key, nasal rural singing style and ties words together to give the song the feel of a playful lecture. He emphasizes that the M-1 is good for both urban and rural guerrilla warfare and that its advantage is that it can be used with a bayonet. The song cheerfully proclaims that learning to sing each of these verses means one fewer man in enemy lines. This sing-along clearly explains technical details, and its catchy melody with verses that rhyme makes it easy to memorize. Great emphasis is put on doing things "with care" and "correctly," all the while stressing the simplicity of the action. The technicality of the weapon is not for a specialized few, says the song; it can be mastered by the common man. While cheerful and didactic, the song also reveals a certain paternalistic vanguardism, where the nonlettered masses are exhorted to behave in a modern, rational, and careful manner.[18] This resembles the disciplining processes that, according to Foucault, created the modern subjectivities and their "docile bodies" in eighteenth-century Europe (138). Training people for war becomes an act of training them for modernity.[19]

Overall the album *Guitarra Armada* divides the critics. Some celebrate these songs as an extraordinary example of how music can be used didactically (Landau 246; Pring-Mill 179) and call them a "milestone" in the Nicaraguan New Song movement (Scruggs, "Nicaragua" 764). Others, on the contrary, in otherwise eulogistic reviews of the musical legacy of Carlos and Luis Enrique Mejía Godoy, consider these songs their least accomplished (Mántica; Mora Lomeli). More than anything, this mixed reception points to several dilemmas and tensions at the core of the songs: political and aesthetic tensions that arise in the context of a didactic poetics and a firm belief in the use of violence. The songs explain the functional logic of firearms but simultaneously try to transform the weapon, poeticize it, or feminize it in order to stress that revolutionary insurgent violence is different from other forms of political violence. Another tension is the one between revolutionary rhetoric of liberation and empowerment and—due to the didactic purpose of the songs—the apparent paternalistic and militaristic tendencies. One can say this is a logical consequence of the attempt to popularize armed struggle—no planned, organized revolution without a certain militarism and paternalism—but it also shows how early on there were already fissures in the revolutionary discourses.

The act of drawing weapons closer has political consequences. It invites the weapon into one's midst. In Luis Enrique Mejía Godoy's lullaby for a rifle,

"Canción para un fusil," as he prepares the weapon for battle, he promises it a place in his home once the enemy is defeated. They will tend the new cornfield, eat at the same table, and the rifle will be able to sleep next to his children. Born out of the urgency and emergency of the times, these songs of insurgency carry the danger of perpetuating a logic of militarism. It invites the weapon into the intimacy of life, but how will it leave again? These tensions can only be resolved or appear to be resolved within a powerful discourse about the end of violence. The enchanted, animated rifle that appears in the years of insurrection becomes even more important in the years after the triumph.

## Rifles and Auroras: Nature, War, and Enchanted Modernity

In the Sandinista discourse the projection of a nonviolent future materialized in what I call the idea of an "enchanted modernity." Contrary to Max Weber's well-known conceptualization of modernity as leading to the "disenchantment of the world" ("Entzauberung der Welt") ("Wissenschaft" 510), the Sandinistas envisioned a romantic, transformative, nonpositivist national project in which spirituality, nature, and politics converged. It was truly transformative and, as such, metamorphosis was a key element in this narrative: rifles shooting auroras, rifles full of flowers, militants converted into trees and animals, trees and animals converted into militants. These vivid images were a visualization of a quintessential logic of many twentieth-century liberation and guerrilla movements: the firearm as the harbinger of a new dawn.

Weber conceived of modernity as the establishment of the nation-state and a well-functioning bureaucracy and economy, accompanied by a further rationalization of society, which leads to disenchantment. True to the tradition of cultural pessimism in German thought, this is a foremost skeptical look at the consequences of rationalism, which holds that political and scientific developments will lead to "disenchantment," meaning both secularization and an end of magic (Jenkins 12; Schluchter 9). One can ask whether Weber's ideas can be applied to Latin America, since his analysis was developed through a focus on Europe and the United States, and many academics have rightly pointed out that the experience of modernity in Latin America differs from traditional accounts of European and North American modernity, stressing its peripheral, decentered, heteroclite, asynchronous, and culturally heterogeneous character (García Canclini; Martín Barbero, "Modernidad"; Richard; Rincón; Sarlo). But despite these important theorizations of Latin American difference, the Weberian concept of modernity continues to be very powerful in the Latin American collective imagination. Even critical revisions of the idea of modernity in Latin America in the light of postmodernism make mention of Weber's conception as the underlying principle of many discourses on modernity in the region (García Canclini 22–23; Beverley, Aronna, and Oviedo 2, 7). A primarily Weberian conception of modernity leads to the common discourse of lack in Latin America, of yet having to fully achieve modernity. In my analysis I play on Weber's ideas not to reinforce this imaginary of lack but to demonstrate how a particular Latin American political project formulated a different vision, one that defied the notion of modernity inevitably leading to disenchantment.

In many ways Sandinista politics were modeled on classical modernization theories, combining both capitalist and socialist models. Saldaña Portillo has shown how deeply Sandinista politics were enmeshed with twentieth-century developmentalist narratives (10). Also, a former Sandinista vice president Sergio Ramírez talks in his memoirs about the revolution's "ambition for modernity" ("ambición de modernidad") (*Adiós* 238). Yet since the Sandinistas were nationalists, they also wanted to create a political project of their own, something uniquely and genuinely Nicaraguan. The intentions of doing something unique does not mean that they necessarily succeeded, as it would be a mistake to assume that the Sandinistas created something entirely new (Chávez 173). In many ways they did not break with the past—just as many Sandinista artists did not break with the old patriarchs of poetry such as José Coronel Urtecho and Ernesto Cardenal. Yet in the idea of enchantment lies the political desire for a different type of modernity: Nicaragua's very own utopia.

In *Nicaragua and the Politics of Utopia,* Daniel Chávez proposes a semiotic rectangle to understand Sandinista utopian discourses, consisting of four corners: modernity and the people as elements of one partial opposition and nature and technology as those of another, all of which are temporarily mediated within the Sandinista discourse of the New Man (8, 173). This rectangle also contains a neutral utopian, which "is the projection of a realizable future in which the contradictions of the mediating complex term will be resolved" (6). In my view an enchanted modernity precisely represents this neutral utopian. An enchanted modernity is the promise of a nonviolent future, a state where tensions and contradictions are resolved. It manifests in a nonpositivist worldview, a convergence of the political and the religious sphere, including rituals of sacrifice for the foundation of the new society, as well as a conception of the world in which the human is part of nature. This vision of modernity heavily built on romantic ideas, so precisely the European-American literary tradition that rejected positivism and intended to recuperate magic. The San-dinista project aimed at escaping European rationalism and is thus also not unlike the literary (counter)narrative of magical realism, whose "lure" was "that it reenchanted the world by drawing into literature popular beliefs and practices as a form of dissent from post-Enlightenment rationalism" (Franco, *Decline and Fall* 159).[20] The enchanted modernity as such is thus not solely a Sandinista invention, but rather the revolution, drawing heavily on the ro-mantic tradition, is one of the strongest *political* expressions of a desire for a different modernity in Latin America.

While also present in many Sandinista writings, this desire becomes most apparent in the music. On the album *Guitarra Armada* the most explicit vision for such an enchanted modernity appears in the Sandinista anthem "Himno de la unidad sandinista." The song by Carlos Mejía Godoy is a cheer-ful tune that conjures unity and optimism—onward to the future. In this rel-atively conventional marching tune, a high-pitched choral adagio suddenly interrupts, which projects the idea of an enchanted modernity. He rephrases the title of Tomás Borge's book *Carlos, el amanecer ya no es una tentación* and predicts that the new dawn will no longer be a dream, but that a new sun will rise "which will illuminate the whole earth" ("que habrá de iluminar toda la tierra"). This new dawn will come "with mighty rivers of milk and honey" ("con caudalosos ríos de leche y miel"). In his postrevolutionary account *Adiós muchachos*, Ramírez references that idea with some irony and titles the chap-ter that deals with the numerous failed economic politics of the Sandinistas "Rivers of Milk and Honey." In the anthem, however, the proposed project is still intact. Modernity will cease to be a desire and will be imbued with en-chantment, irradiating and animating the world. Through the sudden flaring up of the adagio in the song, reminiscent of Gregorian chants, the coming of modernity is represented almost like a theophany.

Some, like Comandante Cero, Edén Pastora, have mocked the song pre-cisely for this adagio, saying that it gave the song an old-maidish feel, but Carlos Mejía Godoy defended it by saying that "at the moment it fulfilled its function" ("que en su momento cumplió con su función") (Sánchez, "PJCH"). The function, I believe, was the incorporation of a Christian aesthetic, since fear of atheist Marxists ran high. The song projects a convergence of the polit-ical and the religious spheres. This was further affirmed through Luis Enrique Mejía Godoy's song on the album "A Gaspar," dedicated to the Spanish priest Gaspar García Laviana, fallen in 1978. Later this convergence of the religious and political spheres should hold true when several priests held high political offices in the Sandinista government. Contrary to liberal, secularist ideals of nineteenth-century Latin America, and infuriating the anti-communist Vatican, Ernesto and Fernando Cardenal and Miguel D'Escoto headed, respectively, the ministry of culture, of education, and of foreign affairs.

Yet nonsecularization was not the only element of the Sandinista vision for an enchanted modernity. Important for conciliating tensions in the utopian discourse was the idea of transformation: the transformative power of immolation as well as the animation and transformation of objects (examples of which we have already seen in the previous section). Within the possibility of metamorphosis, technology and nature, people and modernity are all able to converge. Chávez argues that the importance of nature in Sandinista texts has to do with the need "to propose a utopian refoundation of the relationship of the individual and of society to the natural world" (176), given that previous regimes were centered on extractive and exploitative practices of the land and the people. The "reencounter with nature legitimates a horizon of utopian images for reclaiming a strong and renewed bond with the national, indigenous, and popular roots of Nicaraguan history" (177). While I agree with his assessment, it is only one aspect of the importance of nature in the Sandinista discourse. Communing with nature is key for justifying the millitants' ethics of sacrifice, and for transforming violence, for giving it this halo of redemption. In the brothers' songs all of this combined brings about the desired modernity. Nature and technology forged together in war bring about an enchanted modernity.

Sacrifice and death were seen as means to bring about a different modernity. Sacrifice was one's offering for a better world and made death merely the beginning of new life. Immolation and communion with nature thus become key tropes of the Sandinista discourse, most vividly in the music, but they later appear in fictionalizations of the Sandinista struggle—for example, Gioconda Belli's *La mujer habitada*. *Guitarra Armada* ends with songs about how immolation brings about a process of transformation. "El zenzontle pregunta por Arlen" by Carlos Mejía Godoy is among the most lyrical revolutionary songs, and its aesthetics and tone differ considerably from the rest of the album. It is a song about death, mourning, and sacrifice, and it plays on the Amerindian myth that fallen warriors become hummingbirds. The song is a duet between a mockingbird (a *zenzontle*, sung by a female voice) and a motmot (a *guardabarranco*, sung by Carlos). They chirp about the whereabouts of Arlen Siu, a Chinese-Nicaraguan Sandinista militant and singer who was killed by the National Guard in 1975 at age twenty.

An intertextual reference to Rubén Darío's "El poeta pregunta por Stella," in which the poetic I asks a lily about the whereabouts of Stella's soul (White 554), this is a song of mourning but also of revolutionary resilience. It is a delicate, dulcet, and melancholic song characterized by light marimba and flute tones that create a sense of frailty and tenderness. A change from minor to major key in the chorus, however, gives the solemnity an optimistic twist (Landau 256). In the song it turns out that Arlen Siu has not died but rather has undergone multiple metamorphoses. Where she died, a spring emerged. But she has also become a water lily and a butterfly. Her transformations illustrate that her spirit and the purity of her conviction have survived. Some critics only see one transformation (she has become a natural spring) and view the other beings as creatures in solidarity with the revolution (White 555) or as poetic comparisons for the beauty of Arlen (Bello 158). I, however, understand the song as expressing the possibility that Arlen has the ability to convert into numerous states, but most often she appears as a colorful butterfly and continues to fight.

Again, the feminine element is used to soften the bloody implications of armed struggle, but the song is more significant as it relates to the idea of an enchanted modernity. In the world conveyed in the song, the human is not increasingly estranged from nature due to processes of rationalization; rather, the human is (re)submerged into nature, it has become nature again, forming part of the enchantment. Arlen's sacrifice makes the transformation possible, both of herself and the world. It brings about an enchanted modernity in which nature is not the premodern Other but is inherently fused with the enterprise of war and modernity. This idea materializes in the endearing image of a hummingbird commanding officer who leads his guerrilla troop of butterflies: "a butterfly is doing clandestine work and her superior is a hummingbird" ("anda clandestina una mariposa y su responsable es un colibrí"). This catapults nature into the modern sphere and enchants war, merging nature, technology, people, and modernity.

Metamorphosis is also a main theme in Carlos Mejía Godoy's song "Comandante Carlos Fonseca" on the album *Guitarra Armada*. This song is dedicated to the Sandinista guerrilla leader who died in combat in 1976 and "every Sandinista militant and much of the country could sing [the song] by heart in the 1980s" (Judson 225). The song, which contains some fragments of Borge's *Carlos, el amanecer ya no es una tentación* (80), celebrates Fonseca as a virile leader who has defied death. While Borge's original text mentions in the same paragraph that after Fonseca's death, his head was cut off and brought to Somoza (80), the song omits this gruesome episode. The song instead focuses on the transformative power of martyrdom. The bullet that pierced his heart in Zinica spilled his blood across Nicaragua. His death, his saintly and affectionate offering, brings about an enchanted modernity, a "free and luminous Nicaragua" ("Nicaragua libre y luminosa"). He and his "rifle shooting auroras" ("carabina disparando auroras") will always be remembered as the harbingers of the new dawn.

This martial song is full of war metaphors, but what is important in the song is not war but rather the transformative power of sacrifice. Fonseca's blood is the offering for the new bright modernity that awaits Nicaragua and thus even the firearm is transfigured. The firearm has completely lost its rationalist, lethal quality and instead is enchanted—the bullets converted into auroras—but continues to be a modern object of technology. As such, this aurora-shooting firearm is the ultimate symbol of the desired enchanted modernity. The music plays an important role in conveying this lyrical content. It is a melodramatic song, full of masculine resolve and declamatory gestures, but within the musical arrangement of the crescendo, the whispers, the full-throated chorus, the soft piano, violin, and flute sounds, the new order seems attainable and the firearm becomes the artifact of a new dawn, of an end of violence, an enchanted modernity.

After the triumph the Mejía Godoy brothers continued to work on this projection of an enchanted modernity, both the result and redemption from armed struggle. For the second anniversary of the revolution, together they produced the already mentioned cantata-suite *Canto épico al FSLN,* which mythologizes the Sandinista armed struggle. The whole FSLN leadership became involved in the preparations of the magnum opus, making it "one of the first official histories that the Sandinistas produced" providing "a unique non-linear perspective of the war that weaves political analysis, spirituality and storytelling into a historical narrative" (Landau 261). Scruggs considers this double album the most memorable and ambitious musical composition in Central America ("Legado").[21]

The saga begins with the mythical origins of the Sandinistas. *Canto épico al FSLN* starts with Sandino and then narrates how nature witnesses and applauds the birth of the Frente. "El nacimiento" compares the FSLN guerrilla, the politico-military organization, to a corn cob whose kernels have become revolutionary bullets, fusing war with pre-Columbian conceptions of genesis (White 559). The epic piece connects nature and war, recounting in the song "Los árboles" how different trees join the insurrection. They come to greet the newborn, bless it, and conjure the power of nature to help the revolution. The trees can be seen as an intertextual reference to Pablo Antonio Cuadra's *Siete árboles contra el atardecer* (White 562) and even to the Ents, insurgent treelike creatures in J.R.R. Tolkien's *The Lord of the Rings.* The reference to these trees commonly found in Nicaragua naturalizes and nationalizes the revolution, expanding it to the entire territory. The song mentions the ceiba, the holy Mesoamerican tree, uses the Caribbean *palo de mayo* rhythm and mentions Kilambé in the north (White 563). The song thus symbolically incorporates those northern and Caribbean regions with predominantly indigenous and Black communities into the revolutionary projects, even though the Sandinistas were already starting to clash with these communities because of their top-down colonialist-revolutionary projects in those regions. Later, parts of the Miskito, Sumo, and Rama people and other peasants would join the Contra to fight the Sandinistas, but within the music the revolutionary utopia, the convergence of all forces within an enchanted modernity, remains intact.

The urban indigenous element from the Pacific side is celebrated in the songs about Monimbó, the site of indigenous artisan resistance against Somoza in 1978. In an earlier song, "Vivirás Monimbó," from before the insurrection, this resistance is depicted as part of a long line of indigenous defiance against white invaders that continues on: "Where the Indian fell, flowered a granadillo tree" ("Donde el indio cayó, floreció el granadillo"). *Canto épico* takes this idea up in the song about Camilo Ortega, who died during the insurrection at Monimbó. It is a rhythmic song, marked by the sounds of the *atabales,* indigenous drums that were used during the Monimbó insurrection, which are featured in the lyrics: "The *atabales* resounded, the marimbas fluttered" ("Sonaron los atabales, tremolaron las marimbas"). Camilo is fully immersed, joined by birds in his fight, and brings about an enchanted future as he marches toward the new dawn. Again, the blood sacrifice has a transformative effect. Camilo's blood now flows and flowers in the dragon fruit trees and the laughter of the children of the new Nicaragua. In Cabezas's *testimonio,* guerrilla fighters go through a process of animalization in the mountain, hardening, becoming closer to nature (Chávez 184). In the Mejía Godoy brothers' music the transformation is absolute. In these revolutionary-ecological songs, the Frente is supported by the entire country, communes with the people and the land, guerrillas become trees and animals, and animals and trees join in the fight.[22]

In the song "Repliegue"—about a tactical retreat on June 27, 1979, when Sandinista troops evacuated thousands from Managua, bringing them covertly to Masaya—nature also helps. Thousands move quietly through the night, careful not make any noise, "and the command was followed even by nature" ("y la orden fue cumplida hasta por la naturaleza"). The cicadas and mosquitoes are quiet, holding their breath together with the fleeing humans. Sung in whispers that erupt in vehement chants, the song has an immense theatricality, expressing the fear experienced and the sensation that nature could betray them, but nature is on the side of the Sandinistas.

The notion of the FSLN guerrilla communing with nature becomes most apparent in "Pablo Úbeda," a song about the *guerrillero* Ricardo Cruz, who died in 1967 (White 562). In it, Cruz (aka Pablo Úbeda) continuously escapes the repressive forces of the Somoza regime and appears to be everywhere and nowhere at the same time. He is so elusive that the sergeant starts to believe that he is a *cadejo,* a mythical being from Central American folklore that haunts travelers. The refrain tells the listener that Úbeda has the ability to convert himself into plants like sword grass and sandbur and into animals: a parrot, a rabbit, an iguana, an armadillo, or a coati. All these plants and animals have qualities that are useful for a *guerrillero,* as Steven White has noted: the burr of the sandbur, the swiftness of the rabbit, the endurance and adaptivity of the iguana, the armor of the armadillo (563). This refrain is sung in a crescendo whisper by male voices, accompanied only with very soft albeit fast and rhythmic strumming on a guitar's muted strings. Through this musical arrangement, the song conjures an atmosphere of mystique and suspense (evoking the fear of the National Guard in light of Úbeda's elusiveness). The Guard will never find him because he disappeared into the mountain. For Pablo, however, nature is not a *locus terribilis;* he is part of it and is aided by it. They all help him: the swamp, the corn field, the wind, the Pleiades. The Guard shoots into the coffee field, but Úbeda slips out "serenely, quietly by the edge of the sugar field" ("sereno, pajito, bordeando el cañal"). One could criticize this twentieth-century reenactment of the noble savage but, within the logic of the Sandinista discourse, it merely stresses the organicity of the fight as well as the enchantment at its core.

This enchantment also transforms technology. Like the aurora-shooting rifle in the song about Fonseca, the firearm appears transformed in "Comandante Marcos," a song about Eduardo Contreras, guerrilla fighter and mastermind of the Tercerista faction of the FSLN, also killed in 1976. In the song by Luis Enrique Mejía Godoy, Contreras is converted into a saint and the weapon turned into a vessel of beautiful rather than lethal objects. He has a rainbow across his chest, "the sash of the chosen ones" ("la banda celeste de los elegidos"). When he disarms his rifle—lubricating it with the rays of the moon— his magazines reveal carnations and irises instead of bullets. The association is again that the rifle in the right hands—those of the chosen ones—is magically transformed. Although it is a violent tool, the rifle, as symbolized by the flowers, bears possibility of nonviolence, of peace.

Even inorganic matter becomes enchanted and militarized in the process, like in the female solo piece "La catedral de León," also on the album *Canto épico.* In a first-person narration the cathedral tells her story of how she joined the fight in the battle for León in 1979. The righteousness of the cause as well as the vulnerability of the *muchachos* makes the cathedral join. The sanctity of armed struggle moves even great stones: "I left behind my role as monument . . . and I became a militia combatant" ("abandoné mi rol de monumento . . . y me hice miliciana combatiente"). The cathedral becomes a fort for the *muchachos,* every stone protecting them. The cathedral comes to life and as a weapon of obstruction takes part in the war. This results in a new dawn, a revolutionary, enchanted modernity that envelops everything: the city, the animals, the air. The enchanted modernity transfigures the city, even its colonial baggage. The cathedral remembers that the air was full of rifles and songs, the colonial mansions overflowed with red and black flags, and swallows celebrated in her eaves. The envisioned modernity is always conceived as a colorful dawn, a paradisiacal place. From the grass to the rivers, the humming birds to the armadillo, from the rifle to the cathedral, both organic and inorganic matter converge in the grand enchanted-modernizing current of revolution. They bring about a societal state that is apparently cleansed of all wrongdoing, even of the violence required to reach this enchanted state. No longer do rifles shoot bullets but auroras and flowers.

## Militarism and the Elusiveness of Peace

Yet instead of an end of violence, the Sandinistas soon saw themselves in a war with several fronts: disgruntled ex-Sandinistas to the south, ex–National Guard financed by the United States to the north, and to the east, the resistance by indigenous groups such as the Rama, Miskito, and Sumo, who perceived the FSLN as an invading, colonizing force. Soon the country started to spend nearly half of its budget on weapons, and the militaristic logic that came with armed struggle started to permeate the public sphere: military parades, a vertical organization of society, and the nine commanders making up the Dirección Nacional who did not take off their uniforms. Part of the militarism can be explained by the external and internal aggression, but it was also a result of the militarism acquired during the insurgent years. The militarism that came with the direct violence in the Sandinista Revolution ended up undermining its utopian aspirations. Although influenced by the Cuban Revolution, the Sandinista discourse and poetics created their very own militarism, which utilized exuberant, poetic, and romanticized imagery to communicate bellicose content. The Marxist axiom that revolutionary violence is justified because it will lead to a nonviolent future needs certain narrative devices to appear feasible and convincing. In the Sandinista discourse these included the semantic transformation of violence as well as the sketching of the future society in poetic terms. Motivated and inspired by the urgency of the time and cause, music in part *created* this particular militaristic logic, in part *reflected* the sentiments of an epoch.

Ultimately, the songs show how in lyrical disguise militarism strolls in. The image of the corncob as a provider of innumerable bullets, the insurgent Ent-like trees, and the guerrilla troop of birds and butterflies are symptoms of the totalizing discourse of revolutionary violence. Poetic images that are used to convey the organic and spontaneous character of the armed struggle and to project the enchanted character of the envisioned project of modernity end up militarizing even nature. This project enlists nature, enchanting and totalizing war, and a militaristic logic starts to permeate all spheres of life: the rifle sleeping next to the children, the rifle as the only means for true, righteous politics, a paternalistic authoritative rhetoric of discipline clashing with the emancipatory, liberating spirit. And this militarism was present from early on.

This was not classical right-wing militarism but a left-wing guerrilla militarism. It appeared, for example, in the song "No se me raje mi compa" written by Carlos Mejía Godoy in 1974, a clandestine song, taped on cassette, not professionally produced and recorded until the 1980s (C. Mejía Godoy, "Interview"). It is probably his most bellicose song, exhibiting a violent militaristic logic and aesthetic. It speaks of different *muchachos,* among them Leonel Rugama, dressed in military green, determined and serene in their decision to fight for the *patria.* The refrain expresses this fierce determination through numerous, full-throated male voices that are only accompanied by clasps and few rhythmic chords on the guitar. It is a patriarchal war song, which tells men not to shrink back and not to be mediocre (*chusmón*).

The accordion in the bridge adds a certain nostalgia to the song, expressing a yearning for these saintlike, pure, and serene *muchachos,* who are already fey and not of this world anymore. These *muchachos* are determined in their will to sacrifice themselves. This determination is manifest both in confronting the enemy—uttering no other words during torture than affirming one's militancy and in confronting the supposed inner enemy. The last strophe reveals how in the discourse of armed struggle the militant is also expected to direct violence against oneself. The song references a saying often attributed to the Cuban communist Julio Antonio Mella (1903–1929), later popularized by Che Guevara: "If I advance, follow me; if I halt, push me; if I retreat, kill me" ("Si avanzo sígueme, si me detengo empujáme, si retrocedo mátame" (Cortés Camarillo). In the song the quotation is expanded and adapted to Nicaraguan Spanish through the use of *voseo.* This slogan has traveled much and undergone some strange transformations. The original quotation is attributed to Henri de la Rochejaquelein, a leader of the royalist, Catholic Vendeán insurrection after the French Revolution, who supposedly said: "My friends, if I advance, follow me! If I retreat, kill me! If I die, avenge me! ("Mes amis, si j'avance, suivez-moi! Si je recule, tuez-moi! Si je meurs, vengez-moi!") (Lescure 25). Later, it was attributed to Julio Antonio Mella. It also became the slogan of the Kaibiles—a feared, elite Guatemalan troop founded in 1975—the only alteration being from "push me" ("empújame") to "urge me on" ("aprémiame"), which according to one journalist is a code word for torture under the Kaibiles (Bardini). That the slogan could so easily travel from royalist to communist and from leftist guerrilla to right-wing, counterinsurgent elite troops, is startling and calls into question the Sandinista discourse of armed struggle as a sanctified act of love.

One could also argue that the appropriation by the Kaibiles is just another sign for the schizophrenic counterinsurgency techniques that demoralize by seizing the slogans of the other side. Landau, for example, was surprised to hear Carlos Mejía Godoy's "La tumba del guerrillero" playing on the Contra radio (262). Despite this very real possibility, Mella's slogan nonetheless holds a painful reminder of internal violence within the Left, as, for example, Salvadoran poet Roque Dalton being killed by his own comrades. As Jean Franco puts it: "The absurdity of Dalton's death continues to haunt the Left" (*Cruel Modernity* 133). The absolute military/guerrilla logic has no respect for human life, only for the higher cause and discipline. In this song it becomes clear that the engagement is absolute and the offering of one's life is the prerequisite for the sanctity of armed struggle. This means also putting oneself in the hands of one's controlling and purifying comrades. Here the comrades are the "network of surveillance" of a "disciplinary society" (Foucault 176, 218). They become the revolutionary Panopticon.

One, of course, needs to hear and analyze this music in context—in this case, that of a fight against a bloody dictatorship—but the music reveals not only the many tropes necessary to negotiate revolutionary violence but also the tensions and dangers imminent in popularizing a logic of armed struggle. Both Carlos and Luis Enrique Mejía Godoy stated that their songs were simply an expression of the moment, born out of it and a chronicle of it. Carlos affirmed that he had made war songs when the times had called for it and songs for peace when it was necessary to sing about peace (C. Mejía Godoy, "Interview"). Both brothers were very critical of the Servicio Militar Patriótico, the conscription during the 1980s. Luis Enrique stressed his utter disdain for firearms. Only when I pushed a little further did he marvel that he now claimed to hate weapons after having made songs like "Canción para un fusil"; however, he also reiterated the need for armed struggle as the only possible path under the Somoza dictatorship (L. E. Mejía Godoy, "Interview").

The music of the Mejía Godoys was first and foremost a music of guerrilla warfare, its structure of feeling is that of insurgency. When in the mid-1980s the revolutionary state had to continue to fight its own share of insurgent forces (the Contra), the influence of the music waned. This was due to a number of reasons: the economic crisis that affected consuming power, state support, and the quality of the recordings; war-weariness and revolutionary fatigue; an increasing disconnect of music concentrated mainly in the capital (Scruggs, "Politics of Erasure" 259; Scruggs, "Nicaragua" 764; Wellinga, *Entre* 109–111). The songs of the Mejía Godoy brothers produced a powerful tale of guerrilla and collective, popular warfare, in which the firearm was the primary tool for change. But instead of the rifle lightening the firmament with the new dawn, over the years the weapon became the despised symbol of a never-ending war and a revolutionary militaristic state that sapped the originally liberating spirit. The Sandinista Revolution yearned for enchantment but ended in profound disenchantment.

In 1985, Carlos Mejía Godoy published the album *Tasba Pri,* meaning "free land" in Miskito and also the name of the forced Sandinista relocation project in the Caribbean. It contains his most famous song about peace, "Cuando venga la paz." Based on a poem by Gioconda Belli, the song takes on the difficult task of imagining a future society of nonviolence amid the bloodiest years of the Contra War (Scruggs, "Legado"). It is sung from the perspective of two militant lovers. The lovers appear to be separated and dream of being reunited and of retiring to the mountain with their children. The promise is that they will finally be able to rest and that they will enjoy peace by dedicating themselves to long nights of love-making. This song uses idyllic, almost pastoral images of an enchanted nonviolent society, but the *sostenuto* style make them appear faint, like a washed-out postcard. Once peace reigns, the prairie will smile, the rivers will sing, and the roads will be covered in flowers. Once workers and peasants are in power, the lovers will finally be able to love each other in full liberty.

The song expresses a nostalgic longing for the future and for an end of violence—in particular, the end of war. The imagery and poetics move away from the militaristic images, and no weapons appear in the song. This song was written while the Sandinistas were still in power but here the revolution seems to be already in the past, ready to be memorized but not lived anymore. The song displays a war fatigue, but the lovers promise each other that they will tell their children how they got involved in the revolution and that they will sing the old guerrilla songs for them. In its celebration of its own revolutionary mystique—the war songs—the song foreshadows the nostalgic gesture of later memoirs of former revolutionaries, which keep certain discourse intact and do not question the violence at the core of armed struggle. Although the song is about obtaining peace, about nonviolence, the intense desire and nostalgic feel of the song make it appear to be an impossible dream. Enchanted modernity has become lost in reverie. The song is the promise of nonviolence, which, in repeating over and over again "Once peace comes" ("Cuando venga la paz"), appears to become ever more distant. Even the notion of the revolution as love-making has become fissured—the revolutionary lovers do not seem to be able to reach each other. The revolutionary discourse has reached its own impasse because it cannot fulfill its promise of nonviolence.

## CHAPTER 5

# HIDDEN ARSENALS

## DEMOBILIZED COMBATANTS AND THE POSTWAR STATE OF MIND

Throughout the 1990s hidden weapon caches were discovered across the Central American isthmus. Sometimes the arms were not properly stored and an explosion revealed the weapons depot. The most famous case was *el buzonazo*, when in 1993 a bomb went off in a warehouse in Managua. It revealed a secret weapon cache of the Salvadoran guerrillas, which factions who were distrusting the peace process had hidden in case they needed to take up arms again. During the 1990s more than a hundred such weapon depots, allegedly from the guerrillas, were discovered throughout the region (Kingma 7). The military also had its issues with its weapon storage sites. Reports abound of storage sites exploding or weapons being stolen or illegally sold and ending up in the drug war (Godnick 17; Proceso digital; Petrich; Proceso, "Hallan en El Salvador").

These arsenals allegorize the complexity and volatility of the postwar situation in Central America. Thousands of soldiers and guerrilla fighters in Nicaragua, El Salvador, and Guatemala were demobilized in the 1990s, tens of thousands of firearms rendered. Yet the vestiges of war remained: violence, trauma, individual and collective guilt, right-wing and left-wing militarism. Political processes often came up short in working through the complex legacy of the wars. In a context of widespread impunity, oftentimes it was fiction that offered "symbolic acts of reparation" by filling a void (A. P. Rodríguez, "Diasporic Reparations" 33). Yet not all postwar texts have wanted to fulfill that function. In fact, postwar literature has been accused of producing many depoliticized, easily consumable short novels, or nostalgic militant memoirs (Arias, *Taking Their Word* 21–25, 221). But it is also true that literature, maybe more than any other institution, has taken on the task of representing and reflecting on the pain, anger, and nostalgia of Central American postwar societies. For this endeavor, coming to terms with the metaphoric and literal soldier within society is key. Hence, ex-combatants and their arsenal have become a common figure in Central American postwar literature, to the point that I see the emergence of a new subgenre in the region: the demobilized combatant novel.

One of the most emblematic examples of this subgenre is the aptly titled *El arma en el hombre* (2001) by Horacio Castellanos Moya. The novel is about a demobilized soldier from the Salvadoran army named Robocop, who after the war works as a hired delinquent and security guard for several isthmian criminal organizations with links to the military. Another emblematic set is the novels *Managua, salsa city (¡Devórame otra vez!)* (2000) and *Y te diré quién eres (Mariposa traicionera)* (2006) by Franz Galich. These are about Pancho Rana, a demobilized soldier from the Sandinista army, who from private security guard turns into a private detective, delinquent, and avenger. In the violent aftermath of the wars, both characters roam Central America equipped with a heavy arsenal of grenades, assault rifles, and rocket launchers. The novels constitute an astute critique of the devastating and violent effects of neoliberal modernity, yet ultimately they eschew a thorough engagement with the legacy of militarism within society as a whole. In these novels with their action movie aesthetics the ex-combatants either remain abject citizens, Rambo-like killing machines, alien to the society that bore and trained them, or they retain the glorious halo of the figure of the *guerrillero*.

I contrast these novels with the short stories "La noche de los escritores asesinos" (1997) by Jacinta Escudos and stories from *De fronteras* (2007) by Claudia Hernández, which show more experimental approaches to the figure of the ex-combatant. Escudos's story is a bitter yet forceful inquiry into women's liberation and war as well as a critique of the (gender) violence in the guerrilla organization and lettered circles. Hernández's grotesque-fantastic stories omit any high-tech weaponry and instead leave the reader with the echoes of violence, with wounds, and desires for recognition and compassion.

## *The Postwar Battlefield: Weapons, Violence, and Discourse*

The armed conflicts of the 1970s and 1980s left militarized, disenchanted, and uprooted societies across Central America. More than three hundred people were killed and over two million displaced (Kurtenbach 95). Partly financed by outside powers, army sizes and defense spending had grown exponentially during the 1980s.[1] Following formal, political peace agreements in the three countries in which most of the fighting took place—1990 in Nicaragua, 1992 in El Salvador, 1996 in Guatemala—and a Democratic Security Treaty with Honduras in 1995, regular and irregular armed forces were demobilized, after which states and citizens began a process of disarmament. The peace agreements involved reducing armed forces that had more than quadrupled during the 1980s (Pearce, "From Civil War" 594) as well as demobilizing and disarming nonstate combatants.

In Nicaragua sixty-five thousand soldiers of the regular Sandinista army and twenty-three thousand Contras, the irregular reactionary combatants, were demobilized. By 2004 the Nicaraguan army, once ninety thousand soldiers strong, was reduced to sixteen thousand; it disarmed by selling part of its arsenal and air force. The Contras handed in an estimated 14,920 small arms, 4 heavy machine guns, 1,265 grenade launchers, 1,310 grenades, 138 mines, and 112 missiles—all of which were destroyed in situ (Wrobel and UNIDIR 31). In El Salvador thirty thousand members of the army and eight thousand of the guerrilla organization Frente Farabundo Martí para la Liberación Nacional (FMLN) were demobilized. In a decade-long standoff the FMLN had essentially become an army with a firepower comparable to that of the Salvadoran army (Castañeda 102). FMLN fighters surrendered 8,268 assault rifles, over 500 machine and submachine guns, 662 grenades launchers, 379 mortars and cannons, 74 missiles, 140 rockets, more than 9,000 grenades, and over 5,000 explosives (Godnick and Laurance 8). The disarmament process also involved the generally successful clearance and destruction of more than 9,000 landmines laid by the FMLN (Godnick and Laurance 8, 27-28). However, factions of the FMLN did not trust the truce and were reluctant to give up their arsenal, which led to the aforementioned existence of many hidden weapon depots mostly in Nicaragua and El Salvador.

In Guatemala twenty-four thousand so-called military commissioners and approximately thirty-six hundred guerrillas of the Unidad Revolucionaria Nacional Guatemalteca (URNG) were demobilized. The URNG in Guatemala was the smallest of the Central American guerrillas and never well armed. In 1997 the fighters turned in 1,665 small arms including assault rifles and light machine guns, 159 crew-served weapons, 147 grenades, 1,390 mines, 934 bombs and rockets, and 1,720 kilograms of explosives.[2] Despite these returns, 642 combatants never showed and never surrendered their weapons (Godnick and Laurance 26). In 1996 the Guatemalan government agreed to reduce the armed forces by a third (Kingma 2). However, it was not until 2004 that steps were taken to downsize the army from 27,000 to 15,500 members and to cut military spending (Rogers 13).[3]

Some assistance in the form of money or reintegration programs was provided to the demobilized combatants but that does not mean that demobilized combatants have found a place in society. For many, finding employment in war-torn countries has not been easy. Some ex-combatants organized themselves in veteran groups, providing mutual support and demanding social assistance, at times bridging former political divides. Others, especially in Nicaragua during the 1990s, rose up in arms again in the form of *recompas*, *recontras*, or *revueltos* (both sides mixed together).[4] Other ex-combatants have found employment in the private security sector, which has grown exponentially due to the heightened security concerns of the population. In fact, by 2000 private security officers exceeded those of the public sector in all Central American countries (Godnick 3). Unresolved structural problems such as poverty and inequality, exacerbated by widespread implementation of neoliberal policies following the wars and an increased influx of local and transnational crime, fueled a violent environment on the isthmus. The guerrilla and counterinsurgent wars have given way to new, far more diffuse wars and multifaceted violence (Kurtenbach 95; Pearce, "From Civil War" 589). At the same time, the increased news coverage about crime has heightened the sense of insecurity among Central Americans (Moodie 96; Oettler 27–28).

While the old arsenals have not been completely eliminated, new weapons are pouring into the region. In fact, arms imports have increased in the past decade (Godnick and Laurance 20; World Bank 21). The number of small and light arms circulating in the region appear high—estimates range from 1.3 million to 4.5 million—yet Central American nations are by far not as armed as other nations (Kurtenbach 104; Godnick 4; World Bank 20).[5] However, both the presence of military-grade weaponry, in particular grenades, as well as the disproportionately high number of intentional homicides are what makes the presence of this weaponry a severe security problem.[6] Statistics for intentional homicide per one hundred thousand inhabitants are consistently high by global comparison, especially in Honduras, Belize, El Salvador, and Guatemala, and in El Salvador, Guatemala, and Honduras 70 percent of homicides are committed with firearms (UNODC, *Crime and Development in Central* America, 16). It appears that the early 1990s were more impacted by the war vestiges, while the 2000s were more impacted by narcoviolence (Godnick vii, 25; World Bank 12, 15, 32). The *Global Study on Homicide* from the United Nations Office on Drugs and Crime (UNODC) finds that "there was a steady decline in homicide rates in Central America from 1995 to 2005, [but that] the subregion has experienced a sharp increase in the homicide rate since 2007" (25), indicating that the growing drug trade is indeed an enormous factor fueling the current violence.[7] Contrary to common perception, the threat by youth gangs is largely exaggerated. While their numbers are high (estimates range from sixty-nine thousand to five hundred thousand) and they are perceived as an enormous threat by the population, they are less organized then generally assumed and they account for only a small percentage of the region's crime, and little evidence exists of their involvement in the international drug trade (Kurtenbach 105; World Bank 59–62).[8] Among social scientists describing the situation, it has become common to speak of "social violence" or a widespread diffuse "culture of violence" in comparison to the former political violence, pointing to the high levels of violence without a clear political motive, such as economically motivated or domestic violence (Duhalde 93; Godnick vii, 11, 18, 29; Pearce "From Civil War" 591, 608). The risk with such affirmations seems to me to be that, as an analytical category, "culture of violence" is both vague and reminiscent of older criminological approaches about the innate criminality or violence of a population. Sabine Kurtenbach has written that "even in war, violence is not just instrumental for the 'master cleavage' (that is, the conflict patterns at the macro-level) but resembles a mixture of privatized, economic and political forms of violence at the micro level" (103). Ellie Moodie has further criticized the discursive whitewashing of violent acts in El Salvador, which makes it appear as if present violence has no relation whatsoever to previous conflicts and simply results from "'common,' everyday, domestic concerns" (89).

Instead, approaches that view the current violence in relation to the previous violence seem more adequate for describing the current situation. Castellanos Moya predicted in 1993 that "without a transformation of the social and political structures, without a redistribution of income, war will find new manifestations" ("sin una transformación de las estructuras sociales y políticas, sin una redistribución del ingreso, la guerra encontrará nuevas manifestaciones" (quoted in Kokotovic, "Neoliberalismo" 206). In the current violence several issues overlap and resurface: remnants of the prewar violence (such as authoritarianism and white/mestizo racism), war violence and trauma, as well as the ongoing negative effects of exploitative geopolitics and transnational market politics. As such, what ails Central America is not a "culture of violence" or "social violence" but a violence of unresolved political, social, economic, and historic problems.

Looking at this violence as one of unresolved issues means placing more analytical power on the topic of militarization—a society's permeation with military values and attitudes. The military has indeed played an important role in Central America. As Kurtenbach has pointed out, Central American armies "traditionally have been the central pillar of the state as—side by side with the Catholic Church—they used to be the only national institution with a presence in most of the territory and control of the rural areas" (103). When guerrillas rose against military right-wing governments, they deepened processes of militarization from the left. Dirk Kruijt, in an extensive study of Central American guerrilla movements that draws on interviews with over seventy former guerrilla commanders, comes to the conclusion that "it is the soldier in them that prevails" (75). When he asked about their final evaluation of the guerrilla years, most commanders talked less about the achievements or defeats in relation to former ideals. Instead, they recalled war maneuvers and heroic acts, insisting that they could still teach the army a trick or two. Part of this seems to point to a "will to elude the defeat" (Avelar, *Untimely Present* 21), yet it also points to a heavily militarized conception of politics. What prevails are not ideals but battle tactics.

This is where literature comes into play. Arturo Arias has noted in many Central American postwar texts a similar "ethical refusal to assimilate the past, assimilate the dead, assimilate the political defeat within a coherent and explicative historical narrative" ("rechazo ético a asimilar el pasado, asimilar a los muertos, asimilar la derrota política, dentro de una narrativa histórica coherente y explicativa" ("Post-identidades" 122). Arias, in this critique, uses Sergio Ramírez's historical fictions as an example, and many militant memoirs could be added to this category. Memoirs and historical fictions tend to take on a nostalgic or escapist tone. Yet simultaneously a more angry, scathing, and experimental fiction emerged that explored "the (im)possibilities of human coexistence *with* the violence" ("las [im]posibilidades de la convivencia humana *con* la violencia") (Ortiz Wallner and Mackenbach 82, italics in the original). Fiction, as opposed to the testimonial voices and the realist register predominant during the revolutionary times, has made a powerful return in current Central American literature (Ortiz Wallner; Shea). Generally this literature, often referred to as postwar literature, explores the full potential of fiction and is associated with such writers as Horacio Castellanos Moya, Jacinta Escudos, Rodrigo Rey Rosa, Claudia Hernández, and Franz Galich, among others.[9] Both the nostalgic-escapist memoirs and historical fictions as well as the disenchanted-furious and at times cynical short stories and novels make up the two sides of the current complex and prolific literary production on the isthmus. One recurrent topic is the demobilized militant or combatant. Chapter 3 discussed two such autobiographical postwar accounts by former militants, Gioconda Belli and Sergio Ramírez; this chapter explores examples of postwar fiction, focusing on a particular subgenre that I call the demobilized combatant novel. This subgenre has the following thematic characteristics: (1) at least one of the protagonists is a demobilized combatant, from either right-wing or left-wing factions, often special forces; (2) the protagonists' relationship with their weapons figures prominently in the narrative; (3) some kind of trauma manifests itself in the narrative, which is either addressed or ignored; (4) the text has a transnational or postnational scope, meaning that the plot either involves several countries, diasporic communities, and border crossings or the nation is no longer an important category; (5) negative passions such as wrath and revenge are prevalent in the protagonists; (6) phallocentric, aggressive heteronormative sexuality and masculinity predominate in the texts; and (7) the plot features drug trafficking and delinquency—in particular, criminal elites.

Formal and structural characteristics in the subgenre include a noticeable orality, created through colloquial registers and the use of mainly monologues and dialogues, which create a sense of immediacy and of access to the mind(set) of the demobilized combatant. There is also an action-movie aesthetic or recurring references to this type of movie; the novels often end in a violent showdown or face-off. These texts share many characteristics with the *novela negra* or *nueva novela policíaca latinoamericana*—often the demobilized soldier is the new "detective" revealing conspiracies.[10] Examples of this kind of novel abound.[11]

## Weapon and Man: Tools and Allegories of the Postwar Period

Whereas Gioconda Belli nostalgically remembers those days when she carried a rifle, in these demobilized combatant novels, the protagonists still rely on their weapons in the postwar period to make a living and to engage in delinquent and insurgent action. The demobilized combatants continuously return to and amass heavy weapon arsenals; weapons are their tools of the trade. Meanwhile, the demobilized soldiers themselves are allegories of war time and postwar violence, human weapons, tropes of a violence of unresolved conflicts and the legacy of militarism. The short novel *El arma en el hombre* is told in first-person by a demobilized soldier named Robocop. Being 190 centimeters (about 6 feet 2 inches) tall and sturdy, he was recruited by force to the Salvadoran army, where he quickly moved up to special forces and became a sergeant. After being demobilized, he is left with a severance check and a few weapons he hid during the war. He gets involved in a demobilized combatant group demanding indemnization.

With a friend Robocop starts stealing cars, until a former mayor, Linares, hires them for special operations. They carry out assassinations under the pretense that these are army orders, although they are in fact assignments by private individuals and crime circles. Since his assassination of a former guerrilla commander results in a public outcry, Robocop has to go into hiding and becomes part of the private security detail of a rich landowner in Guatemala, working alongside former Kaibiles, Guatemalan special forces. He returns to El Salvador shortly thereafter, but the police are on his trail, and they capture and torture him. Linares's contacts liberate Robocop but subsequently try to kill him because he has become a liability. He manages to escape the assassination and leave the country, ending up as a guard at a poppy plantation along the Guatemalan-Mexican border with former Salvadoran guerrillas. The novel ends with a massive attack on the plantation by security forces. Robocop, gravely injured—a piece of shrapnel having torn off part his face—is offered a new identity, new body, and new job as a special-ops agent by a Chicano DEA officer, formalizing and finalizing his conversion into a mercenary and cyborg.

Taken together, *Managua, salsa city* and *Y te diré quién eres* have all the elements of demobilized combatant novel. The plot of *Managua, salsa city* takes place during a single violent night in Managua and involves continuous deceit. A woman and a man meet at a bar and pretend to be people they are not: Guajira, a prostitute and gang member, pretends to be a guileless girl; Pancho Rana, former special ops of the Sandinista army, pretends to be rich by using the belongings of the couple for whom he works as a security guard. They fall in love without wanting to but are soon attacked by Guajira's gang (led by an ex-Contra) and then by a group recently returned from Miami who want to rape Guajira. A shootout ensues and it seems like the only survivors are Guajira and the Miami returnee Cara de Ratón, who gets to keep Guajira and the diamonds that Pancho Rana was trying to steal.

The sequel, *Y te diré quién eres*, is a more structurally complex novel, with a plot that develops over a longer period of time, told through different characters and perspectives. The reader discovers that Pancho Rana survived the attack. He tries to recover Guajira, who is raped several times by Cara de Ratón and then partners up with her rapist and becomes a pimp and leader of a human-trafficking ring in Central America. It turns out that the rich American-Nicaraguan couple with ties to the Somoza regime (for which Pancho Rana has been working since *Managua, salsa city*) makes their money from smuggling diamonds. Rana manages to convince them that he heroically defended their home against a group of robbers, so they keep him on their payroll as bodyguard and detective. Officially, Rana is in charge of recovering the diamonds stolen in the first novel, but he uses his position to try to find Guajira. His search takes him through several Central American countries, at times in the company of different allies: the transvestite Chobi-Xaquira and a new comrade-in-arms El Brujo, an ex-guerrilla from Guatemala. Rana never finds Guajira; instead his quest uncovers a political-economic network of criminal elites. The novel ends with a spectacular showdown: simultaneous attacks on the Nicaraguan Congress, an airplane, and the US embassy—carried out by six demobilized combatants.

Weapons define the protagonists of these demobilized combatant novels. After the peace agreements, weapons are the only things Robocop has left: two AK-47s, one M-16, eight grenades, magazines, and a pistol. Weapons frame his entire possible range of action, he cannot imagine himself beyond weapons. Robocop's weapon arsenal, although lost at times, is the only constant in the novel—in contrast to his changing employers and his chaotic zigzag through Central America full of blurry political signs. He quickly acquires new firearms. He carries weapons with him in a backpack, always returns for them, and, fearing an imminent attack on the plantation, sleeps with an AK and a radio-transmitter hugged to his body. Rana's relationship with firearms is a central element too. The final battle in *Managua, salsa city* involves revolvers, rifles, and grenades, and in Y *te diré quién eres*, he is constantly obtaining new weapons and accessing old hidden weapon caches. The coordinated attacks at the end of the second novel involve assault rifles, grenade launchers, mortars, and even surface-to-air missiles.

The postwar is presented as a battlefield with omnipresent violence and a neoliberal logic of precarization: the State is absent and one single entrepreneurial ideology prevails. In the neoliberal postwar era, Robocop and Pancho Rana are left to fend for themselves and thus they rely on the only skill set they know: the use of weapons of destruction and surveillance. Weapons have lost the connotation of political artifacts; they appear foremost as tools of these "violence workers" (Huggins, Haritos-Fatouros, and Zimbardo). They only occupy a position not alienated from their labor when they act out of their own accord as avengers. Since the state offered little to no support, private security, crime, or transformation into a mercenary are their only options. Quite pragmatically and dynamically, Robocop adapts to the new times and sells his labor on the transnational market. He offers his services in El Salvador and Guatemala and ends up in the United States. Galich's novels also depict a neoliberal universe of poverty, inequity, and political neglect. This context has all figures trying to make it on their own—through the use of violence (Kokotovic, "After the Revolution" 26; Gianni). Pancho Rana dabbles with insurgency, precarious labor, and criminality. He works as a private guard, a detective, and kidnapper. El Brujo in Y *te diré quién eres* follows a similar trajectory; the former *guerrillero* first works in the sale of hidden war arsenals, then in private security, and then in kidnapping, until he joins Rana in his plan for revenge. The use of weaponry corresponds mainly to an economic logic.

### The Disavowal of the Language of Revolution

The violence of the war years and its ideological justifications now appear devoid of political meaning. The three novels continuously mock the political language of the war, speaking from the depths of the Central American postwar *desencanto*. The notion of *desencanto* has often been used to describe

Central America in the postwar period. For war-fatigued and suffering societies, the end of the wars meant relief. Yet it also meant that a period of hope—that the century-old patterns of inequality, injustice, and exploitation could change—came to a bitter end. As Jean Franco puts it: the "end of the utopian is a mild way of describing what has been lived in much of Latin America as historical traumas, in the aftermath of which both politics and culture have been irrevocably dislocated" (*Decline and Fall* 260). In Central America these ruptures and shifts were particularly dramatic.

In *El arma en el hombre* the postwar period produces strange inversions of roles: the former counterinsurgent soldiers mobilize themselves to fight for unfulfilled indemnity rights. Robocop at first is reluctant to affiliate himself with these social movements, since he distrusts any revolutionary rhetoric that in his eyes is "subversive" or "terrorist." He joins them nonetheless and repeatedly appropriates symbols of the left. In a symbolic occupation of the Congress by a group of demobilized combatants, Robocop—ex-military, reactionary, brutal, racist—dons a ski mask like the Zapatistas from Chiapas, which creates a media flurry (Castellanos Moya, *El arma* 21). Then, during a mission in Guatemala, he yells "Let your mother surrender" ("Que se rinda tu madre"; 94), which is precisely what the Nicaraguan poet-*guerrillero* Leonel Rugama yelled before dying, riddled by bullets by the National Guard in 1970. This is the bizarre new postwar world order: the reactionary soldier apparently turned into the new guerrilla. The novel thus slyly insinuates that perhaps both sides were not that different to start with.

Not only the political language of the left is in crisis; that of the right is too—at least partially. Robocop barely ever speaks of homeland or honor. The absence of these essential military codes puts their validity into question. Being demobilized meant to go from exemplary citizen, the soldier as "defender of the homeland" in the militarist-nationalist discourse, to abject citizen, discarded and rejected. Robocop's acts are not too different from those committed during the war, but the signs have changed. The waning importance of *la patria* shows that the nation as category has lost importance and leaves the door open to become a true mercenary. The only language that remains intact is the seemingly apolitical language of counterinsurgency. It continues to work as a justification of Robocop's own violence—he only speaks of subversives and terrorists. However, as William Castro has observed, Robocop's actions constantly undermine his anti-terrorism discourse, since he is the terrorist of the story (127).

Robocop denies any interest in politics (16), yet he is a man marked by military ideology. His worldview consists of enemies, surveillance, *la ley del más fuerte*, discipline, and action. He is a man of actions rather than words, and his conception of politics is that it is just "wordiness" ("palabrería"; 19). He thus presents a military worldview that sees itself above politics. Brian Loveman and Thomas Davies have argued that Latin American militaries always conceived of "politics" as a problem that the military could fix by imposing its rule (3). According to the military, only an end of politics—understood as "conflict among personalist factions and later, political parties over ideological formulas and the spoils of rule"—could bring stability and development (3). The military saw itself above politics, because it only had the best interest of the fatherland in mind.

Since Robocop's identity hinges upon a militaristic logic, demobilization was his own personal process of disenchantment. It left him adrift. He yearns to go back to the stability that the military routine provided. In his postwar employments, Robocop finds his own military-pastoral idyll, when he guards the poppy plantation together with former guerrilla fighters—again, the novel's iconoclastic gesture suggesting the guerrilla and army might not be so different after all. The poppy plantation is described as an enchanted homosocial idyll, where Robocop seems to find some tranquility after all the turmoil. He describes it as a dreamlike place amid the clouds where trees and magical flowers abound, where he lives his second military life: daily training, a clear routine, surveillance (86). There is in him a desire to return to the previous order of the military life: "Once I had the rifle in my hands, running, following the orders of command, I started to feel warm. At last I managed to be again what I had desired. I was not in shape, but that did not matter either" (86).[12] The attack on the plantation by US forces is his personal expulsion from paradise.

In Galich's novels the political language of the wars is in crisis, too. Instead of a paradisiacal new dawn promised by the Sandinista discourse, Nicaragua appears as a hellish battlefield, where nothing has changed: "here in hell, I mean, Managua, everything is still the same: the panhandling, glue-sniffing boys, the sissies and the whores, the pimps and the politicians, the thieves and the police (who are the same as the politicians, be it sandinards or liberards or conservatards, christiards or whateverthefuckards, sonsofbitches partners of the Devil)" (2).[13] The ideologies that have defined the history of Nicaragua matter no more; the struggles in their name were meaningless endeavors; the poor are still poor, and only the rich benefited. *Managua, salsa city* itself represents a national allegory, in which Guajira is Nicaragua, the coveted nation, and both sides, Sandinistas and Contras, die in an attempt to save her or possess her. Those who get to keep the loot are members of the oligarchy who had fled to Miami after the triumph of the Sandinista Revolution (Gianni).

The sequel *Y te diré quién eres* contains multiple diatribes against "that stupid war" ("esa guerra estúpida") and against the elites who got rich through the revolution while the poor were left in misery (49, 93, 168, 178). Pancho Rana's reaction is pure sarcasm when he sees the Monument to the Popular Combatant, the giant statue in Managua of a brawny man raising an AK-47 toward the sky, irreverently renamed "Big Doll" ("el Muñecón") or "Hulk." Rana mocks the inscription of this statue that reads: "Only workers and peasants will go until the end." He exclaims: "Whatever! Of course, only the workers and the peasants went until the end, but the end of the world—that is because they were left knackered in the very end: dead, wounded, mutilated, or crazy, and the worst of it all, in misery, because where we were left, there is only hell" (48).[14] He makes fun of the military authoritarianism of the Sandinistas by changing the call-and-response "National Direction—command us!" ("Dirección Nacional—ordene!") to "National Direction—milk!" ("Dirección Nacional—ordeñe!")—achieved through converting the "n" to a "ñ" (48). Similarly, the Patriotic Military Service (Servicio Militar Patriótico), the controversial obligatory military service implemented by the Sandinistas in the 1980s, is derided by referring to sex work as "Patriotic Sexual Service" ("Servicio Sexual Patriótico," 82).

Rana, in contrast to Robocop, does not appropriate symbols of the neo-Zapatistas but wants nothing to do with them: "No, I'm no longer interested in any of that, I give a rat's ass about the Zapateros, now it's just me and what's in my pocket" ("No, a mí ya no me interesa nada de eso, me vale un saco de turcas los Zapateros, ahora soy sólo yo y lo que tengo en la bolsa"). He disavows the ideologization of armed struggle. Of the last attack that closes _Y te diré quién eres_, he says: "No, guys, this is nothing political, that's over, that belongs in the past. This is, simply and purely, revenge" ("No hombres, esto no es nada político, eso ya pasó, pertenece al pasado. Es simple y crudamente, una venganza") (Galich, _Y te diré_ 169, 187–88). Yet despite these declarations, the final act of revenge is an insurgent act—a collective revolt against authority that involves coordinated attacks against the embassy and the Congress, targets similar to those of the Sandinista commandos in the 1970s. This leaves the reader with the blurry (a)political signs of the postwar period.

The actions of Robocop and Pancho Rana constitute a form of precarious, violent semipolitical acts of survival, anger, and revenge. Political ideology is generally absent or mocked in their discourse. The only thing that remains from the wars are the weapons, the actual firearms, and these two men: human killing machines.

## The Human Weapon as Problematic Allegory

Firearms appear as mere tools, devoid of any political meaning, yet the figures of Robocop and Pancho Rana—the humans who have become weapons—do have a symbolic function. They are personified allegories of war and postwar violence as well as militarism. In both cases, noms de guerre have taken over their previous self. Only once does the reader find out their civilian name: Juan Garcia Peralta in the case of Robocop, and Francisco de Jesús González Macís, in the case of Chico Chú, alias Pancho Rana, alias Pancho Sapo, alias the Nicaraguan and Central American Rambo (Castellanos Moya, *El arma* 69; Galich, *Y te diré* 23, 40 130–31, 136, 139). In both cases 1980s movies about the US military police state are the reference points for their war names: *RoboCop* (1987) and the Rambo character from *First Blood* (1982). These nicknames synthesize their allegorical function and meaning as war machines, underscore the novels' action movie aesthetic, and point to the political and cultural exportation of US militarist culture. From its title and paratext, Castellanos Moya's novel clearly announces itself to be a novel about "the weapon in the man." The cover contains a photograph of the futurist statue *Unique Forms of Continuity in Space* (*Forme uniche della continuità nello spazio*, 1913) by Italian sculptor Umberto Boccioni. Violent, strong, angular, dynamic, and cast in bronze, it is a statue of a superhuman, its bellicosity indicated through a headgear resembling a soldier's helmet, while its massive thighs move forward with determination. An example of the fascination with war and technology of Italian Futurism, the statue is a menacing figure of a machine being, an expression of pure action and barely contained violence.

This idea is continued in the novel's epigraph: "In the spear I have my black bread, in the spear my Ismarian wine, and I drink reclined on the spear" ("En la lanza tengo mi pan negro, en la lanza mi vino de Ismaro, y bebo apoyado en la lanza"). This is a fragment of a poem by Archilochus (711–664 BC) about the experience of a mercenary. It announces the idea of a violence worker, he who earns his bread with a weapon. It alludes to the possible symbiosis between weapon and man, to the point that the weapon becomes his prosthesis and he cannot live without it. All his activities happen supported by, reclined onto the weapon, intoxicated with it. Robocop only exists through the weapon. The novel is an intent to imagine and visualize this man, who lives reclined on his weapon arsenal; it is an attempt to face the war, violence, and the militarism he represents.

Castro has argued that *El arma en el hombre* is marked by a radical gesture. The work presents the reader with the most unlikely *testimonio*: that of a right-wing soldier. The *testimonio* was the dominant genre of committed literature in the 1980s in Central America.[15] Castellanos Moya has declared that he dislikes the *testimonio* (Buiza 152), yet his literary opus is marked by an ongoing negotiation with the genre from *El asco* to *Insensatez*. *El arma en el hombre* also produces a complex revision of *testimonio*, since it shares a number of characteristics with the controversial genre. Robocop narrates in the first person, in an oral style. He speaks from a state of emergency—that of the postwar—not unlike the "urgency" (Yúdice 44) or "state of emergency" (Beverley, "Real Thing" 281) that scholars have identified as key factors in the speech act of the *testimoniante*. Although Robocop insists on not wanting to talk, he nonetheless tells his story several times. This speaks of an irrepressible urgency to tell his story. Robocop is a traumatized victim of violence and, as other *testimoniantes* before him, tells his story to survive, since the narration we read appears to be the account he gives the DEA in order to save his life (Cortez *Estética* 92).

Yet from the beginning, the novel problematizes the testimonial subject and breaks with the conventions of the genre. First, it is a *testimonio* of someone who does not want to stand in his singularity for a broader collective: "I just want to make it clear that I am not your average demobilized [combatant]" ("nada más quiero dejar en claro que no soy un desmovilizado cualquiera") (Castellanos Moya, *El arma* 11). This is the opposite of "an affirmation of the individual self *in a collective mode*" (29), which is an element Beverley once identified in his provisional definition of the *testimonio* in "The Margin at the Center" (1989). The text does not present the reader with a typical or expected *testimoniante*: a subaltern, oppressed, or revolutionary subject—a woman, a child, a victim of violence, or a political activist such as Omar Cabezas. Robocop is both victim and perpetrator of violence. While *testimonios* of reactionary forces exist—as, for example, *Una tragedia campesina: Testimonios de la resistencia* (mentioned in chapter 3)—here the reader is faced with the apparent *testimonio* of an extremely violent, remorseless right-wing ex-soldier. As Castro has illustrated, the novel thus confronts *testimonio* criticism "with what would be (one of) its *abject* subjects" (123). The novel gives voice to a testimonial subject, from whom a left-leaning audience does not want to hear.

Given his violent impositions, it is hard to see Robocop as a subaltern, but he is often the subaltern within the story. His subalternity manifests itself in the precarious constitution of his subjectivity; he is unable to guarantee his own subjectivity since it hinges upon the military institution (Cortez, *Estética* 95). Even though Robocop desperately claims, "I'm not an ignorant peasant, like most of the troop" ("No soy un campesino bruto, como la mayoría de la tropa" (*El arma* 10), since, as he argues, he was born in the capital and went to school until eighth grade, the elites and military use his lack of education to manipulate him in a paternalistic manner. The elites use but despise him. He walks up to the office of one of the bosses from criminal elites "under the condescending gaze of elegantly-dressed executives and secretaries" ("ante la mirada despectiva de ejecutivos y secretarias elegantemente vestidos"; 104). The paternalism of the names of his bosses (*tío* and *don*) underscores the feudal-capitalist power relations between them and him (Castro 127). Most importantly, he is eternally subaltern because of his military grade: "By literalizing 'subalternity' in the figure of Robocop, the soldier-for-hire, the novel refashions the idea of 'subalternity' as a category through which the *testimonio* is built, disconnecting from its association with leftist political agendas" (Castro 132).

The novel thus deconstructs the figure of the subaltern as merely a projection for the left. Castro sees an extraordinary push for inclusion in the novel: "By incorporating the radically differentiated Other—in a word the *abject* of *testimonio* criticism—the novel instantiates solidarity *in itself*. . . . this strategy insists on 'solidarity' as an instrument of *radical inclusion*, of unification across difference, and not merely across sameness or political affinity" (124, italics in the original). In Castro's reading, the blurring of signs is not a cynical stance but rather a sign of the radically inclusive gesture of the text: "Thus, the subaltern or revolutionary subject of *testimonio* is not entirely absent from this narrative. Rather, he is displaced; re-placed *within* the figure of Robocop, more important, *interwoven* with it" (133, italics in the original). Castro argues that the novel blurs the lines between real and representational subalternity (128) and that it "resituates or reformulates . . . the figure of the testimonial subject by converting it into an *alias*" (131). In his reading, Robocop is just an alias—not meant to represent anything "real."

This is where I differ from Castro. Precisely this alias-like, stereotypical representation undermines the radical proposal of the novel. There is no humanity and complexity in this character. Castellanos Moya seems unable or unwilling to imagine the militarist, right-wing Other as a genuine subject that truly has humanity. Robocop is one-dimensional, a character originally from another novel, *La diabla en el espejo* (2000), where he appears as the hired assassin of Olga María, a member of the Salvadoran high society. There he is described as "a tall, brawny guy, a whopper, who didn't wear beard or mustache, with his hair short, as if he were a cadet . . . he walked like Robocop, that police robot that you can see on TV" (*La diabla*, 16).[16] Later he is described as "a raging lunatic who doesn't know how to do anything other than killing" ("energúmeno que lo único que sabe hacer es matar") (*La diabla*, 35). In *El arma en el hombre* Robocop barely evolves from this first description in *La diabla*.

Maybe the point is precisely that there is no depth to the soldier, that he is pure action, that humanity has been brainwashed out of him. Yet this seems a proposition too simple both in terms of literature and politics. The reader does not learn much about Robocop before he became Robocop, so his perversion and inhumanity do no generate a sense of true tragedy and loss. While the brief reference to training in the School of the Americas implies that he was taught brutal counterinsurgent methods, we do not learn about his training, nor who or how he was before. Although we get a sense of his trauma, we never get to know Juan García Peralta.[17] He is as unknown as the little peasant man who hands Sergio Ramírez an old rifle in a demobilization ceremony in San Carlos.

The movie *RoboCop* is about the internal fight between human and machine. Whereas in the film the cyborg's humanity saves him, in the novel the use of the name Robocop primarily serves the purpose of highlighting his lack of humanity. Donna Haraway has argued that the cyborg myth can be a creative space from which to reimagine society. In *El arma en el hombre*, however, Robocop is not a complex cyborg in which machine and human are in an eternal struggle, but just an inhuman(e) killing machine. This is what ultimately undermines the radical proposal of the novel.

The representation of Pancho Rana is different. He expresses anger, enjoys life, is ingenious and skilled with words. This is one of the greatest contrasts in the constitution of both figures. While Robocop is monosyllabic and restrained, the language of Pancho Rana and his brothers in arms is exuberant, imaginative, full of puns. Also subaltern, and used and abused by the criminal elites of Central America, Rana tends to follow his own agenda. He uses his assignments to settle war and postwar scores. Yet he is similarly marked by war and weaponry. Rana yearns for the times of war—"a time when he felt powerful with his folding AKA, the magazines, and his Makarov" ("una época en la que se sentía poderoso con su Aka plegable, los magazines y su Makarov") (Galich, *Managua* 26).

The reference to Rambo underscores that Rana is a war machine but also that he is a traumatized, misunderstood, discarded veteran. The Rambo played by Sylvester Stallone is a manifestation of the Vietnam war in the United States, and his figure is neither a clear defense nor condemnation of war. In fact, particularly in the first film, *First Blood* (1982), the argument is more complex than usually associated with the Rambo figure. The first film is about a Vietnam veteran harassed by the police in a small US town. He had come there to visit his brother of arms, who, without Rambo knowing, has died due to Agent Orange exposure. The harassment at the hands of the police triggers a flashback in Rambo, traumatized by torture endured as a prisoner of war. As a result, Rambo attacks the police officers and escapes to the forest. The subsequent war between fascist police officers and Rambo—a special-ops soldier trained in guerrilla and counterinsurgent warfare—results in the death of several police and destruction in town. The movie ends with Rambo, the war machine, sobbing on the shoulder of his former superior officer and saying that he is unable to adapt to civilian life and that nobody understands him. The film contains several common tropes of postwar narratives: the return of the combatant, the violent potential of the war veteran, the rejection of the latter by society. The movie underscores the trauma of the war veteran at the same time that, as Kathleen McClancy shows, it provides a troublesome acquittal of the atrocities committed during war by omitting Rambo's Vietnamese victims and converting him into the victim of the war (503–19).

Pancho Rana resembles the Rambo figure of the movie in that both are traumatized war veterans unable to adapt to civilian life. This shows the trauma of the demobilized combatant. Even though Pancho Rana, a former member of Sandinista special forces, can still kill in cold blood, the images of the war haunt him. He dreams of war and, during the attack to the residential home in Managua in the first novel, he merges images of the war into this postwar battle scene. Even when he has sex, he can only conceive of it in war metaphors (Galich, *Managua* 64, 84). His trauma also manifests in his physical reactions to violence—he sweats profusely.

The figure of Rambo resurrects the idea of insurgency and guerrilla warfare. The Rambo film series was an enormous and surprising success in war-torn Nicaragua in the 1980s. Even though the movies were not projected in theaters in Nicaragua, people flocked to watch them on video (Lancaster 191). Although the Contra War ravaged the country, the Nicaraguan youth were apparently eager to watch a Hollywood movie about an anticommunist war machine, murderer of Vietnamese guerrillas. This seems surprising at first sight, but is less so if one thinks of youth grown up in war times. Furthermore, Rambo fulfills many characteristics of the masculine guerrilla ideal emphasized by the Sandinista discourse: he has been trained in guerrilla methods and can survive in the mountains. In addition, in the movie Rambo represents a countercultural figure in the US context because of his "drifter" appearance.

Whereas Robocop is the ghost of counterinsurgency, Pancho Rana (alias the Central American Rambo) is the ghost of insurgency. The novel narrates that he was among the *recompas* who took up arms again in the 1990s—a reference to an actual attack on Estelí in 1993. Then he leaps toward insurgency again at the end of the second novel (Galich, *Y te diré* 58, 61, 186). Despite all the disillusionment imprinted in Galich's novels, the Sandinista guerrilla ideal is never fully deconstructed. Despite his sexist and violent flaws, Pancho Rana remains the hero of the narrative: the avenger who redeems the oppressed. Galich's novels quote several revolutionary songs by Carlos Mejía Godoy. Both *Managua, salsa city* and *Y te diré* make reference to the song

"No se me raje mi compa"—one of Carlos Mejía Godoy's most violent and militaristic songs (analyzed in previous chapters) (*Managua* 68; *Y te diré* 170). In the novels the song is an intertextual reference that moves between nostalgia and mockery. It underscores what the novel keeps intact: the ideal of a violent warrior masculinity. A certain nostalgia permeates Galich's novels: a hopefulness for the return of the hero, a desire to return to the times of the revolution—despite the initial statements about the Sandinistas being "partners of the Devil" ("socios del Diablo") (Galich, *Managua* 2). Pancho Rana dreamily pictures Guajira with a weapon on her shoulder ("armas al hombro"; 8)—not unlike the famous photograph of "La miliciana de Waswalito." He recalls the military parades of the Sandinistas of the 1980s with nostalgia: the artillery in formation, the rejoicing audience yelling, "One single army," and the feeling of power giving him goose bumps (62). Nostalgia and militarism are entwined.

In the representations of violence and militarism, Robocop and Pancho Rana ultimately turn out to be problematically allegorical figures. The novels condense part of the violent and militaristic history of Central America in the 1980s and 1990s in these single characters. This is evidently part of the literary configuration of these characters, but it poses a problem to the extent that it makes it appear as though one single violent individual can be responsible for the violence that has devastated the region during the war and postwar years. The Robocop figure amalgamates El Salvador's recent history. His battalion, named Acahuapa, resembles the infamous Batallón Atlácatl, responsible for several massacres during the war in El Salvador. He continues the bloodshed during the transition and the postwar periodl: the murder of the guerrilla commander Antonio Cardenal in 1991, just before the signing of the peace accords in El Salvador, and the assassination of a former guerrilla named Célis (Castellanos Moya, *El arma* 30, 38). The latter is reminiscent of the murder of Francisco Velis in 1993, gunned down as he dropped his daughter at kindergarten, which is generally viewed as a postwar settling of scores or as an attempt to destabilize the country. Then there is the trail of devastation Robocop leaves behind during his travels through Central America. In a similar vein, Pancho Rana appears solely responsible for violent acts during the war, insurgent violence of the *recompas*, and then a wave of postwar violence in Nicaragua, Honduras, El Salvador, and Guatemala. Thus the diffuse violence of the postwar period is placed on a few people. Both novels point to the criminal elites behind the demobilized combatants, but the direct violence emanates only from these few individuals. To individualize violence in such a manner exonerates society of its complicity and the collective guilt of war and its problematic legacy during the postwar period.

This also weakens the novels' critique of militarism. In the case of Robocop, the figure remains such a stereotypical war machine that the reader does not have to accept him and the violence and militarism he represents as an intimate part of society. No act of radical inclusion and solidarity is called for; instead, the *weapon in the man* can be safely stored in the action movie register, far away from the Self. In the case of Pancho Rana, the novel formulates a critique of militarism and authoritarianism by mocking the revolution's slogans but simultaneously presents a certain nostalgia for the revolution's militarist culture and for the figure of the redeemer of the oppressed. It is a contradictory take, and it cannot shake the militarism that accompanied armed struggle. In Castellanos Moya's novel the demobilized combatant is abject and remains abject. In Galich's novel, despite his extreme violence, the demobilized retains part of the halo of the heroic *guerrillero*. Both representations thus ultimately eschew a candid engagement with the pressing issue of militarism.

## Letters, Arms, and Gender Reloaded

When it comes to the arsenals of Central America's postwar literature, two topics resurface: the relationship between the intellectual and the man of arms and the relationship between gender and war. The demobilized combatant novels by Galich and Castellanos Moya establish an overlap between weaponry, military identity, and an aggressive heteronormative and misogynist identity. Robocop operates from a phallocentric, misogynist perspective wherein women are traitors and he is the virile man who discharges into disposable, female bodies. Robocop's hegemonic masculinity remains intact throughout; he is able to sexually perform even with the screaming Guadalupe, whom he detests. He is the penetrator and does not allow himself to be penetrated. Under threat of death he refuses to let the mistrustful plantation overseers check his rectum for surveillance devices. His masculinity is contrasted with that of the Mexican narcos, whom he describes as effeminate, weak, sentimental addicts who wear gold chains, carry lots of luggage, and use weapons decorated with gems.

Also in Galich's novels women primarily play the role of "whore" and "traitor," key tropes of misogyny—even though, as Vinodh Venkatesh has analyzed, there is room for some ambiguity (*The Body*, 101). Although the novels display some attempts to break the sexist, heteronormative frame—in *Managua, salsa city*, Guajira is the gang leader, and in *Y te diré quién eres*, the transvestite Chobi-Xaquira plays an important role—ultimately the figure of Pancho Rana reaffirms traditional gender roles.[18] The descriptions of sex are focused on phallic pleasure. In the beginning, Guajira seems to be an independent woman (Galich, *Managua, salsa city* 14), but throughout the narration she loses agency and ends up being an exploiter of women. Robocop and Rana share an "extreme masculinity" (Franco, *Cruel Modernity* 15). Both *El arma en el hombre* and *Y te diré quién eres* contain brutal scenes of women's murders. Robocop establishes a relationship with a prostitute named Vilma over the course of several months, but after encountering her again in Guatemala, sleeping with her, and telling her his story, he executes her without a second thought. Pancho Rana murders the prostitute Gata during intercourse: ejaculating inside her and breaking her neck.

"La noche de los escritores asesinos" in *Cuentos sucios* (1997) by Jacinta Escudos provides a powerful counternarrative to these misogynist scenes, albeit similarly violent. The almost forty-page text tells the story of Boris and Rossana, former guerrilla members and former lovers turned writers. The text simultaneously critiques militarism, epistemic intellectual violence, and the lack of gender equality in revolutionary and postwar Central America. In contrast to the demobilized combatant novels by Castellanos Moya, Galich, and others, Escudos's protagonists technically are not demobilized combatants because they left the armed organization of their own accord before the war had ended. Nonetheless, just like the other ex-combatants, they also needed to reinvent themselves professionally after leaving the guerrilla ranks. Yet, as the story suggests, this was easier for them than for Castellanos Moya's Robocop and Galich's Pancho Rana. They came from a different class in the first place—many guerrilla fighters in Central America were from educated, wealthier sectors—which facilitated their transition into legal, civilian employment. Having more social capital, Rossana and Boris do not become hired assassins or security guards; rather, they are able to find a less alienating and more prestigious and autonomous profession: writing.

As writers, they engage in a violent struggle to have their voices heard. Rossana starts a prolific writing career in exile and eventually returns to her home country. Upset at her success, Boris, also now a writer (yet by his own admission an unsuccessful and untalented one), returns to destroy Rossana. In the male-dominated lettered sphere, Boris's socializing skills—more than any literary talent—help him gain fame as a writer. After Rossana rejects him again, he badmouths her and closes off publication space for her. One day he forces himself into her home, revolver in hand, and tries to rape her. In the ensuing fight over the firearm he shoots her, a crime of which he is acquitted by claiming self-defense. The story ends with Rossana at his doorstop, revolver in hand, shooting him to put an end to this "ridiculous story" ("ridículo cuento"; 123).

This is the superficial plot but the complex structure of the text (including different voices and narrative levels) introduces several doubts into the narration. The story is framed and interrupted by a third-person narration as well as interpolated by another first-person narrative voice in italics. The main narrator appears to be Boris, who writes a short story about their relationship as if he were telling his story to his cell mate before his acquittal. His story is interspersed by annotations, diary entries, and comments that appear to be Rossana's. Yet these could also be part of Boris's overall short story in which he invents Rossana's thoughts about him, appropriating her voice. Most critics have read the main part as entirely Boris's fabrication (his voice and Rossana's imagined voice) and the third-person narration, which opens and closes the narration, as showing how Rossana ultimately reappropriates the narrative voice by killing Boris (Kokotovic, "After the Revolution" 43–45; Shea). Another reading views the whole story, including Boris's, as a fabrication created by Rossana, who would thus maintain control over the narration the entire time (Padilla 142). Given this uncertainty about narrative voices—the reader has to constantly wonder who is speaking/writing—one can only make a "tenuous and problematic reading" of the text (141).

Even though their transition into civilian life appears easier than that of Robocop and Pancho Rana, Escudos's story still depicts these individuals as heavily impacted by the war logic and its violence. Rossana, we learn, is not the woman's birth name but the nom de guerre that she kept even after leaving the guerrilla forces (Escudos 88). Both are individuals who in the postwar period still carry firearms with them and ultimately use violence to solve conflicts, even though their firearms and their violence are on a smaller scale than those of former special-ops soldiers. They do not have high-tech weapon caches, but just as for Robocop and Pancho Rana, the firearm continues to be their prosthesis: "Reflections of my days in the guerrilla, what can you do? One gets so used to go around carrying a weapon that one cannot do a thing without it. That piece of metal is part of your body, it is your hand, your partner, your guardian angel" (107).[19] Boris blames the ex-soldiers and ex-policemen for the current violence in his home country, but the ex-*guerrilleros* reveal themselves to be equally violent and still under the spell of the war (107).

Through the figure of Boris, heavily politicized masculinities such as the heroic *guerrillero*, the revered *letrado*, and the sensitive poet are all simultaneously dismantled and destroyed. Boris is a profoundly unlikable, self-involved character who is a far stretch from the idealized New Man. Escudos uses Rossana to deconstruct the romantic image of the austere *guerrillera*. According to Boris's narrative voice, Rossana was "authentically humble. Oh, how *fake* naïve, romantic, loyal, that is, all that you can imagine a movie or soap opera heroine to be, that's how she was. Noble. Repugnantly noble. I think she copied herself from fiction characters" (88, italics in the original).[20] The interjection of "fake" in italics can be interpreted as an annotation about her by Boris, as a comment by Rossana about Boris's depiction of her, or as a sly, cynical comment by Rossana about her guerilla austerity having been a phony performance. This skeptical gesture is repeated when Boris's account of Rossana as an idealistic, saintlike *guerrillera* is in the end commented by another voice in italics that says, "I must confess that all of this is not true" ("Tengo que confesarte que todo esto no es cierto"; 89). It is unclear who is speaking, yet what is certain is that the epic, self-sacrificing hero, whether feminine or masculine, has become a questionable entity in the postwar period.

The postwar society appears as inhabited by violent creatures moved not by higher ideals but by petty passions. Boris's and Rossana's relationship is "symptomatic of the violent and embittered period of transition" (Padilla 142). The militarized postwar society is also reflected in Boris's revenge fantasies. He thinks of insinuating an affair between Rossana and her former guerrilla commander so that his wife will have her shot. Similarly, Boris thinks of suggesting to a military officer, now a friend, that Rossana killed one of his relatives so that the officer will send the death squads after her. He imagines ways to make Rossana suffer: "Kill her, destroy her, beat her up, spit at her, degrade her . . . corner her, torture her, tear off her skin bit by bit, make her swallow the piss of the guards, be there standing, in a corner of the dungeon, while all the battalion's soldiers raped her" (112–13).[21] These horrid fantasies speak not only to his profound misogyny but also to the memory of the unspeakable violence committed during the state's counterinsurgent war. They speak to the collective trauma of a society in which brutal torture became the margin of possible experience and behavior.

Although the short story retains the memory of the atrocities committed by the right, the story is also reminiscent of one of the darkest episodes of the Salvadoran guerrilla: the brutal murder of Comandanta Ana María (Mélida Anaya Montes) in 1983 by her own comrades, followed by the suicide of Comandante Marcial (Cayetano Carpio). Cayetano Carpio commanded the Fuerzas Populares de Liberación (FPL), the most important FMLN faction, while Mélida Anaya Montes was second-in-command. They differed considerably in their political strategies: Anaya Montes wanted to incorporate into their program the possibility of a negotiated solution, to which Carpio was strictly opposed. He saw long-term war as the only possibility (Kruijt 64). During this internal power struggle, Anaya Montes was found dead in Managua, stabbed multiple times with an ice pick. The brutality of the murder was allegedly meant to suggest that the Salvadoran right had murdered her. However, the Sandinista investigation found Carpio to be behind the conspiracy to murder her, and he subsequently committed suicide. Conspiracy theories about these two deaths abound, and the entire affair was never fully clarified. The uncertainty of accounts and voices as well as the pettiness and brutality of the treatment among comrades echo in Escudos's story. Not only does the text point to the gender discrimination women suffered within the guerrilla; it also shows the power of direct and epistemic violence by conflating them: "Killing on paper is easy, he thinks . . . And when he tries to imagine how it would be, to in real life take a weapon, aim it at someone and shoot, in contrast to pressing the keys of the typewriter . . . he thinks it is not too different" (114–15).[22]

Both writing and violence are ultimately about power: "the revolver in my hand, absolute power over the entire world" ("el revólver en mi mano, poder absoluto de todo el mundo"; 115). In this story the *letrado* is not removed from the violence anymore; the revolver hides in the drawer of his writing desk (107). As the title "La noche de los escritores asesinos" suggests, the writer himself or herself has become a murderer. The lettered city is portrayed as a violent, male-dominated network that enables and indulges men with little talent: "you talk a lot, move some contacts, say provocative things . . . publish a book and sit to watch as you grow a reputation of intellectual" ("hablas mucho, revuelves algunos contactos, dices cosas provocativas . . . publicas un libro y te sientas a echar fama de intelectual"; 103).

War violence (gun), lettered violence (pen), and domestic violence (fist and penis) are equated. Boris recounts how, when they were still a couple, he sometimes hit Rossana to force her to sleep with him (92). He invades her home with a revolver in hand trying to rape her, a crime of which he acquits himself by writing a note in the newspaper and using a male network to draw an image of her as an irrational, deranged woman—the prime tool of patriarchy to silence a female voice. Against these overlapping types of violence, the woman raises her gun/pen. Female agency and desire ultimately interrupt the phallocentric equation as represented by Boris. "And you think that with a gun in your hand you will seduce me and take me to bed?" ("Y piensas que con una pistola en la mano vas a seducirme y llevarme a la cama?"; 118), asks the italicized voice, then Rossana pulls the trigger and unravels the entire story. Violence appears here as the only means to liberate oneself from male authority and voice (Kokotovic, "After the Revolution" 44–45). A woman can only interrupt the male discourse if she takes up the pen/gun and destroys the man and male narration. Violence has both an oppressing and liberating dimension in the short story (Cortez, *Estética* 169).[23]

Escudos's expertly crafted story is a powerful counterweight to the many denigrated and murdered female characters in recent Central American postwar literature. It offers a counterpoint to female figures who, without a second thought, are killed after or during the sexual act by ex-combatants. These scenes might have been written as a social critique, yet in their absolute disregard for human dignity and intimacy, they are as powerful as they are violent and perverse. In the demobilized combatant novels, the women become the most disposable bodies of all: after the men deposited their stories and sperm in them, they are annihilated in cold blood by the protagonists and thus in a sense also by the writers of these scenes. Escudos's story underscores how the act of writing can be a violent act. The intersection of epistemic and direct violence—pens and gunstored in the same drawers and taken up by the same hands— makes the intellectual as violent as the soldier. The ending fully dismantles the oftentimes sublime position that intellectual figures attribute themselves in relation to violence. Violence is often that of the irascible, abject, subaltern masses, about which the intellectual writes with a mix of intrigue and disgust. The overlap of gun and pen in Escudos's story is thus a critique of the writer and the militarism in left-wing middle- and upper- class milieus that only see reprehensible violent behavior in the masses and in the right, but not in themselves.

## *Wounds*

While the demobilized combatant novels are full of assault rifles, grenade launchers, and revolvers, not one firearm appears in the collection of short stories *De fronteras* (2007) by Claudia Hernández.[24] If violence is committed within a story, it is committed with simple tools or bare hands. Nonetheless, the collection is full of the consequences of direct violence: cadavers, mutilated bodies, and traumatized minds. By omitting the main instrument of direct violence the text points to the echoes of firearms, to the profound wounds and voids they leave behind.

Despite their deterritorialized character, these short stories have generally been read in relation to the violent and desolate postwar state of mind in Central America.[25] María Catalina Rincón Chavarro has argued that the stories offer a critique of the normalization of violence because the stories make the reader question the protagonists' indifferent behavior toward the omnipresent violence. Misha Kokotivic has put emphasis on the "deadpan tone" narrators use to describe characters "doing fantastic things in the most mundane ways," arguing that this "raises questions about what passes for ordinary or exceptional in El Salvador's postwar social order" (Kokotovic, "Telling Evasions"

72). Next to the nonchalance with which the stories comment on the crude and absurd realities of the postwar state of emergency, the omission of high-tech weaponry is key. The lack of firearms exposes the crude bare-life situation of the (post)war period quite differently than the demobilized combatant novels. Acts of direct violence, if they appear in the narration at all, are committed with bare hands, broken glass, or rope. Many stories do not show the violent acts, only their echoes: cadavers, traumatized bodies and minds—somewhat similar to Nellie Campobello's *Cartucho.*

One short story, "Manual del hijo muerto," gives instructions for putting together one's child if it returns home dead, tortured, and mutilated: "It is especially exciting to reconstruct the body of the dead child (24–25 years) that left home complete two or seven days ago" ("Causa especial emoción reconstruir el cuerpo del niño [24–25 años] que salió completo de la casa hace dos o seis días") (Hernández 107). Narrated in "bureaucratically euphemistic language" (Kokotovic, "Telling Evasions" 64), the manual also provides instructions on how to grieve: "Cry every time someone mentions his name" ("Llore cada vez que alguien mencione su nombre"; 109). There is no perpetrator and no weapon—only a mutilated cadaver and a numb society that has forgotten how to grieve.

Cadavers turn up everywhere. "Hechos de un buen ciudadano I" and "Hechos de un buen ciudadano II" narrate the pragmatic deeds of a "good citizen" when cadavers suddenly appear in his home. In "Hechos de un buen ciudadano I," the corpse of a woman appears in his kitchen out of nowhere; she appears to have died a violent death, but there is no perpetrator, no weapon. The "good citizen" puts an ad in the newspaper to find the "owner" of the cadaver and the state apparatus only calls to make sure he assumes responsibility for any hygiene issues and to congratulate him on his deeds. After nobody claims the body, he decides to give it to another man who was looking for a dead male relative and they make the female body stand in for that of the missing relative by putting heavy objects in the coffin. In "Hechos de un buen ciudadano II," others find cadavers in their homes and call the "good citizen" to ask for advice. He tells them to bring the corpses to him, shows them how to clean them, and together they place another ad in the newspaper for a total of twenty cadavers. Cheerfully, they sit together and wait for calls. Seven bodies are never claimed, and the protagonist ends up converting them into a stew for the poor. Again, society applauds him for his deeds as a "good citizen."[26] Although some have argued that the bodies point to state terror and the lack of accountability for war crimes (Kokotovic, "Telling Evasions," 56, 60), I read the stories as pointing to the sensation of a diffuse violence, the kind of violence that has characterized Latin America after the Cold War. This violence brings forth cadavers everywhere, although generally there is no official war; the violence is far more ambiguous and difficult to "read" than the politically motivated violence of the war years. While I concur with Rincón Chavarro's and Kokotovic's analyses regarding Hernández's critique of the normalization of violence, I would go even further and propose that just below the surface of these dark and seemingly cynical stories lies a profound desire for a different type of *convivencia*. In these stories the foundation for this new *convivencia* emerges from compassion for the Other. Many of Hernández's beings share a common desire: to be recognized in their subjectivity and suffering. Mutual recognition becomes a form of healing, not by sweeping aside painful experiences and memories (as the amnesty laws did), but by acknowledging physical and psychological wounds and by accepting Otherness. Instead of a logic of annihilation of one's opponent, they envision a process of recognition based on reciprocity, compassion, and empathy.

Hegel's dialectic of recognition puts forward arguments on how human beings become self-aware through recognition. His master-slave dialectic from *Die Phänomenologie des Geistes* holds that we need the Other to become self-aware. Hegel first stresses the need of the slave/bondsman (*Knecht*) to fight the master (*Herr*) to become recognized (156–58). This idea is also taken up by Frantz Fanon, who in *Black Skin, White Masks* says that "man is human only to the extent to which he tries to impose his existence on another man in order to be recognised by him" (216). Foreshadowing his justification of anti-colonial violence in *The Wretched of the Earth* (73, 84), Fanon argues that a violent struggle is necessary for the oppressed subject to become human in itself and for itself. However, along with the idea of struggle, both Hegel and Fanon point to a second dimension that stresses the need for mutual recognition and reciprocity. Hegel writes that self-awareness can only happen through both gestures; it is dependent upon the actions of the self and the Other: "because what has to happen can only come about through both" (153).[27] It is through this reciprocity that the human can, in the end, attain "consciousness-in-itself for itself," as Fanon puts it (*Black Skin* 222). The initial struggle could lead to the loving embrace of the self and the Other (222). Fanon highlights that this coming together, this encounter, is dependent on the recognition of "alterity" (222) or, as we might say today, difference. Later postcolonial thinkers such as Homi K. Bhabha have deplored Fanon's "deep hunger for humanism" and ridiculed it for being "as banal as it is beatific" (120).

It is, however, precisely this idea of mutual recognition dependent on the acknowledgment of difference that I want to emphasize in relation Hernández's stories. The idea of recognition and embrace of the Other comes to the forefront in the short story that opens *De fronteras*, "Molestias de tener un rinoceronte." It is a story about a man who has lost his arm and has since become the involuntary owner of a small rhinoceros. His missing arm refers us to a possible war trauma, as it is a wound often inflicted by firearms and landmines, both of which were employed in the heavily armed Salvadoran conflict. Even though the text makes no direct mention of the war or specific places—we only know that the two roam the streets of "pretty and peaceful cities" ("ciudades bonitas y pacíficas"; 11)—the story *can* be read as dealing with an ex-combatant, given his physical and psychological trauma and his anger that clashes with the seemingly peaceful surroundings that the man and rhinoceros inhabit—either a city to which the man migrated or a Central American postwar city. The small rhinoceros appeared on the day the man lost his arm and has followed him ever since. They cause quite a spectacle on the streets: "The people in these pretty and peaceful cities are not used to seeing a guy with one arm too few and one rhinoceros too many jumping around him" (11).[28] People congratulate the man on his rhino, but he always tells them that he does not want the animal, that it is not his and that they can have it. Since the strangers do not want to accept the animal, the man tries to lose it through other means. He leaves it at his grandparents' place, but the rhino only wants to follow him. Annoyed, he tries to abandon the rhino in "a region dominated by the night" ("una región dominada por la noche"; 12), but again the rhino runs back to him. Finally the man accepts the rhino's company and love. Ultimately, he, who has gone through great pains to establish that he does not need anyone's company or help, finds comfort in the fact that it is *he* whom the animal chooses to follow: a man with a mutilated, hurt body, rather than the other humans who "are complete" ("están completos"; 12).

Like other stories in *De fronteras*, "Molestias de tener un rinoceronte" alludes to violence but does so by omitting the violent act itself. The mutilated limb represents "a violent act enunciated not as an act but as a result" ("un acto violento no enunciado como acto, sino como resultado") (Rincón Chavarro). Only the echo remains, the hollowness, the void, the pain. The rhinoceros, meanwhile, seems to be a substitute for something that was lost through armed violence: not only an arm but also humanity, compassion, and tenderness. The man observes: "It follows me. It accompanies me. It gives me its short, gray company and caresses me with that horn of his" ("Me sigue. Me acompaña. Me da su compañía bajita y gris y me acaricia siempre con ese su cuerno"; 12). Through the recognition of the rhino—through its love and its acceptance of the man's difference—the man becomes whole again. He talks of others as people who "are complete," ("están completos" 12), implying that his state is that of *estar incompleto*, being incomplete. It is only at the end, when he has accepted the rhino's love and can admit his fondness of the animal, that he talks about himself as "being incomplete" ("ser incompleto"; 13). He has come to accept his trauma, first through the struggle with the rhino and then through the rhino's love, which signifies a tender recognition of the man's existence and suffering. The man thus was able to move on from an unstable state of *estar* to a stable existence of *ser*.

Significantly, the rhino does not return the man to a pretrauma state, just as Hernández's stories do not yearn for a society that could conceal its scars or return to some lost identity. Rather, still aware of his trauma but in acceptance of it, the man has attained a "consciousness-in-itself for itself," as Fanon would call it (*Black Skin* 222). Although the protagonist calls the animal such names as "problem with horn" ("problema con cuerno") (Hernández 13), in my reading, the rhino represents the emergence of hope. The man caresses the rhino with "its horn that points to the future" ("su cuerno que apunta hacia el futuro"; 12). But this is not the goat's horn—*cuerno de chivo*, the nickname for the AK-47—that leads toward the future as it did in revolutionary times. Instead, it is the loving rhino's horn. There is deep sadness in the story but also great tenderness as the man develops a relationship with the animal and starts to reciprocate its love: "I was filled with joy when I heard its little steps stumbling toward me" ("me alegré al oír su pasos pequeños atropellándose en mi búsqueda"; 12) and later "I smile when I see it" ("sonrío cuando lo veo") and "when I come home I caress it with the fingers I'm missing and let it sleep under my shadow" ("[l]o acaricio al llegar a casa con los dedos que no tengo y le permito dormir bajo mi sombra"; 13). The rhino's unconditional love helps the traumatized man and gives him self-worth.

As previously mentioned, Hernández's stories can also be interpreted outside the context of Central America. The allegorical nature of this story allows it to resonate in almost any country where former combatants, weapons arsenals, and war trauma still permeate daily life. With some guidance, students of mine in the United States were able to interpret the story in relation to post-traumatic stress disorder, the companion animal programs for US veterans, or the imaginary friend of a disturbed mind. The story thus ultimately can speak *to* and speak *of* the deep war trauma of the heavily militarized United States. Next to the issue of trauma, it is a story about the reintegration of former combatants within society. How willing is a society to engage with ex-combatants and their wounds? In the story nobody wants to know about the lost arm, only about the rhino. Society leaves the man to deal with his trauma on his own. Only the rhino recognizes the man in his suffering, and with its sheer size, the rhino pushes people to engage with the man and his trauma (Kokotovic, "Telling Evasions" 58f). As Ana Patricia Rodríguez puts it: "the appearance of the rhinoceros signifies the magnified spectacle of living trauma in everyday contexts" (*Dividing the Isthmus* 227). The rhino is the elephant in the room: the guilt of a society that pushes individuals to war, dehumanizes them through military training and war, and then refuses to recognize their trauma and to truly engage with them.

The questions of war legacy and reintegration resurfaces in the story "Carretera sin buey," which can be read allegorically as dealing with a former combatant, in this case his guilt and awareness of the harm he has caused.[29] Again, the story features no firearms, and the violence is instead committed with a car and a broken bottle. It tells of a man who tries to absolve himself of striking and killing an ox with his car by becoming an ox. The story is told in a first-person plural narration by people who, while driving in a car, encounter a man standing on a road pretending to be an ox. They stop, listen to his story, and then offer suggestions on how the man can deepen his transformation. They recommend he put on horns, undress himself, dull his gaze, and castrate himself. He does so willingly in order to free himself from the pain of having killed the ox by replacing it. Yet the people in the car, the narrators, are concerned that the man might never manage to become fully animal because his eyes still have a certain shimmer and a gaze that evokes his human soul and intellect. In the end, the people drive on, leaving the man to his endeavor.

Yansi Pérez has argued that this story subverts mourning by making literal "what mourning proposes at a more metaphorical and symbolic level" and says that this story presents "a perverse fantasy of a mourning that only accepts total restitutions." Although this is a valid point, I read the literalization more positively, as proposing a reflection on the possibility of restorative justice. The Latin American pleasure for wordplay suggests that the man is indeed an ox, an idiot, for wanting to turn himself into an animal by means of emasculation. Yet there is also an urgency in his task to understand and fill the void he has left. Restorative justice generally involves victims, offenders, and the community, with a focus on repairing and empowering the community and holding it accountable for helping in this process (Johnstone and Van Ness 7). Restorative justice is "geared less toward stigmatizing and punishing the wrongdoer and more toward ensuring that wrongdoers recognize and meet a responsibility to make amends for the harm they have caused" and on "tangible ways" to address the injury and needs of the victims (Johnstone and Van Ness 7). The ox-man's motifs and actions display a form of restorative justice that confronts the reality of death in all its details and accepts one's guilt by trying to fill the void. He yearns to feel the Other, recognizing the void that the death of the other being, the ox, has left. He does not seek vindictive, punitive justice for himself but seeks to replace the loss he has caused. Such restorative justice represents a concept that differs considerably from modern justice systems. It is not a justice of revenge, nor does it fit with the modern principle of incarceration. Instead of exclusion through state-ordered death or prison, it is concerned with integration.

This logic differs from the demobilized combatant novels by Castellanos Moya and Franz Galich, which are concerned with settling old feuds from the war and annihilating the opponent. In "Carretera sin buey," a different logic comes to the fore, one of recognition and restitution instead of revenge and annihilation. Many critics have read "Carretera sin buey" more as a critique than a proposal, as a story critical of powerful elites or outside agencies defining and commanding the marginalized being (Cortez, *Estética* 155, 158; Kokotovic, "Telling Evasions" 67). Kokotovic reads the story as referring to the "unacknowledged cost of pacification," during which the poor majority in Central America was "called upon to pay for restoring" peace ("Telling Evasions" 67, 69). Although it is possible to read "Carretera sin buey" within a critical framework of empire and domination, such a reading overlooks the potentially radical proposal of the story, which advocates healing through a particular form of restitution. Read under this light, the story asks the question of what it would mean to truly accept the guilt of having taken the life of another being. What would an individual or a society have to do to engage with the individual and collective guilt accrued in a context of war?

While my reading differs from those of Kokotovic and Cortez, it is undeniable that in the story the people who stop only hesitantly, give recommendations, and then drive off play an odd role in this process. In this sense I agree with Kokotovic's and Cortez's critique of the role of elites or outside advisers in the peace-building process. If a society is truly invested in facilitating the reintegration of its violent perpetrators, people have to engage with them, just as they have to engage with their own guilt. They cannot merely say a few words from a position of power and then drive off. The concern for reintegration and reconciliation cannot be a fleeting concern, a passing interest. A society has to be willing to engage compassionately and emphatically with its ex-combatants and war legacy. Instead of fixating on only the most explicit and spectacular violence and trauma—like in the demobilized combatant novels or the act of emasculation—a society must also consider the grief, pain, and guilt tied to more nuanced, overlooked, or unseen remnants of the past.

In Hernández's stories there are no shiny metallic objects, no AK-47s, no colts or grenades to distract our immediate attention. Firearms can have a distancing effect, the text reminds us, and the stories deny readers that potential distraction and leave them with cadavers and bare violence. Nonetheless, weapons linger and resonate throughout the text: as echo, wound, void.

FIGURE 6.1. Soldier displaying a confiscated golden firearm to the press. *La Jornada*, August 19, 2010. Photograph by José Antonio López. José Antonio López/*La Jornada*/México.

## CHAPTER 6

# GOLDEN AK-47s AND WEAPON DISPLAYS

## THE PROPS OF THE DRUG WAR

A man clad in military uniform holds up an ornate firearm. Most of the assault rifle has been bathed in gold; the grips and hand-guard appear to be made of hand-carved wood. The curved magazine, characteristic of Kalashnikov-type rifles, is also gilded. The golden cock on the front on the barrel amplifies the rifle's hypermasculine, phallic, and flamboyant character. The baroque exuberance of the weapon contrasts with the plain simplicity of the standard army fatigues of the man holding it. Here the army is not showing off its newest equipment, but rather exhibiting the exotic Otherness of its assumed opponent. What looms behind the rifle is the mythical figure of the narco: a powerful man, economically and militarily potent.

This golden AK-47 is a trophy of war. It is on display; its meaning more discursive than lethal. Most likely, the rifle would malfunction in a shootout because of its decoration, but this is relatively irrelevant for its significance. The weapon more than anything is a stage prop in the propaganda wars of the current armed conflict in Mexico. Within narcoculture—the cultural and material production around the real and imagined traits of the lifestyle of those involved in the illegal drug business—the firearm functions as a celebratory prop of unrestrained consumption and fatalistic bravado. The Mexican government forces use the firearm to establish a clear Other—the narco as alien to society, an enemy of the state and decent people—and to present itself as society's upstanding defense against the moral, cultural, and political decay and danger of the narco figure. They also use it to imply that the narco is a *naco:* a tacky nouveau rich, whose bad taste and ostentation reveals his lower-class upbringing. Exposing these weapons underscores the exotic and lower-class nature of the narco enterprise in opposition to the attitudes and actions of established elites. This makes it easy to locate these narcos and *nacos* on the outside of civil society.

This photograph of the gilded AK-47, which appeared on the front page of *La Jornada* on August 9, 2010, presents clear dividing lines, but the reality is far more complicated (figure 6.1). The drug war in Mexico (*guerra contra el narco*) is a complex conflict with blurry battle lines and often indiscernible actors. Parts of the state apparatus are involved in managing the drug business and militarizing the country, making the state only one more actor in the conflict, not the heroic antagonist of evil criminal organizations operating outside of the state. Even though there are many aspects of the business that are done without guns or do not necessarily need guns (such as agricultural, industrial, and financial services), the powerful iconography of the narco always involves firearms. The state apparatus often appears and acts in relation to weaponry, too. All sides make heavy use of weaponry—both in battle and discourse—making the firearm a central and confusing symbol of the conflict. To better understand the significance of weapons, it is important to keep in mind the distinction between different values of an object that I developed on the basis of Jean Baudrillard's object value-system (detailed in the introduction). I distinguish between an object's functional value as a tool, its economic value as a commodity, its spectral value as an echo, and its symbolic values as an artifact, trope, and prop.

All these different uses are present in the drug war. The firearm is a crucial tool and commodity of the drug war; however, since this is a war fought both on the military and the discursive realms, the symbolic significance of firearms cannot be stressed enough. This chapter analyzes literature, visual culture, music, and material culture to elucidate the symbolic uses of firearms—in particular, the use of firearms as props. This means that the firearm is used no longer for its original lethal function and purpose but for performative purposes. Firearms are used as props by political actors and cultural agents, both within official government and cultural discourses. The focus on performative uses is not to downplay the very real numbers of people killed in the conflict or the very real problem of the US weapons market fueling the conflict, but rather to shed light on a conflict also fought very much on the level of discourse and propaganda. In this theater of war, weapons become objects to stage positions and assumed truths of this war, making them ultimately highly specious symbols.

## Trafficking Death: The Firearm as a Commodity in the Drug War

During the Mexican Revolution, Martín Luis Guzmán decried that the merchants in the US border towns "equipped [Mexicans] for life and death" ("nos equipaban para la vida y para la muerte) (*El águila* 174) since both wine for parties and weaponry for battles were acquired in places such as El Paso and Nogales. Although Mexican merchants are the ones providing US Americans with drugs today—be it psychoactive drugs in the pharmacies in the Mexican border towns or the vast quantities of illicit narcotics smuggled into the

United States—one flow has not changed its course. The US market is still the major provider of weaponry for Mexico, continuing the long-standing pattern of the US market providing Mexico with firearms in times of unrest (Andreas 294; DeLay 8).

As in most border regions, smuggling has been a common activity in the US-Mexico border region for many decades, with goods flowing in both directions. In the nineteenth century, mainly agricultural products were smuggled from the Mexican side, while from the US side, primarily industrialized consumer products made their way into Mexico (Díaz 35; Ramírez-Pimienta, *Cantar* 22). Smuggling was not too difficult as the border was always porous. In the early twentieth century, border flows increased. During the Mexican Revolution, weapons poured into Mexico from the US side. In the meantime, prohibition efforts in the United States—the 1914 Harrison narcotics law and the 1919 Volstead Act—created both a drug tourist industry on the Mexican side of the border and an increased contraband toward the United States, mainly of alcohol and, to a lesser degree, opiates and marijuana (Knight, "Narco-Violence" 119; Serrano 136).

Throughout the twentieth century, demand for narcotics in the United States increased, as did the share Mexican merchants held of this market. During World War II, the United States encouraged Mexican poppy and marijuana production—for morphine and rope, respectively—and then in the 1960s and 1970s students and returning soldiers of the Vietnam War created a bigger market for narcotics (Andreas 308; Astorga, *El siglo* 101–12). US interdiction efforts, internationalized under President Nixon, did not eradicate drugs. Rather, they constantly displaced and rerouted drug production and trafficking, creating greater incentives and ever more daring, risk-prone entrepreneurs (Andreas 275, 290). Originally only cultivated in Sinaloa, production of marijuana and poppy became common in several Mexican states (Astorga, *El siglo* 107–12). The successful fight against the Colombian cartels and Caribbean trafficking routes in the 1980s and early 1990s made Mexico the main transit route for Andean cocaine. Furthermore, NAFTA in the 1990s probably contributed to the rise in drug trafficking because the increased border traffic made it easier to smuggle merchandise (Muehlmann 12). Over time, Mexican merchants started to control over 80 percent of the product entering the US market: heroin starting in the 1970s, partly due to the successful clampdown on Turkish production; cocaine by the 1990s after the demise of the Colombian cartels; and methamphetamine by the mid-2000s (Gootenberg 9; Serrano 139–40; Muehlmann 113).

As the importance of the Mexican narco business grew, so did the armed violence. The story of drugs, once made illegal, seems inseparable from that of arms. An armed conflict has been brewing since the 1970s but escalated during the presidency of Felipe Calderón (2006–2012). Calderón, a weakened president because of the allegations of fraud during the election, used the narco war as a means to create legitimacy and power (Serrano 153). He declared a war on drug-trafficking organizations and militarized the country. Since 2006, an estimated 170,000 people have lost their lives in the war (*El País,* "Año 11 de la guerra contra el narco"). The war is partly acted out through a violent spectacle, in which violence "takes elaborate and ritualized forms that draw on the medium of the corpse as central to the semiotics of terror" (Muehlmann 86). Severed heads are placed next to written messages, corpses are hung from bridges, or bloodied corpses covered in money are exposed to the press. This violence imprinted on the body brings the weapon out of focus. But firepower is the lethal power and threat that lies behind what is being done to the bodies after being forced into submission by firearms. Homicides committed with firearms have doubled in Mexico since 2006, and the homicide rate overall is on the rise: between 2001 and 2006 only a quarter of intentional homicides were committed with firearms, and now it is 55 percent (Arriaga Carrasco, Roldán Álvarez, and Ruiz Mendoza 17). While not the only means to kill, firearms are the main tools used to perpetrate violence.

The vast majority of these firearms comes from the United States. The massive firearms production as well as the lax weapon laws in the United States undercut the very strict laws in Mexico, where civilians are allowed to keep arms at their homes but they are generally not allowed to bear them outside of the home, neither in concealed nor open carry. Citizens in Mexico may purchase firearms only for home defense, hunting, sports, and collection. One has to apply for a permit to the military to be allowed to own a gun; another permit is necessary to transport weapons. There is only one shop where civilians can legally purchase firearms: the Dirección de Comercialización de Armamento y Municiones operated by the Ministry of National Defense, located in Mexico City. The type of guns a civilian can own are restricted; many rifles and bigger calibers are restricted to exclusive use by the military (SEDENA).

Enforcement of these laws is an issue, however. In 2005—the numbers are surely higher today—the *Small Arms Survey* estimated that next to the 4.49 million firearms registered in Mexico, there were another 10 million unregistered firearms ("Annexe 1").[1] As the high numbers of unregistered firearms show, there is a thriving black market. Weapons come from US retail, Mexican security forces, and old Central American stockpiles (*Small Arms Survey,* "Captured and Counted" 312). The share of the US market as country of origin of the weapons used by drug-trafficking organizations in Mexico is disputed. The 2013 *Small Arms Survey* mentions data in the range of 68 percent (295) but explains that given the data gaps they can only state that "the US civilian market is a significant source of weapons" (298).[2] The type of weapons sought in Mexico has changed over the years: from mainly handguns in the late 1990s to more powerful long guns by 2010 (289).[3] The higher numbers of assault rifles seized in Mexico could, as some studies suggest, be related to the end of the US federal assault weapons ban in 2004 (Young 24–25).

Confusion exists on whether narco organizations are able to obtain military-grade weapons or not. The *Small Arms Survey* emphasizes that criminal organizations in Mexico do not have an armament equitable to that of a state army, despite what is often claimed ("Captured and Counted" 300). They have mainly rifles, long guns, a few heavy machine guns and explosives but generally no heavy anti-tank, missile, and anti-air heavy weaponry (300). However, by Mexican standards the narco organizations do own a vast military-grade arsenal, because in Mexico many of the rifles used by alleged criminals are of exclusive use of the military (Ley Federal de Armas de Fuego y Explosivos, Article 11).[4] In the United States, however, many of these weapons can be legally purchased by civilians and then make their way into Mexico.

Attempts by the United States to curb gun smuggling have been haphazard. In 2006 the Bureau of Alcohol, Tobacco, Firearms and Explosives (ATF) started Project Gunrunner, a pilot project focused on straw purchasers and corrupt gun dealers (Young 31–32). This turned into Operation Fast and Furious, a 2009 attempt by the ATF to catch gun traffickers higher up on the ladder by letting weapons through the border and tracing them. But the ATF quickly lost track of the weapons and more than two thousand got into Mexico (32–34), two of them appearing at the site of a homicide of a border patrol agent and in a hideout of Joaquín Guzmán (aka El Chapo), alleged leader of the Sinaloa cartel. The Fast and Furious debacle made the ATF an international laughingstock and caused turmoil within US agencies as well as diplomatic tensions.

But there is an even bigger issue when we talk about firearms as a commodity in the drug war. In general, the story told about weapon flows from the United States only tells one side—that of illicit flows to criminal organizations. It does not tell the story of massive flows of weapons into the hands of the Mexican government—through US financial and military aid and through legal purchases in the United States and elsewhere.[5] Overall, the Mexican military budget has increased from $2 billion in 2006 to $9.3 billion in 2009 (Paley, *Drug War* 66). Mexico used to buy more weapons from European arms dealing nations, but lately it has increasingly turned to the US market—with a sharp increase in spending to $400 million in 2006, double from previous buys, to spikes of almost $1 billion in 2009, and $1.2 billion in 2012 (Lindsay-Poland).[6] In 2015 the Mexican government under President Enrique Peña Nieto went on what security experts called a military "buying binge" (Lindsay-Poland), acquiring Black Hawks and Humvees and other military equipment from the United States. The year 2015 also stands out because, while Mexico used to buy mainly through commercial sales in the United States, that year Mexico spent more than $1 billion at the Pentagon's Foreign Military Sales program (Gagne).

Other arms-dealing countries have provided weapons, too. The German company Heckler and Koch caused a scandal by circumventing German law that prevents German firms from selling weapons to conflict zones or governments with a human rights violations record. Heckler and Koch was thus prohibited from selling rifles to states in conflict such as Chiapas, Chihuahua, Guerrero, and Jalisco but did so nonetheless. Some GS-36 rifles were found with the Iguala police implicated in the forced disappearance of the forty-three rural college students of Ayotzinapa in 2014 (*Proceso* "Confirman envío ilegal"). Furthermore, by German law, Heckler and Koch was only allowed to export ten thousand GS-36 rifles to Mexico if the Mexican government were going to destroy an equal number of their older weapons. As proof, images of the destruction of firearms were created with the presence of a Mexican officer, a member of the German embassy, and an employee from Heckler and Koch. But it appears that overall the Mexican government only destroyed about six hundred revolvers and seven hundred rifles—among them many AK-47s, which are not part of the official equipment of the government forces (Leyendecker). This last episode shows again how in this complex armed conflict weapons are also used for highly performative acts.

## The Firearm as a Nebulous Symbol and the Indistinctness of Actors

There is a recurring scene in the novel *Contrabando:* armed men attack a village, a gathering, a ranch, or a field; they shoot, kill, or kidnap, but it generally remains unclear whether the perpetrators are narcos or government forces (Rascón 14–23, 41, 87, 100). The novel by Víctor Hugo Rascón Banda, which many consider to be the best Mexican narco novel to date, thus captures one of the main problems of the current Mexican armed conflict: the indistinctness of the combatants of the war and the blurring of insurgent and counterinsurgent violence. Everyone seems to carry a weapon, but it is not always clear for what purpose: to break the law, to upkeep the law, to defend the state apparatus or to challenge it, or none of the above—just to guarantee oneself a piece of the enormous pie that the drug business represents? The novel thus destroys what Oswaldo Zavala has called the powerful "simulacrum of truth" that drug-trafficking organizations are exterior to the Mexican state apparatus and civil society and that state forces and violent nonstate actors are easily distinguishable (343).

Key to this narrative is the idea of cartels (Astorga, *El siglo* 130), which implies a powerful organization and monopoly status. This does not reflect the fluctuating, dispersed, and often compartmentalized drug operations. Rather, the "cartel myth was created and perpetuated by politicians, journalists, and law enforcement agents looking for a simple and easily identifiable target" (Andreas 280). This turned into what Dawn Paley has called the "the cartel wars discourse"—a narrative that the current war is only a turf war between competing cartels. This narrative relies primarily on government sources, has "a guilty-until-proven-innocent/victims-were-involved-in-drug-trade bias," and is based on the assumption "that cops involved in criminal activity are the exception, not the rule, and that more policing improves security" (Paley, "Repressive Memories").

Reality is much more complex. For one, for a long a time the narco business was semicontrolled or at least "milked" by the elites (Knight, "Narco-Violence" 128). There is an "incestuous relationship between criminals and the state apparatus" and "the imbrication of police and narcos . . . is a staple, structural feature of the flourishing narco-economy" (120–21). Further adding to this confusion is the fact that during the presidency of Vicente Fox Quesada, more than one hundred thousand soldiers defected from the armed forces (Serrano 155). Ex-military, both from the Mexican and Guatemalan special forces, turned into one of the most violent and feared groups of the war: Los Zetas (154). Whereas in Colombia the violence work has generally been undertaken by disenfranchised youth, in Mexico it was often easier to use ex-policemen or ex-militaryy (Astorga, *El siglo* 165). Moreover, certain firearms are acquired by drug-trafficking organizations to impersonate government personnel (*Small Arms Survey*, "Captured and Counted" 293).

When President Felipe Calderón changed the strategy from one of semi-clandestine negotiation and repression to one of heavy armed confrontation and sent the military into many parts of the country, violence skyrocketed and so did human rights violations by the military. President Enrique Peña Nieto (2012–2018) outwardly seemed to take a different stance than his predecessor and showed a less militarist demeanor, but he further increased the military budget, and vast regions of Mexico remain under siege. Adding to the confusion is that in recent years several paramilitary self-defense groups (*las autodefensas*) emerged in parts of Mexico. They were either criminalized and attacked or incorporated by the Mexican state apparatus, further complicating the blurry frontlines of this conflict.[7] While some have called the conflict a "criminal insurgency" (Sullivan), in many ways it is the counter-insurgent tactics that have unleashed the horrific violence in the past several years, begging the question: "Who are the insurgents in this war?" (Paley, "Repressive Memories"). Paley says that the insurgents can only be seen in relation to the government and its counterinsurgent tactics, constructed by it. She suggests thinking of the Mexican drug war more in relation to the "repressive memories" of the counterinsurgent violence in Central America, as a continuation of that state-sponsored violence in which "state forces . . . were using the specific language of insurgency when in fact the entire population was being targeted." So, rather than an insurgency, the so-called drug war is an ongoing violent process of counterinsurgency and paramilitarization—a context far more complex and political than that presented by the "cartel war discourse."

While many Mexican narconarratives draw heavily on the cartel wars discourse and indulge in noir and detective novels about the excitingly immoral narco underworld, the novel *Contrabando* depicts the conflict in precisely these political terms necessary to develop a better critical understanding of the conflict. The novel has been acclaimed as the best Mexican narconovel to date because of its experimental narrative strategies and its focus on the victims (Palaversich). I have argued elsewhere that the novel's strength lies in its highly political, nonmoralistic treatment of the drug war (Esch). Written around 1991 but published posthumously in 2008, the novel draws sketches of drug-related violence in the mountainous region of Chihuahua in the 1980s.[8] The novel tells the story of a writer who returns to his home village to write a script for a *ranchera* movie but finds himself enmeshed in an increasingly violent region—witnessing violent episodes and hearing many witness accounts of violence, generally told by the relatives of the dead. He struggles to depict the real-life drug-related violence in a movie and theater play he is writing, both scripts of which are included in the novel. The writer encounters a region that is under siege. His entry and exit from the Sierra Tarahumara is marked by military checkpoints and confrontations with the military, who—the irony—are looking for alcohol and weapons being taken into the *ley seca* mountains but not for the narcotics coming out of it.

Maybe it is precisely because the novel is closer to the "repressive memories" of the 1980s that it is able to offer a viewpoint different from hegemonic discourses. In fact, the protagonist repeatedly compares what he sees to movies of the Vietnam War and the Salvadoran civil war. In the chapter "El río de la muerte" the protagonist and his father visit an acquaintance at a river and suddenly helicopters appear and attack the marijuana fields and the people along the river. The ensuing scenes of violence and destruction remind the protagonist of a war movie (100). In another episode the protagonist is nap-ping and has a dream that he is an actor in a movie about the Salvadoran civil war, which was still ongoing in the period depicted in the novel (207–8). He wakes up and finds himself in the midst of the new Mexican civil war. His driver did not stop at a military checkpoint and the military opens fire on the vehicle—killing the driver and wounding the protagonist and his father (208).

The narrator witnesses in Chihuahua low-intensity warfare within a military-controlled zone, carried out by different armed men characterized by their indistinctness. The novel's multiple testimonial voices particularly stress the indistinctness of narcos and *judiciales,* the most fearsome branch of the Mexican police due to its criminal and violent practices, nominally abolished in 2002: "They were taken by the narcos, they took them. Or the police" ("Se los llevaron los narcos, se los llevaron. O los judiciales") (Rascón Banda 41). "At this point we don't know if they were narcos with judicial IDs or *judiciales* looking like narcos" ("a estas alturas no se puede saber si fueron narcos con credenciales de la Judicial o judiciales con facha de narcos"; 87). The police even face off against each other, as in the chapter "Yepachi massacre," when an entire family is killed in a battle between federal and local *judiciales.*

*Contrabando* neither glorifies nor condemns narcos. In the novel they are neither heroes nor beasts but ordinary people. Although the novel has a chapter called "Retratos en blanco y negro," nothing in the novel is black and white. Just as the state is not easily separated from narcobusiness, neither is civil society. There is a pervasive discourse in Mexico that narcos are sepa-rate from society, but the "drug trade does not exist separately from society. It functions through networks of ordinary people attempting to survive in the starkly unequal social and economic conditions of the US-Mexico border-lands" (Muehlmann 18). This is the world the novel represents: a poor rural area where many people get involved in poppy and marijuana cultivation as a means of survival, social mobility, or for increased consumption. The text consistently stresses the humanity of narcos (Rascón Banda 9, 48). The novel thus makes it difficult to view the narco as either the terrible or the glorious Other. It does not permit the distancing that, as Juan Villoro has noted, is so common in Mexico's collective discourse, in which the narcos are always the Others, seemingly outside of civil society. There is no such distancing in *Con-trabando,* which shows how the narcobusiness starts to permeate a society on different levels.

The firearm is the only artifact that most clearly identifies one as partic-ipant of the business and the conflict—despite the fact that there are many people in this business who do not carry a weapon to do their part (money laundering, for example) and that there are many people (in particular, gov-

ernment forces) who carry weapons and most adamantly deny any involvement with the business. Carrying a weapon identifies one as a participant in
the conflict, showcasing one's firepower and willingness to use violence, but
without necessarily clarifying one's affiliation or allegiance. This means that
the weapon is an artifact of identification but specious. It becomes even more
nebulous when it appears in relation to women in the conflict. An iconic image of the drug war is a photo of Alma Chávez, a ministerial police agent in Ciudad Juárez from March 2009. The photo was on the front page of the Mexican
news magazine *Proceso* titled "Bienvenidos a Ciudad Juárez," which included
a cover story on the additional five thousand soldiers being sent into Ciudad
Juárez as part of Operativo Conjunto Chihuahua, the most visible moment of
the massive militarization of the country under Calderón.[9]

It is a powerful photo: a woman with a dynamic strut and some swagger,
the AR-15 strapped to the shoulder but with a firm grip on the upper receiver,
the gaze hidden behind sunglasses. Only the paper tissue in her hand, maybe used to pat dry the face for the photo op, destroys the careful arrangement. This photo can be interpreted as a performance of state power, where
the weapon is an artifact for the *mano dura* politics and the determination
of the state—showcasing its willingness to use heavy firepower to defeat the
threat of the narco, an unafraid stance, a strong state clearly distant from the
narcobusiness. Here the "simulacrum of truth" of the state's exteriority to the
narcobusiness is reenacted through the female presence in the government
forces, since it is generally assumed that female police officers are less corrupt-
ible. She is the state fighting the forces of evil. Yet to some degree, the image
undermines the orchestration. In the photo the AR-15 designates the officer as
a participant of the conflict, whereas the only object distinguishing her from
the narcoworld is the badge on her belt. Yet her other demeanor and appearance—the firearm again is the confusing artifact—could make her seem to be
the sassy *narca* of novels and movies.

Indeed, this is a very different representation of women and Ciudad Juárez.
Instead of the common narratives of woman as victim, murdered, the victimized maquiladora worker, here appears a powerful woman. At the same time,
because of her enormous sex appeal, she does not threaten the heterosexual
patriarchal order. It remains intact. News reporters were quick to point out
that the officer was "a flirt" ("coqueta") and, after the photo appeared, she
started to receive flowers from government officials and alleged narcos (Valdez Cárdenas 188). It was good theater, in which the female body adorned by a
firearm was used not to expose the violence of Juárez but to hide it—after all,
this is the iconic photo of the moment when the troops effectively took over
the city, causing the numbers of deaths to soar to unprecedented numbers.

FIGURE 6.2. Mural commissioned by the Secretaría de la Defensa Nacional
(SEDENA), 2009. Photograph by Sophie Esch.

This photo stands in contrast to the story of María Susana Flores, who
died in a narco-related shootout with the Mexican military in November 2012
in Sinaloa. She was reportedly found dead with an AK-47 lying next to her.
Because of the assault rifle, her beauty queen title "Mujer Sinaloa 2012," and
her alleged relationship with one of the drug traffickers, the case gained national prominence. Flores's case had all the ingredients of a good narco story:
criminals, beauty, sex, rifles, and Sinaloa. Social media was full of debates
over whether she had shot the weapon herself, whether she was a "fallen woman," or whether the attorney general of Mexico was incriminating an innocent
companion of the narcos (*Proceso,* "Miss disparó"). Many compared the news
story to fictional accounts such as Arturo Peréz Reverte's novel *La reina del
sur* (2002) and Gerardo Naranjo's movie *Miss Bala* (2011). Yet what called my
attention was the deep misogyny that ran through the entire debate on social
media. Comment threads were filled with remarks like "she had it coming,"
"whore," "bitch," "those women that want it all easy are very common," "any
well-brought-up woman would not hang out with narcos" ("ella se lo buscó,"
"zorra," "perra," "esas mujeres que todo lo quieren fácil, abundan," "cualquier
mujer educada no andaría con narcos").

The other recurring speculation was that Flores could not possibly have
shot the rifle. Given the deep involvement of Mexican state officials and the often contradictory or false information provided to the public about narcos, the
public's skepticism toward government statements is understandable. But part
of the disbelief likely also stems from the fact that Flores was a woman. Admit-
ting that she shot the rifle would give her agency, whether we agree with her
actions or not. Maybe the AK-47 was hers, maybe she fired at the military. Yet
the "victim" and "whore" narratives—variations of the fallen woman—deny
her any subject position of her own. She is just the *bulto* (the bundle) carried
along by evil beasts, used for pleasure and then as a human shield, as some

comments suggested. The woman with the rifle remains a problematic category. Her radical implications drown in a sea of misogyny and symbolic politics.

## Arms Arrangements: The Firearm within Official Government Discourses

This is how the Mexican military would like to see itself: soldiers with torches
and assault rifles rushing to burn and destroy poppy and marijuana fields,
supported by troops in helicopters and planes. The Mexican flag is above them
and the Mexican eagle joins in the battle cry. This mural is at the entry of
the Museo de Enervantes, a nonpublic museum used for training purposes
by the Mexican military (figure 6.2). It is an epic and propagandist display
with a social-realist aesthetic, an affirmation of the military's self-image as
leading the good fight, defending the nation, battling drug cultivation. Even
though the mural was painted by a member of the military in 2009, its iconography appears to be more from the 1970s when the US-masterminded and
-financed Operation Condor promoted eradication campaigns in the mountains of Sinaloa and other northern states. As such, this mural points to the
long trajectory of this war in Mexico and government intent to control the
narrative. As the war intensified since 2007, this became even more important. In Calderón's *guerra contra el narco,* the firearm becomes a pivotal artifact and prop within the competing narratives about this war.

The government uses the firearm as an artifact to claim its monopoly on
violence and to present itself as the only legitimate violent actor in the conflict. During Calderón's presidency, from the conservative Partido de Acción
Nacional (PAN), the state represented itself in a bellicose fashion and in a
highly moral manner. Massive public ad campaigns on government buildings
or in newspapers featured policemen and soldiers clad in protective gear and
holding powerful firearms. The firearm became an artifact of the heroic forces
fighting evil—a trope of righteousness. In 2011 the government even financed
a TV show, *El equipo,* about incorruptible federal policemen and women. The
motto of the show: "They know that good conquers evil" ("Ellos saben que el
bien vence el mal") (Televisa).

Whereas the government's firearms are symbols of legitimate use of force
and moral superiority, the golden AK-47s are indecent immoral weapons.
These golden and silver weapons, on display in the Museo de Enervantes,
frame the narco figure as a dangerously excessive actor, his bad taste and excess a threat to the social order of the good people. During Calderón's presidency it became common to showcase these firearms to the press, sometimes
along with alleged narcos, following a "carefully orchestrated script" (Carlin
507). In elaborate arrangements the government showcased the entire arse-

nals seized in raids of houses of supposed narcos. In these, the government highlighted and oftentimes aggrandized the firepower of the narcos and the threat that they represent, foregrounding the machine guns and other military-grade weaponry. For example, they generally put 50-caliber sniper rifles in the front, even though drug-trafficking organizations rarely have that kind of firepower (*Small Arms Survey* "Captured and Counted" 292). The state apparatus used these weapon arrangements to create dangerous criminals, both in terms of their firepower and their morals.

Another obvious form of using firearms as a prop was the installation of a message at the Mexico-US border. In February 2012, in Ciudad Juárez, the federal government of Calderón revealed an enormous sign built out of destroyed weapons facing the United States that said in English: "No More Weapons." When revealing the sign, Calderón offered a discourse that condemned the US weapons market. Although it is important to denounce the flow of weapons from the United States, this was a populist trick to divert attention to the United States and away from the government-led militarization of the country under Calderón. The functional value of the firearm here has little importance; the weapon is used as a prop in an international theater play directed toward the Mexican interior.

During the war years, several art installations using firearms or modifying firearms have popped up.[10] In these artworks, of different caliber and quality, there is a tendency to work with a simple equation of "Weapons are bad, let's make something else, something good out of them." Art like this is easily imitated by the government. The military, for example, has even sponsored their own anonymous artist, who melded firearms into the emblem of the Mexican Colegio Militar (Peña Sánchez). This installation at the Colegio and the sign at the border show how easily such art can be appropriated by a government intent on depoliticizing and moralizing the narrative.

There existed, however, other art—visual, not plastic, and less focused on only the firearm itself—that countered state attempts to control the narrative. "Mexican Jihad," a Tumblr installation by Mexican artist and DJ Alberto Bustamante, was artistic antipropaganda that cleverly exposed the performative dimensions of the war and the governmental militarism.[11] Created during Calderón's presidency, and no longer online since 2016, the blog offered one of the most compelling visual commentaries about the Mexican drug war. It went "beyond simplistic, neatly drawn lines of 'war' and clear-cut camps of good versus evil by training its focus on the visual 'war' narrative; one in which very little is known about how people are killed and why" (García). The Tumblr installation offered a critique of the government discourse and of "the press for reprinting the images with little or no scrutiny, and [of] the public for buying into the entire package" (García). Most tellingly, "Mexican Jihad" starts with the mural from the Museo de Enervantes and ends with it but, with an onslaught of images, it slowly takes apart that heroic image. The Tumblr installation features numerous images and gifs, but only very few feature objects or people associated with narcoculture: El Chapo, Jesús Malverde, narco tanks, Polo shirts, El Kommander. Absent are the gilded rifles. What dominates the installation are displays of militarism and weaponry by the Mexican government. The government force is not represented through one single weapon but through a massive show of force. The spectacular narco weapons are not the focus here; rather, the spectacle of the state is highlighted: tanks, helicopters, sophisticated equipment, the full force of an army.

The majority of images feature President Calderón, often clad in military uniform and accompanied by army generals, inspecting military equipment, or overseeing military parades. Calderón appears as what he was and what he wanted to project: a president of war. Through the arrangement of the images in Tumblr, the PAN president looks like a mixture of a twentieth-century dictator, a warlord, and also a propaganda buffoon, riding upright on a jeep like a Hollywood action hero or awkwardly and anachronistically riding a horse leading the troops. Many of these images stem from the Fiestas Patrias celebration in September 2012—in particular, a show titled "Ceremonia Magna: Pensamientos de la Patria" at the Colegio Militar. These are odd images for a Mexican public used to a repressive but generally not overtly militarist PRI regime.[12] By zooming in on the militarism, the Tumblr installation changes the narrative of the drug war.

Everything in the Tumblr exhibition points to the state as the main perpetrator of the violence. Photo after photo shows the executive celebrating war and firepower. The army also appears as invading the public sphere. Several photos feature street scenes disrupted by the presence of military vehicles. Then there is another photo of a street ad announcing the visit of Pope Benedict XVI in 2012, featuring the slogan "Our hope resounds in all of Mexico" ("Nuestra esperanza suena en todo México"), in front of a military vehicle with a soldier who is pointing a mounted machine gun. Also, the infamous photo of capo Arturo Beltrán Leyva's exposed body is slipped into the scroll art, as a reminder of the military's violence.[13] What also appears is an image of the already mentioned border installation "No More Weapons." This exposes the hypocrisy of the government discourses, since it is the state apparatus that brings the weapons to Mexico street scenes. Taking from his other craft as a DJ, Bustamante rearranges and mixes snippets of the drug war narrative, so controlled by the government, and creates a new story. Using the government propaganda itself, the installation puts the images of the narco war on its head.

When Enrique Peña Nieto took office in 2012, in a deliberate break with Calderón's PR strategy, he shifted from his predecessor's overt PR campaign to a covert one intent on hushing the violence. Alleged narcos are no longer paraded before the press, weapon arrangements no longer exposed, and the press has been asked to publish less on crime and violence. Supposedly, this is done not to glorify narcos but to reshape Mexico's image abroad. Consequently, the "No More Weapons" sign at the border was taken down in 2015; the mayor of Ciudad Juárez argued that it did not help bilateral relations and commerce (Olivas). In many ways this is the return of the PRI many hoped for and many others were afraid of. Like President Carlos Salinas de Gotari in the 1990s, this PR strategy is about presenting Mexico as a reliable and safe country, good for foreign investment. What has returned, too, is a state violence more easily readable as political violence, as, for example, the cases of violent repression of leftist activists such as the forced disappearance of forty-three students from Ayotzinapa in 2014 and the murder of Rubén Espinosa and Nadia Vera in 2015.

While the militarization has not stopped and the violence is ongoing—there were over sixty thousand homicides in the first three years of Peña Nieto's presidency only (Redacción Sin Embargo), the clampdown on the press has come with attempts to obscure crime data (Á. Delgado, "Los muertos"). What appears to have also increased is the practice of alleging enemy fire to justify or obscure government aggression and executions. For a long time the Mexican government has used weapons and drugs to create drug traffickers (Astorga, *Mitología* 34, 41), but under Peña Nieto some flagrant cases were revealed. There is, for example, Tlatlaya in June 2014, where the military executed presumed criminals alleging a battle took place but then had to admit it was actually an extrajudicial execution, or Apatzingán in January 2015, where sixteen civilians were shot but none of them had long weapons, most only sticks (Castellanos, "Fueron").

This, of course, does not mean that theatricality has left Mexican national politics. In *Symbolism and Ritual in a One-Party Regime,* Larissa Adler de Lomnitz, Rodrigo Salazar Elena, and Ilya Adler provide an insightful analysis of rituals under the old PRI regime. This would need to be expanded and updated to include the different performative constructions of the Mexican government after 2000: under the Panistas Fox and Calderón and the return of the PRI under Peña Nieto. The forced clampdown under Peña Nieto is its own theater, which was strategically broken with heavily televised and manipulated images and footage of the capture of El Chapo in 2016. These performances of sovereignty—through public display of executions and cadavers, or nowadays the exhibition of alleged criminals, constitute "a spectacularization of the law, a sovereign performance" ("una espectacularización de la ley, un performance soberano") (Quintana Navarrete). But Peña Nieto's strategy meant an attempt to push into less visible spheres the war that under Calderón had been brought out into the open. Hence firearms were generally suppressed. Instead of the overtly militarist demeanor of Calderón, the covert repressive state politics of the PRI returned.

## The Ballad of the AK-47: Violent Life, Paramilitarism, and Legitimacy

Not only do firearms appear in the officially propagated state discourses and their reflections and revisions in literature and the arts; they also appear in so-called narcoculture, the cultural and material production around the real and imagined traits of the lifestyle of narcos. Often donning glamorous 1980s aesthetics, narcoculture presents a by now common image of the luxurious life of narcos along the coordinates of expensive guns and clothes, surgically altered female bodies, and exotic animals. Influenced by Mexican B movies, *Miami Vice,* and the legend of Colombian capo Pablo Escobar, a potent imaginary surrounds Mexican narcos: men with mustaches, hats, shades, gold chains, leather boots, Western-style shirts or Ralph Lauren Polo shirts, showy SUVs, and a bust of narco saint Jesús Malverde dangling on the headboard.

These readily assumed coordinates of narcoculture do not mean that this is an organic culture stemming out of the world of drug trafficking. While these images seem to define a subculture, they are in fact created by consumers, providers, media, civil society, and the state apparatus: a powerful narcoimaginary. The truth is that we know very little about narcos—a point that haunts Zavala's critique of Mexican narconarratives. Anthropological research such as Shaylih Muehlmann's *When I Wear My Alligator Boots* is changing this, but her study also shows that although there is a way to gain access to the rural poor implicated in the drug business, a similar access to narcoelites is much more difficult to obtain. Keeping this complexity and our own ignorance in mind, the following two sections trace the meaning of firearms in the narcocultural imaginary—particularly in corridos and in material narcoculture.

Firearms are a staple in narcocorridos. As discussed in chapter 1, *corrido* is a broad descriptor for folk ballads associated with the borderlands and the

North. The genre resurfaced in the 1970s in the form of the so-called narco-corrido—Los Angeles being the main production hub.[14] Even though corridos referencing drug trafficking date back to the 1930s and smuggling even earlier (Ramírez-Pimienta, *Cantar* 22), they started to become massively successful in the 1970s. Narcocorridos play on staples of earlier corridos: the outlaw and the rebel. But now the *narcotraficante* is the main protagonist of the songs; and instead of horse and pistol, the AK-47, the AR-15, and the latest *carro* or *troca* are the attributes of this modern outlaw (96).

## The Many Functions of Narcocorridos

Just like the *corridos de la revolución*, narcocorridos have an aura of authenticity and veracity. This idea is most famously voiced in the opening lines of the song "Jefe de Jefes" by Los Tigres del Norte, which states that corridos "are the true facts of our people" ("son los hechos reales de nuestro pueblo") and that they tell "the honest truth" ("la pura verdad"). Although most scholars refute the narcocorrido's truth claims (Simonett, "Transnational Dimension" 228; Villalobos and Ramírez-Pimienta 136), many also agree that their narrative, while not necessarily veracious, is often counterhegemonic (Valenzuela Arce 222), "a narrative form of geopolitical intervention, reflection, and critique" (Muniz 56), or a means for marginalized populations to insert themselves discursively into narratives of globalization (Cabañas 520, 524).

Zavala, however, argues that just like the Mexican literary narconarratives he criticizes, narcocorridos reinforce "the convenient discursive illusion that drug cartels threaten civil society and its government from without" and thus make it impossible to incorporate "a critique of the state's responsibility in drug trafficking" (347). Given the heterogeneity of the narcocorrido genre, this is an overgeneralization.[15] Rather than repeating the government discourse, narcocorridos are, as Luis Astorga has pointed out, a means to express ideas outside the governmental discourse, but with some restraints; the narcocorridos operate within a clear framework of what is sayable—for example, they indicate government involvement and corruption but do not name officials (*Mitología* 37).

The narcocorrido is a heterogeneous genre that, as Ramírez-Pimienta has identified, resists any single or totalizing reading ("De torturaciones" 309). It would be a mistake to want to pin down the position of an entire genre with hundreds of minor and major bands and interpreters and a history of several decades and of enormous heterogeneity (Wellinga, "Cantando" 142). This is impossible, just as it would be impossible to say that all hip-hop or all rock is counterhegemonic or a sellout. Sometimes narcocorridos talk about actual events and characters, sometimes about fictional ones. Sometimes they are commissioned by drug traffickers themselves to sing their glories; more often they are created by composers and singers to entertain, to tell a story, to make money. Instead of romanticizing the songs as the authentic voice of the people or condemning them as simple propaganda, we have to see music as a dynamic entity, shaped by market and political contexts, always adapting. Through catchy tunes, witty lyrics and storytelling, narcocorridos try to appeal to different audiences—rural, urban, delinquent, intellectual, young—and fulfill several functions at the same time.

Los Tigres del Norte, the most famous and successful corrido band with multiple Latin Grammys, are an excellent example of this multilayered negotiation. Los Tigres display social consciousness by producing many corridos about migration, they appeal to a broad audience by consciously omitting swear words, and they play with the notion of taboo by selling albums of *corridos prohibidos,* which were never actually prohibited (Ramírez-Pimienta, *Cantar* 94f; 105). Especially one of their songwriters, Teodoro Bello, managed to solve the moral-commercial dilemma of singing about delinquency and violence by creating ambiguous lyrics. Enunciating without saying became part of their market rationale, their appeal, and legitimacy (101, 109).

One common criticism, often made by government officials, is that narcocorridos glorify violence and thus spread violence. Against the idea that corridos cause violence, Muehlmann has argued that instead they "heighten awareness of the violence connected to the war on drugs" (87), rightly pointing out that there is a difference between representation of violence and actual violence (92). Based on her anthropological research, she argues that corridos are "real" in the sense that they reflect a reality of violence (102). It is violent business, all-encompassing, leading to a violent life and possibly a violent death; as such, they are an expression of a reality of violence.[16] Narcocorridos are first and foremost artistic creations. Often they are a reflection of and on violence, but within their own logic of market and political concerns. It is a complex music that generally fulfills several functions at the same time, which range from criticism and celebration to entertainment, and a music that, through puns and coded, witty language, appeals to different audiences simultaneously.

## The Meaning of Firearms in Narcocorridos

While it is difficult to create an encompassing narrative about the narcocorrido genre, we can highlight certain trends—in relation to specific contexts or groups. Several emblematic songs illustrate how the meaning of the assault rifle and the negotiation of violence undergoes various transformations over time. At first, only remarked upon in passing, the firearm over the years becomes the ever more prominent artifact and trope of a violent life and a symbol of an archaic-postmodern narcomodernity—until it starts to appear mainly as a tool of paramilitarist groups. In "Contrabando y traición" by Los Tigres del Norte from the early 1970s, the song that revived the genre and created a new mass appeal through the narco topic, the firearm has only an implicit relation to the trade. In this corrido Emilio and Camelia successfully smuggle marijuana in their car tires, but the corrido ends in a violent altercation when Emilio tells Camelia that he will go to his love in San Francisco. She then shoots him seven times. The firearm is a part of their violent life, but not essential for smuggling or defending their turf. Rather, similar to "Adelita," this is a melodramatic romance song, told on the backdrop of a violent context. The firearm is not used to settle scores between competing parties but to avenge betrayal in the context of romance.

It is only in later corridos that the firearm becomes more prominent, in "Cuerno de chivo," for example. The song was written by famous composer and songwriter Paulino Vargas in 1977 and recorded and performed by many such as Chalino Sánchez and groups like Los Broncos de Reynosa. In the song the AK-47, nicknamed "goat's horn" for the shape of its magazine, becomes the crucial accessory of the narco and acquires a broad symbolic meaning. The firearm is an artifact of resistance against the federal state, reminiscent of similar discourses in earlier bandit and rebel corridos from the north, since the singer says that he will resist federal police ("federales") with his AK-47. The song establishes a transnational geography: border crossings and an odyssey through the United States (El Paso, Sacramento, Chicago) to sell cocaine. The AK-47 is the seductive siren of adventure and economic independence but also a tragic symbol of the proximity of death, because one of the holders of an AK-47 winds up dead, killed with an Ak-47: "This is the ballad the goat's horn sings" ("Esta es la balada que canta el cuerno de chivo").

The firearm is thus a symbol of bravado and precariousness—the artifact and trope of a violent life. The reference to weapons often underscores one's willingness and threat to use violence (see, for example, Los Tigres del Norte's song "Lo que sembré allá en la sierra" on the album *Jefe de Jefes*). Yet next to the power bestowed by the firearm lies the issue of precariousness, of insecurity, and the proximity of death. In later songs—for example, in "118 balazos" by Valentin Elizalde, himself killed in an ambush in 2006—firearms are a symbol of a precariously violent life. The first-person narrator says that he has already survived three attempts on his life; 118 bullets have been shot at him but so far God and the Virgen de Guadalupe have protected him. In "El primo" by Los Tucanes de Tijuana, on the album *Tucanes de Plata*, there is a sense of fatality associated with the firearm and the drug business; the protagonist wants to leave the violent business, but he can't because by now there is "gunpowder in his blood" ("Ya pólvora trae mi sangre").

Often the rifle is a trope used to connect with the image of a rural and idyllic life, as for example in "Pacas de a kilo" from the album *La garra de . . .* by Los Tigres de Norte, which is also illustrative of Bello's ambiguous songwriting. The song extends the metaphor of the AK-47 as a goat's horn to tell a story of narcolife as good old *serrano* life. Modern technology—assault rifles and airplanes—is combined with images of nature. The narrator tells of an idyllic childhood in the mountain, where he roamed free and learned math by counting the sacks of produce. The sacks counted are bales of marijuana, just as the "cattle without ticks" ("ganado sin garrapatas") and "with sheep tails" ("con colitas de borrego") are code words for high-quality marijuana: without seeds ("ticks") and with its leaves sticking out, easily cut out ("tails"). Similar to guerrilla songs, the association of arms with animals creates legitimacy, only that here they are not wild animals but domesticated farm animals within an agroindustiral enterprise, just like the drug business. This song, full of pastoral images, starts with the sounds of a rooster crowing, a cow mooing, and a horse neighing. In this sense it almost resembles The Beatles' "Good Morning" from *Sgt. Pepper's Lonely Heart Club Band,* which features a wide array of animal voices. Only that "Good Morning" talks about the predictable tranquil urban life of office workers, whereas "Pacas de a kilo" paints an image of the adventurous yet idyllic rural life of the narco.

Many double entendres equate and interlace the life of a peasant and a narco. The nature references formulate a critique of the government, which protects the narrator, since the pines giving him shade can be understood as referring to pine trees or the lodgings of the Mexican president, nicknamed Los Pinos. It is also a song good for dancing, making the double entendre of the song a triple entendre, since it has a catchy, danceable melody, and the emphasis on words such as "very close" ("pegadito") and "pretty-looking" ("chulas") lend themselves to dancing closely with a partner. It is the perfect example of attracting different listeners by fulfilling different functions. This song "defined a new style" of corridos, which was soon imitated by groups like Los Tucanes de Tijuana, for example, in their song "Mis tres animales" about heroine, cocaine and marijuana (Wald 289). In "El balido de mi ganado" from the album *Los Poderosos* by Los Tucanes de Tijuana, which starts with the bleating of actual goats, the weapons appear as animals, the bleating turns into the bursts of firearms. Yet the song also relates the rural narco life with globalization and transnational trade routes, because the narrator sings that he got the firearms from China. Omar Rincón has argued that the narco figure is simultaneously premodern, modern, and postmodern; archaic because it is connected to the land and ideas of *compadrazgo,* modern because of its capitalist enterprise, and postmodern because of its focus on immediacy and consumption (5–6).

The most important narcocultural symbol of this simultaneous triple modernity is the lavishly decorated baroque golden or silver, diamond-encrusted firearm. "Temible cuerno de chivo" by Los Incomparables de Tijuana praises a luxurious silver-plated AK-47.[17] The silver AK-47 is a symbol of initiation; Rodrigo is accepted into the circles of the *valientes.* The Commander Aguilera gifts it to Rodrigo, saying that it is a weapon for a "man of courage" ("valiente") and stressing its decorations and silver incrustations and its grenade launcher. He tells the history of this weapon; it has killed fourteen soldiers and three bandits. As such, the song also points to the blurry battle lines of this conflict and to the topic of paramilitarism. The protagonist has a military rank (commander), and he speaks about the weapon killing both soldiers and bandits. Except for the general association of the golden rifle with the narcoworld, it is unclear whether Commander Aguilar is the commander of an official military troop or of a paramilitary troop.

The most recent corridos tend to reflect the (para)militarist logic even more clearly. As the conflict turned more violent, so did the corridos. In particular, the self-denominated Movimiento Alterado has created particularly violent and graphic songs. Like most narcocorridos, they are produced again in California, relatively removed from the bloodshed in the Mexican northern and central states. The Movimiento Alterado is a recent development and in many ways a musical representation of the escalation of the conflict during the Calderón years (Ramírez-Pimienta, "De torturaciones" 306, 320). The songs by the Movimiento Alterado are "war chants" characterized by "hyperviolence" ("cantos de guerra," "hiperviolencia," 321). In these songs the singers rarely talk about cultivation and trafficking, but only about violence work and at times drug consumption. These songs tend to take on more of a military standpoint; the weapon is far less an artifact but mainly a tool. The song "10 tiros por segundo" from the album *El Katch* by El Komander, for example, celebrates the firepower of the AK-47, describing its technical details such as shots per minute and magazine capacity and admonishing listeners to always have a round in the chamber. Here the AK-47 is no longer an icon of insurgency but presented as the favorite tool of "the mafia"—a tool of organized crime, ideal for settling scores and carrying out executions.

These songs are not about daring *narcotraficantes* who manage to fool the border patrol, but about brutal soldiers who enjoy war and are good at kidnappings and executions. They are full-blown battle songs, aimed at giving listeners a powerful rush. The most famous example is "Sanguinarios del M1," sung by several Movimiento Alterado artists. This is a song about an army invading towns, about long caravans of vehicles driving to battle; the fighters, high on narcotics, are heavily armed, uniformed, and operate in battle formation. Besides a brief reference to the Sinaloa Federation and its alleged leaders El Mayo and El Chapo, no explicit reference to drugs and drug-trafficking appears in the song—only weapons and war. In this song the functional logic of the firearm is at the center: to execute, to kill, to make people suffer and agonize. The BuKnas sings about handling an AK-47 and a bazooka, about blowing off heads and the pleasure of killing: "We are bloodthirsty . . . we like to kill" ("Somos sanguinarios . . . nos gusta matar"). Here a paramilitarist state logic appears as they do these things "to control" and "to traumatize" ("para controlar"; "pa' traumatizar").

The song is unapologetic in its celebration of violence. Earlier songs are more romanticizing, the rifle the curious artifact of the individual narco, but here it is a tool of the work of a paramilitary group. As such, it can be seen as a representation and expression of the ever more violent escalation under Calderón and the appearance of mercenary groups composed of former military such as Los Zetas. Nonetheless these songs are an artistic representation, a part of the violent narcoimaginary that sells so well—not necessarily an organic representation from within a drug-trafficking or mercenary organization. Yet it certainly shows a shift in the representation of firearms and rifles within the narcocorrido genre. Within this notion of sick and disturbed violence propagated by the Movimiento Alterado, the songs still express a desire for legitimacy.[18] They do so by invoking heroes of the Mexican Revolution. Especially Villa is the ideal for playing up northern culture and legitimacy, as he is the ultimate bandit-turned-rebel. Many corridos have for long played on the power of the image of the social bandit, and many use key coordinates of the northern dimension of the revolution, referring to being *valiente y serrano*.[19] Bands like Los Tigres del Norte have made albums featuring songs of the revolution such as "Siete leguas" and "La Valentina" (Ramírez-Pimienta, *Cantar* 113). But it is in the songs by the Movimiento Alterado, the most violent, that appear the most explicit references to Pancho Villa. They sing that the fighters have Villa on their minds when they engage in heavy battle with bazookas and assault rifles (for example, "Sanguinarios del M1"). In the song "Estrategias de guerra," from the album *Impactos de arranque,* the group Voz de Mando implies that only the weaponry has changed, but that the narcos are heirs of Villa; instead of carbines, they use assault rifles and grenade launchers; instead of bandoliers, bullet-proof vests; instead of horses, armored vehicles. As Juan Carlos Ramírez-Pimienta has indicated, while they celebrate the modern technology, they always return to the powerful image of Villa, comparing the narco commander to him, alluding to a nonexistent anachronistic cavalry: "always riding in the front" ("siempre cabalgando al frente") ("De torturaciones" 314). Just as the postrevolutionary regime always used dead rebels to create legitimacy, the latest narcocorridos draw on these figures to legitimize the actions of narcos.

This makes for a confusing aesthetics: so like the Mexican state and so like the outlaw. The narcos are not revolutionary insurgents, they are armed businessmen and mercenaries, but the discourses surrounding them invoke insurgent images and they are being combated with counterinsurgent techniques. In the meantime, counterinsurgency, while not successful in the stated aim of curbing drug trafficking, has helped the state apparatus to militarize big stretches of the country in an unprecedented manner. As a cultural and political phenomenon, this is difficult to read. The rifle is again a blurry signifier, a chameleon of meaning. What happens if we take material narcoculture into account, if we try to interpret actual golden rifles?

## Golden AK-47s: The Kitsch and Politics of Material Narcoculture

Once more, it is unclear whether the golden firearms represent a subculture that emanated organically from the narcoworld or whether it was invented in the media and then adopted. Yet they are a central part of material narcoculture and the narcoimaginary. Instagram accounts of alleged narcos showcasing golden weapons pop up and then disappear again. Golden and silver rifles are repeatedly found during raids of houses of alleged narcos. The section "Narcocultura" in the Museo de Enervantes—curated, of course, by a problematic curator, the Mexican military—is full of golden and silver rifles and pistols with elaborate engravings and decorations.[20] The Calderón government used golden weapons to underscore the indecency and tacky, exotic Otherness of narcos. Yet these firearms have to be interpreted differently if we analyze them not with regard to government propaganda but as part of a subculture constructed in relation to the drug-trafficking business, as a possibly organic expression of a narcoculture. Then the kitsch reveals an unapologetic stance, a disregard of what is considered bad taste by other strata or society and a means to stand out. "I don't like what's cheap" ("no me gusta lo corriente") sing Los Matadores del Norte in "De Sinaloa a Durango," talking about the narrator's semiautomatic handgun with golden handle plates. There is a class dimension to these weapons. Similar to the golden chains in hip-hop culture, the weapon celebrates social mobility and power. Narcocorridos are songs of social mobility (Ramírez-Pimienta, *Cantar* 84), and the golden rifle is a brash artifact of the ascent.[21] But whereas the golden chains of hip-hop culture reveal only economic success and brazen consumption, the golden rifle does not obviate the violence but rather puts it in the center.

The golden rifles are primarily props as their usefulness is questionable. Since they have parts bathed in gold and elaborate decorations, for which the barrel needs to be made smaller, there is a high probability that they would malfunction in a shootout. To some degree, they are thus an example of what Sayak Valencia Triana has called "decorative violence" ("violencia decorativa")—that is, a phenomenon that converts weaponry in decorative items or military goods into civilian ones. There is a long history of decorative weapons used as symbols of power, such as the decorated swords of kings. Golden rifles abound in visual presentations of narcocorrido bands, at least those known for their heavier, more violent *corridos perrones* (not those by Los Tigres del Norte). Album covers of singers of *corridos perrones,* such as Lupillo Rivera, often feature golden AK-47s with extra-long magazines, triple the size of a normal magazine (Edberg annex). These extend the metaphor of a horn and highlight the hypermasculine phallic character: a long golden firearm shooting an extra round of sperm. The Movimiento Alterado, too, is often depicted with golden assault rifles, pistols, or cartridges.

This representation on covers of narcocorrido bands contrast with the few photographs we have of alleged narcos. There is one photo of El Chapo Guzmán, which before his second and third capture was the only picture that circulated of him.[22] The photo was found in a raid and for a long time was used for Most Wanted posters. It shows El Chapo with simple clothes, a cap, a hunter's vest, and a regular AR-15—not a golden AK-47—hanging over his shoulder but also held with both hands. At his side stands a man said to be called Don Juanito (Valencia), dressed in fatigues, cap, sunglasses, an AR-15 dangling off his shoulder and a walkie-talkie in hand. Don Juanito's martial outfit is interrupted by the fact that he is wearing open-toe sandals. This photo has little to do with the imagined extravagant life of the narco. El Chapo seems very much like a foot soldier, not like the leader of a powerful organization. The photo once more points to the indistinctness of actors of the drug war, since both—because of their outfit—could also well be members of a regular army. Moreover it stands out because of its lack of epic quality. El Chapo is not the charismatic caudillo of old, but he looks somewhat uncomfortable and shows no flash or verve. The supposedly *real* narco is far less ostentatious and exuberant than the *narcocorridistas* playing narcos.

This does not mean that the golden rifles are only a narcocultural fiction, however. All the golden and silver rifles in the Museo de Enervantes come from somewhere. Somebody is producing them, somebody is buying them. And somebody is displaying them—in a museum, albeit closed to the public. This once more makes the firearm in the drug war an ambivalent and nebulous symbol—an attractive one, eagerly gobbled up, rarely critically analyzed.

In Latin America and beyond, exists a fascination with narcoculture and its extravagance. Rincón has argued that the fascination speaks of "societies of exclusion in which one can only catch sight of the dream of modernity by means of the paralegal" (2). But this criminal from-rags-to-riches story becomes an exoticizing cliché: "Latin America ends up becoming another stereotype, another theme park: of very macho narcos and very slutty beauties, both horizons of sin, after the desire for capital, both ironies of being a Latino in these times when one is modern any way one can" (30).[23] To be as modern "any way one can" reveals an important aspect of narcocultural modernity—namely that the state has lost importance as interlocutor between projects of modernity and citizenry.

The golden rifles baffle many leftists. Leftist newspapers such as *La Jornada* readily displayed images of golden rifles during the years of heavy government propaganda, such as the image at the opening of this chapter. During 2010–2011, *La Jornada* at least three times featured golden weapons as the main photo on their cover page—the photos were always from press conferences of arms confiscated and exhibited by the Mexican government. The photos had hardly any framing in the form of captions or commentary, so it is difficult to discern the intended purpose of the golden firearms on the front page. It is unclear whether this is a newspaper uncritically buying into government propaganda, fascinated with these modern outlaws, or a newspaper hoping for a new insurgency, or simply trying to sell through violence. The radical left generally looks favorably on insurgents, but they do not know how to interpret these insurgent entrepreneurs who aim at emulating state functions.[24]

The golden rifle is a confusing symbol and the lack of interpretation is not only owed to an embeddedness of thought in government discourses, but also to the prop's slippery symbolic nature. These weapons are a deliberate excess, "perhaps the most explicit mesh of kitsch, retro, and porn" (Muniz 66). The golden rifles express power—symbolic military power and real power of consumption—and they fit the triple temporality of the narcomodernity, which is simultaneously anachronistic-medieval, modern-consumerist, and postmodern-ambivalent. They are "the signs of power and the neoliberal mystique" ("los signos de poder y de la mística neoliberal") (Valenzuela Arce 156). They are both artifact and prop of a neoliberal modernity, determined by violent spectacle and global consumption. The golden AK-47 thus creates an impasse for thinking about insurgency, counterinsurgency, the state, and the market. Similar to the Mexican and the Nicaraguan revolutions, it stands for a violent dynamic where modernity is accessed through the firearm but the coordinates have shifted. The golden AK-47 announces a political-economic entity simultaneously constructed through firepower, power of consumption, and occupation of state functions.

FIGURE C.1. Frank Orozco, *El Monumento al Combatiente Popular*, 1984.
Photograph by Sophie Esch.

## EPILOGUE

# THE LONG SHADOW OF THE RIFLE

In the center of Managua, amid empty lots, ruins of the 1972 earthquake, and government buildings, stands a statue of a man. Nine meters tall, the cast iron statue is that of a bare-chested, eerily muscular man who in one hand holds a pickax and with the other thrusts an AK-47 into the sky (figure C.1). The Monument to the Popular Combatant, as it is officially called, was revealed in 1984, for the fifth anniversary of the Sandinista Revolution. The statue's inscription reads: "Only the workers and peasant will go to the end" ("Sólo los obreros y los campesinos irán hasta el fin"). Managuans responded with irreverence to its martial sternness—they commonly refer to it as "The Hulk."[1] Whereas the comic book Hulk operates with sheer strength and fury, the Managuan Hulk showcases the importance of tools and raises once more the question of the firearm as artifact.

The statue's AK-47, so ominously or auspiciously erect into the sky, is an artifact of symbolic and spectral significance. As it points skyward, it seems to fulfill Carlos Mejía Godoy's promise of a "rifle-shooting auroras"—the statue is a memorial to a dream, the search for utopia through arms, and the disintegration of that dream. It is a specter of insurgency and counterinsurgency. The statue was a paradox and a premonition. It praised the worker in a land with few workers and praised the popular combatant and the peasant at a moment when—during the Contra War—popular combatants and peasants were fighting against the revolutionary regime that erected it. It features the AK-47, the iconic rifle of insurgency, even though it was the rifle of the Sandinista state combating Contra insurgents. "Only the workers and peasants will go to the end," predicts the inscription and, in the end, peasants—through filling the ranks of the Contra revolution—decided the outcome of the Sandinista Revolution. Six years after the erection of the statue, the FSLN lost the elections, ousted from power in part by those it allegedly wanted to get into power.

The statue is also a Cold War memorial and a reminder of the eternal geopolitics influencing the Central American isthmus. The statue—its socialist-

realist aesthetic and Kalashnikov rifle a deferential nod to the Soviet Union—
was erected as a symbol against US intervention, since an invasion seemed
imminent (González Centeno). It was a warning that if the United States
dare invade Nicaragua, an armed population like this popular combatant would wait for them.[2] But instead of a full-scale US invasion, the Nicaraguan people suffered the consequences of a drawn-out conflict between
Sandinistas and Contras, the latter equipped with arms by the Reagan
administration.

The past, present, and future that collide in contradictory ways in the
statue are a reminder of the complex legacy of armed struggle in present-day
Latin America where the rifle continues to haunt the left.[3] Nowadays many
leftist intellectuals have moved away from the idea of armed struggle. As Jean
Franco put it, after the end of the Cold War it became "hard to backtrack
and discover the moment when armed struggle was not an idle project [but]
regarded as realistic [and] necessary" (*Decline and Fall* 87). With the end of
the guerrilla period, the notion of armed struggle was hastily dismissed to
make way for neoconservative and neoliberal politics. Yet the conditions that
led to armed struggle in Latin America—inequality, injustice, violence—did
not suddenly disappear (Castañeda 4). They still affect current societies. John
Beverley thus has rightly argued that "the question of . . . armed struggle is
not only about the Latin American past but also about its political present
and future" ("Rethinking the Armed Struggle" 48). And while Latin American countries are still trying to come to terms with the violence of the Cold
War period, they are being ravaged by the violence of the current drug wars.
Latin America thus appears haunted by the reality and the memory of the
rifle.

In this context my book follows complicated lines of inquiry. Through cultural analysis, it looks to understand the many meanings behind taking up
arms for political means and offer a deeper understanding of armed struggle
when its heyday in Latin America is long over. Offering a complex critique of
arms, I highlight the precarious, affective, and egalitarian nature of many insurgent acts and critically examine the latent militarism and profound trauma
present in these armed political acts. Through my analysis, I am able to show
that the firearm is a key artifact of political struggles in Mexico and Central
America. It becomes an artifact of different symbolic-political uses and meanings: an artifact for participation and recognition within the state, a prosthesis
for citizenship, an artifact for militancy, as well as an artifact for participation within modernity. The book thus captures a modernity aspired, fulfilled,
modified, and seen through the rifle, a modernity imagined, realized, and ne-

gotiated at gunpoint, a modernity mirrored in and haunted by the rifle. Alberto Ribas-Casasayas and Amanda L. Petersen have stressed the importance of ghosts in Hispanic literature and argued that they "communicate something in connection with the region's tortuous relationship with modernity" (4). By looking at the symbolic meaning of the firearm and its spectral presence in the form of echoes and wounds, this book shows that not only people but also things and their ghostly echoes tell us something about the region's narratives of modernity, citizenship, and militancy.

In this book I developed my own framework to analyze material culture by looking at both the material object itself as well as the cultural production about it and by distinguishing the different values of the object as tool, commodity, artifact, trope, prop, and echo. This framework can inform other studies of material culture, while highlighting cultural production as central to creating the meaning of an object.

I make my findings through literature and music, through the particular space of thinking about the world, of imagining and feeling the world that is opened up by literature and music. By drawing attention to cultural representations of weaponry, this book leaves the reader with many symbolically powerful and meaningful scenes created in the literary, musical, and visual works: the little girl who puts the frozen blood of her dead friend into his blue linen jacket; the gestures of the no-longer anonymous Perfecto Olivas who extends his sarape and leaves his forehead uncovered to face the firing squad; a woman, her face blackened by gun powder, who throws herself into combat; women raped under the threat of the rifle; *muchachos* facing off against machine guns, tanks, and airplanes; rifles shooting auroras and fallen guerrilla fighters turning into insurgent fauna and flora; an old peasant handing a young *guerrillero* ammunition from the times of Sandino's army; violent incursions of armed troops of unclear affiliation in the sierra of Chihuahua; and also the little rhinoceros running toward a man missing an arm.

Because it is a book about literature and music, I hope it leaves the reader not only pondering the political-literary meaning of these scenes but also savoring the language of texts and songs: the lyrical restraint of Nellie Campobello; the melodies and the wit of the corridos of the revolution; the precise wordiness of Martín Luis Guzmán; the exuberant sincerity of Gioconda Belli and Omar Cabezas; the deliberate and eloquent discourse of Sergio Ramírez; the catchy tunes of the Mejía Godoys and their romantic-violent worlds full of cheerful lyricism and militant idealism; the monosyllables of Horacio Castellanos Moya's Robocop; the irrepressible slew of anger and pop culture references in Pancho Rana's universe of sex, dance, and war; the bitterness of Jacinta Escudos's fighting narrators and lovers; the detached tone and compassionate gaze of Claudia Hernández's stories; the tragic tone of the *testimonios* of violence gathered by Víctor Hugo Rascón Banda; the melodramatic, boisterous, and violent ballads of the AK-47 and the thrill and rush of the nauseous *corridos alterados.*

The shadow of the rifle looms large, haunting not only the militant left but also lettered circles. Juan Pablo Dabove has analyzed the "monsters" haunting the Latin America's lettered cities: identities other than the white, urban, male *letrado,* often grouped under the term "bandit" (*Nightmares* 1–2). He shows how the trope of the bandit was used to define the lettered city but also challenge it; it was central to defining opposition between "the paradigms of bandit/citizen and outlaw violence/state violence" (7). This book follows similar lines of inquiry but focuses on the object firearm and the figure of the insurgent. Instead of the bandit trope in relation to nation-building in the long nineteenth century, I discuss peasant insurgency, guerrilla warfare, and the drug war in relation to material culture, the construction of political subjectivities, and modernity in the twentieth and twenty-first centuries.[4] In this context, the rifle appears as an artifact that intrigues the lettered city on both political and affective levels.

This book highlights many scenes of *encuentros* and *desencuentros* between people of letters and people of arms: the intellectual looking upon the fleeting images of men with arms in a camp of *la bola;* Villa teaching an intellectual how to shoot a firearm; the dance of the rifle and the pistol of angry Zapatista troops in the Ministry of War; a poet shooting a heavy machine gun in Cuba, Fidel Castro looming over her; a *letrado* receiving a rusted FAL from a poor Contra peasant; and the violent pistols and pens of former *guerrilleros* in postwar El Salvador. The rifle is a key symbol to see the Other but also to construct oneself.[5] Questions of power, solidarity, and self are central to these narratives of insurgency. Support, mediation, autonomy, condemnation, defense, or an inquiry into the reality of the violence are among the many possible positions literature can take in the face of armed violence. Often these questions are addressed via the depiction of the relationship between *letrados* and people in arms in the literary text itself. The many *(des)encuentros* of *letrados* and *armados* depicted in the texts are a means to explore the complex interactions between the literay and the political field. Often the observation of the distance between the two is one of the main achievement of the literay texts, honest and artful acknowledgments of ignorance, misunderstanding, and distrust.

There is, nonetheless, in many of these texts a desire to bridge this distance between *letrado* and *armado,* between *ciudad letrada* and *campo armado;* to bring them together or reconcile them. Not surprisingly, education has always been one of the major aims and achievement of many Latin American revolutions. The focus on public education in the postrevolutionary regime profoundly changed Mexico (Vaughan), and the literacy campaign is one of the undisputed achievements of the Sandinistas. During the National Crusade Against Illiteracy in 1980, the revolutionary regime sent out teenagers into the rural areas to teach peasants basic reading and math and lowered illiteracy drastically, at least temporarily. This was a moment when the imagined opposition between city and countryside, civilization and barbarism, between literacy and illiteracy, was bridged.[6] It was a moment of encounter, not only because peasants learned to read and write, but also because the young people acquired new knowledge. The young *brigadistas* learned about their own country. Similar to the peasants of *la bola* in the Mexican Revolution who got to know the country via train, in this instance the young educated generation from the city got to know their country: the speech, knowledge, life of rural folks.

Often the social and political changes fell short of the hopes and aspirations of the agents of revolution, but maybe these short moments of encounter, of mutual recognition and learning, are what remains as the most important legacy of these twentieth-century revolutions—even though their legacy seems so frail under the current regimes in Mexico and Nicaragua. In the 1990s unknown persons placed a bomb at the foot of the Monumento al Combatiente Popular. It damaged statue's footing and legs but did not tumble it. Environmental corrosion did further damage, but the statue still stands (*El Nuevo Diario*). It still stands despite the determined endeavor of conservative, neoliberal regimes that followed the Sandinista rule to erase revolutionary symbols and murals across the country and rename plazas, markets, and streets that had been named after Sandinista martyrs.

Another statue also survived the politics of erasure: the Monumento a Sandino. The statue, designed by poet and sculptor Ernesto Cardenal, was erected in 1990, the year of the transition of power. It is a silhouette of the peasant general with his wide-brimmed hat, built on top of the Loma de Tipiscapa. The peasant insurgent overlooks Managua from the same hill from which the Somoza clan once ruled the country and where it once tortured political prisoners. It seems that the erection of the statue was a frantic move of the Sandinistas to preserve the memory of the revolution, knowing what was to come. It meant that this particular revolution ended not with the tumbling of a statue but with the erection of one. The statue was a sign that Central America would no longer be haunted by the watchful eyes of dictators on hills overlooking the capitals—the frightening atmosphere that Cardenal had re-created in his poem "Hora Cero" from 1958. Today Managua is no longer "aimed at by machine guns" ("apuntada por las ametralladoras"; 27). Instead, it is haunted by the shadow of the peasant insurgent. Its significance ranges, as Sergio Villena Fiengo has pointed out, between "paternal, protective image" "intimidating vigilant specter," and "tragic emblem of the revolution" (26, 33).[7]

Yet despite its different meanings in the ever-changing urban landscape of Managua, the statue fulfills one of the Sandinistas great discursive maneuvers: to make Sandino a national hero. The statue, even though it does not have its arms wide open, is reminiscent of the Christ the Redeemer statue in Rio de Janeiro (Villena Fiengo 26). Sandino, the redeemer, stands over Managua as the hope and promise of a salvation from imperialism, inequality, and authoritarianism. Sandino is now a hero recognizable even without a rifle. His hat is enough to remind people of his legacy and the legacy of insurgency in Nicaragua. The rifle is not the only artifact making a man or an image of insurgency iconic. Head gear is also key: Zapata's sombrero, Sandino's sombrero, Guevara's beret. Yet the rifle is the shadow behind the silhouette. The threat and reality of peasant insurgency materialize through sombrero and rifle. As such, even though the transition to formal democracy is often celebrated as the ultimate achievement of the Sandinista Revolution, in the end its legacy might be a lot closer to the Mexican Revolution: leaving the nation with the legacy of peasant insurgency. Villa, Zapata, and Sandino might have been appropriated by different groups and regimes for different purposes throughout the twentieth century, yet the shadow of these insurgents and their rifles looms large.

These rifles have shaped sociopolitical developments and literary traditions of Central America and Mexico in the twentieth and twenty-first century and carry a message to this day. The looming shadow of firearm is a reminder of the insurgent potential of the citizenry—a reminder that as long as societies remain deeply unequal, people will rise up and take up arms in quests for participation, recognition, or survival. It is a reminder to democracies "of the revolutionary forces to which they owe their existence," to quote Walter Benjamin once more ("Critique of Violence" 244). The specter of the rifle means that we have to rethink the role of difference and dissent in the construction of more inclusive and equal societies.

# *NOTES*

## *INTRODUCTION*

1. Tellingly, Cervantes's *Don Quijote de la Mancha,* considered the first modern novel (printed in 1605), offers a mournful and humorous reflection on this weapon in the eponymous character's famous discourse on arms and letters. Don Quijote, the fervent reader, appears to favor arms over letters in his discourse, yet he laments that the firearm—that "diabolical invention" and "wicked machine" ("invención diabólica," "maldita máquina," Part part 1, Chapter chapter XXXVIII38)—forecloses the heroic path of the knight who acquires fame through his sword skills. A way of life is being swept away by modernizing regimes. Aptly so, two other modern inventions— the printed book and the novel genre—are the ones to capture the profound impact of the firearm.

2. Kurz's account does not fully explain why the discovery of gunpowder in China centuries earlier, probably in the ninth century AD (Parker 83), did not lead to a similar firearms-led expansionism. This question is still debated by historians.

3. Academics have long pointed out that the experience of modernity in Latin America differs from traditional accounts of European and North American modernity. Beatriz Sarlo in *Una modernidad periférica: Buenos Aires, 1920 y 1930* and Jesús Martín Barbero in "Modernidad y posmodernidad en la periferia" stress the peripheral and decentered character of Latin American modernity. Néstor García Canclini in *Culturas híbridas. Estrategias para entrar y salir de la modernidad* highlights cultural heterogeneity as the marking experience of Latin American modernity. In "Latinoamérica y la posmodernidad," Nelly Richard refers to the heteroclite elements of the modern experience in the region (277). In *La no simultaneidad de lo simultáneo: postmodernidad, globalización y culturas en América Latina,* Carlos Rincón underscores the asynchronous insertion of Latin America into world history and economy. In spite of these theorizations of Latin American difference, the Weberian concept of modernity continues to be very powerful in the Latin American collective imagination. Even critical revisions of the idea of modernity in Latin America in the light of postmodernism such as *Culturas híbridas* and *The Postmodernism Debate* make mention of Weber's conception as the underlying principle for many discourses on modernity in the region (García Canclini 22–23; Beverley, Aronna, and Oviedo 2, 7).

4. In an already vast cultural corpus, I have excluded film in order not to overburden the book. What interests me is drawing a bridge between the study of literature and song. Yet photography is also included in the corpus, as it is impossible to talk about the symbolic significance of weaponry without at least selectively analyzing several iconic images featuring weaponry.

5. Throughout the nineteenth century until today, insubordinate groups in Mexico have used US arms to resist state projects, be they Apaches, Comanches, Kiowas, or Yaquis; the insurgents of the Mexican Revolution; or drug-trafficking organizations (DeLay 15).

6. I thank Ana Catarina Teixeira for pointing out that "Cold War" is a misnomer.

7. From the original Spanish: "el regalo precioso de encontrar su sitio; de encontrar que . . . con sólo una 30–30 como única propiedad, su vida era pertinente precisamente por el hecho que ellos eran los dueños de ella." Unless otherwise noted, all the translations in this book from the original Spanish and German sources into English are my own.

8. About the relationship between technology and peasants or subalterns, see also Legrás, *Culture and Revolution* 124–25, 151.

9. In *Everyday Forms of State Formation,* the historians Gilbert Joseph and Daniel Nugent put great emphasis on the fact "that the state is not a thing, an object one can point to," stressing the process of continuous negotiations and processes that make up a state, constituted through "forms, routines, rituals, and discourses of rule" (19–20). They make an important point, but I contend that the state apparatus (made up of state institutions and officials) often functions as just such a "thing," symbolizing the state. Yet a state is more than its apparatus; it is constituted through a territory, people, violence, and as Joseph and Nugent point out, through rituals of rule.

10. *Los de abajo* is one of the earliest writings about the revolution, originally published in 1915 in the form of sequels in border newspapers. While the first (sequel) edition expresses this idea of war for war's sake in an affirmative and explicit manner, the second edition only harbors a trace of this idea. The first, shorter version from 1915 had a revolutionary, highly allegorical ending: the peasant leader Demetrio Macías pointed his rifle, forever in an eternal struggle against injustice (Aguilar Mora, *Una muerte sencilla* 49–50). The revised version of 1920 is far more disillusioned in its overall tone. It introduces new figures, such as the disloyal poet Valderrama. Also, the ending has lost its allegorical dimension. It no longer points toward a never-ending quest for social justice through insurrection. In the revised edition, Demetrio is no longer the peasant who stands for all justice-seeking peasants (Aguilar Mora, *Una muerte sencilla* 49–50). He is just a man who, after a futile succession of skirmishes and carnage, is left dead, rifle in hand. Ignacio Sánchez Prado furthermore points out that stylistic changes (vernacular language and a conversion into past tense) between the two editions "have a clear ideological consequence: the assertion of the difference

between the rationality of the lettered class and the barbarism of the troops, and a change of the novel's "reality effect" from the experiential sense of the present to the preterit's connotation of established history" ("Novel, War" n.p.).

11. There were some slippages, though: the popular tribunal against a former private secretary of Somoza during the insurrection as well as the assassination of Anastasio Somoza Debayle in 1980 in Asunción were deviations so great that long testimonial novels such as *Sombras nada más* (2002) by Sergio Ramírez and *Somoza: Expediente cerrado: La historia de un ajusticiamiento* (1993) by Claribel Alegría and D. J. Flakoll were dedicated to them, albeit after the FSLN's electoral defeat.

12. In this case, the English translation is not my own: "der Zwang zur allgemeinen Verwendung von Gewalt als Mittel zu Zwecken des Staates" (Benjamin, "Zur Kritik der Gewalt" 40).

13. The English translation is not my own: "jammervolle Schauspiel, weil sie sich der revolutionären Kräfte, denen sie ihr Dasein verdanken, nicht bewußt geblieben sind" (Benjamin, "Zur Kritik der Gewalt" 46).

14. From the original: "Rechtsetzung ist Machtsetzung und insofern ein Akt von unmittelbarer Manifestation der Gewalt" (Benjamin, "Zur Kritik der Gewalt" 57).

15. The idea of intervening politically through arms might also have to do with the legacy of *caudillismo* in Latin America—the legacy of politics being shaped by military strongmen in the aftermath of the independence wars. Yet designations such as banditry and *caudillismo* point to the problem of who has the power to say what the armed act means and who is able to create a discourse of legitimacy. The term "banditry" is often used to criminalize rural insurgency (Dabove, *Nightmares*; Hobsbawm), whereas the term *caudillismo* is used to criticize personalist, regionally anchored politics or to berate Latin American nations for their supposedly inherent authoritarianism.

16. For a discussion of (post)revolutionary citizenship in Mexico, its scope, expectations, and gendered dimensions, see Olcott (11–12, 32–59).

17. Pratt advocates a scheme in which the military sphere is one of hyperconsumption, unproductivity, fighting, and destruction, and the civilian-domestic sphere is one of hyperproduction, reproduction, work, and construction. Both spheres have to be seen as equally important components of war ("Mi cigarro" 161). The military sphere is dependent on the civilian sphere, not merely for moral support as nationalist narratives frame it but for actual material support (161).

18. I was unable to obtain the reproduction rights for this photograph, but it can be viewed online through an image search of "La miliciana de Waswalito."

19. From the original Spanish: "cuando la metralla furiosa bramó . . . la ciudadanía por primera vez la verdad sesionó." In the songs by the Mejía Godoys, the word *metralla* is used interchangeably with *fusil* (rifle).

20. The term "violent nonstate actors" is used by the military and international

organizations to refer to armed actors who do not belong to a state apparatus and thus use violence without the state's legitimization. However, I am more inclined to speak of nonstate and semistate actors because the lines with regard to the state are often blurry. There exists a long history of violent nonstate actors intervening in state formation in the Americas. These range from colonial outlaws such as pirates and maroons to the classical bandit of the nineteenth century, to revolutionaries, guerrilla fighters, and drug traffickers.

21. From the original Spanish: "Un indígena guatemalteco sujeta la rama que lleva como si fuera un fusil, y apunta a la oscuridad. La silueta engaña."

22. The region today know as the Mexican nation-state forms part of the geographical entity North America but also part of the historic-cultural region known as Mesoamerica—a term anthropologists use to refer to the shared cultural traits among pre-Columbian populations in Central Mexico, the Yucatán Peninsula, and the Central American isthmus. During the colonial period these regions were incorporated into the viceroyalty of New Spain, which stretched from what is today known as the US Southwest to the isthmus of Panama, with Mexico City as the capital. Within this administrative colonial-feudal entity, the captaincy general of Guatemala—which included present-day Chiapas, Guatemala, Belize (which came under British rule over time), Honduras, El Salvador, Nicaragua, and Costa Rica—had a certain level of autonomy. In 1821, New Spain declared its independence from Spain, and the remaining regions for a short time comprised the Mexican empire, until the southern entities declared their independence from Mexico in 1823 in the form of the United Provinces of Central America. Between 1838 and 1840 these entities broke into the five independent nation-states that currently exist.

When it comes to defining Central America today, people tend to speak of either five, six, or seven countries: the five original Central American provinces that became independent first—Guatemala, Honduras, El Salvador, Nicaragua, and Costa Rica—joined later by independent Panama in 1903 and by independent Belize in 1981. Belize is sometimes not included because of its late independence from Britain and also because of its predominantly English-speaking population in contrast to the other predominantly Spanish-speaking nations—a problematic move ignoring the reality that all Central American nations are multilingual nations with native speakers of Spanish, English, and numerous indigenous languages. This brings up another issue of contention. Most Central American countries also form part of the Caribbean; however, the nation-states tend to negate their Caribbean coastlines. These predominantly Black, indigenous, and often English-speaking regions are at times referred to as "the Atlantic" and are generally poorly connected to the interior and the Pacific side, where the criollo and mestizo elites reside. To make definitions even more unstable, the southern parts of Mexico—Chiapas and the Yucatán Peninsula—are sometimes included in the definition of Central America because of the shared Mesoamerican (in particular Maya) cultures in Mexico, Guatemala, Belize, and Honduras. Throughout this book, when I talk about "Central America," I refer to the region comprised of seven countries, interconnected with Mexico in numerous ways.

23. The 2017 publication *México ante el conflicto centroamericano* edited by Mario Vázquez Olivera and Fabián Campos Hernández offers an important comprehensive overview of the complex interactions during that period.

24. People from Latin America and Europe flocked to Nicaragua. The solidarity movements supporting the Nicaraguan Revolution are only comparable to those of the Spanish Civil War (Ramírez, *Adiós* 14). The solidarity at times even bridged Cold War divides; there were strong solidarity movements in East and West Germany (see Harzer and Volks).

25. For an excellent discussion of the advantages and perils of Mexican state support for literature in the recent years, in particular CONACULTA and FONCA, see Sánchez Prado's "Mexican Literature."

26. Some writers such as the Guatemalans Luis Cardoza y Aragón and Augusto Monterroso even made it their permanent home. Monterroso, one of the most original Latin American literary voices, is sometimes even claimed in anthologies as a Mexican author (L. Zavala). Cardoza y Aragón and his wife, Lya Kostakowsky, were important members of the intellectual life in the capital. They donated their house and art collection to the Colegio de México.

27. In 2015, for example, the Mexican Fondo de Cultura Económica provided financial support so that Central American literature could present during the International Book Fair in Guadalajara (Agencia EFE). For several years the book fair Centroamérica-Chiapas, organized by the Universidad Nacional Autónoma de Chiapas, has provided spaces for exchange.

28. Ramírez already played an enormous role in the promotion of Central American literature by founding the important Editorial Universitaria Centroamericana (EDUCA) in 1968 and the Editorial Nueva Nicaragua in 1981.

29. And then there is Juan Rulfo, of course. Ramírez notes that, for him, reading Rulfo provided a relief from the *costumbrismo* prevalent in the region; he says it made him see the rural sphere in a new light (*Señor de los tristes* 127).

30. There were also some dissonances. Mexican corrido singer Lupillo Rivera made a cover of "Tus perjúmenes mujer," a Nicaraguan folk song made famous by Carlos Mejía Godoy, who disliked that Rivera had changed some of the Nicaraguan Spanish lyrics (El Universal).

31. We could, for example, read the *novela de la revolución* and later works on the revolution by Juan Rulfo, Elena Garro, and Carlos Fuentes not as revolutionary literature but as postwar literature and compare it to the current Central American postwar literature: full of nostalgia, trauma, and disappointment. Or we could com-

pare specifically testimonial literature from Mexico and Central America. Or, since Mexico City was so important for political exiles, we still need comprehensive studies of the representation of Mexico City in works of authors of the Central American diaspora—for example, Monterroso's *Pájaros de Hispanoamérica* and Castellanos Moya's exile novels *La diáspora* and *El sueño del retorno*. Or we could read literature dealing with the current conflicts for references to the other region: in Rascón Banda's *Contrabando*, for example, the narrator compares experiences of the violent drug war in the mountains in Chihuahua to the Salvadoran civil war (207–8). Or in Castellanos Moya's *El arma en el hombre*, the Salvadoran former soldier Robocop despises the, in his view, effeminate Mexican narcos. Or there is Élmer Mendoza's famous *Un asesino solitario*, which could be read in relation to the Central American demobilized combatant novel I discuss in this book. In Mendoza's novel the protagonist makes fun of his leftist friend who, after the uprising of the Zapatistas, gets together with friends "to analyze the meaning of the wooden rifles and the ski masks" ("para analizar el significado de los rifles de palo y de los pasamontañas") (50).

The prolific indigenous literatures of the region demand further circulation and study, an important task currently undertaken by several scholars (see, for example, Arias, "Nahuahtlizando"; Chacón). Other works include writings by Latino authors from Mexico and Central America (Arias, *Taking Their Word;* Rodríguez, *Dividing the Isthmus*) as well as the increasing Central American and Mexican literary and filmic production on the perilous trajectory of Central American immigrants through Mexican territory.

32. In "Relearning the Revolution: The Contemporary Relevance of the novela de la revolución in the University Classroom," Cheyla Samuelson shows what it can mean for Mexican American students to read the literature of the Mexican Revolution (63–81). Personally, I will always remember the Salvadoran American student who told me that she knew her grandmother had grown up picking bananas but before taking my class she had never heard of the United Fruit Company.

33. Since 2000, California State University University–Northridge has a Central American Studies program. In 2015 it became the first Department of Central American Studies in the United States, and their major in Central American Studies is transnational it in its focus (Morgan n.p.). While positions for researchers working on Central American culture and literature are still scarce, there is a growing number of Centroamericanists on the isthmus itself and beyond, in Mexico, Chile, the United States, and Europe.

34. Mexican literature alone has several annual academic conferences in the United States, plus many other conferences in Mexico. Central American literature and culture have two congresses every other year that generally take place in Central America, sometimes in the United States. Both *A History of Mexican Literature* published by Cambridge University Press and the book series *Hacia una historia de las*

*literaturas centroamericanas* published by T&G Editores constitute concerted efforts to create a critical literary history of these literatures. In Mexico, academic interest in Central America is also growing—beyond the Central Americans who have long studied at institutions of higher education in Mexico and made important contributions to academic life there. Even though it is surprisingly recent, it is a good sign that in 2017 the Colegio de Michoacán celebrated the first meeting of graduate students working on Central America in Mexico.

## CHAPTER 1. CARBINES AND CARTRIDGE BELTS

1. Or he will be the state. As Legrás has pointed out, "often the lag between concept and image is the very meaning of the photograph" (*Culture and Revolution* 146). For an extensive interpretation of the iconic photograph, see Vargas Santiago. Among other things, he argues that the formal *charro* pose and attire is intended to defy the elite's view of Zapata as a "savage" and bandit as well as to highlight his higher status within the rural community, since Zapata was not a peon but a ranchero who worked his own small piece of land (444–445). Macías-González and Rubenstein argue that the hypermasculinity of these photographs of armed men is a means to make up for the lack of social status of the subjects in the photographs (11). These are excellent observations, yet I believe that the meaning of the objects and the posture run deeper: the rifle as the artifact to affirm the peasant before the state.

2. Unless otherwise noted, I generally refer to the second, longer edition from 1940 (republished in 2000). Regarding the changes Campobello made between the first and the second editions, refer to Aguilar Mora, *El silencio* 101–12, and Parra 54, 69.

3. I thank my colleague Francisco Leal for pointing out this sensory quality of the text.

4. The historiography of the revolution can be divided into roughly four phases and currents: (1) the orthodox populist current starting in the 1930s that sees the revolution as a nationalist and populist movement, a heroic gesture of the peasantry; (2) the revisionist current that, influenced by the experience of the repressive regime of 1968, stressed the continuities between the old and the new regimes and stressed its methods of co-optation of the masses; (3) the neopopulist view that stresses the popular and peasant character of the revolution; and (4) the relational view focused on how negotiations between bureaucratic apparatus, social movements, and popular culture shaped the Mexican state (Joseph and Nugent, *Everyday Forms* 5–12). In this book I work from a neopopulist and relational perspective.

5. The PRI reign was shortly interrupted by two presidents from the conservative Partido Acción Nacional (PAN). When the PRI returned to power in 2012, it continued a process of neoliberalization started under President Salinas de Gortari (1988–94) and, through a number of swift legal reforms, the party dismantled long-standing

revolutionary achievements such as the protection of the energy sector from private and foreign capital (del Valle and Tarica n.p.).

6. Regarding the photo of Villa and Zapata in the presidential seat, see Gollnick; Legrás, *Literature and Subjection;* Noble; and Williams, *Mexican Exception.*

7. Great disagreement exists on what constitutes this genre. It is most commonly believed that the corrido is a further development of the *romance español* that came with the colonizers to Mexico (Simonett, "Transnational Dimension" 221–22) and that it started to become an important musical form in the nineteenth century. A famous dispute among folklorist is on whether the corrido developed its current characteristics in the Mexico-US border region (Américo Paredes's position) or in the center of Mexico (Vicent Mendoza's position) (Giménez and Héau 364). The question of the origin of the corrido is related to that of its form. Giménez and Héau have pointed out that the corrido cannot be defined because its form and style varies according to the region and that it is just an imprecise descriptor for popular song (26). The form and musical style of corridos varies (sometimes accompanied by a guitar, a *trío norteño,* or larger ensembles for the different *sones* from the center), and they have been sung by *ranchera* singers, giving them a more emotional, theatrical style. While many different forms exist, corridos are often associated with a matter-of-fact style, "a deadpan language and performance style" (Simonett, "Transnational Dimension" 223). Corridos often rely on familiar formulas such as the singer asking permission to sing, announcing the story he will tell, or bidding farewell at the song's conclusion (224). Expressions such as "Please allow, my dear listeners," or "With this one I say goodbye" ("Permítanme, señores" and "Con esta me despido"), point to the live performance and oral origins of the corrido. I define them as political, lyric-focused ballads that often tell a story, mostly in the context of conflict.

8. "La Valentina" actually dates from 1909, before the war, but became popular in 1914 (Herrera-Sobek 108–9).

9. Some attribute the corrido to an anonymous author from the late 1910s, but others credit Genaro Núñez as the composer, which would make it a corrido composed *after* the armed phase (Kohl 68). The periodization of corridos is a difficult task. Because of the anonymity of some writers and composers, the sometimes informal production of the corridos, and their numerous versions, it is hard to know when and how they were originally performed.

10. The English translation is not my own. This is the original in German: "weil sie sich der revolutionären Kräfte, denen sie ihr Dasein verdanken, nicht bewußt geblieben sind" (Benjamin, "Zur Kritik der Gewalt" 46).

11. See for example Avelar's discussion of Jacques Derrida's reading of Benjamin in *The Letter of Violence* (79–106).

12. Only over time did insurgents acquire a level of uniformization. Villa's elite troops, Los Dorados, were named after their golden cartridges and their flashy khaki-colored uniforms customized on the US border. The Zapatistas, given their cultural

background and limited funds, marched in coarse peasant garments with rifles, cartridges, big-brimmed hats, and banners of the Virgen de Guadalupe.

13. For a detailed account of the struggle for female suffrage in Mexico, see Olcott 159–200.

14. In her work about *soldaderas* and Afro-Mexican women, Arce shows how they are often denied in official discourse but viewed with "ongoing fascination (in the popular imagination)," leading to "the stunning paradox that constitutes their simultaneous absence and presence" (3).

15. For a more extensive discussion of the Adelita and the Cucaracha trope, see Arce 83–98.

16. Arce points out that *soldadera* became "a word what was socially unacceptable" (65), devaluing women's military importance. Over her hovered "the phantasm of prostitution" because "in traditional, patriarchal and mestizo Mexican society, to be outside of the home is to be public, and to be public is not constitutive of a middle-class *mujer decente*" (70, italics in the original).

17. In Azuela's *Los de abajo,* La Pintada represents the female combatant. She dresses extravagantly and has sex whenever it suits her, which marks her as a "fallen woman" or whore—in accordance with moralist patriarchal stories used to police female liberty and sexuality. She runs with, drinks with, and kills with the rebels. She defies the domestic sphere, as symbolized by the novel's other female figure—Camila, a true *soldadera* in the sense that she reluctantly accompanies the men and cares for them but does not engage in combat. When La Pintada kills Camila, she is almost killed by her comrades and expelled from the rebel band. Left by the road, the character is dropped from the storyline. La Pintada is an intriguing literary figure because she does not conform to the gender norms around her, but her presence is ultimately rejected, both within the plot and through the negative depiction of her in the novel (Thornton, *Women and the War Story* 68–73). See also Arce 99–101.

18. Several feminist interventions in the 1980s and a new edition by Era with an exceptional foreword by Jorge Aguilar Mora in 2000 have brought *Cartucho* to the attention of a greater audience. Over the last two decades many studies about the author's life and texts have been published. Her greater prominence now stands in contrast to how she was forgotten during her life. Near the end of her life, Campobello was medicated and held hostage by a couple responsible for taking care of her; her death (probably in 1986) was hidden by the couple so that they could continue to take advantage of her financial means. When years later this case was brought to court, one of the perpetrators was sentenced to twenty-seven years in prison, but the verdict was quickly overturned; he was absolved, and the case was closed in 2002 (Pratt, "Mi cigarro" 153, 184).

19. From the original Spanish: "Ella ni con una ametralladora hubiera podido pelear contra ellos. . . . Los ojos de Mamá, hechos grandes de revolución, no lloraban, se habían endurecido recargados en el cañón de un rifle de su recuerdo."

20. The first edition ended here. The second part was added in the second edition of *Cartucho.*

21. In many ways "Mamá" is also the manifestation of a revolutionary *mater dolorosa.* The catholic-national impetus is affirmed by *Cartucho*'s ending with Nellie and her mother walking toward the church, "where the Virgin received her" ("donde la Virgen la recibía") (161). This ending scene constitutes a dissent from the consolidation of the revolutionary project by the elites in the 1920s and 1930s, when the fervent politics for secularization under president Elías Calles caused another uprising: the Cristero War (1926–29).

22. Thinking of the archive in relation to the Mexican Revolution is particularly appropriate because an important action of *la bola* was to burn the archives, to destroy the power of the old state apparatus.

## CHAPTER 2. PISTOLS AND PAREDÓN

1. Huntington has argued that rather than a novel of *los de arriba,* it is a novel of somebody aspiring to power, somebody close to power but not in control (141).

2. From the original Spanish: "de no sé qué esencia de México, en el trajinar de hombres que se movían allí entre las sombras, seguros de su marcha, insensibles a su suerte y con el rifle al hombro o la cadera hecha al peso de revólver. ¡Ambiente de misterio, hombres de catadura y alma misteriosas!"

3. Martín Luis Guzmán (1887–1976) was both intrigued and confused by the Mexican Revolution. He was part of the Ateneo de la Juventud, a group of young intellectuals who tried to pit classical Greek notions of virtue, beauty, and popular education against Díaz's positivist, technocratic elite (Parra 85). The revolution took Mexican intellectuals by surprise, and they did not know what to make of it. Far more than his fellow *ateneístas* Alfonso Reyes and José Vasconcelos, Guzmán was open to exploring the challenge that the armed insurrection of the populace represented to the self-conception of the intellectual (Legrás, "Martín Luis Guzmán" 427; Parra 20; Pineda Franco, "Entre el exilio" 31–32). He actively participated in the revolutionary struggle, which forced him into exile several times (for his support of Madero in 1913, Gutiérrez in 1915, and de la Huerta in 1922). Still, Guzmán—impacted by Domingo Faustino Sarmiento's *Facundo* ([1845]) and José Enrique Rodó's *Ariel* ([1900])—was also very much concerned with the need to "civilize" (educate) and thus control the perceived barbarian elements in the nation. The tension between lettered parochialism and intellectual receptiveness runs through Guzmán's novels as well as his life.

*El águila y la serpiente* (1928) reflects on the relationship between violence and power through ambivalent representations of Villa. He continued to struggle to render Villa in literary form, especially in the artificially folksy *Memorias de Pancho Villa* (1951). His temporarily censured novel *La sombra del caudillo* (1929) is a condemnation of authoritarian *caudillo* politics under Álvaro Obregón; yet late in Guzmán's life he accommodated himself within the PRI regime. He defended the student massacre in 1968 and became a senator in 1970 (Domínguez Michael 208). This complex literary and political legacy thus represents a prime example of the difficult relationship of Mexican intellectuals with the armed phase of the revolution and the regime that followed it. In *The Man Who Wrote Pancho Villa*, Nicholas Cifuentes-Goodbody provides a compelling reading of the complex intertwined relationship between the author and his works—in particular, of Guzmán's successful and failed attempts to use his writing strategically to create an extraliterary persona and to secure political and literary positions.

4. Some have doubted the fictional and novelistic nature of the text. Written during exile in Spain and first published in the form of different *entregas* in US American-Mexican newspapers (such as *La Prensa* in San Antonio and *La Opinión* in Los Angeles; some parts were also published in the Mexican *El Universal*; Pineda Franco, "Entre el exilio" 35), most early critics doubted if it in fact could be called a novel, pointing to the text's episodic, testimonial style (as related by Leal 83). Others, not questioning the text's fictional and novelistic nature, have celebrated its high literary artifice and complex narrative strategies (Cortínez 221; Megenney 116) and Guzmán's "narrative framework of adventure and suspense" (Parra 81). Guzmán uses different narrative genres, such as the short story, the detective novel, and the spy novel, to maintain tension and attention throughout his text. Legrás indicates that the work is not as accessible as most people think and stresses that the "prejudice that assumes that testimonial texts do not demand much reading work to unveil their meanings has kept Guzman's [sic] novel in a sort of hermeneutical limbo" (*Literature and Subjection* 127).

5. Numerous chapters deal with Villa: "Primer vislumbre de Villa," "La pistola de Villa," "Pancho Villa en la cruz," "La fuga de Pancho Villa," "El sueño del compadre Urbina," "A la merced de Pancho Villa."

6. For a reading of the animalization in relation to sovereignty, affect, and mercy, see Abeyta.

7. From the original Spanish: "es una manifestación inequívoca y decidida del deseo de que no se le confunda a él ni con la plebe, ni con los caudillos analfabetos, ni con los líderes corruptos de la Revolución."

8. From the original Spanish: "La violencia y la barbarie misma, la animalidad con que se representa a Pancho Villa no son simplemente rechazados sino reinscritos y reinterpretados a través de un discurso que a la vez que los incorpora los domestica."

9. Benito Juárez created the *rurales* to fight bandits (Knight, *Mexican Revolution*, vol. 1 33), and Porfirio Díaz even developed an international propaganda campaign refuting the idea of epidemic banditry in Mexico because it did not fit his desired image of a modern country (Frazer 60).

10. From the original Spanish: "Este hombre no existiría si no existiese la pistola ... La pistola no es sólo su útil de acción: es su instrumento fundamental, el centro de su obra y su juego, la expresión constante de su personalidad íntima, su alma hecha forma."

11. Nigel Thrift declares that there is in fact "no stable definition of affect" (59) and discusses four translations that range from "embodied practices" (60) to "a notion of drive" (61), "the property of the active outcome of an encounter" (62), and "a deep-seated physiological change written involuntarily on the face" (64). Gregory Seigworth and Melissa Gregg offer a range of different definitions, saying that affect is "found in those intensities that pass body to body (human, nonhuman, part-body, and otherwise)," the "visceral forces beneath, alongside, or generally *other than* conscious knowing, vital forces insisting beyond emotion" (1); they say affect can be a "*force* or *forces of encounter*" and that it is a "potential: a body's *capacity* to affect and to be affected" (2). Mabel Moraña uses "afecto" interchangeably with "affect" and talks about it as a "a deterritorialized, fluctuating and impersonal form of energy" ("forma desterritorializada, fluctuante e impersonal de energía"; 323) that works in the social sphere. While the English-speaking debates on affect stress the bodily, impulsive aspect separating it from such words as "feelings" and "emotions," the emotional and affective aspect is precisely what constitutes "afecto" in Spanish, defined by the Real Academia de la Lengua Española solely as "Cada una de las pasiones del ánimo, como la ira, el amor, el odio, etc., y especialmente el amor o el cariño."

12. From the original Spanish: "Al disparar, no será la pistola quien haga fuego, sino él mismo: de sus propias entrañas ha de venir la bala cuando abandona el cañón siniestro. Él y su pistola son una sola cosa. De su pistola han nacido, y nacerán, sus amigos y sus enemigos." Cifuentes-Goodbody also notes "the unity between gun sight and eyesight" in this scene (78).

13. This is a key scene, and one Guzmán later rewrites in *Memorias de Pancho Villa*—where he writes that he did not plan of abandoning Villa (805)—in order to rewrite his own life and to affirm his political-literary position through the ghost of Villa (Cifuentes-Goodbody 150–51).

14. Abeyta also points out that "generally, critics have overdetermined Guzmán's Arielism" (109).

15. Lomnitz argues that being executed also generally had a class dimension. Hanging or mass firing squads were common for lower classes and rank-and-file combatants, while individual firing squads were reserved for notables and officers (*Death* 585). Yet the literary texts do not corroborate that distinction. *Cartucho*, in particular, narrates many individual *fusilamientos* of rank and file.

16. The novel overall is highly critically of Obregón, a criticism Guzmán further expands in *La sombra del caudillo*.

17. From the Spanish original: "Tic-tic, tiqui . . . Villa no apartaba los ojos del movimiento que estaba trasmitiendo sus órdenes doscientas leguas al norte, ni nosotros tampoco."

18. From the original Spanish: "trataba de adivinar el momento preciso en que las vibraciones de los dedos deletrearan las palabras 'fusile usted inmediatamente.'"

19. Not only were trains used as means for troop transportation, but the trains controlled by the northern armies also guaranteed supply lines to the main purveyors of firearms: the US border towns. Crucial for war logistics, trains were nonetheless also used as destructive weapons themselves. The Villistas, for example, employed the *máquina loca,* a locomotive loaded with explosives that they crashed into enemy trains. Given its centrality to the war, it should not come as a surprise that the rail system was severely affected by the revolution: entire railroad tracks were demolished, and "3,873 railroad cars, 50 locomotives, and 34 passenger cars" as well as about "1,250 miles of telegraph lines" were destroyed (Aguilar Camín and Meyer 71f). See also Ruffinelli, "Trenes revolucionarios."

20. Michael Abeyta points out that the violent descriptions could "serve as an inoculation against the contagion" (102), the danger of romanticizing Villa and his followers (121), but the novel shows the contrary: slowly the man of letters becomes more like the man of arms.

21. From the original Spanish: "Ese capítulo ha sido juzgado como prueba de la vesania 'pequeñoburguesa' de Guzmán, de su incomprensión ante las fuerzas populares, cuando es una formidable llamada de atención sobre la irrupción de los otros en la vida de México."

## CHAPTER 3. RIDDLED BY BULLETS

1. Later on, due to the numerous fissures, inconsistencies, and debacles in the revolutionary process in the 1980s, this project appears in literature as an "uninhabited utopia," as Werner Mackenbach has pointed out (*Unbewohnte* 503). Leonel Delgado has argued that nowadays to talk of the Sandinista Revolution in idealist terms of hopes and dreams followed by disillusionment seems a cliché, given that the revolution had from the beginning apocalyptic dimensions ("Memorias apocalípticas" 110).

2. From the original Spanish: "cómo las armas automáticas expulsaban con una gran velocidad los casquillos, . . . cómo saltaban pedazos de concreto, cemento, madera, vidrios, pintura, cuando centenares de miles de impactos de bala golpeaban contra la casa."

3. From the original Spanish: "empezaron a disparar sobre la casa todos los guardias, la tanqueta insistentemente, y el avión, que casi rozaba la casa, disparaba, y entonces veíamos cómo iban reduciendo a escombros la casa en cuestión de segundos."

4. From the original Spanish: "vemos salir por la puerta central de la casa a Julio

corriendo, disparando en ráfaga contra la Guardia y, segundos después, cómo Julio se empieza a doblar y disparando y doblándose más y disparando y doblándose más, hasta caer al suelo."

5. There is also a certain dose of penis envy in relation to the rifle when Cabezas eyes the more powerful rifle of his friend El Gato, who has an AR-15, while Cabezas himself only has a M-1 carbine (182).

6. From the original Spanish: "es parte tuya el fusil en la montaña, dormís con tu arma, caminás con ella, te bañás a la orilla de ella, hacés ejercicio con ella, arma helada, arma aceitosa, arma al hombro, arma en la mano, arma con sarro, arma apoyo, arma limpia, arma mojada . . . En la montaña el arma se vuelve un pedazo tuyo, como un miembro más, y uno de los miembros más importantes."

7. See her book *Nicaragua, June 1978–July 1979*.

8. Just as the Frente tried to look for legitimacy in the peasant arsenals on the countryside, they also did so within the urban masses, and the indigenous neighborhoods in particular were symbolically significant. Cabezas's *testimonio*, before concentrating on the mythical mountain space, points to an urban axis of resistance that starts not only in the university but also in the indigenous neighborhood Subtavia in León, where political organizing begins around urban bonfires (55).

9. From the interview with Ramírez: "Desde el discurso político de la Revolución el pueblo pobre, el pueblo artesano, campesinos, la gente marginal es el pueblo al que la Revolución va a redimir. El discurso de la Revolución a su vez asume que ese pueblo por tratarse de la Revolución que los va a redimir, este pueblo está de lado de la Revolución, entonces es una asunción a priori que se da una simbiosis pueblo-revolución que se responden mutuamente, eso termina siendo una falacia, no? Porque una parte de ese pueblo se voltea en contra de la Revolución en armas, los campesinos pobres toman las armas contra de la Revolución."

10. Stephen Henighan points out that the exchange before the execution in Ramírez's novel *Sombras nada más* can be read in relation to this scene (533).

11. From the original Spanish: "lo vi subir a la tarima . . . vestido en hilachas y descalzo, el fusil viejo sostenido por un mecate en lugar de correa. Entonces advertí que entre nosotros había un inmenso abismo difícil de salvar."

12. From the original Spanish: "el ejército campesino de la 'contra' representaría una de las contradicciones más evidentes entre la razón estatal revolucionaria y la representación [o ausencia de representación] subalterna."

13. Henighan calls it a "watered-down, liberal-democratic residue of the project of a nation restructured in order to reverse the oppression of the poor" (509).

14. In the German translation by dtv, the war context is ameliorated in the paratext. The cover features a close-up head shot of Belli herself—curly-haired, smiling, and beautifully aged—and the title is *Die Verteididgung des Glücks* (The defense of happiness).

15. From the original Spanish: "todos parecíamos niños en tienda de juguetes, tocando y examinando los fusiles automáticos, semi-automáticos, las subametralladoras y las pistolas puestas a nuestra disposición." And: "El estruendo sacudía cada una de mis articulaciones y me dejaba en la cabeza un silbido insoportable, agudo, desconcertante."

16. Henighan points out that Belli also constructs herself with masculine identity in the book, conforming to the Nicaraguan concept of being masculine as being active (506).

17. Belli uses the subject position of woman (especially of the mother) to judge the attitude of the commanders: "they had become infatuated with the seductive image that they had created of themselves: the image that they saw reflected in the eyes of the crowd on the day of the triumph. They believed they were tremendously astute, skillful, a blend of mischievous children of politics and heroic and virile wandering knights" ("se habían quedado prendados de la imagen seductora que se crearon de sí mismos: la imagen que vieron reflejada en los ojos de la multitud el día del triunfo. Se sentían enormemente astutos, hábiles, una mezcla de niños traviesos de la política y de caballeros andantes heroicos y viriles"; 362). Where Campobello's child narrator is fascinated with the game of the revolution, in Belli's work the mother figure perceives that power is not a game.

18. From the original Spanish: "En ese instante, comprendí, físicamente, lo que significaba «tomar el poder». Me inundó una sensación indescriptible que era a la vez deslumbre, orgullo y humilde agradecimiento de que la vida me hubiese concedido ese día en mi historia. Cuando uno sueña con cosas como cambair el mundo, no hay poder más hermoso que sentir que es posible hacerlo."

19. Just like Guzmán, who gets an invaluable tip from Villa, Belli gets a tip from an instructor in Cuba, to aim with the left eye even though she is right-handed (*El país* 115).

20. From the original Spanish: "Vestida de verde olivo con mi subametralladora al hombro—Bayardo decía que la llevaba como si fuera un bolso." And later in the paragraph: "Me gustaba ver a las muchachas con uniformes verde olivo y botas militares impecablemente lustradas. Muchas de ellas se pintaban los labios y hasta llevaban las uñas pintadas de rojo. Eran el símbolo de un tiempo nuevo para las mujeres de mi país."

21. This is another aspect Ramírez has in common with Belli. Both writers refer to important figures and texts of the Spanish literary tradition (e.g., *El Cid Campeador, Historia verdadera de la conquista de Nueva España, El Quijote*), looking for their place within the Hispanist lettered tradition. This is somewhat surprising for former revolutionaries of national struggles with heavy anticolonial undertones.

22. From the original Spanish: "Nadie habría cogido un fusil para hacer una revolución a medias. . . . Tampoco se triunfa con las armas para conquistar un poder de corto plazo, cuando se trata de barrer con la historia."

23. From the original Spanish: "Sus palabras se convierten, de manera efectiva, en la memoria con la que los nicaragüenses, seguramente, recordarán la revolución y se reconocerán como nación."

## CHAPTER 4. SONGS OF GUERRILLA WARFARE AND ENCHANTMENT

1. I hereby follow Judson's example to talk of "folk popular" (213) to translate the range of meaning of the Spanish "popular."

2. The work of Scruggs offers the most thorough engagement with Carlos Mejía Godoy's work ("Socially Conscious"; "Politics of Erasure"; "Nicaragua"; "Música y el legado"). Landau follows suit in his dissertation from 1999. There are also essays by O. Cortez; Judson; Mántica; Mora Lomeli; Pring-Mill; Sturman; Ureña; Zambrana; and several texts that discuss the relation between music and liberation theology (Bello; Guerrero Pérez; García Irles; Scruggs, "Las misas"). In most major academic works on cultural aspects of the Sandinista Revolution, however, the revolutionary music is either not mentioned or only done so in passing (Beverley and Zimmermann; Chávez; Dawes; Wellinga, *Entre*). Only Whisnant dedicates several pages to the music, but with little analysis.

3. From the original Spanish: "Yo no sé cuánto debe la Revolución a las canciones de Carlos Mejía Godoy, que lograron organizar un sentimiento colectivo del pueblo [y preparar] ese sentimiento para la lucha."

4. From the original Spanish: "Hoy la revolución queda para muchos, dentro y fuera de Nicaragua, entre las nostalgias de la vida pasada y los viejos recuerdos, y se evoca igual que se evocan los amores perdidos; pero ya no es más una razón de vida. A veces, en casas de amigos en el extranjero . . . suena, como un homenaje que me pagan, y se pagan ellos a sí mismos, la música de aquellos tiempos, las canciones revoluciona-rias de Carlos Mejía Godoy que escucho con tristeza opresiva, con un sentimiento de algo que busqué y no logré encontrar."

5. This was not only an artistic endeavor but also a political one, since it was an effort to preserve a patrimony and—much like the German romantics, the brothers Grimm—an attempt to invent a nation through the collection of its folk-popular rural culture.

6. From the original Spanish: "Carlos Mejía Godoy no le canta al pueblo. El pueblo canta en él y por él y con él. La voz popular. Voz y canto del pueblo."

7. Many particularities of Nicaraguan Spanish, with its strong influences from Nahuatl and its inclination for word plays and double meanings, appear through-out the album. It featured the cover smash hit "Son tus perjúmenes mujer," the song of the forgetful "Clodomiro el ñajo," and the playful mazurka "Cuando yo la vide."

8. In 1983 the Concert for Peace that protested against the Contra War brought fa-

mous Latin American Nueva Canción and Nueva Trova musicians—such as Mercedes Sosa, Silvio Rodríguez, Chico Buarque, and Amparo Ochoa—to Managua, where they performed with Carlos and Luis Enrique Mejía Godoy (see the album *Abril en Managua,* various artists). The music created a transnational space of belonging. Carlos Mejía Godoy's music was a big hit in Spain (Landau 225, 229), and he toured several times in Europe playing solidarity concerts. Hermann Schulz, editor and important intermediary for Nicaraguan literature in Germany, recalls the following episode: "When Tomás Borge sat on our couch in Wuppertal for the first time after his five-year imprisonment, he took a transistor radio out of his bag and played the cassette with the newly created 'Anthem of the FSLN' by Carlos Mejía Godoy for us. He had tears in his eyes" (105, my translation). Langenburg, from the Dutch solidarity movement, recalls: "It was easy to support Nicaragua especially with such good music coming out of there. . . . . The songs drew us a picture of this little corner of the world where we could make a difference with our support" (quoted in Landau 233). As such, the music of the Mejía Godoys also became that of an internationalist generation fascinated with this revolution. This space of identification was not free of misunderstandings or romantic projections though. Scruggs points out that Carlos Mejía Godoy's music, because of its vernacular and double entendre, was even difficult to understand for Spanish speakers who were not Nicaraguan ("Socially Conscious" 51). An example of the music's romantic projection is the back cover text of *Nicaraguan Epic* (1989), a British compilation of poems by Julio Valle-Castillo, and the lyrics of the *Canto épico al FSLN* in Spanish and English. Here the music becomes a space of hope under Thatcherism: "And for us in Britain, this late-twentieth-century epic, whose quest is justice and social joy, is astonishingly cheering and a sorely needed inspiration."

9. Carlos Mejía Godoy decided not to mention famous guerrilla leader Edén Pastora on the Sandinista musical saga *Canto épico* because, at the time of composition in 1981, the former Comandante Cero and soon-to-be counterrevolutionary Alianza Revolucionaria Democrática (ARDE) leader had become a dissident and left the country (E. Sánchez, "PCJH").

10. Carlos Mejía Godoy, in a public letter to First Lady Rosario Murillo, wrote: "In the dramatic context that our people live, again threatened by a family dictatorship [ . . . ], I cannot permit that these songs, inspired precisely in the sacrifice and immolation of thousands of Nicaraguan brothers, be used as musical background in order to continue—from the platforms decorated with flowers—the most shameful tragicomedy of the recent years" ("En el contexto dramático que vive nuestro pueblo, amenazado nuevamente con otra dictadura familiar [ . . . ], no puedo permitir que las canciones, inspiradas precisamente en el sacrificio e inmolación de miles de hermanos nicaragüenses, sirvan de fondo musical, para continuar—desde las tarimas enfloradas-la tragicomedia más vergonzosa de los últimos años" ("Carta de Carlos Mejía Godoy a Rosario Murillo" ).

11. The music appealed to the revolutionary, nationalist sentiment. After decades of disdain for Nicaraguan culture during the Somoza years, young people in Nicaragua were eager to listen to something that they felt was autochthonously Nicaraguan (Scruggs, "Politics of Erasure" 258).

12. Carlos Mejía Godoy continued to strengthen this relationship through his music, most notably with *Misa campesina nicaragüense,* which was inspired by Ernesto Cardenal's contemplative peasant community on the Solentiname archipelago. For all of Latin America this mass was a key expression of liberation theology (Scruggs, "Las misas").

13. Juan Pablo Gómez has criticized the postrevolutionary storytelling for omitting responsibilities by alleging that everything happened spontaneously, while in fact the several popular insurrections were planned and supported by the guerrilla organization. This tendency can already be perceived in songs by C. Mejía Godoy, in "Cristo ya nació en Palacagüina" and in "Quincho Barrilete," a smash hit about a child laborer who will one day leave his kite behind and fight, a song that Gómez also mentions critically in his analysis of the incorporation of children into armed struggle.

14. Paradoxically, this worked in the opposite direction and also became the anthem for the exiles coming home from Miami in the 1990s, who conceived of Nicaragua now finally being free, making it the unofficial national anthem for all (Ramírez, "Interview").

15. In a similar vein, "Un tiro 22" by Carlos Mejía Godoy puts emphasis on how affect changes the bullet. The bullet that comes from the "tortured heart" will hit its target ("corazón torturado"). This bullet aims better than those "shot without love, without hate" ("disparadas sin amor, sin odio").

16. At the same time, the music, alternating between single and choral voices combined with light chord and flute sounds, adds a playfulness to the song, distancing it from the brutality of war. This lightness transmits a sense of easiness regarding the disarming and handling of this firearm.

17. This comes from the liner notes of *Guitarra Armada,* in a clandestine message by Carlos to guerrilla commander Henry Ruiz (perrerac.org).

18. This is similar to the slogans in many postcolonial countries that continuously remind people what they should do—"Don't cut trees," "Wash your hands," "Don't litter"—and which seem to work under the assumption that the uncivilized masses have to be educated for modernity.

19. The most obvious attempt at instilling military discipline is the song "Memorándum militar 1–79" by Luis Enrique Mejía Godoy, which once again has a cheerful tune supported by light marimba sounds. His voice reminds listeners in a strict tone to study daily and to disarm and oil the rifle. The song reminds listeners of combat strategies such as using camouflage, establishing barricades and sectors of fire, properly communicating with the commanding officer, and forgoing lynch justice. It might

be that the greater emphasis on discipline in his songs is due to his socialization in the communist party in Costa Rica. Scruggs, for example, criticizes the tendency of his songs to sound like pamphlets ("Legado").

20. The possibility of enchantment is also the reason the revolution had such enormous appeal in the world: it was the promise of a somewhat better modernity. Even though there are valuable arguments that in fact the modern world (particularly Europe and North America) is not as disenchanted as it appears (Jenkins 19), this does not lessen the validity of the argument about the peculiarity of this historic Latin American project, since the argument here is about *ideas, imaginaries,* and *narratives* about modernity and not about modernity as an empirical state.

21. This saga of armed struggle is also ambitious in its geographical reach. Along with the brothers' ability to merge different societal spheres, they also represented the entire country musically: not only the northern mazurka and the *sones de pascua* and the marimba from the Pacific west and south but also the Caribbean *palo de mayo* (White 557).

22. Ecology was also a main focus of the songs of Nicaraguan Trova musicians Dúo Guardabarranco (Sturman 258–65; White 577–95).

## CHAPTER 5. HIDDEN ARSENALS

1. US military aid alone grew from $10 million in 1979 to $283.2 million in 1984. Throughout the 1980s, El Salvador alone received $3.9 billion in development and military aid from the United States (Pearce, "From Civil War" 594-95). The Sandinistas and leftist guerrilla movements received aid from Cuba, the Soviet Bloc, in addition to Latin American, European, African, and Asian countries sympathetic to their cause, as well as international solidarity movements.

2. In 2000 de-mining processes in Guatemala appeared to be ongoing (Godnick and Laurance 8, 27–28).

3. Guatemala, Honduras, and El Salvador rely heavily on the army to implement their "mano dura" politics against youth gangs. Costa Rica, which does not have an army but a militarized police, has actually increased its military spending in the 2000s (Rogers 13–14).

4. There were seven thousand (re)armed Contras in 1994 and a group of four hundred ex-soldiers in 1997; about fifteen hundred people died between 1990 and 1994 because of these insurgencies (Pearce, "From Civil War" 590; Pearce, "Peace-building" 59). The northern and Caribbean regions of Nicaragua continue to experience forms of armed insurgency and rural banditry (Godnick 28).

5. If one calculates the number of civilian firearms per 100 residents, no Central American nation is among the most armed. The top three places are occupied by the United States (89/100), Yemen (55/100), and Switzerland (46/100). The Central Amer-

ican countries come in as follows: Panama (21.7/100, rank 26), Guatemala (13.1/100, rank 49), Belize (10/100, rank 62), Costa Rica (9.9/100 rank 64), Nicaragua (7.7/100, rank 77), Honduras (6.2/100, rank 88), and El Salvador (5.8/100, rank 92).

6. This includes military weaponry such as large-caliber machine guns, rocket launchers, mortars, and grenades. A large amount of grenades in civilian and military hands constitutes a particular concern in Guatemala and El Salvador, where accidents and crimes involving grenades are common (Godnich and Laurance 23).

7. Central America has become the main drug corridor in the past two decades. Increased controls and interdiction in the Caribbean as well as the strengthening of Mexican narco-organizations has led to an estimated 90 percent of cocaine getting to the United States through the Central America–Mexico corridor (World Bank 12). While there is some marijuana and poppy cultivation on the isthmus, the main drug trafficked is cocaine (12). Although the "region is a conduit, a transit corridor that neither produces nor consumes significant amounts of cocaine" (32), the firearms-related violence that accompanies drugs trafficking heavily affects the region (13–14).

8. Youth gangs tend to not be as heavily armed as commonly assumed. Among them, makeshift weapons are common: easily discarded and disposable pistols made out of metal tubes and springs, called *armas hechizas* or *chimbas*, as well imitations of 9mm pistols called *tacos* (Godnick 8). That youth gangs are not the main perpetrators of the large-scale criminal operations does not mean, however, that young people are not often perpetrators and victims of violence. The majority of the victims of violence in the region (60 percent) are young men between the ages of fifteen and thirty-four (except in Costa Rica, where they account for 40 percent). A World Bank study found that "young people, particularly young men, comprise the bulk of both perpetrators and victims of violence" (3).

9. Critics disagree on whether to label contemporary Central America literature as "postwar literature" (Cortez, *Estética*; Mackenbach, "Después"). I consider it an adequate albeit broad description for the recent literature that has been so clearly impacted by the wars and the violence that followed. This vast and heterogeneous literature, in response to the desolation of the (post)war period, embarks on numerous identitary, artistic, and political explorations that extend beyond the national.

10. What Kokotovic calls "neoliberal noir centroamericano" coincides largely with the demobilized combatant novel, making it both a subgenre of Central American postwar literature and the Central American expression of the recent vitalization of detective and noir novels in Latin America ("Neoliberal Noir").

11. *Que me maten si* (1997) by Rodrigo Rey Rosa deals with the doings of former military and guerrilla fighters in Guatemala and Belize and the failed attempt to deal with the trauma of the civil war. *The Tattooed Soldier* (1998) by Héctor Tobar, the first Guatemalan-American novel, tells of the violent encounter of two Guatemalan immigrants in Los Angeles at the time of the 1992 Rodney King riots. One is a former

member of the special forces and the other is a widower, whose wife and daughter were killed by this soldier. Such texts as *Tu fantasma, Julián* (1992) by Mónica Zalaquett and *Verano rojo* (2010) by Daniel Quirós Ramírez show some elements of the demobilized combatant novel. Also, the Mexican novel *Un asesino solitario* by Elmer Mendoza can be read as a demobilized combatant novel, since its protagonist is a recently fired violence worker of the Mexican Ministry of Interior turned freelance assassin (19). Similar to the Central American novels, it expresses a disdain for leftist ideology after the end of the Cold War (25).

12. From the original: "Una vez con el fusil en mis manos, trotando, siguiendo las órdenes de mando, empecé a sentir calor. Por fin lograba volver a ser lo que había deseado. No estaba en forma, pero tampoco importaba."

13. From the original: "aquí en el infierno, digo Managua, todo sigue igual: los cipotes piderreales y huelepega, los cochones y las putas, los chivos y los políticos, los ladrones y los policías (que son lo mismo que los políticos, sean sandináis o liberáis o conservaduráis, cristianáis o cualquiermierdáis, jueputas socios del Diablo)."

14. From the original: "Ve que deaca! claro, sólo los obreros y los campesinos llegaron al fin, pero del mundo, porque quedaron hechos mierdas, en el mero fin: muertos, heridos, mutilados o locos y lo peor, en la miseria, porque donde quedamos sólo queda el infierno."

15. The debate about the *testimonio* genre has occupied a sizable contingent of US academia throughout the 1990s and splits into two main fields. On one side are those who see it as a *political* practice and a nonfictional text that incorporates the assumed "authentic" voice of the subaltern or revolutionary subject and challenges Literature as an institution (Beverley, "Margins at the Center" 24, 27; Beverly, "Real Thing" 270–72). On the other side are those who see it as a primarily *literary* practice, in which the voice of the testimonial subject is mediated through the interaction between the compiler and author and the person giving their "witness" account. In this latter view the text is situated between notions of fictionality and factuality (Sklodowska 95). I adhere to the second group and am skeptical of Beverley's ideas about *testimonio*'s "truth-effect" and its lack of literary aspirations ("Margins at the Center" 25, 27).

16. From the original: "un tipo alto y fornido, un grandulón que no usaba barba ni bigote, con el pelito corto, como si fuera cadete, . . . caminaba como Robocop, ese robot policía que aparece en la television."

17. Robocop appears fatigued and traumatized by the war. His trauma becomes most clear when he is imprisoned and under the influence of drugs to facilitate torture. He suddenly feels anxious and has hallucinations of his estranged mother and sister wanting to hire him to kill his father (63). The invitation to parricide is a manifestation of the guilt and marginalization he feels.

18. Venkatesh notes a "queering of the ex-military masculinity of Rana" both through the presence of the transvestite Chobi-Xaquira and double entendres of the Maná song (105). Ultimately though, Pancho Rana's nonqueer masculinity is affirmed

as ideal. Guajira sees him as "a real man" ("un verdadero hombre") (Galich, *Managua* 26); in his interactions with Chobi-Xaquira he is the "macho-macho" (Galich, *Y te diré* 64), and Pancho Rana dies convinced that the world needs more "machos like us, brave champions" ("machos como nosotros campeones arrechos"; 207).

19. From the original: "Reflejos de mis días de guerrilla, qué quieres. Se acostumbra tanto uno a andar con un arma que ya no puedes hacer nada sin ella. Ese pedazo de metal es parte de tu cuerpo, es tu mano, tu compañera, tu ángel de la guarda."

20. From the original: "auténticamente humilde. Ah, la muy *farsante* ingenua, romántica, leal, o sea, todo lo que te puedas imaginar que es una heroína del cine o de las telenovelas, así era ella. Noble. Asquerosamente noble. Creo que se copiaba de los personajes de los libros."

21. From the original: "Matarla, destruirla, golpearla, escupirla, degradarla . . . acorralla, torturarla, arrancarle en pedacitos la carne, hacerla tragarse los orines de los guardias, estar parado ahí, en un rincón de la bartolina, mientras la violaron todos los soldados del regimiento."

22. From the original: "Matar en papel es tan fácil, piensa . . . Y cuando trata de imaginar lo que sería, en la vida real tomar un arma, apuntarla contra alguien y disparar, en contraposición a apretar las teclas de la máquina de escribir . . . , piensa que no hay mucha diferencia."

23. Cortez has argued that the story's ending is not an invitation to violence but an indication that, in order to build a more inclusive Salvadoran society, one needs to "destroy patterns of colonization" ("destruir patrones de colonización"; 170).

24. *De fronteras* is a republished, revised version of *Mediodía de frontera* from 2002. *Mediodía de frontera* contains three additional stories: "Truque," "Estampa," and "De obsequio."

25. The collection of short stories can also be read as unrelated to the Central American postwar societies. The text avoids any geographical or linguistic hints connecting it to the isthmus and at times hints at migration; only one story contains a vague reference to the tropics and another one to the *voseo* used in Central American Spanish (Hernández *De fronteras* 30, 68).

26. The appearance and treatment of the corpses point to the economic logic permeating social relations. Rincón Chavarro has argued: "the corpse is a product of the act of violence and a product of use" ("el cadáver es un producto del acto de violencia y un producto de uso"). As such, the good neoliberal citizen does not deal with the cadavers in a political but in an economic fashion, disguised as charity. The cadavers are fed to the poor. The utilitarianism of all these actions exposes the perversion and inhumanity of the good citizen's civility.

27. This is my translation from the original German: "weil, was geschehen soll nur durch beide zu stande kommen kann."

28. From the original: "La gente de estas ciudades bonitas y pacíficas no está acostumbrada a ver a un tipo con un brazo de menos y un rinoceronte de más saltando a su alrededor."

29. The title of the story, "Carretera sin buey," plays on the Central American legend of a "Carreta sin bueyes," about a cart without oxen that can be heard roaming the streets at night. It tells the story of a witch who tries to fulfill the last wish of her partner to be buried at the Catholic cemetery. She puts his corpse on a cart and commands oxen to pull it, but the priest refuses to receive the man's body because of her evil, blasphemous witchcraft. The priest forgives the oxen for their participation and they are released, whereas the cart, corpse, and witch continue to roam the streets for eternity. Similar to many of Hernández's stories, this folk tale deals with interrupted processes of mourning; this intertextual reference thus adds an additional layer to the story by pointing to the difficult relationship between individual, society, and mourning.

## CHAPTER 6. GOLDEN AK-47S AND WEAPON DISPLAYS

1. In a global comparison Mexico occupies middle rank with regard to civilian gun ownership; in 2007, Mexico ranked 42 out of 178 countries, with an estimated 15 firearms owned per 100 civilians (*Small Arms Survey,* "Annexe 3").

2. Of the 68 percent traced back to the United States 51 percent were manufactured in the United States and 17 percent imported into the United States (*Small Arms Survey* "Captured and Counted" 296). The study notes that according to conservative estimates "at least 100–200 units per day" are likely smuggled into Mexico (288) and that it is not so much large-scale trade by single international merchants but small purchases in the US border towns that arm the narco organizations (312). This further strengthens the theory that US retail is the main source of firearms not acquired through official channels.

3. From 2009 to 2012, of illicit firearms seized in Mexico, 47 percent were rifles and 17 percent long guns, 28 percent handguns, 6 percent shotguns, and less than 2 percent submachine and machine guns. Of the rifles, 31 percent were Kalashnikov-type rifles and 13 percent AR-15-type rifles (*Small Arms Survey,* "Captured and Counted" 291–92).

4. Nevertheless, the Mexican executive continues to be the best-armed actor in the conflict by far. Yet government discourses tend to aggrandize the arsenal of narcos— an issue to which I return in the section on arms arrangements.

5. Through the Mérida initiative, a security cooperation started by President George W. Bush in 2008 and expanded by President Barack Obama, Mexico received $2 billion in military aid until 2013 (Main).

6. The Mexican army used to rely on European weapons—German G3 and HK rifles and variants of the G36 produced in Mexico, the FX-05 Xiuhcoatl rifles—but recently has started to acquire AR-15 pattern rifles from the US government (Beckhusen).

7. While the government under Peña Nieto also made plans to create a paramilitary police force, the new Gendarmería Nacional, planned to be fifty thousand people strong, in the end was scaled back to five thousand (Wilkinson and Sánchez).

8. The unpublished manuscript won the Juan Rulfo Prize for First Novel offered by the Mexican National Council for Culture and the Arts in 1991, and a theatrical adaptation was presented in 1991. However, although the play was published two years later, the original novel was hidden away in a drawer until it was published posthumously by Planeta in 2008. It is unclear why the manuscript was not published earlier. Some say this is because Rascón Banda never authorized its publication (Moreno de Alba); others say that publishers rejected the manuscript at that time (García Ramírez).

9. I was unable to obtain rights for this image, but an image of the cover page can be viewed at www.proceso.com.mx/proceso-1688.

10. Luz María Sánchez displayed seventy-four audio transmitters shaped like guns playing the sounds of citizens caught in violent events to highlight how citizens take to social media to tell their story of violence (2015, Bienal de las Fronteras, Museo de Arte Carrillo Gil). Pedro Reyes converted voluntarily handed-in firearms into shovels ("Palas por pistolas") and musical instruments ("Disarm").

11. Its title strikes a parallelism with the US war on terror and the Mexican-US drug war, since Calderón called narcos terrorists (García). It possibly plays on US fears of jihadists entering the United States along the Mexican border. But the Tumblr account is concerned mainly with the particular Mexican nationalisms at play in this war and its propaganda.

12. Although the Mexican military did conduct a dirty war against students and guerrillas in the 1960s and 1970s, it was not on the same scale as the murderous military dictatorships in South and Central America responsible for the death or the disappearance of hundreds of thousands of people. While repressive, the PRI was not a military dictatorship but a mostly civilian dictatorship, and the military rarely occupied an important presence in the public-political sphere (except for marches on national holidays). In fact, for a long time and among certain strata in Mexico, the military was one of the most respected government institutions, as the least corrupt institution in contrast with the police or the bureaucratic apparatus. This has changed now, as the military has become the main arm of state-sponsored violence and very visibly so.

13. In 2009 the marines who killed Beltrán Leyva had exposed his bloodied body, pants pulled down and covered in bloody five-hundred-peso bills. Matthew Carlin has pointed out that in the drug war there exists a "shared reliance of a particular aesthetic," meaning that all sides rely on "the use of unrestrained enactments and visual displays of violence," and the case of Beltrán Leyva is the most salient example of this use by the state apparatus (506–7).

14. Narcocorridos are associated with the US borderlands, but just as there were southern corridos during the revolution, there are today ensembles in the center and south of Mexico (McDowell; Ramírez-Pimienta, *Cantar* 191–227; Wald 213–84). It is a markedly transnational music, the music of immigrants that expands the borders of Greater Mexico from Oaxaca to Los Angeles and Chicago. The accompanying music and ensembles are firmly northern Mexican though: *música norteña, tambora,* or *banda sinaloense* (Valenzuela Arce 72).

15. While there are songs that draw clear lines—as in the song "El judicial y el traficante" from *Lineas de a gramo* by Grupo Exterminador, about a showdown between an honest, incorruptible judicial and a drug trafficker—there are others that point to the government involvement, such as "El Águila Blanca" from *Corridos atrevidos* by Banda Sinaloense MS or "Pacas de a kilo," "Jefe de Jefes" by Los Tigres del Norte, the latter among the Tigres's most famous and widely cherished songs.

16. Hermann Herlinghaus has argued that the corridos by Los Tigres do not celebrate violence but that they reject guilt, the most sober stance in a violent globalized context (*Narcoepics* 34–35). This is an overgeneralization since Los Tigres have several moralizing corridos, but it is an interesting idea in terms of how corridos position themselves with regard to violence. In *Poetry and Violence,* John McDowell highlights the ambivalence of corridos in general, not only narcocorridos, when dealing with violence; they celebrate violence, but also try to regulate and heal it.

17. China is the country of origin of the firearm in question. I was unable to corroborate whether China is in fact an important source of golden and silver firearms. The reference in the corridos seems to me primarily a reference to being deeply embedded in globalized networks of trade, of a popular globalization from below. Leaders of *ambulantes* of the poorer inner-city neighborhoods and markets, for example, have tight links to China (Alba and Braig). For the corrido it is curious that here a luxury product is associated with the economy of cheap products, yet this can be seen as an unapologetic stance, that of someone who does not operate within bourgeois conceptions of good taste yet has power of consumption and access to global trade routes.

18. It should be noted that, despite the overt celebration of violence, morality is not entirely absent from these corridos. Tanius Karam Cárdenas has noted the notion of being hyper and being sick in the songs of the Movimiento Alterado, showing that there is an awareness of operating beyond morally accepted behavior. It celebrates a

sick violence, or what Jean Franco would call a cruel violence—one that has lost all taboos but is framed as sick and disturbed by the movement itself.

19. The *narcotraficante* is a figure that appeals because it "challenges both the Mexican military occupation of the region and the US dominance on the border" (Muehlmann 93). Also, "the drug trade allows some people, especially young men, to draw on the sense of pride and defiance that characterizes the popular Northern persona of the *narcotraficante* and the rich cultural matrix from which this figure emerges" (20).

20. One cannot discuss actual golden rifles without referring back to government discourses. The golden and silver firearms lie as trophies of war in a museum closed to the public in order not to glorify narcos, as the military says, but the exhibit has, nonetheless, been featured in many documentaries. Despite the military's claim of not wanting to glorify the narcos and despite the fact that the majority of its rooms are dedicated to the drug eradication, the rifles in the museum's section "Narcocultura" section seem to be its most prized possessions.

21. It is important to remember that next to narcocorridos stand the *corridos del mojado,* which talk about the hardships of being an immigrant. Current corridos thus show two ways of social mobility of lower classes: one thorny, arduous, and long; the other one seemingly easy, fast, but possibly short-lived.

22. I was unable to obtain rights for this image, but it can be found in this 2017 *Business Insider* article: "The Rise and Fall of Joaquín 'El Chapo' Guzmán, the World's Most Ambitious Drug Lord" by Christopher Woody.

23. From the original Spanish: "sociedades de la exclusión donde solo se puede avistar el sueño de la modernidad vía lo paralegal." And elsewhere in the paragraph: "América Latina termina siendo otro estereotipo, otro parque temático: de narcos muy machos y de bellas muy putas, ambos horizontes de pecado, luego del deseo del capital, ambas ironías de ser latino en estos tiempos donde cada uno es moderno como puede."

24. Narcocultural discourses often display a state logic, promising welfare and security. Often the represented narcos appear to operate from a logic of monopoly of violence, of wanting to be obeyed (Rincón 4).

## EPILOGUE

1. In Chapter 5 I discussed that Pancho Rana, the demobilized combatant from Franz Galich's *Y te diré quién eres* mocks the statue's inscription, saying that the workers and peasants went to the end and ended up in misery.

2. In the 1980s, similar to Cuba, one of the tactics of the Sandinistas against a possible US invasion of Nicaragua was to hand out arms to the people (Rushdie 19, 65).

3. The use of force has been an incessantly contentious issue among the many groups and ideologies making up a broadly defined left. While some have viewed it as the only way to end the violence of capitalist-militarist systems, others have categor-

ically opposed any direct violence. Some sought parliamentary means to gain power, whereas others hesitated, because according to their analysis, conditions in Latin America were not right for armed revolution.

4. In his 2017 book *Bandit Narratives in Latin America,* Dabove analyzes the bandit trope in processes of nation-building in the twentieth century.

5. For the question of life writing in relation to revolution, see the excellent works on Guzmán by Cifuentes-Goodbody and on Ramírez by Henighan.

6. Nicaraguan artists, among them the Mejía Godoy brothers, produced an album for the literacy campaign: *Convirtiendo la oscurana en claridad*—the idea of converting darkness into light shows again the often paternalist enlightenment principles with which the Sandinistas operated; nonetheless, it shows the humanist, Arielist idealism at work here.

7. The Spanish original reads: "paternal imagen protectora," "intimidante espectro vigilante," "emblema luctuoso de la revolución."

# BIBLIOGRAPHY

Abeyta, Michael. "The 'Man-Beast' and the Jaguar: Mariano Azuela and Martín Luis Guzmán on Pancho Villa as the Sovereign Beast in *El águila y la serpiente*." In *Equestrian Rebels: Critical Perspectives on Mariano Azuela and the Novel of the Mexican Revolution*, edited by Roberto Cantú, 100–124. Newcastle upon Tyne: Cambridge Scholars Publishing, 2016.

Ades, Dawn. *Art in Latin America: The Modern Era, 1820–1980*. New Haven: Yale University Press, 1989.

Adler de Lomnitz, Larissa, Rodrigo Salazar Elena, and Ilya Adler. *Symbolism and Ritual in a One-Party Regime: Unveiling Mexico's Political Culture*. Translated by Susanne A. Wagner. Tucson: University of Arizona Press, 2010.

Agencia EFE. "La FIL mexicana busca el retorno de la literatura centroamericana al mapa." https://www.efe.com/efe/america/mexico/la-fil-mexicana-busca-el-retorno-de-literatura-centroamericana-al-mapa/50000545-2781210. Accessed June 28, 2017.

Aguilar Camín, Héctor, and Lorenzo Meyer. *In the Shadow of the Mexican Revolution: Contemporary Mexican History, 1910–1989*. Austin: University of Texas Press, 1993.

Aguilar Mora, Jorge. *Una muerte sencilla, justa, eterna. Cultura y guerra durante la Revolución Mexicana*. Mexico City: Ediciones Era, 1990.

Aguilar Mora, Jorge. *El silencio de la Revolución y otros ensayos*. Mexico City: Ediciones Era, 2011.

Aguirre Aragón, Erick. *Subversión de la memoria: Tendencias en la narrativa centroamericana de postguerra*. Managua: Centro Nicaragüense de Escritores, 2005.

Alba Vega, Carlos, and Marianne Braig. "Organización política local y entrelazamientos transregionales del comercio ambulante en la Ciudad de México." *Iberoamericana. America Latina–España–Portugal* 12, no. 48 (2012): 129–41.

Alegría, Claribel, and D. J. Flakoll. *Somoza: Expediente cerrado: La historia de un ajusticiamiento*. Managua: Editorial Gato Negro, 1993.

Alonso, Ana María. *Thread of Blood: Colonialism, Revolution, and Gender on Mexico's Northern Frontier*. Tucson: University of Arizona Press, 1995.

Andreas, Peter. *Smuggler Nation: How Illicit Trade Made America*. New York: Oxford University Press, 2014.

Aragón Rodríguez, William. "'Tenía mucho miedo'—Domingo—La Prensa." *La Prensa*, July 17, 2009. http://archivo.laprensa.com.ni/archivo/2009/julio/19/suplementos/domingo/339197.shtml.

Arce, B. Christine. *México's Nobodies: The Cultural Legacy of the Soldadera and Afro-Mexican Women*. SUNY Series, Genders in the Global South. Albany: State University of New York Press, 2017.

Arendt, Hannah. *On Violence*. New York: Harcourt Brace and Company, 1970.

Arias, Arturo. "Nahuahtlizando la novelística: De infiernos, paraísos y rupturas de estereotipos en las prácticas discursivas decoloniales." *alter/nativas* 1 (2013): 1–29.

Arias, Arturo. "Post-identidades post-nacionales: Duelo, trauma y melancolía en la constitución de las subjetividades centroamericanas de posguerra." In *(Per)Versiones de la modernidad. Literaturas, identidades y desplazamientos*, edited by Beatriz Cortez, Alexandra Ortiz Wallner, and Verónica Ríos Quesada, 121–39. Guatemala: F&G Editores, 2012.

Arias, Arturo. *Taking Their Word: Literature and the Signs of Central America*. Minneapolis: University of Minnesota Press, 2007.

Arriaga Carrasco, Paulina, Maura Luz de Jesús Roldán Álvarez, and Vania Ariadna Ruiz Mendoza. *Mujeres victimas de violencia armada y presencia de armas de fuego en México*. Mexico City: Observatorio Nacional de Violencia Armada y Género (OVAG), 2015.

Astorga, Luis. *Mitología del "narcotraficante" en México*. Mexico City: Plaza y Valdés, 1995.

Astorga, Luis. *El siglo de las drogas: El narcotráfico, del Porfiriato al nuevo milenio*. Mexico City: Plaza & Janés, 2005.

Avelar, Idelber. *The Letter of Violence: Essays on Narrative, Ethics, and Politics*. New York: Palgrave Macmillan, 2004.

Avelar, Idelber. *The Untimely Present. Postdictatorial Latin American Fiction and the Task of Mourning*. Durham, NC: Duke University Press, 1999.

Azuela, Mariano. *Los de abajo*. 16th ed. Mexico City: Catédra, 2003.

Banda Sinaloense MS de Sergio Lizárraga. *Corridos Atrevidos*. Audio CD. Disa, 2009.

Bardini, Roberto. "Cuando los narcos vienen marchando." *Almargen*, October 2005. www.almargen.com.mx/notas.php?IDNOTA=836&IDSECCION=Periodismo.

Baudrillard, Jean. *For a Critique of the Political Economy of the Sign*. Saint Louis, MO: Telos Press, 1981.

Bauman, Zygmunt. *Modernity and the Holocaust*. 1989; reprint, Ithaca: Cornell University Press, 2000.

The Beatles. *Sgt. Pepper's Lonely Hearts Club Band*. Sound recording. Hollywood, CA: Capitol Records, 1967.

Beatty, Edward. *Technology and the Search for Progress in Modern Mexico*. Oakland: University of California Press, 2015.

Beckhusen, Robert. "Mexico Is Arming Itself with U.S. Military Hardware: Rifles, Helicopters, and Humvees." *Medium*, April 1, 2015. https://medium.com/war-is -boring/mexico-is-arming-itself-with-u-s-military-hardware-a57c91b8283a#.8eb 2n5m07.

Belli, Gioconda. *La mujer habitada*. 1988. Mexico City: Editorial Diana, 1989.

Belli, Gioconda. *El país bajo mi piel: Memorias de amor y guerra*. 2001 New York: Vintage Español, 2003.

Bello, Giovanna. "Faith and Revolution in the Latin American Nueva Canción Movement." PhD diss., Catholic University of America, Washington, DC, 2012.

Bendaña, Alejandro. *Una tragedia campesina: Testimonios de la resistencia*. Managua: Editora de Arte, 1991.

Benjamin, Walter. "Critique of Violence." In *Walter Benjamin: Selected Writings 1913– 1926*, edited by Marcus Bullock and Michael Jennings, 236–52. Cambridge, MA: Belknap Press of Harvard University Press, 2002.

Benjamin, Walter. "Zur Kritik der Gewalt." In *Zur Kritik der Gewalt und andere Aufsätze: Mit einem Nachwort von Herbert Marcuse*, 29–65. Frankfurt am Main: Suhrkamp, 1965.

Beverley, John. "The Margin at the Center: On Testimonio (1989)." In *The Real Thing: Testimonial Discourse and Latin America*, edited by Georg M. Gugelberger, 23–41. Durham, NC: Duke University Press, 1996.

Beverley, John. "The Real Thing (1995)." In *The Real Thing: Testimonial Discourse and Latin America*, edited by Georg M. Gugelberger, 266–86. Durham, NC: Duke University Press, 1996.

Beverley, John. "Rethinking the Armed Struggle in Latin America." *Boundary 2* 36, no. 1 (spring 2009): 47–59.

Beverley, John. *Subalternity and Representation: Arguments in Cultural Theory*. 2nd ed. Durham, NC: Duke University Press, 2004.

Beverley, John, and Marc Zimmermann. *Literature and Politics in the Central American Revolutions*. Austin: University of Texas Press, 1990.

Beverley, John, Michael Aronna, and José Oviedo, eds. *The Postmodernism Debate in Latin America*. Durham, NC: Duke University Press, 1995.

Bhabha, Homi K. "Remembering Fanon: Self, Psyche, and the Colonial Condition." In *Colonial Discourse and Post-Colonial Theory: A Reader*, edited by Patrick Williams and Laura Chrisman, 112–23. New York: Columbia University Press, 1994.

Blasi, Alberto. "Al todo por la parte: 'La fiesta de las balas.'" *Latin American Studies Program: Commemorative Series* 2 (1978): 20–47.

Borge, Tomás. *Carlos, el amanecer ya no es una tentación*. Managua: Unión Nacional de Empleados, date unknown.

Braudy, Leo. *From Chivalry to Terrorism: War and the Changing Nature of Masculinity*. New York: Alfred A. Knopf, 2003.

Browitt, Jeff. "Amor perdido: Sergio Ramírez, la ciudad letrada y las fallas en el sandinismo gramsciano." *Istmo: Revista virtual de estudios literarios y culturales centroamericanos* 8 (2004). http://collaborations.denison.edu/istmo/n08/articulos/amor.html.

Buiza, Nanci. "Trauma and Poetics of Affect in Horacio Castellanos Moya's *Insensatez*." *Revista de Estudios Hispánicos* 47, no. 1 (2013): 151–72.

Bujard, Otker, and Ulrich Wirper, eds. *Die Revolution ist ein Buch und ein freier Mensch: Die politischen Plakate des befreiten Nicaragua 1979–1990 und der internationalen Solidaritätsbewegung*. Cologne: PapyRossa Verlag, 2007.

Bull, Stephen. *Encyclopedia of Military Technology and Innovation*. Westport, CT: Greenwood Press, 2004.

Bustamante, Alberto. "Mexican Jihad." Tumblr. *Mexican Jihad*. http://mexicanjihad.tumblr.com/. Accessed May 24, 2015.

Cabañas, Miguel. "El narcocorrido global y las identidades transnacionales." *Revista de Estudios Hispánicos* 42, no. 3 (2008): 519–42.

Cabezas, Omar. *La montaña es algo más que una inmensa estepa verde*. 1982; reprint, Mexico City Siglo XXI editores, 2002.

Campobello, Nellie. *Apuntes sobre la vida militar de Francisco Villa*. Mexico City: Edición y Distribución Iberoamericana de Publicaciones, S.A., 1940.

Campobello, Nellie. *Cartucho: Relatos de la lucha en el norte de México*. 2nd ed. Mexico City: Ediciones Era, 2000.

Campobello, Nellie. *Las manos de mamá*. Mexico City, DF: Grijalbo, 1991.

Cardenal, Ernesto. "Hora 0." In *Nueva antología poética*, 27–51. Madrid: Siglo XXI editores, 2009.

Carlin, Matthew. "Guns, Gold, and Corporeal Inscriptions: The Image of State Violence in Mexico." *Third Text* 26, no. 5 (September 2012): 503–14.

Castañeda, Jorge. *Utopia Unarmed: The Latin American Left after the Cold War*. New York: Alfred A. Knopf, 1993.

Castellanos, Laura. "'Fueron los federales.'" *Aristegui Noticias*. http://aristeguinoticias.com/1904/mexico/fueron-los-federales/. Accessed May 14, 2016.

Castellanos Moya, Horacio. *El arma en el hombre*. Madrid: Tusquets Editores, 2001.

Castellanos Moya, Horacio. *El asco: Tres relatos violentos*. Barcelona: Editorial Casiopeia, 2000.

Castellanos Moya, Horacio. *Baile con serpientes*. San Salvador, El Salvador: Dirección de Publicaciones e Impresos, Consejo Nacional para la Cultura y el Arte, Ministerio de Educación, 1996.

Castellanos Moya, Horacio. *La diáspora*. San Salvador, El Salvador: UCA Editores, 1989.

Castellanos Moya, Horacio. *La diabla en el espejo*. Orense: Linteo, 2000.

Castellanos Moya, Horacio. *Insensatez*. Mexico City: Tusquets, 2004.

Castellanos Moya, Horacio. *El sueño del retorno*. Barcelona: Tusquets Editores, 2013.

Castellanos Moya, Horacio. *Tirana memoria*. Barcelona: Tusquets, 2008.

Castro, William. "The Novel after Terrorism: On Rethinking the Testimonio, Solidarity, and Democracy in Horacio Castellanos Moya's *El arma en el hombre*." *Revista Hispánica Moderna* 63, no. 2 (2010): 121–35.

Cázares, Laura, ed. *Nellie Campobello: La revolución en clave de mujer*. Mexico City: Tecnológico de Monterrey Toluca; Universidad Iberoamericana Ciudad de México, 2006.

Centroamérica cuenta. "Sergio Ramírez." *Centroamérica Cuenta*. www.centroameri cacuenta.com/participantes2/sergio-ramirez-2/. Accessed July 18, 2017.

Cervantes Saavedra, Miguel de. "CVC. 'Don Quijote de la Mancha.'" *Centro Virtual Cervantes*, 1605. http://cvc.cervantes.es/literatura/clasicos/quijote/.

Chacón, Gloria E. "Indigenous Literatures and Epistemologies: The Ordering of the Ancient Word in the Contemporary World." *Diálogo* 19, no. 1 (2016): 5–6.

Chávez, Daniel. *Nicaragua and the Politics of Utopia: Development and Culture in the Modern State*. Nashville, TN: Vanderbilt University Press, 2015.

Cifuentes-Goodbody, Nicholas. *The Man Who Wrote Pancho Villa: Martín Luis Guzmán and the Politics of Life Writing*. Nashville, TN: Vanderbilt University Press, 2016.

Clausewitz, Carl von. "On War. Book I: On the Nature of War. Chapter I. What Is War?" *Clausewitz*. www.clausewitz.com/readings/OnWar1873/BK1ch01.html. Accessed September 2, 2013.

Clausewitz, Carl von. "Vom Kriege. Erstes Buch: Über die Natur des Krieges. Erstes Kapitel: Was ist der Krieg?" *Clausewitz*. www.clausewitz.com/readings/Compare/ VomKriege1832/Book1Ch01VK.htm. Accessed September 2, 2013.

Colom, Yolanda. *Mujeres en la alborada: Guerrilla y participación femenina en Guatemala, 1973–1978: Testimonio*. Guatemala City: Artemis & Edinter, 1998.

Cooke, Miriam. *Women and the War Story*. Berkeley: University of California Press, 1996.

Cooke, Miriam, and Angela Woollacott, eds. *Gendering War Talk*. Princeton, NJ: Princeton University Press, 1993.

Coronel Urtecho, José. *Rapido tránsito (Al ritmo de Norteamérica)*. Managua: Ediciones el Pez y la Serpiente, 1976.

Cortés Camarillo, Felix. "Caiga quien caiga, muera quien muera." *Excélsior*, October 27, 2014. www.excelsior.com.mx/opinion/felix-cortes-camarillo/2014/10/27/989 102.

Cortez, Beatriz. *Estética del cinismo: Pasión y desencanto en la literatura centroamericana de posguerra.*, Guatemala City: F& G Editores, 2010.

Cortez, Beatriz. "Memorias del desencanto: El duelo postergado y la pérdida de una subjetividad heróica." In *(Per)Versiones de la modernidad: Literaturas, identidades y desplazamientos*, edited by Beatriz Cortez, Alexandra Ortiz Wallner, and Verónica Ríos Quesada, 259–80. Guatemala City: F&G Editores, 2012.

Cortez, Otilla. "La exaltación del cuerpo en Chinto Jiñocuago: Canción de Carlos Mejía Godoy." *Carátula: Revista Cultural Centroamericana*, December 2008. www .caratula.net/archivo/N27–1208/Secciones/critica/critica-otilia%20cortez.html.

Cortínez, Carlos. "Simetría y sutileza en la narrativa de Martín Luis Guzmán." *Revista Canadiense de Estudios Hispánicos* 12, no. 2 (1988): 221–34.

Craft, Linda J. *Novels of Testimony and Resistance from Central America*. Gainesville: University Press of Florida, 1997.

Cuadra, Pablo Antonio. *Siete árboles contra el atardecer*. Caracas: Ediciones de la Presidencia de la República, 1980.

Dabove, Juan Pablo. *Bandit Narratives in Latin America: From Villa to Chávez*. Pittsburgh: University of Pittsburgh Press, 2017.

Dabove, Juan Pablo. "Ciudad letrada." In *Diccionario de Estudios Culturales Latinoamericanos*, edited by Mónica Szurmuk and Robert McKee Irwin, 55–60. Mexico City: Siglo XXI, 2008.

Dabove, Juan Pablo. *Nightmares of the Lettered City: Banditry and Literature in Latin America, 1816–1929*. Pittsburgh: University of Pittsburgh Press, 2007.

Dalton, Roque, and Miguel Mármol. *Miguel Mármol: Los sucesos de 1932 en El Salvador*. San Salvador: UCA Editores, 1993.

Dant, Tim. "Fetishism and the Social Value of Objects." *Sociological Review* 44, no. 3 (1996): 495–516.

Darío, Rubén. *Cantos de vida y esperanza: Los cisnes y otros poemas*. Managua: Centro Nicaraguense de Escritores, 2005.

Darío, Rubén. *Prosas profanas*. Madrid: Espasa-Calpe S.A, 2002.

Dawes, Greg. *Aesthetics and Revolution: Nicaraguan Poetry, 1979-1990*. University of Minnesota Press, 1993.

DeLay, Brian. "How Not to Arm a State: American Guns and the Crisis of Governance in Mexico, Nineteenth and Twenty-First Centuries." *Southern California Quarterly* 95, no. 1 (spring 2013): 5–23.

Delgado, Álvaro. "Los muertos de Peña Nieto." *Proceso*, April 8, 2013. www.proceso .com.mx/338473/los-muertos-de-pena-nieto.

Delgado, Leonel. "La biblioteca en la selva: Modernidad y vanguardia en los relatos autobiográficos centroamericanos." In *Tensiones de la modernidad: Del modernismo al realismo—Tomo II*, edited by Valeria Grinberg Pla and Roque Baldovinos, 35–56. Guatemala City: F&G Editores, 2010.

Delgado, Leonel. "De la memoria política, los que se narran y los fragmentos." *La Prensa Literaria*, 2002. http://archivo.laprensa.com.ni/archivo/2002/diciembre/07/ literaria/critica/.

Delgado, Leonel. "Desplazamientos discursivos de la representación campesina en la Nicaragua pre y post-sandinista." *Latinoamérica. Revista de Estudios Latinoamericanos*, no. 58 (June 2014): 33–58.

Delgado, Leonel. *Márgenes recorridos: Apuntes sobre procesos culturales y literatura nicaragüense*. Managua: IHNCA/UCA, 2002.

Delgado, Leonel. "Memorias apocalípticas, administrativas y campesinas: Por una crítica de la memoria del sandinismo." *MERIDIONAL Revista Chilena de Estudios Latinoamericanos*, no. 2 (April 2014): 107–31.

del Valle, Ivonne and Estelle Tarica. "Radical Politics and/or the Rule of Law in Mexico." *Política Común* 7 (July 2015).

Diamond, Jared. *Guns, Germs, and Steel: The Fates of Human Societies*. New York: W. W. Norton & Co, 2005.

Díaz, George T. *Border Contraband: A History of Smuggling across the Rio Grande*. Austin: University of Texas Press, 2015.

Domínguez Michael, Christopher. "Martín Luis Guzmán o el texto de la política." In *Tiros en el concierto: Literatura mexicana del siglo V*, 199–227. Mexico City: Ediciones Era, 1997.

Domínguez-Ruvalcaba, Héctor. *Modernity and the Nation in Mexican Representations of Masculinity: From Sensuality to Bloodshed*. New York: Palgrave Macmillan, 2007.

Dore, Elizabeth. "Culture." In *Nicaragua: The First Five Years*, edited by Thomas Walker, 413–22. New York: Praeger Publishers, 1985.

Dröscher, Barbara. "Las performances autobiográficas en la frontera de lo político y lo literario: Dos memorias (post)sandinistas, Gioconda Belli y Sergio Ramírez." In *Los poderes de lo público: Debates, espacios y actores en América Latina*, edited by Marianne Braig and Anne Huffschmid, 395–409. Madrid: Iberoamericana, Vervuert, 2009.

Dueto Rubén y Nelly. *Cantares de la Revolución*. Audio CD. Multimusic, Phoenix, 2005.

Duffrey, Patrick. "Pancho Villa at the Movies: Cinematic Techniques in the Works of Guzmán and Muñoz." In *Latin American Literature and Mass Media*, edited by Edmundo Paz-Soldán and Debra Castillo, 41–57. New York: Garland Publishing, 2001.

Duhalde, Juan Pablo. "Las muertas por armas de fuego en El Salvador: La reproducción de una cultura de violencia." *Revista del Centro de Investigación Social de Un Techo para Chile* (2011): 87–97.

Edberg, Mark Cameron. *El Narcotraficante: Narcocorridos and the Construction of a Cultural Persona on the U.S.-Mexico Border*. Austin: University of Texas Press, 2004.

El Komander. *El Katch*. Audio CD. Fonovisa Inc., 2009.

El Nuevo Diario. "Monumento al Combatiente Popular: La mole herida" *El Nuevo Diario.* www.elnuevodiario.com.ni/nacionales/325922-monumento-combatiente -popular-mole-herida/. Accessed June 22, 2017.

El País. "Año 11 de la guerra contra el narco en México." *El País.* http://elpais.com/ especiales/2016/guerra-narcotrafico-mexico. Accessed June 30, 2017.

El Universal. "Demanda a Lupillo Rivera por Cambiar 'perjúmenes.'" *El Universal,* July 13, 2003. http://http://archivo.eluniversal.com.mx/espectaculos/46238.html.

Elias, Norbert. *Über den Prozeß der Zivilisation: Soziogenetische und psychogenetische Untersuchungen.* 1939; reprint, Frankfurt am Main: Suhrkamp, 1997.

Elizalde, Valentin. *Corridos entre amigos.* Audio CD. Universal Music Group, 2003.

Engels, Friedrich. "Herrn Eugen Dühring's Umwälzung der Wissenschaft" In *Werke,* by Karl Marx and Friedrich Engels, vol. 20, 136–238, Berlin: Karl Dietz Verlag, 1962.

Enloe, Cynthia H. *Does Khaki Become You? The Militarisation of Women's Lives.* Boston: South End Press, 1983.

Esch, Sophie. "In the Crossfire: Rascón Banda's *Contrabando* and the 'Narcoliterature' Debate in Mexico." *Latin American Perspectives* 41, no. 2 (2014): 161–76.

Escudos, Jacinta. *El desencanto.* San Salvador, El Salvador: Direccion de Publicaciones e Impresos, Consejo Nacional para la Cultura y el Arte, 2001.

Escudos, Jacinta. "La noche de los escritores asesinos." In *Cuentos sucios,* 83–123. San Salvador: Dirección de Publicaciones e Impresos, Consejo Nacional para la Cultura y el Arte, 1997.

Espinosa, Gabriela. "El viaje del país a la ciudad: Martín Luis Guzmán." *Taller de Letras* 28 (2000): 85–106.

Estrada, Oswaldo. *Ser mujer y estar presente. Disidencias de género en la literatura mexicana contemporánea.* Textos de Difusión Cultural, Mexico City: Coordinación de Difusión Cultural, Dirección de Literatura, Universidad Nacional Autónoma de México (UNAM), 2014.

Eyerman, Ron, and Andrew Jamison. *Music and Social Movements: Mobilizing Traditions in the Twentieth Century.* Cambridge: Cambridge University Press, 1998.

Fanon, Frantz. *Black Skin, White Masks.* London: Pluto, 1986.

Fanon, Frantz. *The Wretched of the Earth.* New York: Grove Press, 1965.

Faverón-Patriau, Gustavo. "La rebelión de la memoria: Testimonio y reescritura de la realidad en *Cartucho* de Nellie Campobello." *Mester* 32, no. 1 (2003): 53–71.

Field, Corinne. "Women and War at the Imperial War Museum, London." *Culture24,* October 14, 2003. www.culture24.org.uk/history-and-heritage/military-history/ world-war-two/art18458.

Flores, Tatiana. *Mexico's Revolutionary Avant-Gardes: From Estridentismo to ¡30–30!* New Haven: Yale University Press, 2013.

Foucault, Michel. *Discipline and Punish.* New York: Vintage Books, 1995.

Foucault, Michel. *"Society Must Be Defended": Lectures at the College de France, 1975– 76.* Edited by Mauro Bertani and Alessandro Fontana. New York: Picador, 2003.

Franco, Jean. *Cruel Modernity*. Durham, NC: Duke University Press, 2013.

Franco, Jean. *The Decline and Fall of the Lettered City: Latin America in the Cold War*. Cambridge: Harvard University Press, 2002.

Frazer, Chris. *Bandit Nation. A History of Outlaws and Cultural Struggle in Mexico, 1810–1920*. Lincoln: University of Nebraska Press, 2006.

Freud, Sigmund. "Fetischismus." In *Studienausgabe*, vol. 3, 379–88. Frankfurt am Main: S. Fischer Verlag, 1975.

Fuentes, Carlos. *La muerte de Artemio Cruz*. Mexico City: Fondo de Cultura Económica, 1962.

Gagne, David. "New Strategy, Familiar Result: Militarization in Mexico." *Insight-Crime*. March 25, 2015. www.insightcrime.org/news-analysis/new-strategy-familiar-result-militarization-in-mexico.

Galich, Franz. *Managua, salsa city (¡Devórame otra vez!)*. Panama City: Editora Géminis, 2000.

Galich, Franz. *Y te diré quién eres (Mariposa traicionera)*. Managua: Anamá Ediciones, 2006.

Gallo, Rubén. *Mexican Modernity: The Avant-Garde and the Technological Revolution*. Cambridge: Massachusetts Institute of Technology Press, 2010.

Galtung, Johan. "Violence, Peace, and Peace Research." In *Violence: A Philosophical Anthology*, edited by Vittorio Bufacchi, 78–109. New York: Palgrave Macmillan, 2009.

Gandhi, Mahatma. *Towards Non-Violent Politics and the Relation of Constructive Work to Ahimsa: Discourses at the Five Sessions of the Gandhi Seva Sangh from 1936 to 1940*. Thanjavur: Sarvodaya Prachuralaya, 1969.

García Canclini, Néstor. *Culturas híbridas: Estrategias para entrar y salir de la modernidad*. 1990; reprint, Mexico City: Delbosillo, 2009.

García Irles, Mónica. "Carlos Mejía Godoy: Otra voz canta en Nicaragua." In *Literatura y música popular en Hispanoamérica*, edited by Ángel Esteban, Gracia Morales, and Álvaro Salvador, 391–97. Granada: Universidad de Granada, Asociación española de Estudios Literarios Hispanoamericanos, 2002.

García, Michelle. "Deconstructing Mexico's 'War on Drugs.'" *Dart Center for Journalism and Trauma*, November 23, 2013. http://dartcenter.org/content/deconstructing-mexicos-war-on-drugs#.VjeSrTW34_k.

García Ramírez, Fernando. "Contrabando de Víctor Hugo Rascón Banda, Fiesta en la madriguera de Juan Pablo Villalobos." *Letras Libres*, May 2011. www.letraslibres.com/index.php?art=15440.

Garro, Elena. *Los recuerdos del porvenir*. Mexico City: J. Mortiz, 1977.

Gianni, Silvia. "El turno de los ofendidos." *Istmo: Revista virtual de estudios literarios y culturales centroamericanos* 15, 2007. http://istmo.denison.edu/n15/articulos/gianni.html.

Gilly, Adolfo. *La revolución interrumpida*. 2nd ed. Mexico City: Ediciones Era, 2007.

Giménez, Gilberto, and Catherine Héau. "La representación de la violencia en la trova popular mexicana: De los corridos de valientes a los narco-corridos." In *Estudios sobre la cultura y las identidades sociales*, edited by Gilberto Giménez, 363–425. Mexico City: Consejo Nacional para la Cultura y las Artes (CONACULTA), Instituto Tecnológico y de Estudios Superiores de Occidente (ITESO), 2007.

Girard, René. *Violence and the Sacred*. Baltimore: Johns Hopkins University Press, 1977.

Glantz, Margo. "Vigencia de Nellie Campobello." *FULGOR* 3, no. 1 (2006): 37–50.

Godnick, William. "Stray Bullets: The Impact of Small Arms Misuse in Central America." *Small Arms Survey*, October 2002. www.smallarmssurvey.org/.

Godnick, William, and Edward Laurance. "Weapons Collection in Central America: El Salvador and Guatemala." Working paper. Chapter contribution for the Bonn International Center for Conversion, January 2000.

Goldstein, Joshua. *War and Gender: How Gender Shapes the War System and Vice Versa*. Cambridge: Cambridge University Press, 2001.

Gollnick, Brian. "Pancho Villa: Icon of Insurgency." In *Latin American Icons: Fame Across Borders*, edited by Dianna C. Niebylski and Patrick O'Connor, 21–33. Nashville, TN: Vanderbilt University Press, 2014.

Gómez, Juan Pablo. "La insurrección de los niños: Memoria y perversión." *El Nuevo Diario*, May 2012. www.elnuevodiario.com.ni/opinion/251390.

González, Aurelio. "El caballo y la pistola: Motivos en el corrido." *Revista de Literaturas Populares* 1, no. 1 (2001): 94–114.

González Centeno, Alejandra. "La historia en estatuas." *La Prensa*, February 22, 2015. www.laprensa.com.ni/2015/02/22/boletin/1787004-la-historia-en-estatuas.

González Echevarría, Roberto. *Myth and Archive: A Theory of Latin American Narrative*. Durham, NC: Duke University Press, 1998.

González, Manuel Pedro. *Trayectoria de la novela en México*. Mexico City: Ediciones Botas, 1951.

Gootenberg, Paul. "Cocaine's Blowback North: A Pre-History of Mexican Drug Violence." *Latin American Studies Association Forum* (2011) 43: 7–10.

Gould, Jeffrey. "On the Road to 'El Porvenir': Revolutionary and Counterrevolutionary Violence in El Salvador and Nicaragua." In *A Century of Revolution: Insurgent and Counterinsurgent Violence During Latin America's Long Cold War*, edited by Greg Grandin and Gilbert Joseph, 88–120. Durham, NC: Duke University Press, 2010.

Grupo Exterminador. *Lineas de a Gramo*. Audio CD. Fonovisa Inc., 2001.

Grupo Voces de Durango. *Cantares de la Revolución*. Vol. 2. Audio CD. Ecofon, Phoenix, 2001.

Guerrero Aguilar, Antonio. "La carabina 30–30." *Sabinas Hidalgo*, February 2013. www.sabinashidalgo.net/articulos/de-solares-y-resolanas/8926-la-carabina-30-30.

Guerrero Pérez, Juan José. *La canción protesta latinoamericana y la teología de la liberación: Estudio de género musical y análisis de vínculo sociopolítico y religioso (1968–2000)*. Caracas: Monte Ávila Editores Latinoamericana, 2005.

Guha, Ranajit. *Elementary Aspects of Peasant Insurgency in Colonial India*. Durham, NC: Duke University Press, 1999.

Guha, Ranajit. "The Prose of Counter-Insurgency." In *Selected Subaltern Studies*, 45–84. New York: Oxford University Press, 1988.

Guillermoprieto, Alma. "El hombre molotov." *Letras Libres*, September 1999. www .letraslibres.com/revista/portafolios/el-hombre-molotov?page=0,1.

Gutierrez, Norma. "Firearms-Control Legislation and Policy: Mexico." *Law Library of Congress*. www.loc.gov/law/help/firearms-control/mexico.php. Accessed November 28, 2015.

Guzmán, Martín Luis. *El águila y la serpiente*. 1928; reprint, 5th ed. Mexico City: Editorial Porrúa, 1998.

Guzmán, Martín Luis. *Memorias de Pancho Villa*. 2nd ed. Mexico City: Compañía General de Ediciones, 1951.

Guzmán, Martín Luis. *La sombra del caudillo*. Madrid: Espasa-Calpe S.A, 1929.

Haraway, Donna. "A Cyborg Manifesto Science, Technology, and Socialist-Feminism in the Late Twentieth Century." In *Simians, Cyborgs, and Women: The Reinvention of Nature*, 149–81. New York: Routledge, 1991.

Harzer, Erika, and Willi Volks, eds. *Aufbruch nach Nicaragua: Deutsch-deutsche Solidarität im Systemwettstreit*. Ch. Links Verlag, 2009.

Héau, Catherine. "El corrido y la bola suriana: El canto popular como arma ideológica y operador de identidad." *Estudios sobre las Culturas Contemporáneas* 2, no. 6 (1989): 99–115.

Hegel, Georg Wilhelm Friedrich. *Die Phänomenologie des Geistes*. Leiden: A. H. Adriani, 1907.

Henighan, Stephen. *Sandino's Nation: Ernesto Cardenal and Sergio Ramírez Writing Nicaragua, 1940–2012*. Montreal: McGill-Queens University Press, 2014.

Herlinghaus, Hermann. *Narcoepics: A Global Aesthetics of Sobriety*. New York: Bloomsbury, 2013.

Herlinghaus, Hermann. *Violence without Guilt: Ethical Narratives from the Global South*. New York: Palgrave Macmillan, 2009.

Hernández, Claudia. *De fronteras*. Guatemal City: Piedra Santa, 2007.

Hernández, Claudia. *Mediodía de frontera*. San Salvador, El Salvador: Dirección de Publicaciones e Impresos, Consejo Nacional para la Cultura y el Arte, 2002.

Herrera-Sobek, María. *The Mexican Corrido: A Feminist Analysis*. Bloomington: Indiana University Press, 1990.

Heumann, Silke. "Gender, Sexuality, and Politics: Rethinking the Relationship between Feminism and Sandinismo in Nicaragua." *Social Politics: International Studies in Gender, State, and Society* 21, no. 2 (June 1, 2014): 290–314.

Hobbes, Thomas. *Leviathan*. Edited by Richard Tuck. 2nd revised ed. Cambridge Texts in the History of Political Thought. Cambridge: Cambridge University Press, 1996.

Hobsbawn, Eric. *Bandits*. Revised. New York: New Press, 2000.

Hodges, Michael. *AK47: The Story of a Gun*. San Francisco: MacAdam/Cage Publishing, 2007.

Hollis, Karyn. *Poesía del pueblo para el pueblo: Talleres nicaragüenses de poesía*. San José, Costa Rica: Consejo Superior Universitario Centroamericano, 1991.

Horton, Lynn. *Peasants in Arms. War and Peace in the Mountains of Nicaragua, 1979–1994*. Athens: Ohio University Center for International Studies, 1998.

Huffschmid, Anne. *Diskursguerilla, Wortergreifung und Widersinn: Die Zapatistas im Spiegel der Mexikanischen und Internationalen Öffentlichkeit*. Heidelberg: Synchron, 2004.

Huggins, Martha K., Mika Haritos-Fatouros, and Philip G. Zimbardo, eds. *Violence Workers: Police Torturers and Murderers Reconstruct Brazilian Atrocities*. Berkeley: University of California Press, 2002.

Huntington, Tanya. "*El águila y la serpiente* de Martín Luis Guzmán: Una *mea culpa* revolucionaria." PhD diss., University of Maryland–College Park, 2010.

Jenkins, Philipp. "Disenchantment, Enchantment, and Re-Enchantment: Max Weber at the Millenium." *Max Weber Studies* 1 (2000): 11–32.

Johnstone, Gerry, and Daniel N. Van Ness. "The Meaning of Restorative Justice." In *Handbook of Restorative Justice*, edited by Gerry Johnstone and Daniel N. Van Ness, 1–23. Cullompton, Devon, England: Willan Publishing, 2007.

Jones, Karen R., Giacomo Macola, and David Welch, eds. *A Cultural History of Firearms in the Age of Empire*. Burlington, VT: Ashgate, 2013.

Joseph, Gilbert M., and Jürgen Buchenau. *Mexico's Once and Future Revolution: Social Upheaval and the Challenge of Rule since the Late Nineteenth Century*. Durham, NC: Duke University Press, 2013.

Joseph, Gilbert, and Daniel Nugent, eds. *Everyday Forms of State Formation: Revolution and the Negotiation of Rule in Modern Mexico*. Durham, NC: Duke University Press, 1994.

Judson, Fred. "Central American Revolutionary Music." In *Music and Marx: Ideas, Practice, Politics*, edited by Regula Burckhardt Qureshi, 204–35. New York: Routledge, 2002.

Kampwirth, Karen. *Feminism and the Legacy of Revolution: Nicaragua, El Salvador, Chiapas*. Columbus: Ohio University Press, 2004.

Karam Cárdenas, Tanius. "Mecanismos discursivos en los corridos mexicanos de presentación del 'Movimiento Alterado.'" *Anagramas* 12, no. 23 (June 2013): 21–42.

Karp, Aaron. "Completing the Count. Civilian Firearms." In *Small Arms Survey 2007*, edited by Eric Berman, Keith Krause, Emile LeBruin, and Glenn McDonald, 39–71 (and Annexes). Cambridge: Cambridge University Press, 2007. www

.smallarmssurvey.org/fileadmin/docs/A-Yearbook/2007/en/full/Small-Arms
-Survey-2007-Chapter-02-EN.pdf.

Katz, Friedrich. *The Life and Times of Pancho Villa*. Stanford, CA: Stanford University Press, 1998.

Katz, Friedrich. *The Secret War in Mexico: Europe, the United States, and the Mexican Revolution*. Chicago: University of Chicago Press, 1981.

Katz, Friedrich. "Violence and Terror in the Russian and Mexican Revolutions." In *A Century of Revolution: Insurgent and Counterinsurgent Violence during Latin America's Long Cold War*, edited by Greg Grandin and Gilbert Joseph, 45–61. Durham, NC: Duke University Press, 2010.

Kingma, Kees. "Post-War Demobilization and the Reintegration of Ex-Combatants into Civilian Life." Bonn: Bonn International Center for Conversion, 1997.

Klein, Martina, and Klaus Schubert. "Militarismus." *Das Politiklexikon*. Bonn: Dietz, 2006.

Knight, Alan. "Intellectuals in the Mexican Revolution." In *Intellectuals and Power in Mexico*, edited by Roderic Camp, Charles Hale, and Josefina Zoraida Vázquez, 141–71. Mexico City: El Colegio de México; Los Angeles: UCLA Latin American Center Publications, 1991.

Knight, Alan. "Narco-Violence and the State in Modern Mexico." In *Violence, Coercion, and State-Making in Twentieth-Century Mexico*, edited by Wil G. Pansters, 115–34. Stanford, CA: Stanford University Press, 2012.

Knight, Alan. "Peasant and Caudillo in Revolutionary Mexico, 1910–1917." In *Caudillo and Peasant in the Mexican Revolution*, edited by D. A. Brading, 17–58. Cambridge: Cambridge University Press, 1980.

Knight, Alan. *The Mexican Revolution: A Very Short Introduction*. New York: Oxford University Press, 2016.

Knight, Alan. *The Mexican Revolution*. Volume 1, *Porfirians, Liberals and Peasants*. Lincoln: University of Nebraska Press, 1990.

Knight, Alan. *The Mexican Revolution*. Volume 2, *Counter-Revolution and Reconstruction*. Lincoln: University of Nebraska Press, 1990.

Kohl, Randall. "México en 1810." *Gaceta. Universidad Veracruzana* (September 2010): 68-69.

Kokotovic, Misha. "After the Revolution: Central American Narrative in the Age of Neoliberalism." *A Contracorriente: Una Revista de Historia Social y Literatura de América Latina/A Journal of Social History and Literature in Latin America* 1, no. 1 (2003): 19–50.

Kokotovic, Misha. "Neoliberal Noir: Contemporary Central American Crime Fiction as Social Criticism." *Clues: A Journal of Detection* 24, no. 3 (spring 2006): 15–29.

Kokotovic, Misha. "Neoliberalismo y novela negra en la posguerra centroamericana." In *(Per)Versiones de la modernidad: Literaturas, identidades y desplazamientos*, edited by Beatriz Cortez, Alexandra Ortiz Wallner, and Verónica Ríos Quesada, 185–209. Guatemala City: F&G Editores, 2012.

Kokotovic, Misha. "Telling Evasions: Postwar El Salvador in the Short Fiction of Claudia Hernández." *A Contracorriente* 11, no. 2 (2014): 53–75.

Kokotovic, Misha. "Testimonio Once Removed: Castellanos Moya's *Insensatez*." *Revista de Estudios Hispánicos* 43 (2009): 545–62.

Kotcheff, Ted, director. *First Blood*. Orion Pictures, 1982.

Kruijt, Dirk. *Guerrillas: War and Peace in Central America*. London: Zed Books, 2008.

Kurtenbach, Sabine. "Exploraciones/Explorations. Why Is Liberal Peacebuilding So Difficult? Some Lessons from Central America." *European Review of Latin American and Caribbean Studies* 88 (April 2010): 95–110.

Kurz, Robert. "Der Knall der Moderne. Innovation durch Feuerwaffen, Expansion durch Krieg: Ein Blick in die Urgeschichte der abstrakten Arbeit." www.exit-online.org/link.php?tabelle=autoren&posnr=93. Accessed December 11, 2011.

*La Jornada*. Title page. *La Jornada*, August 19, 2010. www.jornada.unam.mx:8810/2010/08/19/.

Lacina, Bethany. "The PRIO Battle Deaths Dataset, 1946–2008, Version 3.0 Documentation of Coding Decisions for Use with the UCDP/PRIO Data." *Peace Research Institute Oslo*, 2009. www.prio.no/Data/Armed-Conflict/Battle-Deaths/The-Battle-Deaths-Dataset-version-30/.

Lancaster, Roger. *Life Is Hard: Machismo, Danger, and the Intimacy of Power in Nicaragua*. Berkeley: University of California Press, 1992.

Landau, Gregorio. "The Role of Music in the Nicaraguan Revolution: *Guitarra Armada*." PhD diss., University of California, 1999.

Leal, Luis. "La caricia suprema: Contextos de luz y sombra en *El águila y la serpiente*." *Latin American Studies Program. Commemorative Series* 2 (1978): 72–82.

Lear, John. "'¡No vamos a la Revolución!' Civilians as Revolucionarios and Revolucionados in the 1910 Mexican Revolution." In *Daily Lives of Civilians in Wartime Latin America: From the Wars of Independence to the Central American Civil Wars*, edited by Pedro Santoni, 173–201. Westport, CT: Greenwood Press, 2008.

Legrás, Horacio. "El ateneo y los orígenes del estado ético en México." *Latin American Research Review* 38, no. 2 (2003): 34–60.

Legrás, Horacio. *Culture and Revolution: Violence, Memory, and the Making of Modern Mexico*. Austin: University of Texas Press, 2017.

Legrás, Horacio. *Literature and Subjection: The Economy of Writing and Marginality in Latin America*. Pittsburgh: University of Pittsburgh Press, 2008.

Legrás, Horacio. "Martín Luis Guzmán: El viaje de la revolución." *Modern Language Notes* 118, no. 2 (2003): 427–54.

Legrás, Horacio. "Seeing Women Photographed in Revolutionary Mexico." *Discourse* 38, no. 1 (Winter 2016): 3–21.

León Diez, Lorenzo. "Rodolfo Fierro o la sordera de los héroes." *Ciclo Literario* 66 (November 2007). http://www.cicloliterario.com/ciclo66noviembre2007/rodolfo. html.

Lescure, Mathurin. *Mémoires sur la guerre de la Vendée et l'expédition de Quiberon.* Paris: Librairie de Firmin-Diderot, 1877.

Leyendecker, Hans. "Deutsche Waffenexporte: 10000 G36 gegen alte Revolver." *Süddeutsche Zeitung,* September 15, 2015. www.sueddeutsche.de/politik/deutsche-waffen exporte-geschmolzene-kalaschnikows-als-schlechte-inszenierung-1.2649145.

Lindsay-Poland, John. "The Mexican Military's Buying Binge." *North American Congress in Latin America (NACLA),* March 23, 2015. https://nacla.org/ news/2015/03/23/mexican-military%27s-buying-binge-0.

Linhard, Tabea Alexa. *Fearless Women in the Mexican Revolution and the Spanish Civil War.* Columbia: University of Missouri Press, 2005.

Linhard, Tabea Alexa. "A Perpetual Trace of Violence: Gendered Narratives of Revolution and War." *Discourse* 25, no. 3 (2003): 30–47.

Lomnitz, Claudio. *Death and the Idea of Mexico.* Brooklyn, NY: Zone Books, 2005.

Lomnitz-Adler, Claudio. *Deep Mexico, Silent Mexico. An Anthropology of Nationalism.* Minneapolis: University of Minnesota Press, 2001.

Los Broncos de Reynosa. *14 Corridos Exitos de Paulino Vargas.* CD. Warner Music Latina, 2002.

Los Incomparables de Tijuana. *16 Corridos Inigualables.* CD. EMI Musica Distribution, 1998.

Los Incomparables de Tijuana. *Temible Cuerno de Chivo,* 2008.

Los Matadores del Norte. *De Sinaloa a Durango,* 2010. https://www.youtube.com/ watch?v=ijQQ6zRwvkQ.

Los Tigres del Norte. *Contrabando y traición.* CD. Fonovisa, 1995.

Los Tigres del Norte. *Jefe de Jefes.* Audio CD. Fonovisa Inc., 1997.

Los Tigres del Norte. *La Garra de . . .* Audio CD. Fonovisa, 1995.

Los Tucanes de Tijuana. *Los Poderosos.* CD. Cadena Musical, 2002.

Los Tucanes de Tijuana. *Tucanes de Plata.* CD. EMI Music Distribution, 1997.

Loveman, Brian, and Thomas Davies, eds. *The Politics of Antipolitics: The Military in Latin America.* Revised and updated. Wilmington, DE: Scholarly Resouces Inc. Imprint, 1997.

Lund, Joshua, and Alejandro Sánchez Lopera. "Revolutionary Mexico, the Sovereign People, and the Problem of Men with Guns." *Política Común* 7 (July 2015).

Macías, Anna. *Against All Odds: The Feminist Movement in Mexico to 1940.* Westport, CT: Greenwood Press, 1982.

Macías-González, Víctor M., and Anne Rubenstein, eds. *Masculinity and Sexuality in Modern Mexico.* Albuquerque: University of New Mexico Press, 2012.

Mackenbach, Werner. "Después de los pos-ismos: ¿Desde qué categorías pensamos las literaturas centroamericanas contemporáneas?" In *Intersecciones y transgresiones: Propuestas para una historiografía literaria en Centroamérica*, edited by Werner Mackenbach, 279–307. Guatemala: F& G Editores, 2008.

Mackenbach, Werner. *Die unbewohnte Utopie: Der nicaraguanische Roman der achtziger und neunziger Jahre.* Frankfurt am Main: Vervuert Verlag, 2004.

Mackenbach, Werner. "Mentiras verdaderas contra verdades mentirosas: Historia y ficción en la obra novelística de Sergio Ramírez." *OtroLunes: Revista Hispanoamericana de Cultura,* 2009. http://otrolunes.com/archivos/09/html/unos-escriben/unos-escriben-n09-a51-p02–2009.html.

Main, Alexander. "The U.S. Re-Militarization of Central America and Mexico." *North American Congress in Latin America (NACLA).* https://nacla.org/article/us-re-militarization-central-america-and-mexico. Accessed November 9, 2015.

Mallon, Florencia. *Peasant and Nation: The Making of Postcolonial Mexico and Peru.* Berkeley: University of California Press, 1995.

Mantero, José María. "*El país bajo mi piel* de Gioconda Belli como anti-testimonio." *Istmo: Revista virtual de estudios literarios y culturales centroamericanos* 6 (2003). http://istmo.denison.edu/n06/articulos/pais.html.

Mántica, Carlos. "El legado musical de Carlos Mejía Godoy." *Carátula: Revista Cultural Centroamericana* (March 2010). www.caratula.net/archivo/N34–0210/Secciones/critica/el%20legado%20musical%20de%20CMG.html.

Mariscal, Alberto, director. *La chamuscada (Tierra y libertad),* 1971.

Martín Barbero, Jesús. *Communication, Culture, and Hegemony: From the Media to Mediations.* Communication and Human Values. London: SAGE Publications, 1993.

Martín Barbero, Jesús. "Modernidad y posmodernidad en la periferia." *Revista del Centro de Ciencias de Lenguaje,* no. 13–14 (1996): 281–88.

Martínez, Oscar. *Los migrantes que no importan: En el camino con los centroamericanos indocumentados en México.* Barcelona: Icaria Editorial, 2010.

Martínez-Pinzón, Felipe, and Javier Uriarte Centaño, eds. *Entre el humo y la niebla: Guerra y cultura en América Latina.* Pittsburgh: Instituto Internacional de Literatura Iberoamericana, 2016.

Marx, Karl. *Das Kapital. Kritik der politischen Ökonomie.* Cologne: Anaconda, 2009.

Matthews, Irene. "Daughtering in War: Two 'Case Studies' from Mexico and Guatemala." In *Gendering War Talk,* edited by Miriam Cooke and Angela Woollacott, 148–73. Princeton, NJ: Princeton University Press, 1993.

Matthews, Irene. *Nellie Campobello: La centaura del Norte.* Mexico City: Cal y Arena, 1997.

Matthews, Michael. *The Civilizing Machine. A Cultural History of Mexican Railroads, 1876-1910.* University of Nebraska Press, 2013.

Matus Lazo, Róger. "El habla nicaragüense en la creación musical de Carlos Mejía Godoy." *El Nuevo Diario. Nuevo Amanecer Cultural,* January 2009. http://impreso.elnuevodiario.com.ni/2009/01/31/suplemento/nuevoamanecer/10069.

McCaa, Robert. "Missing Millions: The Demographic Costs of the Mexican Revolution." *Mexican Studies/Estudios Mexicanos* 19, no. 2 (2003): 367–400.

McClancy, Kathleen. "The Rehabilitation of Rambo: Trauma, Victimization, and the Vietnam Veteran." *Journal of Popular Culture* 47, no. 3 (June 2014): 503–19.

McDowell, John Holmes. *Poetry and Violence: The Ballad Tradition of Mexico's Costa Chica*. Urbana: University of Illinois Press, 2000.

McKee Irwin, Robert. *Mexican Masculinities*. Minneapolis: University of Minnesota Press, 2003.

Megenney, William. "Martín Luis Guzmán como cuentista en *El águila y la serpiente*." In *Five Essays on Martín Luis Guzmán*, edited by William W. Megenney, 83–120. Riverside, CA: Latin American Studies Program, University of California, Riverside. 1978.

Meiselas, Susan. *Nicaragua, June 1978–July 1979*. New York: Pantheon, 1981.

Mejía Godoy, Carlos. *Cantos a flor de pueblo*. Unknown label, 1973.

Mejía Godoy, Carlos. "Carta de Carlos Mejía Godoy a Rosario Murillo." *La Prensa*, June 2008. http://archivo.laprensa.com.ni/archivo/2008/junio/14/noticias/nacionales/265727.shtml.

Mejía Godoy, Carlos. Interview with author, Managua, Nicaragua, July 9, 2012.

Mejía Godoy, Carlos. *El son nuestro de cada día*. Madrid: CBS, 1977.

Mejía Godoy, Carlos. *Tasba Pri*. LP, Nicaragua: Ocarina, 1985.

Mejía Godoy, Carlos. "El verbo se hizo canto: Yo no puedo callar." *Blogspot Carlos Mejía Godoy*, June 2008. http://carlosmejiagodoy.blogspot.com/2008/06/y-el-verbo-se-hizo-canto-yo-no-puedo.html.

Mejía Godoy, Carlos, and El Taller del Sonido Popular. *Misa campesina nicaragüense*. Managua: Empresa Nicaragüense de Grabaciones Artísticas y Culturales (ENIGRAC), 1979.

Mejía Godoy, Carlos, and Los de Palacagüina. *Monimbó*. Cassette. Managua: Empresa Nicaragüense de Grabaciones Artísticas y Culturales (ENIGRAC), 1986.

Mejía Godoy, Carlos, and Los de Palacagüina. *La nueva milpa*. Casette. Madrid: CBS, 1978.

Mejía Godoy, Carlos, and Los de Palacagüina. *La tapisca*. Managua: Empresa Nicaragüense de Grabaciones Artísticas y Culturales (ENIGRAC), 1985.

Mejía Godoy, Carlos, and Luis Enrique Mejía Godoy. *Canto épico al FSLN*. CD. Managua: Empresa Nicaragüense de Grabaciones Artísticas y Culturales (ENIGRAC), 1981.

Mejía Godoy, Carlos, Luis Enrique Mejía Godoy, and Los de Palacagüina. *Guitarra Armada*. Cassette. Mexico City: Pentagrama, 1979.

Mejía Godoy, Carlos, Luis Enrique Mejía Godoy, and Julio Valle-Castillo. *The Nicaraguan Epic*. London: Katabasis, 1989.

Mejía Godoy, Luis Enrique. *Amando en tiempos de guerra*. LP. Costa Rica: CBS, 1979.

Mejía Godoy, Luis Enrique. *Hilachas de sol*. LP. Costa Rica: CBS, 1972.

Mejía Godoy, Luis Enrique. Interview with the author, Managua, Nicaragua, July 27, 2012.

Mejía Godoy, Luis Enrique. *Para luchar y quererte*. LP. Unknown label, 1975.

Mejía Godoy, Luis Enrique. *Relincho en la sangre: Relatos de un trovador errante*. Managua: Anamá Ediciones, 2002.

Mejía Godoy, Luis Enrique. "Respuesta a Jacinto Suárez de Luis Enrique Mejía Godoy." *El Nuevo Diario*, July 2008. www.elnuevodiario.com.ni/opinion/22808.

Mejía Godoy, Luis Enrique. *Un son para mi pueblo*. LP. Managua: Empresa Nicaragüense de Grabaciones Artísticas y Culturales (ENIGRAC), 1981.

Mejía Godoy, Luis Enrique. *Yo soy de un pueblo sencillo*. LP. Nicaragua: Empresa Nicaragüense de Grabaciones Artísticas y Culturales (ENIGRAC), 1983.

Mendoza, Élmer. *Un asesino solitario*. Mexico City: Tusquets Editores, 1999.

Mendoza, Vicente T. *El corrido de la revolución mexicana*. Mexico City: Fondo de Cultura Económica, 1956.

Mignolo, Walter. *The Darker Side of Western Modernity: Global Futures, Decolonial Options*. Durham, NC: Duke University Press, 2011.

Miranda, Roger, and William Ratliff. *The Civil War in Nicaragua: Inside the Sandinistas*. New Brunswick: Transaction Publishers, 1993.

Monsiváis, Carlos. "No con un sollozo, sino entre disparos (notas sobre cultura mexicana 1910–1968)." *Revista Iberoamericana* 148–49 (1989): 715–35.

Monsiváis, Carlos. "When Gender Can't Be Seen amid the Symbols: Women and the Mexican Revolution." In *Sex in the Revolution: Gender, Politics, and Power in Modern Mexico*, edited by Jocelyn Olcott, Mary Kay Vaughan, and Gabriela Cano, 1–19. Durham, NC: Duke University Press, 2006.

Montenegro, Sofía. "Carteles Políticos—Nicaragua 1979–1990. Las mujeres y la Revolución del 79: Las reliquias hablan." *Centro de Investigaciones de la Comunicación*, March 2006. http://cinco.org.ni/archive/18.pdf.

Monterroso, Augusto. *Pájaros de Hispanoamérica*. Madrid: Alfaguara, 2002.

Moodie, Ellen. "Democracy, Disenchantment, and the Future in El Salvador." In *Central America in the New Millennium: Living Transition and Reimagining Democracy*, edited by Jennifer Burrell and Ellen Moodie, 96–112. New York: Berghahn Books, 2013.

Moore, Robin. "Transformations in the Cuban Nueva Trova, 1965–1995." *Ethnomusicology* 47, no. 1 (2003): 1–41.

Mora Lomeli, Raúl. "Cultura desde abajo en la fuente del coraje." *Envio*, August 1990. www.envio.org.ni/articulo/638.

Moraña, Mabel. "La batalla de las ideas y de las emociones." In *El lenguaje de las emociones: Afecto y cultura en América Latina*, edited by Mabel Moraña and Ignacio Sánchez Prado, 313–37. Frankfurt: Vervuert Verlag, 2012.

Moreiras, Alberto. *The Exhaustion of Difference: The Politics of Latin American Cultural Studies*. Durham, NC: Duke University Press, 2001.

Moreno de Alba, José. "Contrabando, una novela autobiográfica." *Milenio*, December 27, 2008. http://impreso.milenio.com/node/8513598.

Morgan, Shanté. "CSUN Establishes Nation's First Department of Central American Studies." *CSUN Today*. https://csunshinetoday.csun.edu/university-news/csun-es tablishes-nations-first-department-of-central-american-studies/. Accessed July 24, 2017.

Movimiento Alterado, various artists. *Lo mejor del Movimiento Alterado*. Ava, 2012.

Muehlmann, Shaylih. *When I Wear My Alligator Boots: Narco-Culture in the US-Mexico Borderlands*. Berkeley: University of California Press, 2014.

Muniz, Chris. "Narcocorridos and the Nostalgia of Violence: Postmodern Resistance en La Frontera." *Western American Literature* 48, no. 1 and 2 (spring–summer 2013): 56–69.

Muñoz, Rafael. *¡Vámonos con Pancho Villa!* Mexico City: Ediciones Era, 2009.

Nacaveva, A. *Diario de un narcotraficante*. Mexico City: B. Costa-Amic, 1967.

Naranjo, Gerardo, director. *Miss Bala*. 20th Century Fox, 2011.

Navarro-Génie, Marco Aurelio. *Augusto "César" Sandino: Messiah of Light and Truth*. Syracuse, NY: Syracuse University Press, 2002.

Noble, Andrea. *Photography and Memory in Mexico: Icons of Revolution*. New York: Manchester University Press, 2010.

Oettler, Anika. "Discourses on Violence in Costa Rica, El Salvador, and Nicaragua: National Patterns of Attention and Cross-Border Discursive Nodes." German Institute of Global and Area Studies (GIGA) working paper no. 65. Hamburg, 2007. www.giga-hamburg.de/de/system/files/publications/wp65_oettler.pdf.

Olcott, Jocelyn. *Revolutionary Women in Postrevolutionary Mexico*. Durham, NC: Duke University Press, 2005.

Olivas, Juan de Dios. "Retiran mañana letrero 'No More Weapons.'" *El Diario*. June 16, 2015. http://diario.mx/Local/2015–06–16_1fb9d387/retiran-manana-letrero -no-more-weapons/.

Orr, Brianne. "From Machista to New Man: Omar Cabezas Negotiates Manhood from the Mountain in Nicaragua." *Ciberletras*, 2009. www.lehman.cuny.edu/ciberletras /v22/orr.html.

Ortiz Wallner, Alexandra. *El arte de ficcionar: La novela contemporánea en Centroamérica*. Madrid: Iberoamericana; Vervuert, 2012.

Ortiz Wallner, Alexandra, and Werner Mackenbach. "(De)formaciones: Violencia y narrativa en Centroamérica." *Iberoamericana: América Latina–España–Portugal* 8, no. 32 (2008): 81–97.

Padilla, Yajaira. "Setting La Diabla Free: Women, Violence, and the Struggle for Representation in Postwar El Salvador." *Latin American Perspectives* 35, no. 5 (2008): 133–45.

Palaversich, Diana. "¿Cómo hablar del silencio? *Contrabando* y *Un vaquero cruza la frontera en silencio*, dos casos ejemplares del acercamiento ético en la literatura mexicana sobre el narco." *Ciberletras*, 2012. www.lehman.cuny.edu/ciberletras/ v29/palaversich.html.

Paley, Dawn. *Drug War Capitalism*. Oakland, CA: AK Press, 2014.

Paley, Dawn. "Repressive Memories: Terror, Insurgency, and the Drug War in Mexico." *Upside Down World*, October 31, 2013. http://upsidedownworld.org /main/mexico-archives-79/4534-repressive-memories-terror-insurgency-and-the -drug-war-in-mexico.

Paredes, Américo. *"With His Pistol in His Hand": A Border Ballad and Its Hero*. Austin: University of Texas Press, 2006.

Parker, Geoffrey. *The Military Revolution: Military Innovation and the Rise of the West, 1500–1800*. Cambridge: Cambridge University Press, 1988.

Parra, Max. *Writing Pancho Villa's Revolution: Rebels in the Literary Imagination of Mexico*. Austin: University of Texas Press, 2005.

Pearce, Jenny. "From Civil War to 'Civil Society': Has the End of the Cold War Brought Peace to Central America?" *International Affairs* 74, no. 3 (1998): 587–615.

Pearce, Jenny. "Peace-building in the Periphery: Lessons from Central America." *Third World Quarterly* 20, no. 1 (1999): 51–68.

Peña Iguarán, Alina. "La auto-representación del intelectual en la narrativa de la Revolución mexicana." PhD diss., Boston University, Boston, 2010.

Peña Iguarán, Alina. "Próspero entre *El águila y la serpiente*: La auto-representación del intelectual en Martín Luis Guzmán." *Latin Americanist* 55, no. 1 (2011): 93–108.

Peña Sánchez, Jesús. "El hombre que convierte armas en arte." *Vanguardia*, November 21, 2015. www.vanguardia.com.mx/articulo/el-hombre-que-convierte-armas-en -arte.

Pérez, Yansi. "Memory and Mourning in Contemporary Latin American Literature: A Reading of Claudia Hernández' *De fronteras*." *La Habana Elegante*, 2014. www .habanaelegante.com/Spring_Summer_2014/Invitation_Perez.html.

Pérez-Reverte, Arturo. *La Reina del Sur*. Madrid: Punto de lectura, 2002.

Perrerac. "Carlos and Luis Enrique Mejía Godoy: Guitarra Armada (1979)." *PERRERAC*, July 19, 2015. http://perrerac.org/nicaragua/carlos-luis-enrique-meja -godoy-guitarra-armada-1979/2618/.

Petrich, Blanche. "Las armas más letales llegan al narco mexicano desde Centroamérica: EU." *La Jornada*, March 29, 2011. www.jornada.unam.mx/2011/03/29/index .php?section=politica&article=002n1pol.

Pietz, William. "Fetishism and Materialism." In *Fetishism as Cultural Discourse*, edited by William Pietz and Emily Apter, 152–85. Ithaca, NY: Cornell University Press, 1993.

Pineda Franco, Adela. "Afecto, política y experiencia cinematográfica en *El águila y la serpiente*." In *El lenguaje de las emociones: Afecto y cultura en América Latina*, edited by Mabel Moraña and Ignacio Sánchez Prado, 245–55. Frankfurt: Vervuert Verlag, 2012.

Pineda Franco, Adela. "Entre el exilio y el fuego revolucionario: La narrativa de Martín Luis Guzmán de 1925 a 1929." *Revista de Crítica Literaria Latinoamericana* 33, no. 66 (2007): 29–51.

Polit, Gabriela. "Autobiografía, historia nacional y política." *Nueva Sociedad* 170 (2000): 228–32.

Pratt, Mary Louise. "Mi cigarro, mi Singer, y la revolución mexicana: La danza ciudadana de Nellie Campobello." *Cadernos Pagu* 22 (2004): 151–84.

Pratt, Mary Louise. "Violence and Language." *Social Text: Periscope*, May 21, 2001. www.socialtextjournal.org/periscope/2011/05/violence-and-language—mary -louise-pratt.php.

Pring-Mill, Robert. "The Roles of Revolutionary Song—A Nicaraguan Assessment." *Popular Music* 6, no. 2 (1987): 179–89.

Proceso. "Bienvenidos a Ciudad Juárez . . . Proceso 1688." *Proceso*, March 2009. www .proceso.com.mx/proceso-1688.

Proceso. "Confirman envío ilegal de miles de armas alemanas a México." *Proceso*. www.proceso.com.mx/?p=403567. Accessed November 28, 2015.

Proceso. "Hallan en El Salvador arsenal robado a militares y al parecer dirigido a Los Zetas." *Proceso*, October 10, 2013. www.proceso.com.mx/?p=355003.

Proceso. "Miss disparó un 'cuerno de chivo' contra militares, asegura PGR." *Proceso*, December 2014. www.proceso.com.mx/?p=326938.

Proceso digital. "Armas de guerra hacen de Honduras un arsenal sin control." *Proceso digital*, February 19, 2013. http://proceso.hn/2013/02/19/Nacionales/Armas .de.guerra/64579.html.

Quijano, Anibal. "Colonialidad del poder, eurocentrismo y América Latina." In *Colonialidad del saber y eurocentrismo*, edited by Edgardo Lander, 201–46. Buenos Aires: United Nations Educational, Scientific and Cultural Organization (UNESCO), El Consejo Latinoamericano de Ciencias Sociales (CLACSO), 2000.

Quintana Navarrete. "'Misión cumplida': Breve genealogía del performance de soberanía del Estado mexicano." *Horizontal*. http://horizontal.mx/mision-cumplida-breve-genealogia-del-performance-de-soberania-del-estado-mexicano/. Accessed March 9, 2016.

Quirós Ramírez, Daniel. *Verano rojo*. San José, Costa Rica: Editorial Costa Rica, 2010.

Rama, Ángel. *La ciudad letrada*. Hanover, NH: Ediciones del Norte, 1984.

Ramírez, Sergio. *Adiós muchachos: Una memoria de la revolución sandinista*. 1999; reprint, 2nd ed. Santafé de Bogotá: Aguilar, 2000.

Ramírez, Sergio. *El alba de oro: La historia viva de Nicaragua*. Mexico City: Siglo XXI, 1985.

Ramírez, Sergio. *Balcanes y volcanes y otros ensayos y trabajos*. 2nd ed. Managua: Editorial Nueva Nicaragua, 1983.

Ramírez, Sergio. *Confesión de amor*. Managua: Ediciones Nicarao, 1991.

Ramírez, Sergio. Interview with the author, Managua, Nicaragua, July 24, 2012.

Ramírez, Sergio. *Señor de los tristes: Sobre escritores y escritura*. San Juan, PR: La Editorial Universidad de Puerto Rico, 2006.

Ramírez, Sergio. *Sombras nada más*. Madrid: Santillana Ediciones, 2002.

Ramírez-Pimienta, Juan Carlos. *Cantar a los narcos: Voces y versos del narcocorrido*. Mexico City: Temas de hoy, 2011.

Ramírez-Pimienta, Juan Carlos. "De torturaciones, balas y explosiones: Narcocultura, movimiento alterado e hiperrealismo en el sexenio de Felipe Calderón." *A Contracorriente: A Journal on Social History and Literature in Latin America* 10, no. 3 (May 2013): 302–34.

Ramos, Julio. *Desencuentros de la modernidad en América Latina: Literatura y política en el siglo XIX*. Mexico City: Fondo de Cultura Económica, 1989.

Randall, Margaret. *Sandino's Daughters Revisited: Feminism in Nicaragua*. New Brunswick, NJ: Rutgers University Press, 1994.

Randall, Margaret. *Sandino's Daughters: Testimonies of Nicaraguan Women in Struggle*. Revised ed. New Brunswick, NJ: Rutgers University Press, 1995.

Rascón Banda, Víctor Hugo. *Contrabando*. Mexico City: Planeta, 2008.

Real Academia de la Lengua Española and Asociacion de Academias de la lengua Española. *Diccionario de la lengua española*. Vol. 23. Madrid: Planeta Publishing, 2014.

Redacción Sin Embargo. "Suman 65 mil 209 homicidios dolosos a medio sexenio de EPN." *SinEmbargo MX*, January 25, 2016. www.sinembargo.mx/25–01–2016/1606331.

Reed, John. *Insurgent Mexico: With Pancho Villa in the Mexican Revolution*. Saint Petersburg, FL: Red and Black Publishers, 2009.

Reséndez Fuentes, Andrés. "Battleground Women: Soldaderas and Female Soldiers in the Mexican Revolution." *The Americas* 51, no. 4 (April 1995): 525–53.

Restall, Matthew. *Seven Myths of the Spanish Conquest*. New York: Oxford University Press, 2003.

Rey Rosa, Rodrigo. *Que me maten si . . .* Barcelona: Seix Barral, 1997.

Reyes, Pedro. "Disarm." Artist's homepage, Lisson Gallery, London, 2013. http://pedroreyes.net/disarm.php.

Reyes, Pedro. "Palas por pistolas." Jardín Botánico de Culiacán, Culiacán, Sinaloa, Mexico, 2008. http://pedroreyes.net/palasporpistolas.php.

Ribas-Casasayas, Alberto, and Amanda L. Petersen. *Espectros: Ghostly Hauntings in Contemporary Transhispanic Narratives*. Lewisburg, PA: Bucknell University Press, 2015.

Richard, Nelly. "Latinoamérica y la posmodernidad." *Revista del Centro de Ciencias de Lenguaje*, no. 13–14 (1996): 271–80.

Rico, Maite. "Los Mejía Godoy prohíben a Daniel Ortega usar su música." *El País*, June 21, 2008. http://elpais.com/diario/2008/06/21/cultura/1213999203_850215 .html.

Rincón, Carlos. *La no simultaneidad de lo simultáneo: Postmodernidad, globalización y culturas en América Latina*. Bogotá: Editorial Universidad Nacional, 1995.

Rincón, Omar. "Todos llevamos un narco adentro—un ensayo sobre la narco/cultura/ telenovela como modo de entrada a la modernidad." *Revista MATRIZes* 7, no. 2 (December 2013): 1–33.

Rincón Chavarro, María Catalina. "De violencia, de normalización y de fronteras." *Catedral Tomada: Revista de crítica literaria* 1, no. 1 (2013). http://catedraltomada .pitt.edu/ojs/index.php/catedraltomada/article/view/27.

Rivera, Lupillo. *Gabino Barrera: Cartel de Tijuana*. CD. BCI/ Eclipse Music, 2001.

Rodó, José Enrique. *Ariel*. 1900; reprint, Mexico City: Factoría Ediciones, 2000.

Rodríguez, Ana Patricia. "Diasporic Reparations: Repairing the Social Imaginaries of Central America in the Twenty-First Century." *Studies in Twentieth and Twenty-First Century Literature* 37, no. 2 (2013): 26–43.

Rodríguez, Ana Patricia. *Dividing the Isthmus: Central American Transnational Histories, Literatures, and Cultures*. Austin: University of Texas Press, 2009.

Rodríguez, Ana Patricia. "Memorias del devenir: Belli, Cardenal y Ramírez recuentan la historia." *Istmo: Revista virtual de estudios literarios y culturales centroamericanos* 3 (June 2002). http://istmo.denison.edu/n03/articulos/devenir.html.

Rodríguez, Ileana. *Women, Guerrillas, and Love: Understanding War in Central America*. Minneapolis: University of Minnesota Press, 1996.

Rogers, Tim. "Central America's Uneasy Disarmament." *NACLA Report on the Americas* (August 2003): 12–14.

Ruffinelli, Jorge. "Nellie Campobello: Pólvora en palabras." *La Palabra y el Hombre* 113 (2000): 63–72.

Ruffinelli, Jorge. "Trenes revolucionarios: La mitología del tren en el imaginario de la Revolución." *Revista Mexicana de Sociología* 51, no. 2 (1989): 285–303.

Rugama, Leonel. *La tierra es un satélite de la luna*. Havana, Cuba: Casa de las Américas, 1982.

Rulfo, Juan. *El llano en llamas*. Madrid: Visor Libros, 2001.

Rushdie, Salman. *The Jaguar Smile: A Nicaraguan Journey*. New York: Random House, 2008.

Rutherford, John. *Mexican Society during the Revolution: A Literary Approach*. Oxford: Clarendon Press, 1971.

Salas, Elizabeth. *Soldaderas in the Mexican Military: Myth and History*. Austin: University of Texas Press, 1990.

Saldaña Portillo, María Josefina. *The Revolutionary Imagination in the Americas and the Age of Development.* Durham, NC: Duke University Press, 2007.

Samuelson, Cheyla. "Relearning the Revolution: The Contemporary Relevance of the *Novela de la Revolución* in the University Classroom." *Equestrian Rebels: Critical Perspectives on Mariano Azuela and the Novel of the Mexican Revolution*, edited by Roberto Cantú, Newcastle upon Tyne: Cambridge Scholars Publishing, 2016, 63–81.

Sánchez, Chalino. *El Pela Vacas.* Audio CD. Musart, 1995.

Sánchez, Edwin. "Carlos Mejía le debe canto a PJCH." *El Nuevo Diario*, March 2002. http://archivo.elnuevodiario.com.ni/2002/marzo/24-marzo-2002/nacional/na cional4.html.

Sánchez, Edwin. "¿'F' de fuerza insobornable?" *El Nuevo Diario*, July 1999. http://ar chivo.elnuevodiario.com.ni/1999/julio/03-julio-1999/nacional/nacional4.html.

Sánchez, Luz María. "Bienal de las Fronteras—Museo de Arte Carrillo Gil." Present ed at the Bienal de las Fronteras, Museo de Arte Contemporáneo de Tamaulipas, Matamoros, Tamaulipas, Mexico, March 5, 2015. www.museodeartecarrillogil .com/exposiciones/exposiciones-temporales/bienal-de-las-fronteras.

Sánchez Prado, Ignacio M. "Mexican Literature in the Neoliberal Era." In *A History of Mexican Literature*, edited by Ignacio M. Sánchez Prado, Anna M. Nogar, and José Ramón Ruisánchez Serra, 365–78. New York: Cambridge University Press, 2016.

Sánchez Prado, Ignacio M. "Novel, War, and the Aporia of Totality: Lukács's Theory of the Novel and Azuela's *Los de abajo.*" *Mediations: Journal of the Marxist Literary Group* 29, no. 2 (2016). http://www.mediationsjournal.org/articles/novel-war-and -the-aporia-of-totality.

Sánchez Prado, Ignacio M. "Vanguardia y campo literario: La Revolución Mexicana como apertura estética." *Revista de Crítica Literaria Latinoamericana* 33, no. 66 (2007): 187–206.

Sánchez Prado, Ignacio M., Anna M. Nogar, and José Ramón Ruisánchez Serra, eds. *A History of Mexican Literature.* New York: Cambridge University Press, 2016.

Sarlo, Beatriz. *Una modernidad periférica: Buenos Aires, 1920 y 1930.* Buenos Aires: Ediciones Nueva Visión, 1988.

Sarmiento, Domingo Faustino. *Facundo: Civilización y barbarie.* 1845; Madrid: Cát edra, 1990.

Scarry, Elaine. *The Body in Pain: The Making and Unmaking of the World.* New York: Oxford University Press, 1987.

Schluchter, Wolfgang. *Die Entzauberung der Welt.* Tübingen, Germany: Mohr Sie beck, 2009.

Schmitt, Carl. "Der Begriff des Politischen." *Archiv für Sozialwissenschaft und Sozial politik* 58, no. 1 (1927): 1–33.

Schulz, Hermann. *Nicaragua: Eine amerikanische Vision.* Reinbek bei Hamburg, Ger many: Rowohlt, 1983.

Scruggs, T. M. "Las Misas Nicaragüenses: Popular, Campesina, y del pueblo." *Istmo: Revista virtual de estudios literarios y culturales centroamericanos* 17 (2008). http:// istmo.denison.edu/n17/articulos/scruggs.html.

Scruggs, T. M. "Music, Memory, and the Politics of Erasure in Nicaragua." In *Memory and the Impact of Political Transformation in Public Space*, edited by Daniel Walkowitz and Lisa Maya Knauer, 255–75. Durham, NC: Duke University Press, 2004.

Scruggs, T. M. "Música y el legado de la violencia a finales del siglo XX en Centro América." *TRANS—Revista Transcultural de Música* 10 (2006). www.sibe trans.com/trans/a144/musica-y-el-legado-de-la-violencia-a-finales-del-siglo-xx -en-centro-america.

Scruggs, T. M. "Nicaragua." In *The Garland Encyclopedia of World Music: South America, Mexico, Central America, and the Caribbean*, edited by Dale Olsen and Daniel Sheehy. New York: Garland Publishing, 1998.

Scruggs, T. M. "Socially Conscious Music Forming the Social Conscience: Nicaraguan Música Testimonial and the Creation of a Revolutionary Moment." In *From Tejano to Tango: Latin American Popular Music: Essays on Latin American Popular Music*, edited by Walter Aaron Clark, 41–69. New York: Routledge, 2002.

SEDENA (Secretaría de la Defensa Nacional). "Comercialización de armas. Marco legal." 2015. www.sedena.gob.mx/comercializacion-de-armas.

Seigworth, Gregory, and Melissa Gregg. "An Inventory of Shimmers." In *The Affect Theory Reader*, edited by Gregory Seigworth and Melissa Gregg, 1–26. Durham, NC: Duke University Press, 2010.

Serrano, Mónica. "States of Violence: State-Crime Relations in Mexico." In *Violence, Coercion, and State-Making in Twentieth-Century Mexico*, edited by Wil G. Pansters, 135–58. Stanford, CA: Stanford University Press, 2012.

Shaw, Donald. "*El águila y la serpiente*: Arielismo and Narrative Method." *Latin American Studies Program: Commemorative Series* 2 (1978): 1–17.

Shea, Maureen. "Narradoras combatientes en la literatura centroamericana: De la ilusión al desengaño." *Istmo: Revista virtual de estudios literarios y culturales centroamericanos* 15 (2007). http://collaborations.denison.edu/istmo/n15/articulos/ shea.html.

Silva, Marciano. "Corrido Soy Zapatista del Estado de Morelos." *Bibliotecas*. www .bibliotecas.tv/zapata/corridos/corr14.html. Accessed July 4, 2017.

Simonett, Helena. "Los Gallos Valientes: Examining Violence in Mexican Popular Music." *TRANS—Revista Transcultural de* 10 (2006). www.sibetrans.com/trans/ a149/los-gallos-valientes-examining-violence-in-mexican-popular-music.

Simonett, Helena. "The Transnational Dimension of Banda Music: Narco Subculture and Contemporary Influences." In *Banda: Mexican Musical Life across Borders*, 201–54. Middletown, CT: Wesleyan University Press, 2001.

Sklodowska, Elzbieta. *Testimonio hispanoamericano: Historia, teoría, poética*. New York: Peter Lang, 1992.

Small Arms Survey. "Annexe 1: Seventy-Nine Countries with Comprehensive Civilian Ownership Data," in chapter 2, "Completing the Count: Civilian Firearms." *Small Arms Survey*, 2007. www.smallarmssurvey.org/publications/by-type/yearbook/small-arms-survey-2007.html.

Small Arms Survey. "Annexe 3: Civilian Firearm Ownership in 178 Countries, Alphabetical Order," in chapter 2, "Completing the Count: Civilian Firearms." *Small Arms Survey*, 2007. www.smallarmssurvey.org/publications/by-type/yearbook/small-arms-survey-2007.html.

Small Arms Survey. "Captured and Counted: Illicit Weapons in Mexico and the Philippines." In *Small Arms Survey*, 2013. www.smallarmssurvey.org/publications/by-type/yearbook/small-arms-survey-2013.html.

Sommer, Doris. *Foundational Fictions the National Romances of Latin America*. Berkeley: University of California Press, 1991.

Spivak, Gayatri Chakravorty. "Can the Subaltern Speak?" In *Colonial Discourse and Postcolonial Theory: A Reader*, edited by Patrick Williams and Laura Chrisman, 66–111. New York: Harvester Wheatsheaf, 1993.

Sturman, Janet. "Nostalgia for the Future: The New Song Movement in Nicaragua." In *Latin American Popular Culture*, 2nd ed., edited by William Beezley and Linda Curcio, 247–66. Lanham, MD: Rowman and Littlefield, 2012.

Subcomandante Marcos. "Al pueblo de México: Hablaron los hombres verdaderos, los sin rostro. Mandar obedeciendo." *Palabra EZLN*, February 26, 1994. http://palabra.ezln.org.mx/comunicados/1994/1994_02_26_a.htm.

Sullivan, John P. "Criminal Insurgency: Narcocultura, Social Banditry, and Information Operations." *Small Wars Journal*, December 3, 2012. http://smallwarsjournal.com/jrnl/art/criminal-insurgency-narcocultura-social-banditry-and-information-operations.

Taibo II, Paco Ignacio. *Pancho Villa: Una biografía narrativa*. Mexico City: Planeta, 2006.

Taussig, Michael T. *My Cocaine Museum*. Chicago: University of Chicago Press, 2004.

Televisa. "El Equipo—Sitio Oficial." *El Equipo*. http://televisa.esmas.com/entretenimiento/programastv/el-equipo/. Accessed May 30, 2016.

Téllez, Dora María. Email correspondence with the author, August 8, 2012.

Thornton, Niamh. *Women and the War Story in Mexico: La Novela de La Revolución*. Lewiston, NY: Edwin Mellen Press, 2006.

Thrift, Nigel. "Intensities of Feeling: Towards a Spatial Politics of Affect." *Geografiska Annaler* 86 B, no. 1 (2004): 57–78.

Tobar, Héctor. *The Tattooed Soldier*. New York: Penguin Books, 1998.

Tolkien, J. R. R. *The Lord of the Rings*. New York: Ballantine Books, 1973.

Torres, Hugo. Personal conversation with the author, Managua, Nicaragua, July 18, 2012.

Torres-Rivas, Edelberto. *Revoluciones sin cambios revolucionarios: Ensayos sobre la crisis en Centroamérica*. Guatemala City: F&G Editores, 2011.

Townsend, Camilla. "Burying the White Gods: New Perspectives on the Conquest of Mexico." *American Historical Review* 108, no. 3 (June 2003): 659–87.

Traven, B. *Ein General kommt aus dem Dschungel*. Cologne: Kippenheuer und Witsch, 1951.

United Nations Office on Drugs and Crime (UNODC). *Crime and Development in Central America: Caught in the Crossfire*. Vienna: UNODC, 2007. www.unodc .org/documents/data-and-analysis/Central-america-study-en.pdf.

United Nations Office on Drugs and Crime (UNODC). *Global Study on Homicide*. Vienna: UNODC, 2011. www.unodc.org/documents/data-and-analysis/statistics/ Homicide/Globa_study_on_homicide_2011_web.pdf.

Urbina, Nicasio. "Las memorias y las autobiografías como bienes culturales de consumo." *Istmo: Revista Virtual de Estudios Literarios y Culturales Centroamericanos* 8, 2004. http://istmo.denison.edu/n08/articulos/memorias.html.

Ureña, Juan Carlos. *Trovar: Memoria poética de la canción hispanoamericana*. San José: Editorial de la Universidad de Costa Rica, 2013.

Uribe Echevarría, Juan. *La novela de la Revolución Mexicana y la novela hispanoamericana actual*. Santiago: Prensas de la Universidad de Chile, 1936.

Valdez Cárdenas, Javier. *Miss Narco: Belleza, poder y violencia. Historias reales de mujeres en el narcotráfico mexicano*. Mexico City: Aguilar, 2012.

Valencia, Alejandro. "La leyenda del Chapo Guzmán, el hombre que evitaba ser fotografiado, pagaba las cuentas de todos en los restaurantes." *Blog del Narco*, January 2016. www.blog-del-narco.com/2016/01/la-leyenda-del-chapo-guzman-el -hombre.html.

Valencia Triana, Sayak. "Capitalismo gore: Narcomáquina y performance de género." *e-misférica* 8, no. 2 (2012). www.hemisphericinstitute.org/hemi/es/e-misferica-82/ triana.

Valenzuela Arce, José Manuel. *Jefe de jefes: Corridos y narcocultura en México*. Barcelona: Plaza & Janés, 2002.

Valenzuela, Orlando. *Miliciana de Waswalito*. Managua: Publisher unknown, Photography, 1984.

Valtierra, Pedro, and Cuartoscuro. *Entrada del triunfante Ejército Sandinista de Liberación Nacional a Managua en 1979*. Mexico City: Unomásuno, Photography, 1979.

Vanden Berghe, Kristine. "Alegría en la revolución y tristeza en tiempos de paz. El juego en *Cartucho* y *Las manos de mamá* de Nellie Campobello." *Literatura Mexicana* 21, no. 2 (2010): 151–70.

Vanden Berghe, Kristine. *Homo ludens en la revolución: Una lectura de Nellie Campobello*. Madrid: Iberoamericana; Vervuert; Bonilla Artigas Editores, 2013.

Vargas Santiago, Luis Adrián. "Emiliano Zapata: Cuerpo, tierra, cautiverio." In *El éxodo mexicano: Los héroes en la mira del arte*, 440–79. Mexico City: Museo Nacional de Arte (MUNAL), Instituto Nacional de Bellas Artes (INBA), Universidad Nacional Autónoma de México (UNAM), 2010.

Various Artists. *Abril en Managua: Concierto de la paz en Centroamérica*. CD (Concert). Managua: Fundación Mejía Godoy, 2003.

Various Artists. *Convirtiendo la oscurana en claridad*. Recording, 1980.

Various Artists. *The Mexican Revolution: Corridos about the Heroes and Events, 1910–1920 and Beyond*. Audio CD. Arhoolie Records, 1997.

Vaughan, Mary K. *Cultural Politics in Revolution: Teachers, Peasants, and Schools in Mexico, 1930–1940*. Tucson: University of Arizona Press, 1997.

Vázquez Olivera, Mario, and Fabián Campos Hernández. *México ante el conflicto centroamericano: Testimonio de una época*. Mexico City: Centro de Investigaciones sobre América Latina y el Caribe/Bonilla Artiga Editores, 2017.

Venkatesh, Vinodh. "Mirrors, Lipstick, and Guns: Performing Revolutionary Masculinity in *La mujer habitada*." *Hispanic Research Journal* 14, no. 6 (2013): 496–504.

Venkatesh, Vinodh. *The Body as Capital: Masculinities in Contemporary Latin American Fiction*. Tucson: University of Arizona Press, 2015.

Verhoeven, Paul, director. *RoboCop*. Orion Pictures, 1987.

Villena Fiengo, Sergio. "Espectros de Sandino en la política nicaragüense (una interrogación)." *Istmo. Revista virtual de estudios literarios y culturales centroamericanos* 33 (July 2016). www. http://istmo.denison.edu/n33/articulos/04.html

Villalobos, José Pablo and Juan Carlos Ramírez-Pimienta. "Corridos and la pura verdad: Myths and Realities of the Mexican Ballad." *South Central Review* 21, no. 3 (2004): 129–49.

Villoro, Juan. "La alfombra roja." *El Malpensante*, February 2010. www.elmalpensante.com/index.php?doc=display_contenido&id=825.

Virilio, Paul. *Desert Screen: War at the Speed of Light*. London: Continuum, 2002.

Virilio, Paul. *Pure War*. New York: Semiotext(e), 1983.

Virilio, Paul. *Speed and Politics*. Los Angeles: Semiotext(e), 2006.

Voz de Mando. *Estrategias de guerra*. Disa Records, 2010. https://myspace.com/grupo vozdemando/music/song/estrategias-de-guerra-72668425–80148253.

Voz de Mando. *Impactos de Arranque*. CD. Disa, 2010.

Wald, Elijah. *Narcocorrido: A Journey into the Music of Drugs, Guns, and Guerrillas*. New York: Rayo, 2002.

Weber, Max. *Wirtschaft und Gesellschaft; Grundriss der verstehenden Soziologie. Mit einem Anhang; Die rationalen und soziologischen Grundlagen der Musik*. 4th ed. Tübingen: Mohr, 1956.

Weber, Max. "Wissenschaft als Beruf." In *Schriften 1894–1922*, edited by Dirk Kaesler, 474–513. Stuttgart: Alfred Kroener Verlag, 2002.

Weimer, Tanya. "Las imágenes barajadas en *Cartucho* de Nellie Campobello." *Cuadernos Americanos* 134 (2010): 103–23.

Wellinga, Klaas. "Cantando a los traficantes." In *El laberinto de la solidaridad: Cultura y política en México (1910–2000)*, edited by Kristine Vanden Berghe and Maarten Van Delden, 137–54. Amsterdam: Presses Universitaires de Namur, 2002.

Wellinga, Klaas. *Entre la poesía y la pared: Política cultural sandinista, 1979–1990*. Amsterdam: Thela, 1994.

Whisnant, David E. *Rascally Signs in Sacred Places: The Politics of Culture in Nicaragua*. Chapel Hill: University of North Carolina Press, 1995.

White, Steven F. "Los trovadores de la música popular nicaragüense." In *Arando el aire: La ecología en la poesía y la música de Nicaragua*, 525–95. Managua: 400 Elefantes, 2011.

Wilkinson, Tracy, and Cecilia Sanchez. "Mexico's Peña Nieto Unveils Police Unit, Much Smaller Than Envisioned." *LA Times*. www.latimes.com/world/mexico -americas/la-fg-mexico-police-20140823-story.html. Accessed August 2, 2016.

Williams, Gareth. *The Mexican Exception: Sovereignty, Police, and Democracy*. New York: Palgrave Macmillan, 2011.

Williams, Gareth. *The Other Side of the Popular: Neoliberalism and Subalternity in Latin America*. Durham, NC: Duke University Press, 2002.

Williams, Raymond. *Keywords. A Vocabulary of Culture and Society*. Revised. New York: Oxford University Press, 1983.

Williams, Robert R. *Hegel's Ethics of Recognition*. Berkeley: University of California Press, 1997.

Woody, Christopher. "The Rise and Fall of Joaquín 'El Chapo' Guzmán, the World's Most Ambitious Drug Lord." *Business Insider*. www.businessinsider.com/the-his tory-of-el-chapo-guzman-sinaloa-cartel-chief-drug-lord-2017-1. Accessed June 10, 2017.

World Bank. "Crime and Violence in Central America: A Development Challenge." Sustainable Development Department and Poverty Reduction and Economic Management Unit Latin America and the Caribbean Region, 2011.

Wrobel, Paolo, and United Nations Institute for Disarmament Research (UNIDIR). "Disarmament and Conflict Resolution Project. Managing Arms in Peace Processes: Nicaragua and El Salvador." Geneva, New York, 1997. www.unidir.org/ files/publications/pdfs/disarmament-and-conflict-resolution-project-managing -arms-in-peace-processes-nicaragua-and-el-salvador-127.pdf.

Wünderich, Volker. *Sandino: Una biografía política*. Managua: Editorial Nueva Nicaragua, n.d.

Young, Stewart M. "Going Nowhere Fast (or Furious): The Nonexistant U.S. Firearms

Trafficking Statute and the Rise of Mexican Drug Cartel Violence." *University of Michigan Journal of Law Reform* 46, no. 1 (2012): 1-67.

Yúdice, George. "Testimonio and Postmodernism (1991)." In *The Real Thing: Testimonial Discourse and Latin America*, edited by Georg M Gugelberger, 42–57. Durham, NC: Duke University Press, 1996.

Zacarías, Miguel. *Juana Gallo.* Azteca Films Inc., 1961.

Zalaquett, Mónica. *Tu fantasma, Julián.* Managua: Editorial Vanguardia, 1992.

Zambrana, Armando. *El ojo del mestizo o la herencia cultural.* Managua: Ediciones PAVSA, 2002.

Zavala, Lauro, editor. *Relatos mexicanos posmodernos: Antología de prosa ultracorta, híbrida y lúdica.* Mexico City: Alfaguara, 2001.

Zavala, Oswaldo. "Imagining the U.S.-Mexico Drug War: The Critical Limits of Narconarratives." *Comparative Literature* 66, no. 3 (2014): 340–60.

Žižek, Slavoj. *Violence: Six Sideways Reflections.* New York: Picador, 2008.

# INDEX

Note: Page numbers in *italics* refer to figures.